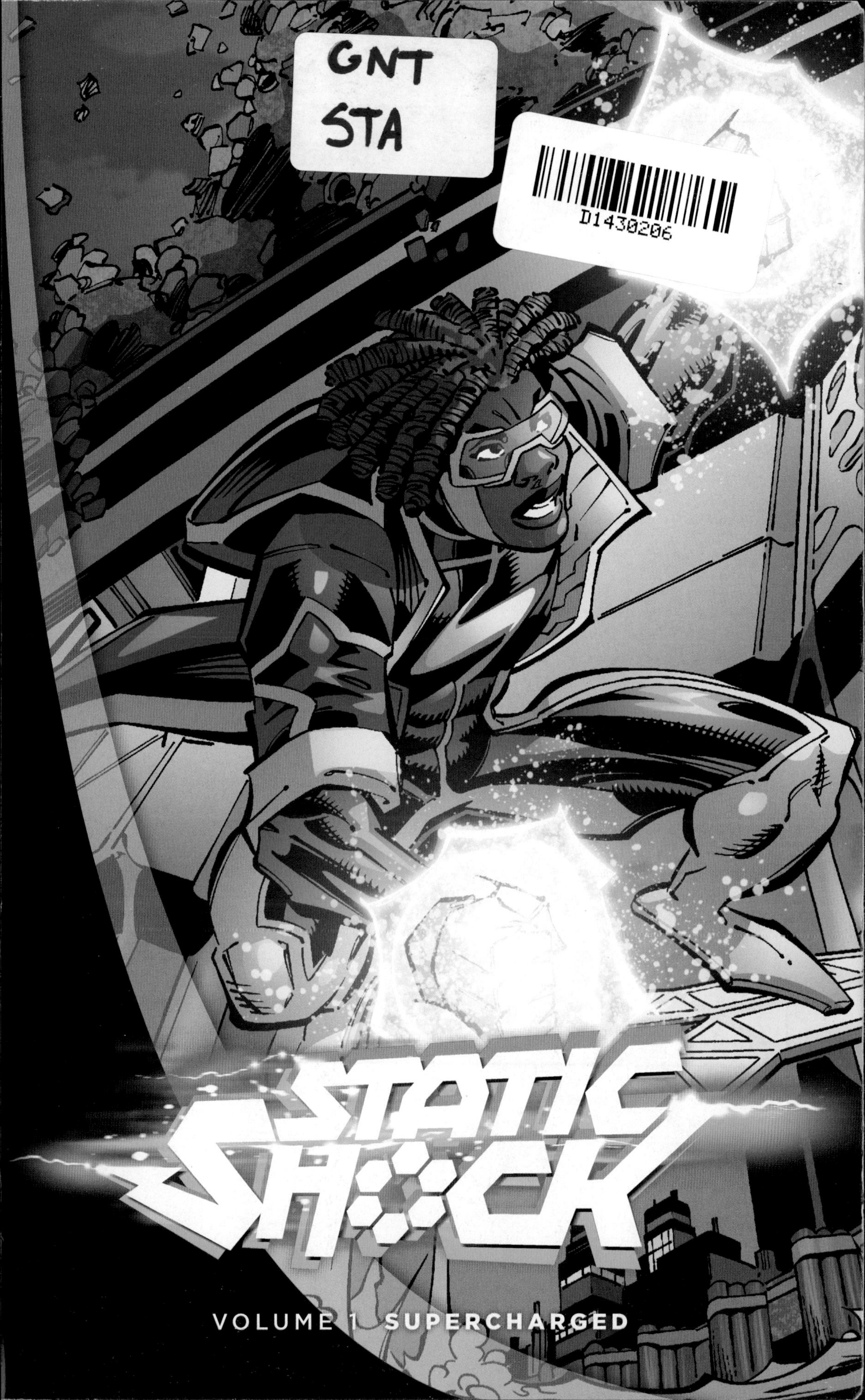
STATIC SHOCK
VOLUME 1 SUPERCHARGED

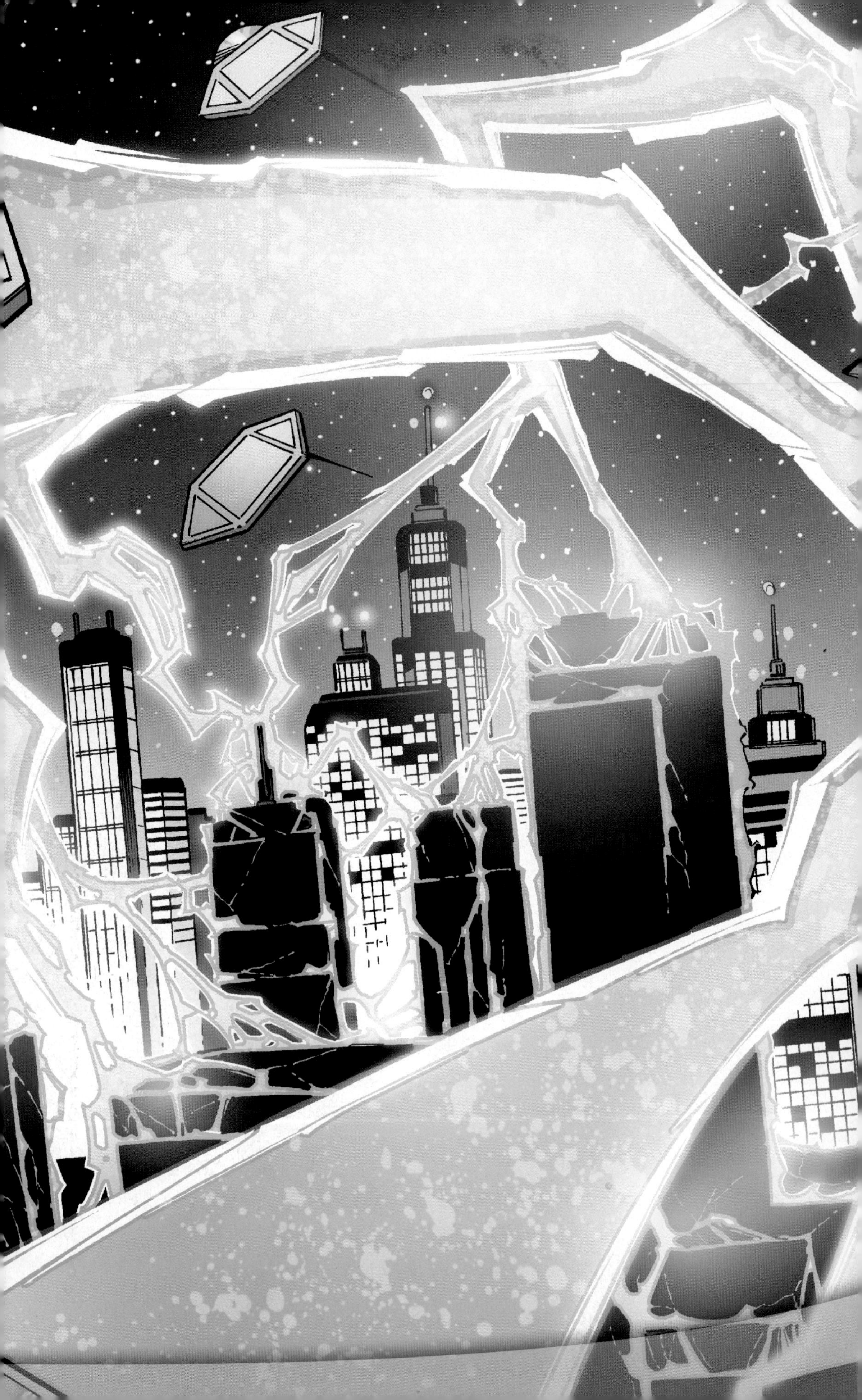

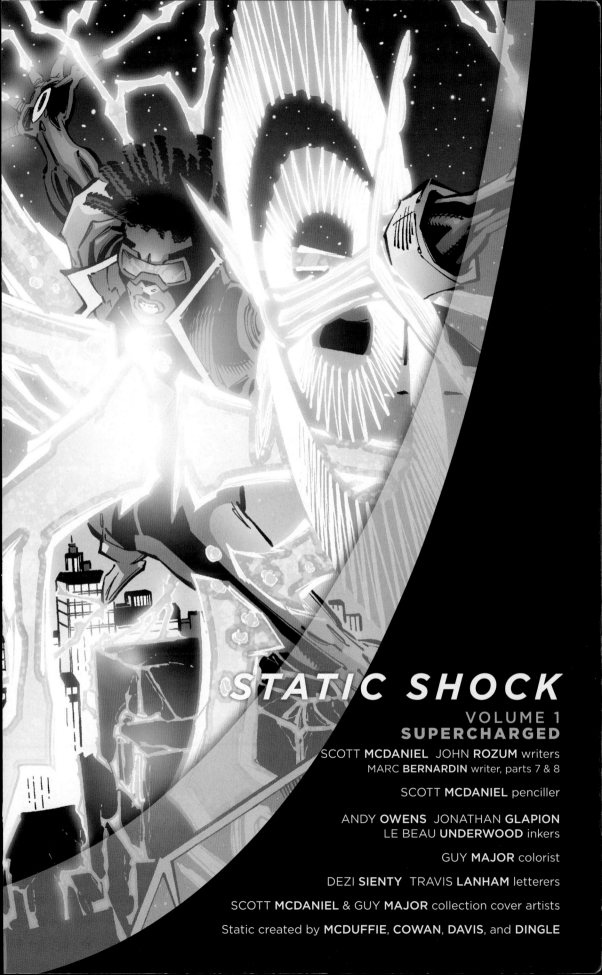

# STATIC SHOCK

## VOLUME 1
## SUPERCHARGED

SCOTT **MCDANIEL**  JOHN **ROZUM** writers
MARC **BERNARDIN** writer, parts 7 & 8

SCOTT **MCDANIEL** penciller

ANDY **OWENS**  JONATHAN **GLAPION**
LE BEAU **UNDERWOOD** inkers

GUY **MAJOR** colorist

DEZI **SIENTY**  TRAVIS **LANHAM** letterers

SCOTT **MCDANIEL** & GUY **MAJOR** collection cover artists

Static created by **MCDUFFIE**, **COWAN**, **DAVIS**, and **DINGLE**

HARVEY RICHARDS Editor – Original Series  ROWENA YOW Editor
ROBBIN BROSTERMAN Design Director – Books  ROBBIE BIEDERMAN Publication Design

BOB HARRAS VP – Editor-in-Chief

DIANE NELSON President  DAN DIDIO and JIM LEE Co-Publishers  GEOFF JOHNS Chief Creative Officer
JOHN ROOD Executive VP – Sales, Marketing and Business Development  AMY GENKINS Senior VP – Business and Legal Affairs
NAIRI GARDINER Senior VP – Finance  JEFF BOISON VP – Publishing Operations  MARK CHIARELLO VP – Art Direction and Design
JOHN CUNNINGHAM VP – Marketing  TERRI CUNNINGHAM VP – Talent Relations and Services
ALISON GILL Senior VP – Manufacturing and Operations  DAVID HYDE VP – Publicity  HANK KANALZ Senior VP – Digital
JAY KOGAN VP – Business and Legal Affairs, Publishing  JACK MAHAN VP – Business Affairs, Talent
NICK NAPOLITANO VP – Manufacturing Administration  SUE POHJA VP – Book Sales
COURTNEY SIMMONS Senior VP – Publicity  BOB WAYNE Senior VP – Sales

STATIC SHOCK VOLUME ONE: SUPERCHARGED

DC Comics, 1700 Broadway, New York, NY 10019
A Warner Bros. Entertainment Company.
Printed by RR Donnelley, Salem, VA, USA. 5/4/12. First Printing.
ISBN: 978-1-4012-3484-3

Library of Congress Cataloging-in-Publication Data

McDaniel, Scott.
Static shock volume one : supercharged / Scott McDaniel ; John Rozum ;
Andy Owens.
p. cm.
"Originally published in single magazine form in Static Shock 1-8."
ISBN 978-1-4012-3484-3
1. Graphic novels. I. Rozum, John. II. Owens, Andy. III. Title. IV.
Title: Supercharged.
PN6727.M265S73 2012
741.5'973—dc23
2012003584

90996 ⊥

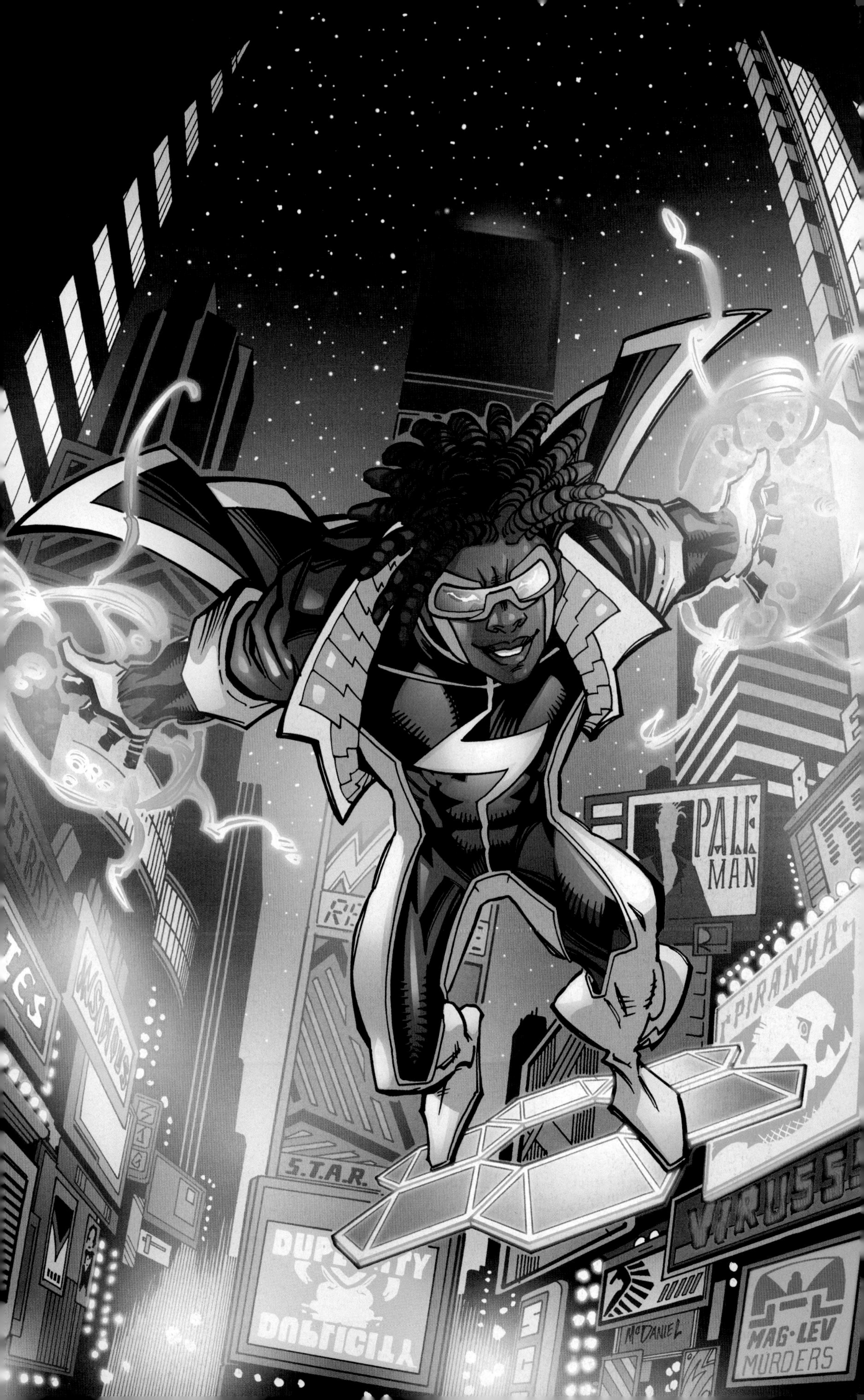
PALE MAN
PIRANHA
S.T.A.R.
McDANIEL
MAG-LEV
MURDERS

cover art by
SCOTT MCDANIEL
& GUY MAJOR

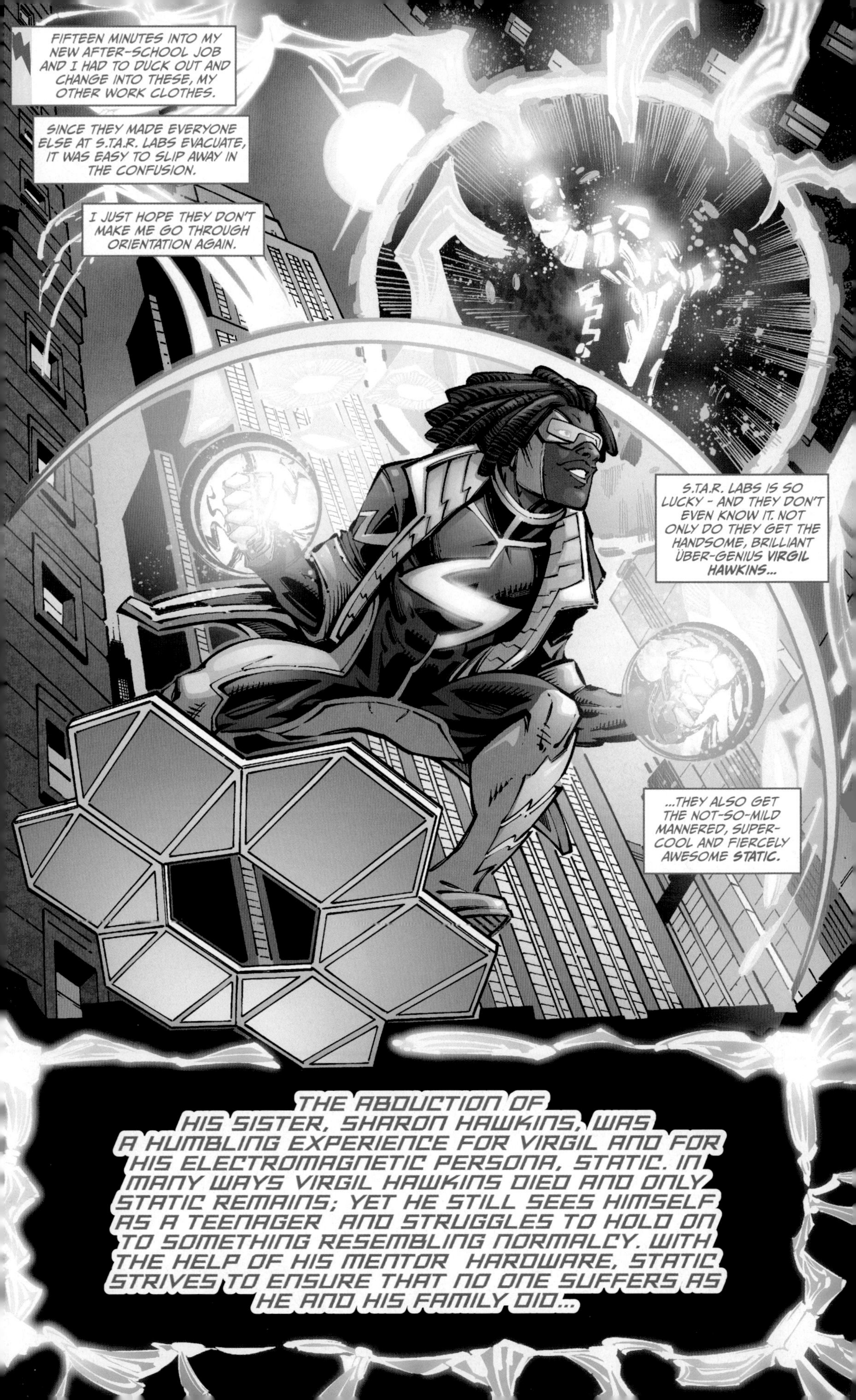
FIFTEEN MINUTES INTO MY NEW AFTER-SCHOOL JOB AND I HAD TO DUCK OUT AND CHANGE INTO THESE, MY OTHER WORK CLOTHES.
SINCE THEY MADE EVERYONE ELSE AT S.T.A.R. LABS EVACUATE, IT WAS EASY TO SLIP AWAY IN THE CONFUSION.
I JUST HOPE THEY DON'T MAKE ME GO THROUGH ORIENTATION AGAIN.
S.T.A.R. LABS IS SO LUCKY - AND THEY DON'T EVEN KNOW IT. NOT ONLY DO THEY GET THE HANDSOME, BRILLIANT ÜBER-GENIUS **VIRGIL HAWKINS**...
...THEY ALSO GET THE NOT-SO-MILD MANNERED, SUPER-COOL AND FIERCELY AWESOME **STATIC**.

THE ABDUCTION OF HIS SISTER, SHARON HAWKINS, WAS A HUMBLING EXPERIENCE FOR VIRGIL AND FOR HIS ELECTROMAGNETIC PERSONA, STATIC. IN MANY WAYS VIRGIL HAWKINS DIED AND ONLY STATIC REMAINS; YET HE STILL SEES HIMSELF AS A TEENAGER AND STRUGGLES TO HOLD ON TO SOMETHING RESEMBLING NORMALCY. WITH THE HELP OF HIS MENTOR HARDWARE, STATIC STRIVES TO ENSURE THAT NO ONE SUFFERS AS HE AND HIS FAMILY DID...

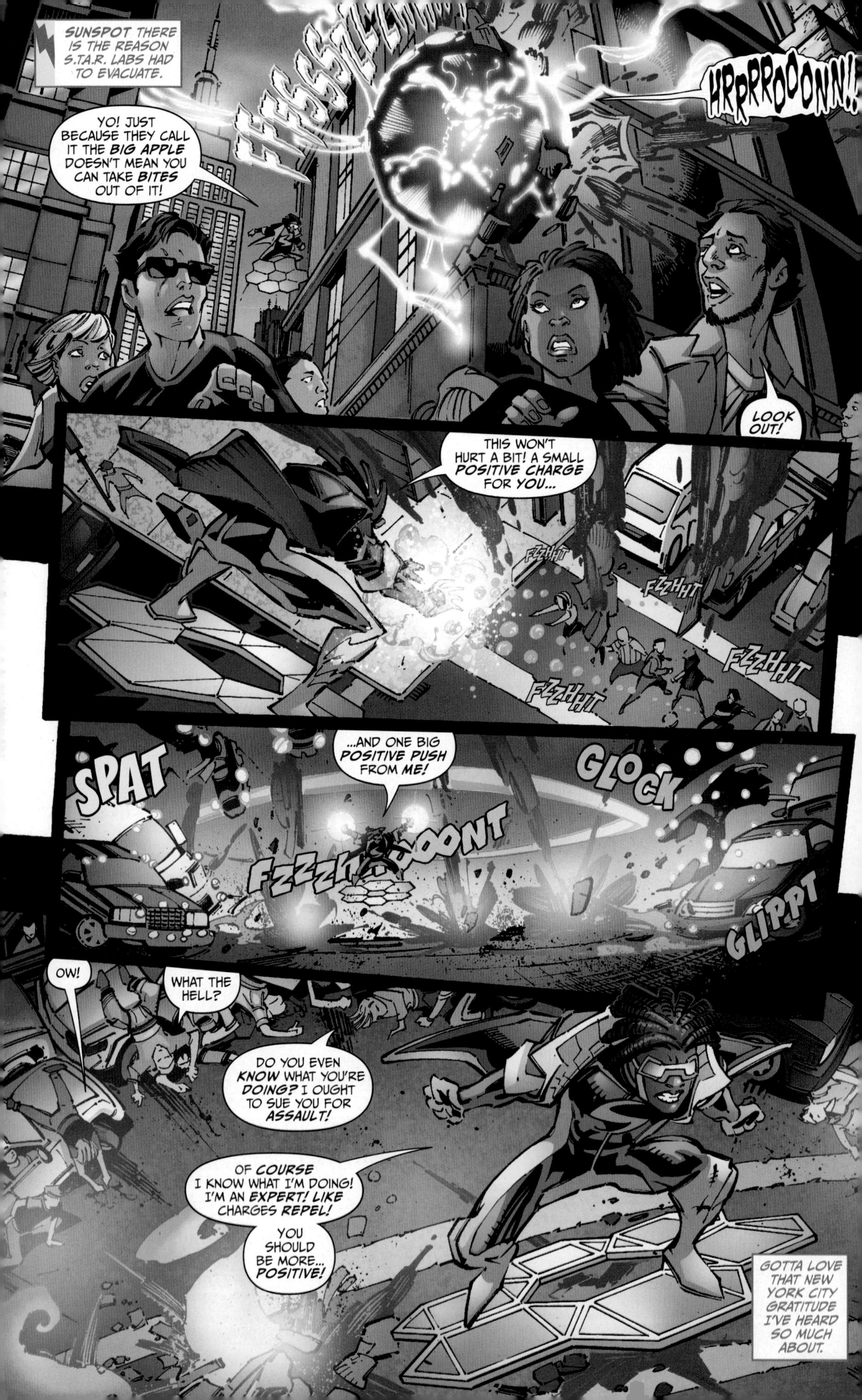
SUNSPOT THERE IS THE REASON S.T.A.R. LABS HAD TO EVACUATE.
HRRRROOONN!!
YO! JUST BECAUSE THEY CALL IT THE BIG APPLE DOESN'T MEAN YOU CAN TAKE BITES OUT OF IT!
LOOK OUT!
THIS WON'T HURT A BIT! A SMALL POSITIVE CHARGE FOR YOU...
FZZHHT
FZZHHT
FZZHHT
FZZHHT
...AND ONE BIG POSITIVE PUSH FROM ME!
SPAT
GLOCK
OONT
GLIPPT
OW!
WHAT THE HELL?
DO YOU EVEN KNOW WHAT YOU'RE DOING? I OUGHT TO SUE YOU FOR ASSAULT!
OF COURSE I KNOW WHAT I'M DOING! I'M AN EXPERT! LIKE CHARGES REPEL!
YOU SHOULD BE MORE... POSITIVE!
GOTTA LOVE THAT NEW YORK CITY GRATITUDE I'VE HEARD SO MUCH ABOUT.

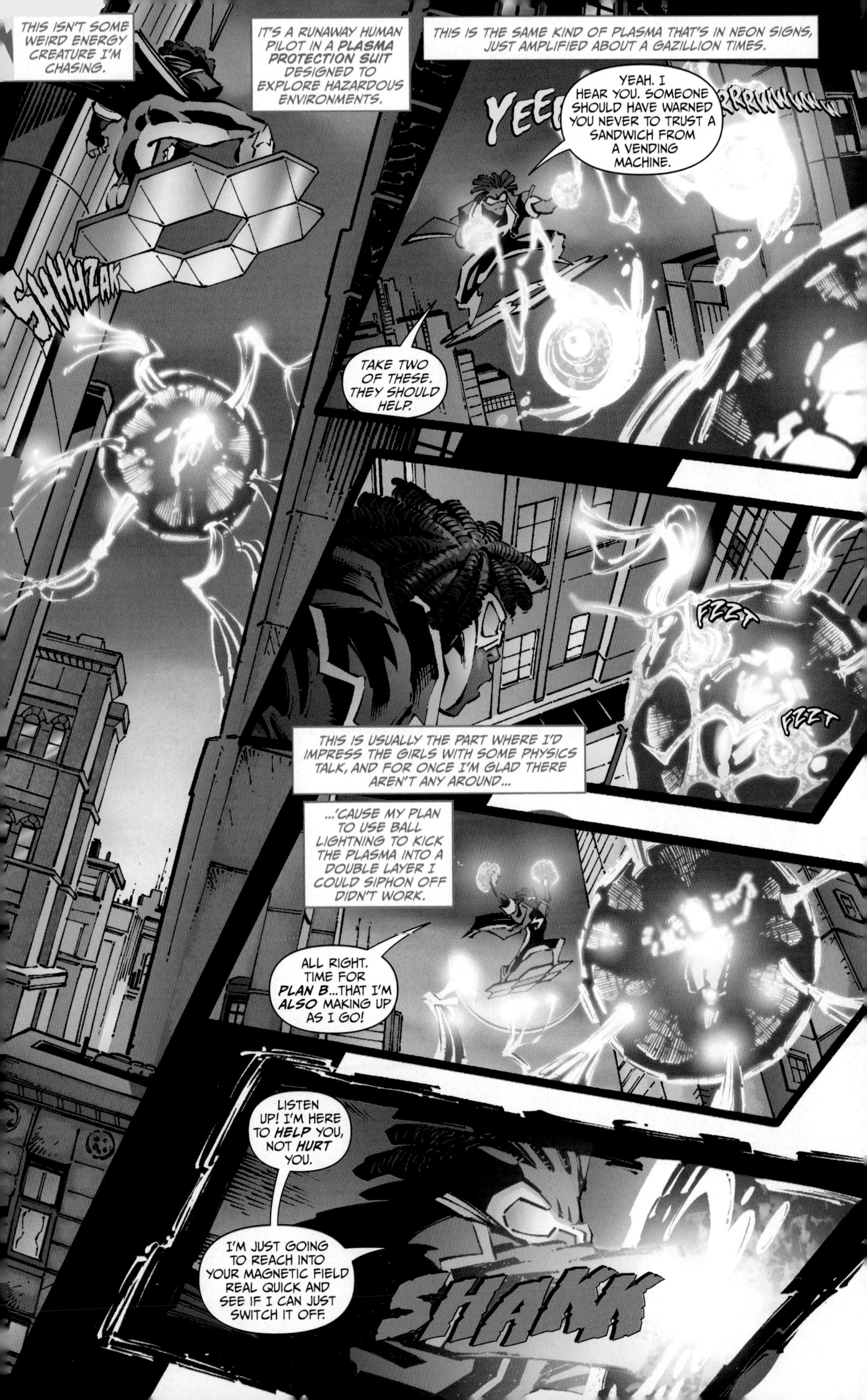
THIS ISN'T SOME WEIRD ENERGY CREATURE I'M CHASING.
IT'S A RUNAWAY HUMAN PILOT IN A PLASMA PROTECTION SUIT DESIGNED TO EXPLORE HAZARDOUS ENVIRONMENTS.
SHHHZAK
THIS IS THE SAME KIND OF PLASMA THAT'S IN NEON SIGNS, JUST AMPLIFIED ABOUT A GAZILLION TIMES.
YEAH. I HEAR YOU. SOMEONE SHOULD HAVE WARNED YOU NEVER TO TRUST A SANDWICH FROM A VENDING MACHINE.
TAKE TWO OF THESE. THEY SHOULD HELP.
FZZT
FZZT
THIS IS USUALLY THE PART WHERE I'D IMPRESS THE GIRLS WITH SOME PHYSICS TALK, AND FOR ONCE I'M GLAD THERE AREN'T ANY AROUND...
...'CAUSE MY PLAN TO USE BALL LIGHTNING TO KICK THE PLASMA INTO A DOUBLE LAYER I COULD SIPHON OFF DIDN'T WORK.
ALL RIGHT. TIME FOR PLAN B...THAT I'M ALSO MAKING UP AS I GO!
LISTEN UP! I'M HERE TO HELP YOU, NOT HURT YOU.
I'M JUST GOING TO REACH INTO YOUR MAGNETIC FIELD REAL QUICK AND SEE IF I CAN JUST SWITCH IT OFF.
SHAKK

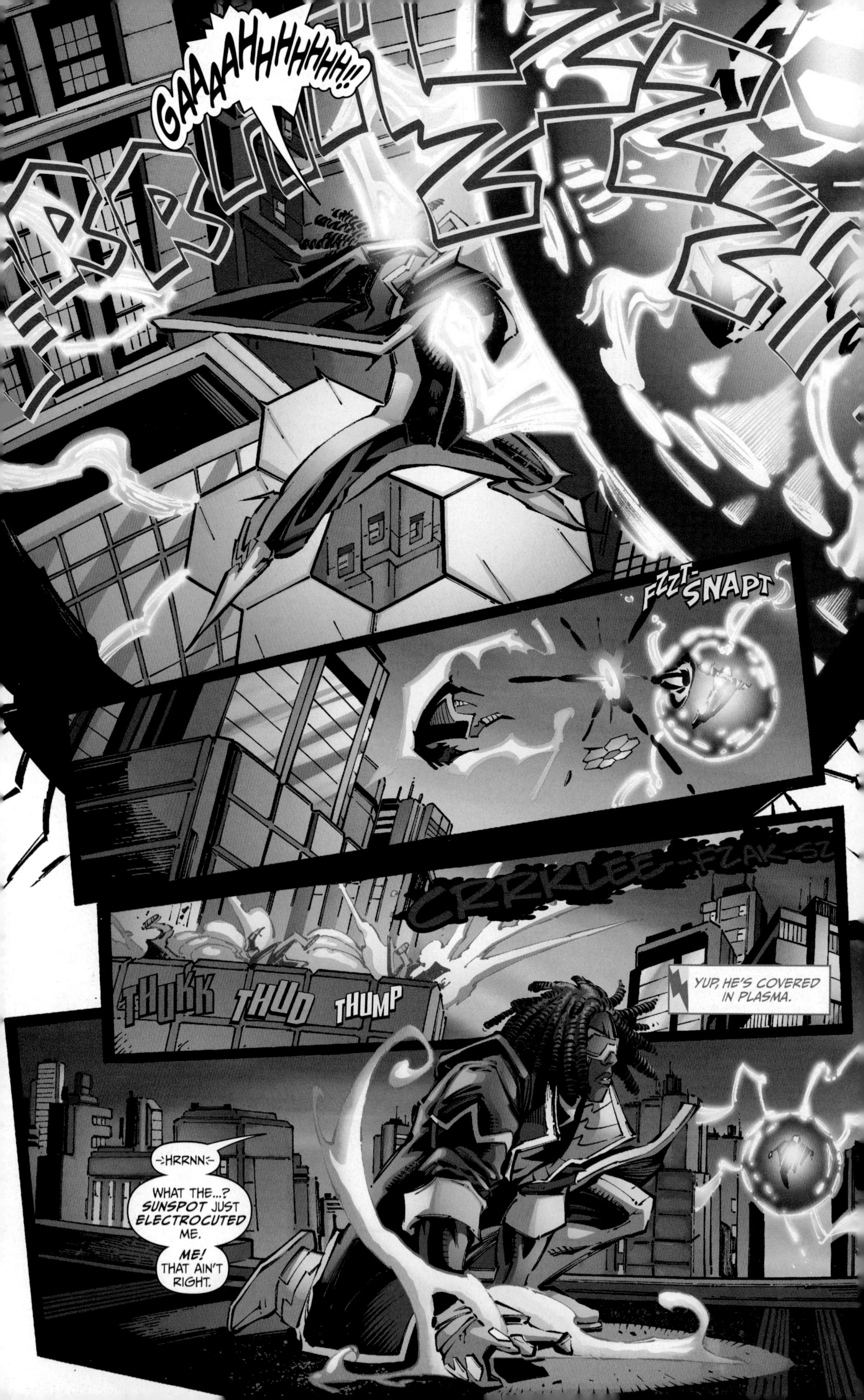
GAAAAHHHHHH!!
FZZT-SNAPT
CRRKLEE-FZAK-SZ
THUKK THUD THUMP
YUP, HE'S COVERED IN PLASMA.
-HRRNN-
WHAT THE...? SUNSPOT JUST ELECTROCUTED ME.
ME! THAT AIN'T RIGHT.

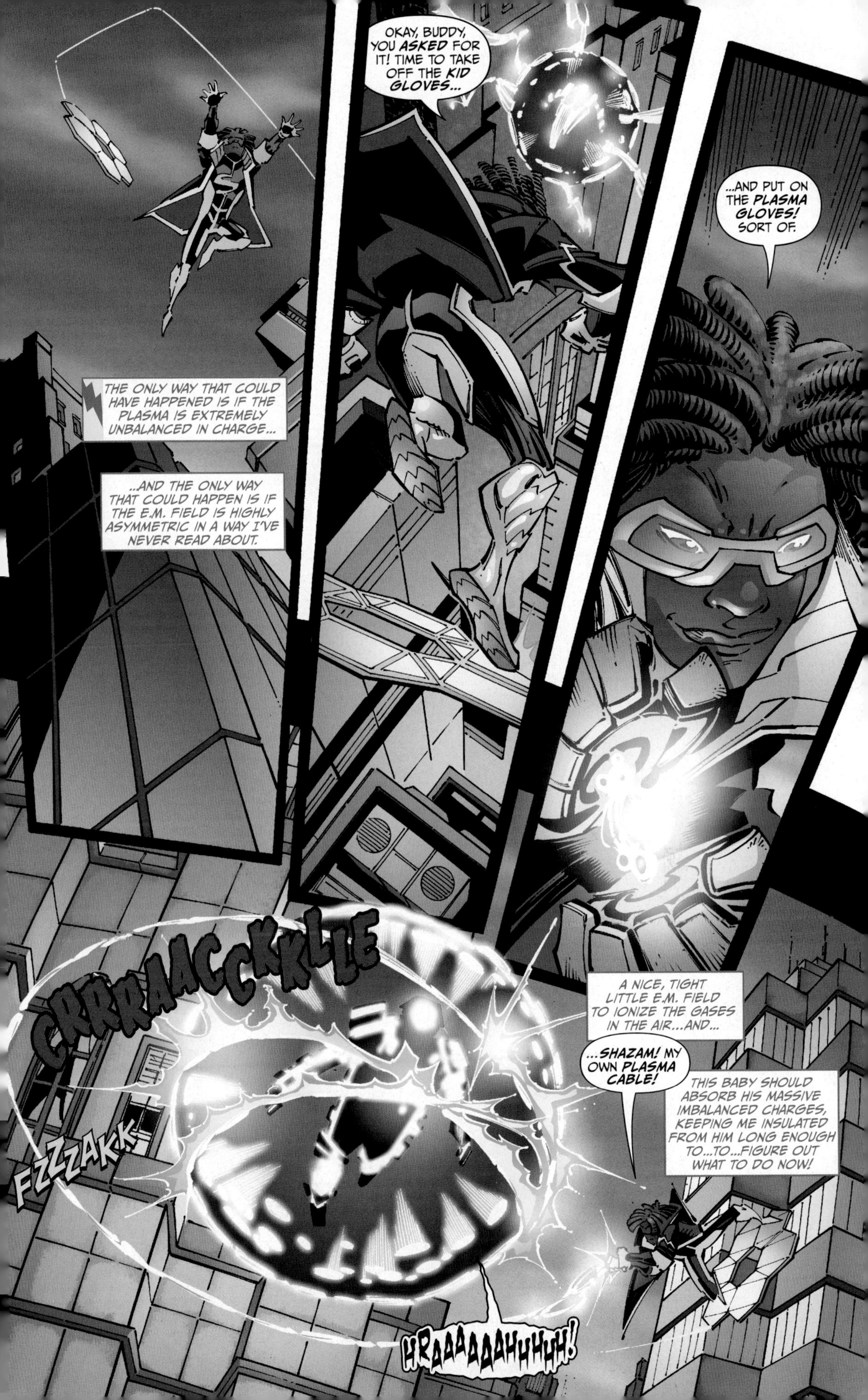

OKAY, BUDDY, YOU ASKED FOR IT! TIME TO TAKE OFF THE KID GLOVES...
...AND PUT ON THE PLASMA GLOVES! SORT OF.
THE ONLY WAY THAT COULD HAVE HAPPENED IS IF THE PLASMA IS EXTREMELY UNBALANCED IN CHARGE...
...AND THE ONLY WAY THAT COULD HAPPEN IS IF THE E.M. FIELD IS HIGHLY ASYMMETRIC IN A WAY I'VE NEVER READ ABOUT.
CRRRAACCKKLLE
FZZZAKK
A NICE, TIGHT LITTLE E.M. FIELD TO IONIZE THE GASES IN THE AIR...AND...
...SHAZAM! MY OWN PLASMA CABLE!
THIS BABY SHOULD ABSORB HIS MASSIVE IMBALANCED CHARGES, KEEPING ME INSULATED FROM HIM LONG ENOUGH TO...TO...FIGURE OUT WHAT TO DO NOW!
HRAAAAAAHHHHH!

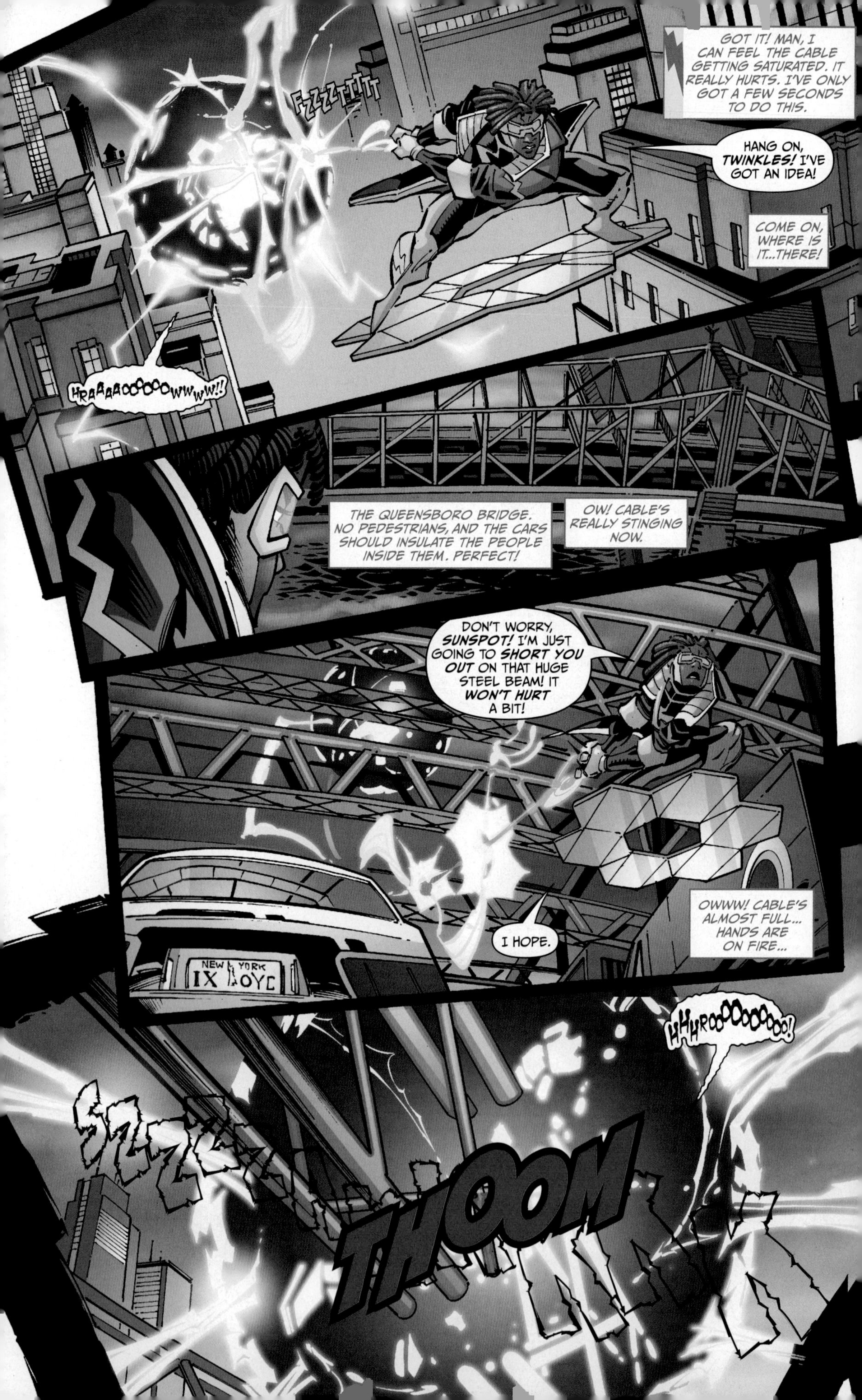
GOT IT! MAN, I CAN FEEL THE CABLE GETTING SATURATED. IT REALLY HURTS. I'VE ONLY GOT A FEW SECONDS TO DO THIS.
FZZZZTTTTT
HANG ON, TWINKLES! I'VE GOT AN IDEA!
COME ON, WHERE IS IT...THERE!
HRAAAAOOOOOOWWWW!!
THE QUEENSBORO BRIDGE. NO PEDESTRIANS, AND THE CARS SHOULD INSULATE THE PEOPLE INSIDE THEM. PERFECT!
OW! CABLE'S REALLY STINGING NOW.
DON'T WORRY, SUNSPOT! I'M JUST GOING TO SHORT YOU OUT ON THAT HUGE STEEL BEAM! IT WON'T HURT A BIT!
I HOPE.
OWWW! CABLE'S ALMOST FULL... HANDS ARE ON FIRE...
NEW YORK
IX AOYC
HHHROOOOOOOOOO!
SZZZZZT
THOOM

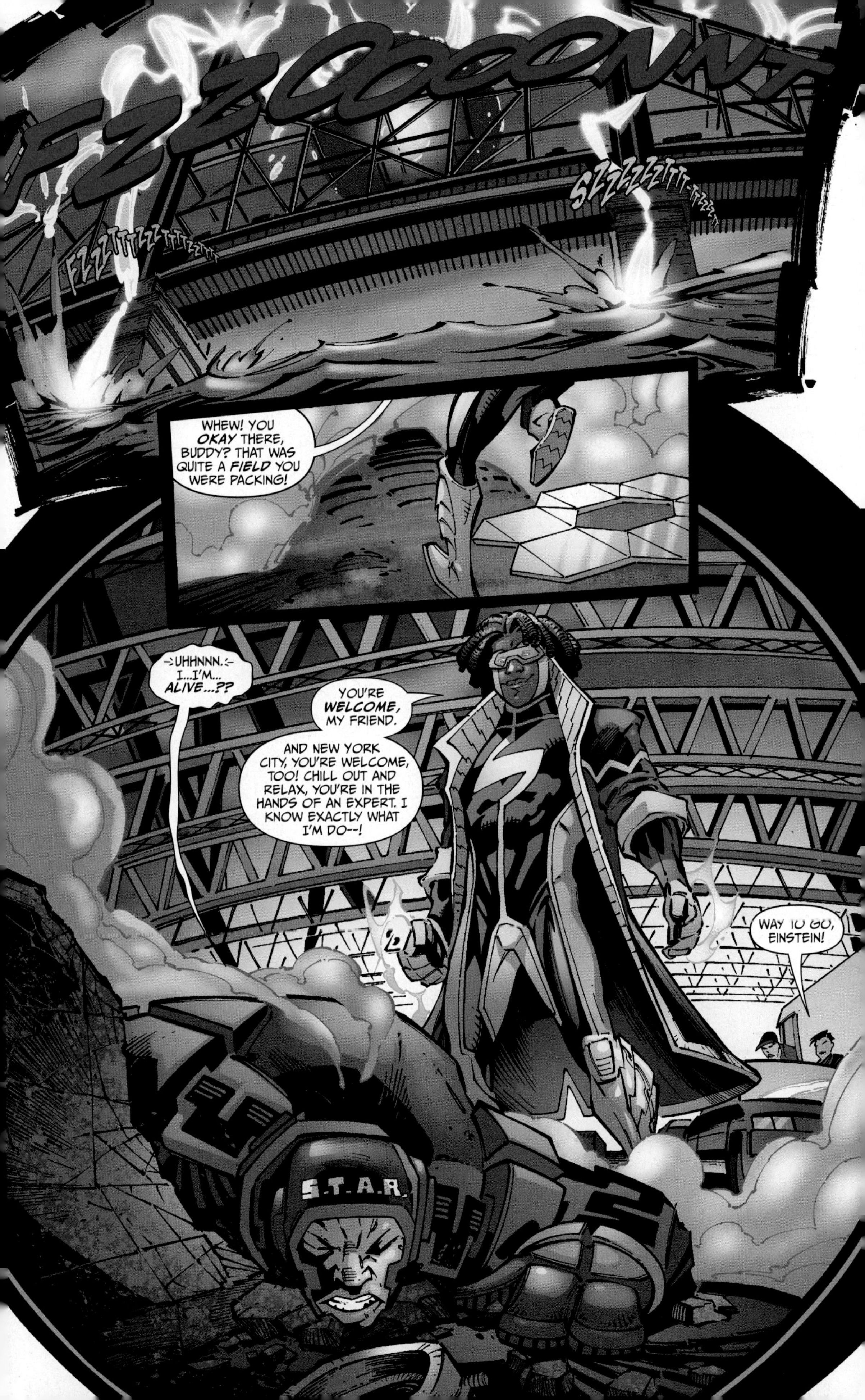
FZZZOOOONNT
FZZZTTTZZZTTTTZZTTTT
SZZZZZZZTTT-TTZZZZTT
WHEW! YOU OKAY THERE, BUDDY? THAT WAS QUITE A FIELD YOU WERE PACKING!
UHHNNN. I...I'M... ALIVE...??
YOU'RE WELCOME, MY FRIEND.
AND NEW YORK CITY, YOU'RE WELCOME, TOO! CHILL OUT AND RELAX, YOU'RE IN THE HANDS OF AN EXPERT. I KNOW EXACTLY WHAT I'M DO--!
WAY TO GO, EINSTEIN!
S.T.A.R.

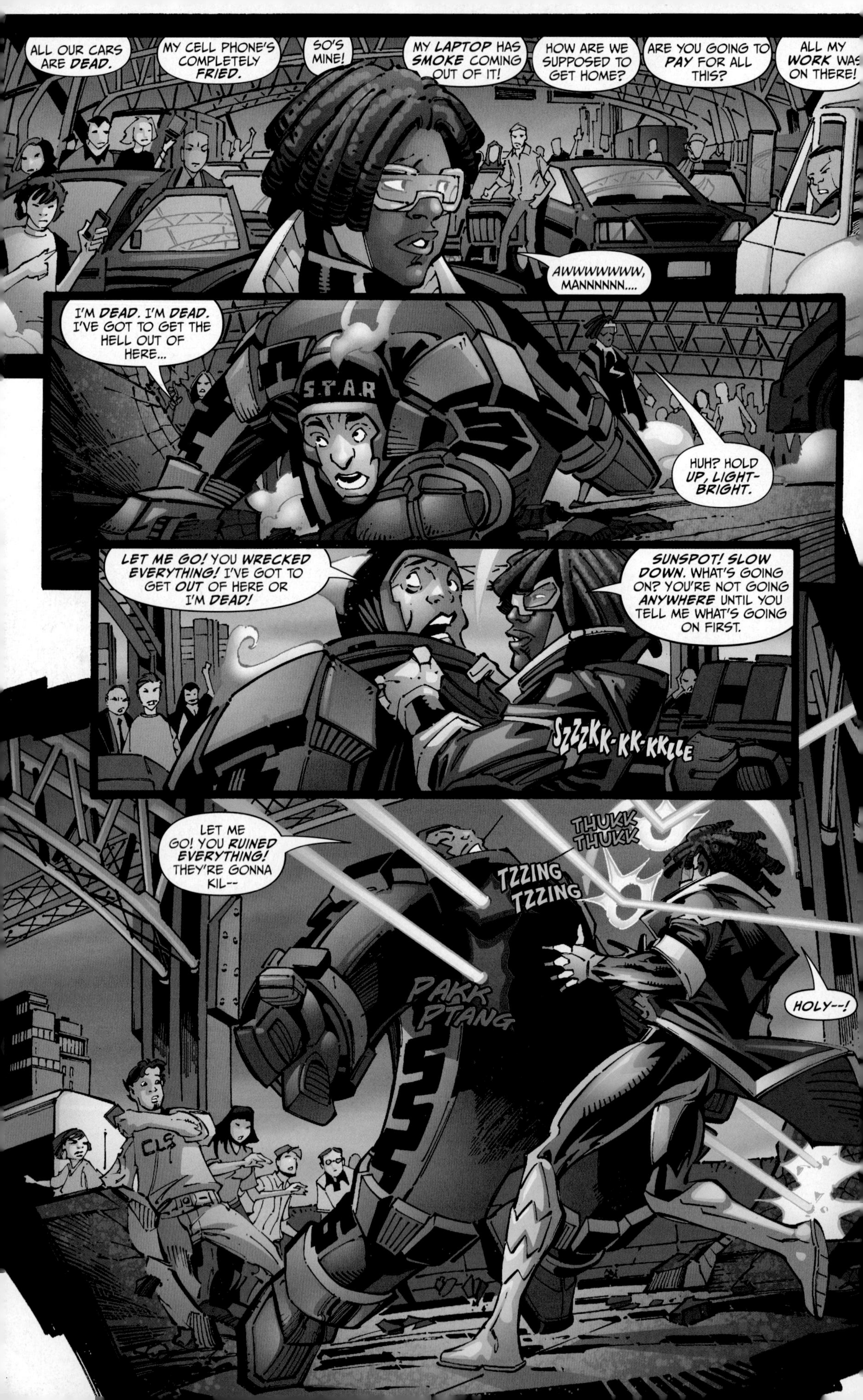

ALL OUR CARS ARE DEAD.
MY CELL PHONE'S COMPLETELY FRIED.
SO'S MINE!
MY LAPTOP HAS SMOKE COMING OUT OF IT!
HOW ARE WE SUPPOSED TO GET HOME?
ARE YOU GOING TO PAY FOR ALL THIS?
ALL MY WORK WAS ON THERE!
AWWWWWWW, MANNNNNN....
I'M DEAD. I'M DEAD. I'VE GOT TO GET THE HELL OUT OF HERE...
S.T.A.R
HUH? HOLD UP, LIGHT-BRIGHT.
LET ME GO! YOU WRECKED EVERYTHING! I'VE GOT TO GET OUT OF HERE OR I'M DEAD!
SUNSPOT! SLOW DOWN. WHAT'S GOING ON? YOU'RE NOT GOING ANYWHERE UNTIL YOU TELL ME WHAT'S GOING ON FIRST.
SZZZKK-KK-KKLLE
LET ME GO! YOU RUINED EVERYTHING! THEY'RE GONNA KIL--
THUKK THUKK
TZZING TZZING
PAKK PTANG
HOLY--!

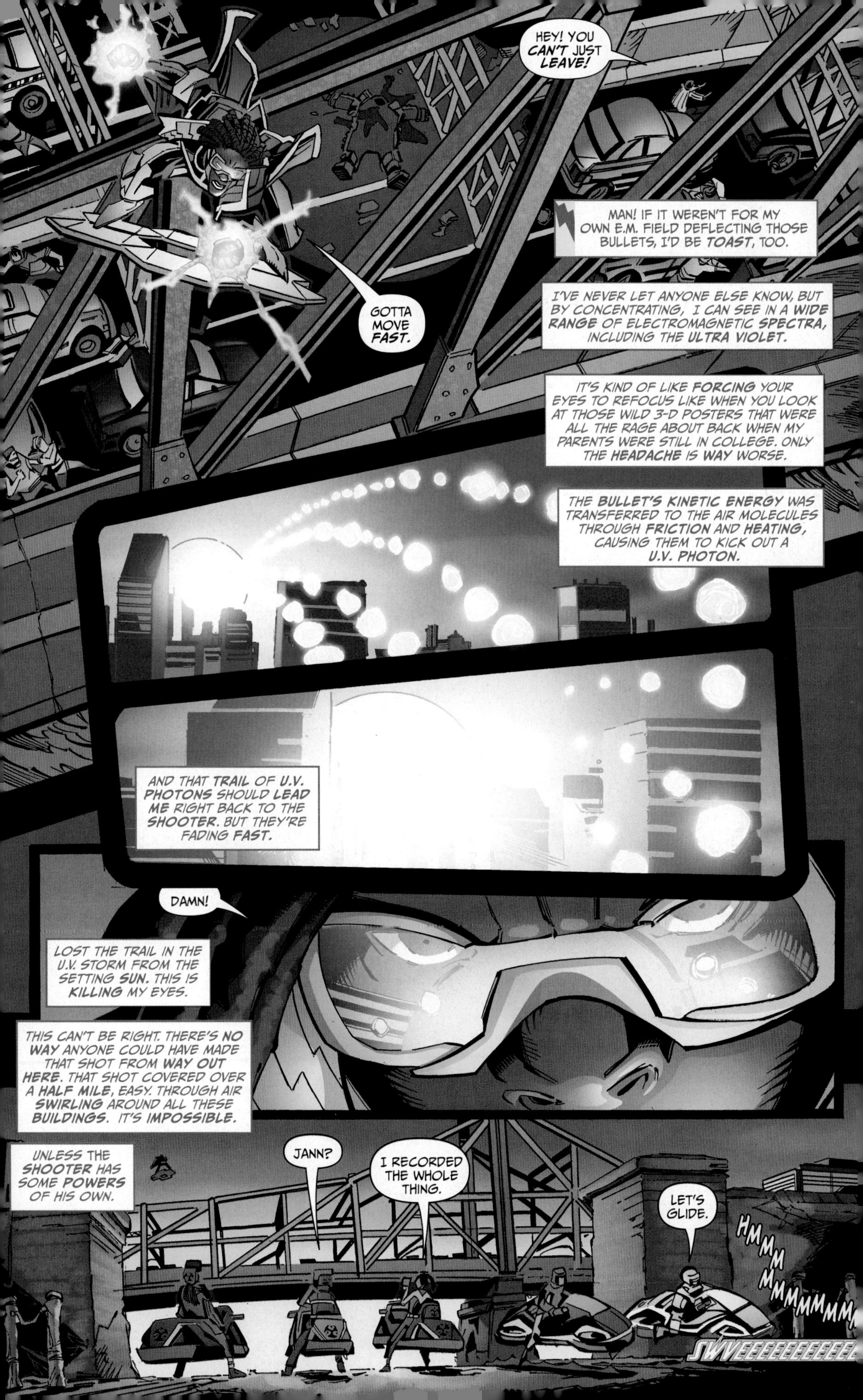
HEY! YOU CAN'T JUST LEAVE!
MAN! IF IT WEREN'T FOR MY OWN E.M. FIELD DEFLECTING THOSE BULLETS, I'D BE TOAST, TOO.
GOTTA MOVE FAST.
I'VE NEVER LET ANYONE ELSE KNOW, BUT BY CONCENTRATING, I CAN SEE IN A WIDE RANGE OF ELECTROMAGNETIC SPECTRA, INCLUDING THE ULTRA VIOLET.
IT'S KIND OF LIKE FORCING YOUR EYES TO REFOCUS LIKE WHEN YOU LOOK AT THOSE WILD 3-D POSTERS THAT WERE ALL THE RAGE ABOUT BACK WHEN MY PARENTS WERE STILL IN COLLEGE. ONLY THE HEADACHE IS WAY WORSE.
THE BULLET'S KINETIC ENERGY WAS TRANSFERRED TO THE AIR MOLECULES THROUGH FRICTION AND HEATING, CAUSING THEM TO KICK OUT A U.V. PHOTON.
AND THAT TRAIL OF U.V. PHOTONS SHOULD LEAD ME RIGHT BACK TO THE SHOOTER. BUT THEY'RE FADING FAST.
DAMN!
LOST THE TRAIL IN THE U.V. STORM FROM THE SETTING SUN. THIS IS KILLING MY EYES.
THIS CAN'T BE RIGHT. THERE'S NO WAY ANYONE COULD HAVE MADE THAT SHOT FROM WAY OUT HERE. THAT SHOT COVERED OVER A HALF MILE, EASY. THROUGH AIR SWIRLING AROUND ALL THESE BUILDINGS. IT'S IMPOSSIBLE.
UNLESS THE SHOOTER HAS SOME POWERS OF HIS OWN.
JANN?
I RECORDED THE WHOLE THING.
LET'S GLIDE.
HMMMMMMMMMM
SWVEEEEEEEEEEEE

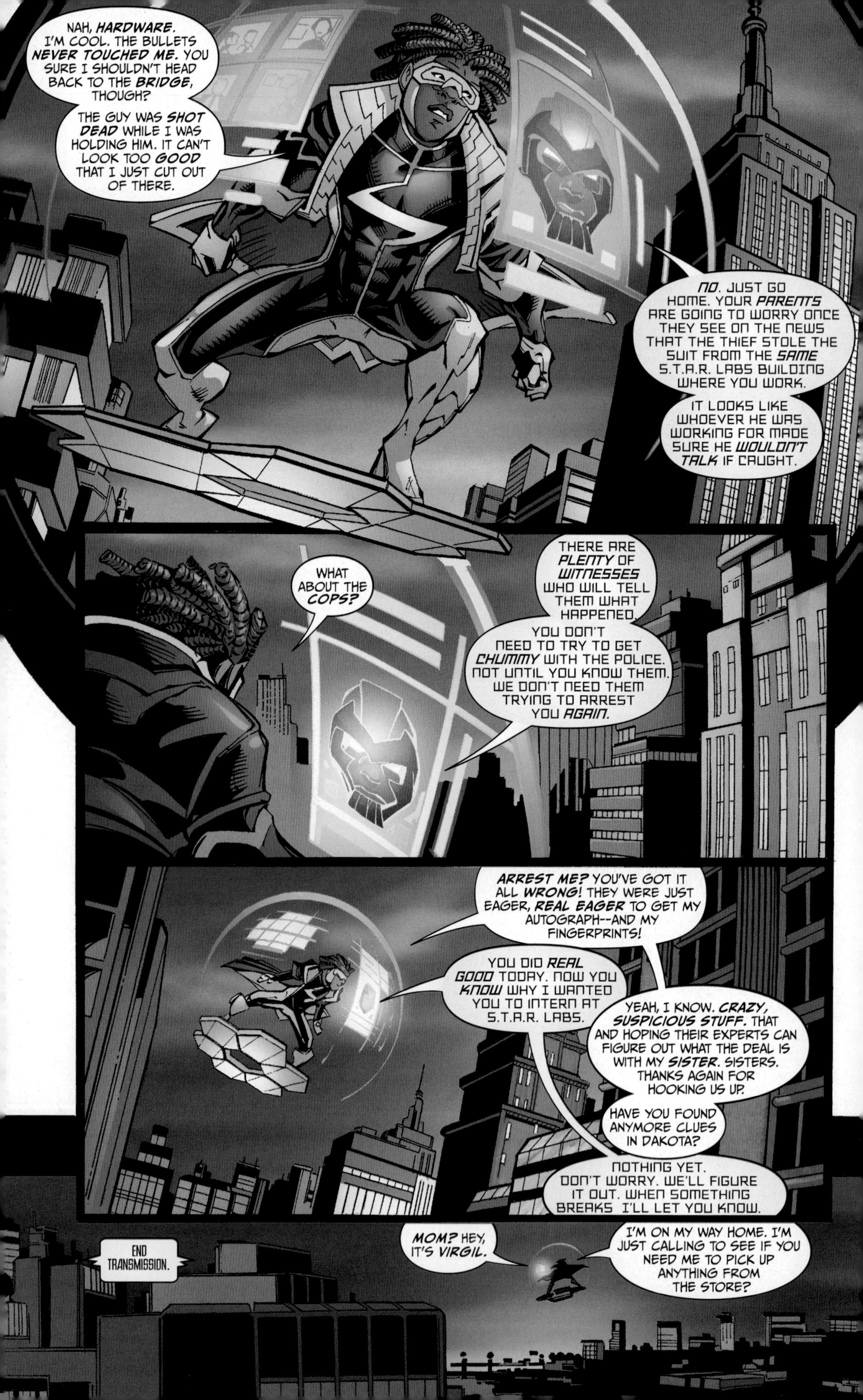
NAH, HARDWARE. I'M COOL. THE BULLETS NEVER TOUCHED ME. YOU SURE I SHOULDN'T HEAD BACK TO THE BRIDGE, THOUGH?
THE GUY WAS SHOT DEAD WHILE I WAS HOLDING HIM. IT CAN'T LOOK TOO GOOD THAT I JUST CUT OUT OF THERE.
NO. JUST GO HOME. YOUR PARENTS ARE GOING TO WORRY ONCE THEY SEE ON THE NEWS THAT THE THIEF STOLE THE SUIT FROM THE SAME S.T.A.R. LABS BUILDING WHERE YOU WORK.
IT LOOKS LIKE WHOEVER HE WAS WORKING FOR MADE SURE HE WOULDN'T TALK IF CAUGHT.
WHAT ABOUT THE COPS?
THERE ARE PLENTY OF WITNESSES WHO WILL TELL THEM WHAT HAPPENED.
YOU DON'T NEED TO TRY TO GET CHUMMY WITH THE POLICE. NOT UNTIL YOU KNOW THEM. WE DON'T NEED THEM TRYING TO ARREST YOU AGAIN.
ARREST ME? YOU'VE GOT IT ALL WRONG! THEY WERE JUST EAGER, REAL EAGER TO GET MY AUTOGRAPH--AND MY FINGERPRINTS!
YOU DID REAL GOOD TODAY. NOW YOU KNOW WHY I WANTED YOU TO INTERN AT S.T.A.R. LABS.
YEAH, I KNOW. CRAZY, SUSPICIOUS STUFF. THAT AND HOPING THEIR EXPERTS CAN FIGURE OUT WHAT THE DEAL IS WITH MY SISTER. SISTERS. THANKS AGAIN FOR HOOKING US UP.
HAVE YOU FOUND ANYMORE CLUES IN DAKOTA?
NOTHING YET. DON'T WORRY. WE'LL FIGURE IT OUT. WHEN SOMETHING BREAKS I'LL LET YOU KNOW.
END TRANSMISSION.
MOM? HEY, IT'S VIRGIL.
I'M ON MY WAY HOME. I'M JUST CALLING TO SEE IF YOU NEED ME TO PICK UP ANYTHING FROM THE STORE?

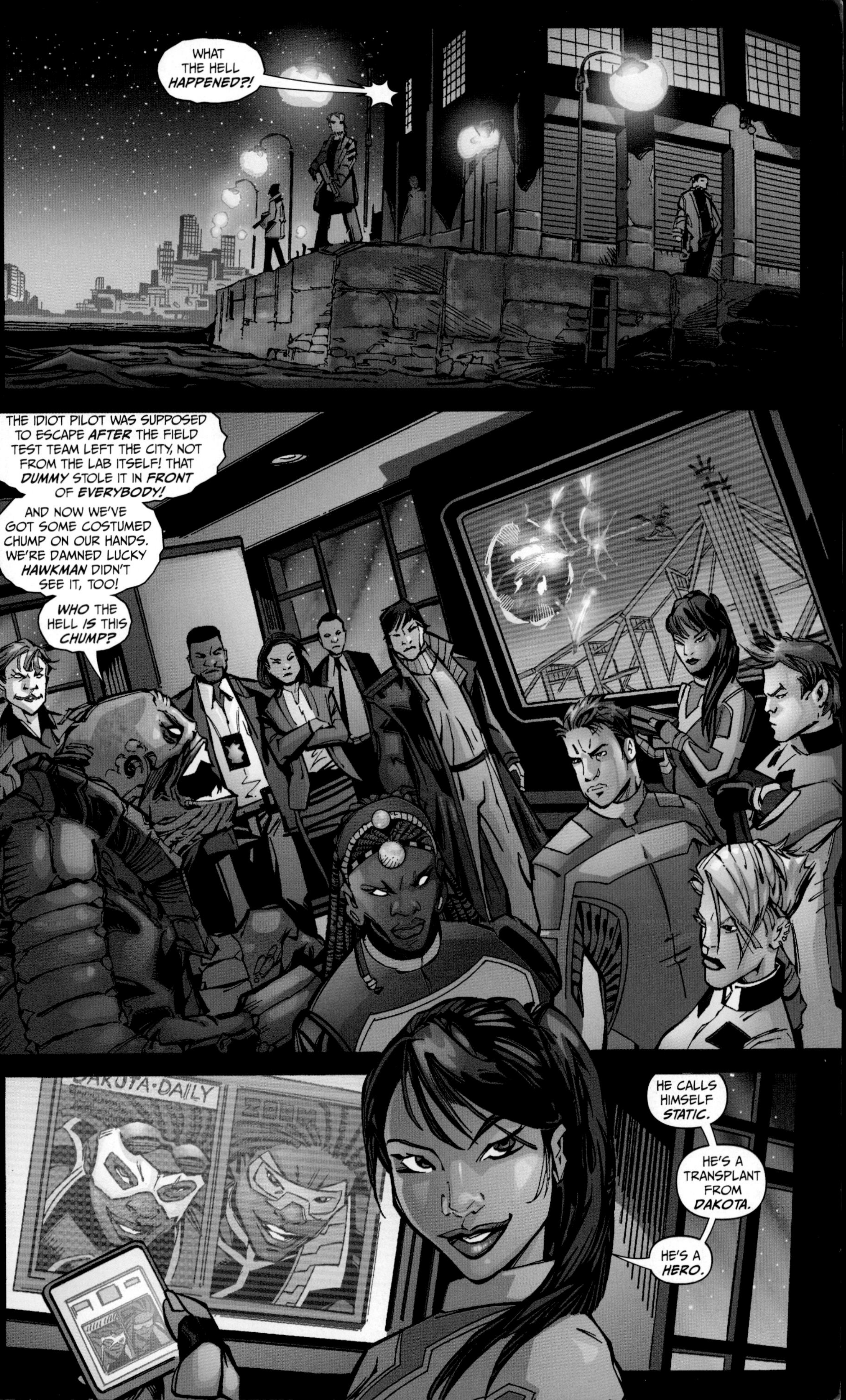
WHAT THE HELL *HAPPENED?!*
THE IDIOT PILOT WAS SUPPOSED TO ESCAPE *AFTER* THE FIELD TEST TEAM LEFT THE CITY, NOT FROM THE LAB ITSELF! THAT *DUMMY* STOLE IT IN *FRONT* OF *EVERYBODY!*
AND NOW WE'VE GOT SOME COSTUMED CHUMP ON OUR HANDS. WE'RE DAMNED LUCKY *HAWKMAN* DIDN'T SEE IT, TOO!
*WHO* THE HELL *IS* THIS *CHUMP?*
HE CALLS HIMSELF *STATIC.*
HE'S A TRANSPLANT FROM *DAKOTA.*
HE'S A *HERO.*

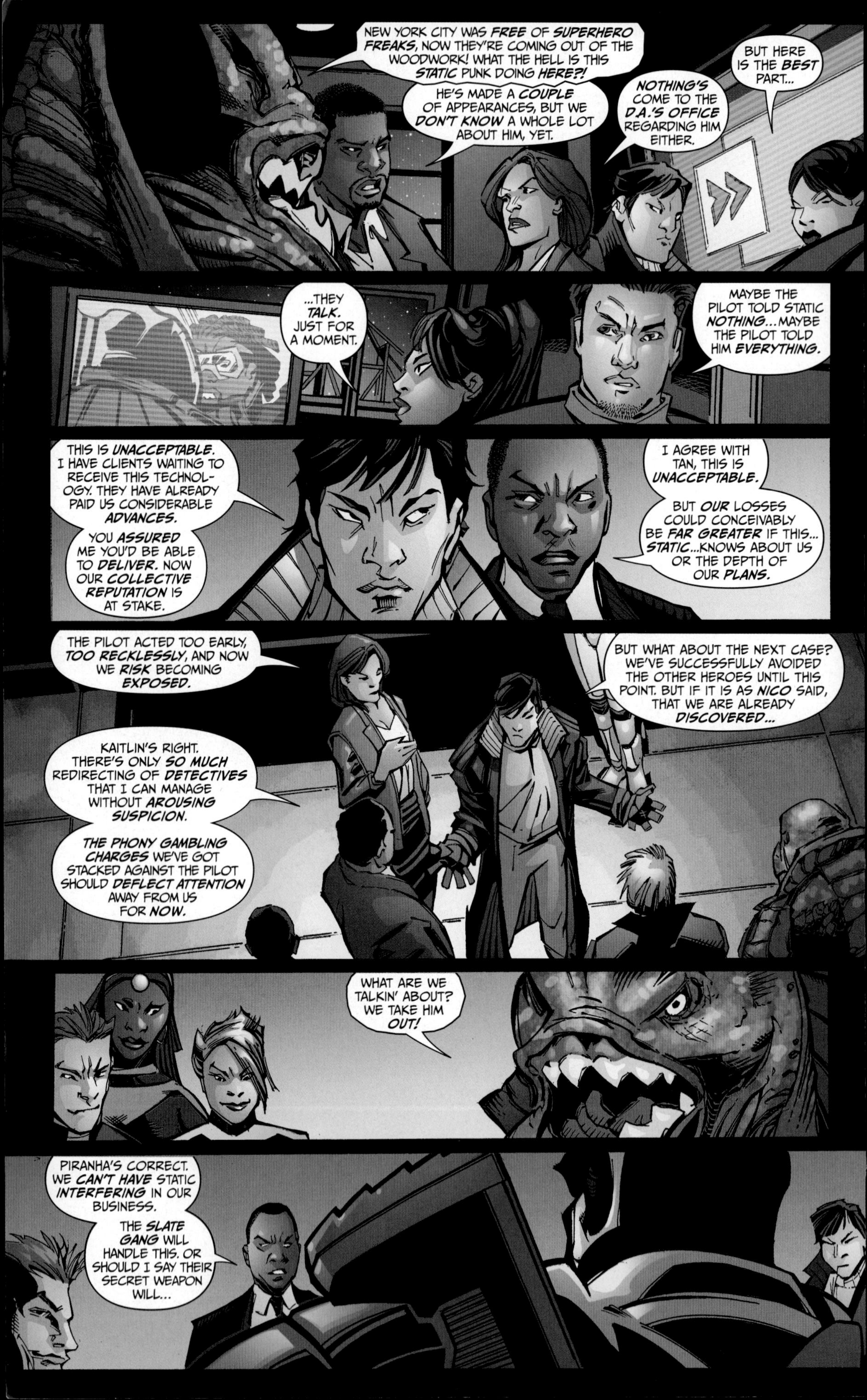
NEW YORK CITY WAS FREE OF SUPERHERO FREAKS, NOW THEY'RE COMING OUT OF THE WOODWORK! WHAT THE HELL IS THIS STATIC PUNK DOING HERE?!
HE'S MADE A COUPLE OF APPEARANCES, BUT WE DON'T KNOW A WHOLE LOT ABOUT HIM, YET.
NOTHING'S COME TO THE D.A.'S OFFICE REGARDING HIM EITHER.
BUT HERE IS THE BEST PART...
...THEY TALK. JUST FOR A MOMENT.
MAYBE THE PILOT TOLD STATIC NOTHING...MAYBE THE PILOT TOLD HIM EVERYTHING.
THIS IS UNACCEPTABLE. I HAVE CLIENTS WAITING TO RECEIVE THIS TECHNOLOGY. THEY HAVE ALREADY PAID US CONSIDERABLE ADVANCES.
YOU ASSURED ME YOU'D BE ABLE TO DELIVER. NOW OUR COLLECTIVE REPUTATION IS AT STAKE.
I AGREE WITH TAN, THIS IS UNACCEPTABLE.
BUT OUR LOSSES COULD CONCEIVABLY BE FAR GREATER IF THIS... STATIC...KNOWS ABOUT US OR THE DEPTH OF OUR PLANS.
THE PILOT ACTED TOO EARLY, TOO RECKLESSLY, AND NOW WE RISK BECOMING EXPOSED.
BUT WHAT ABOUT THE NEXT CASE? WE'VE SUCCESSFULLY AVOIDED THE OTHER HEROES UNTIL THIS POINT. BUT IF IT IS AS NICO SAID, THAT WE ARE ALREADY DISCOVERED...
KAITLIN'S RIGHT. THERE'S ONLY SO MUCH REDIRECTING OF DETECTIVES THAT I CAN MANAGE WITHOUT AROUSING SUSPICION.
THE PHONY GAMBLING CHARGES WE'VE GOT STACKED AGAINST THE PILOT SHOULD DEFLECT ATTENTION AWAY FROM US FOR NOW.
WHAT ARE WE TALKIN' ABOUT? WE TAKE HIM OUT!
PIRANHA'S CORRECT. WE CAN'T HAVE STATIC INTERFERING IN OUR BUSINESS.
THE SLATE GANG WILL HANDLE THIS. OR SHOULD I SAY THEIR SECRET WEAPON WILL...

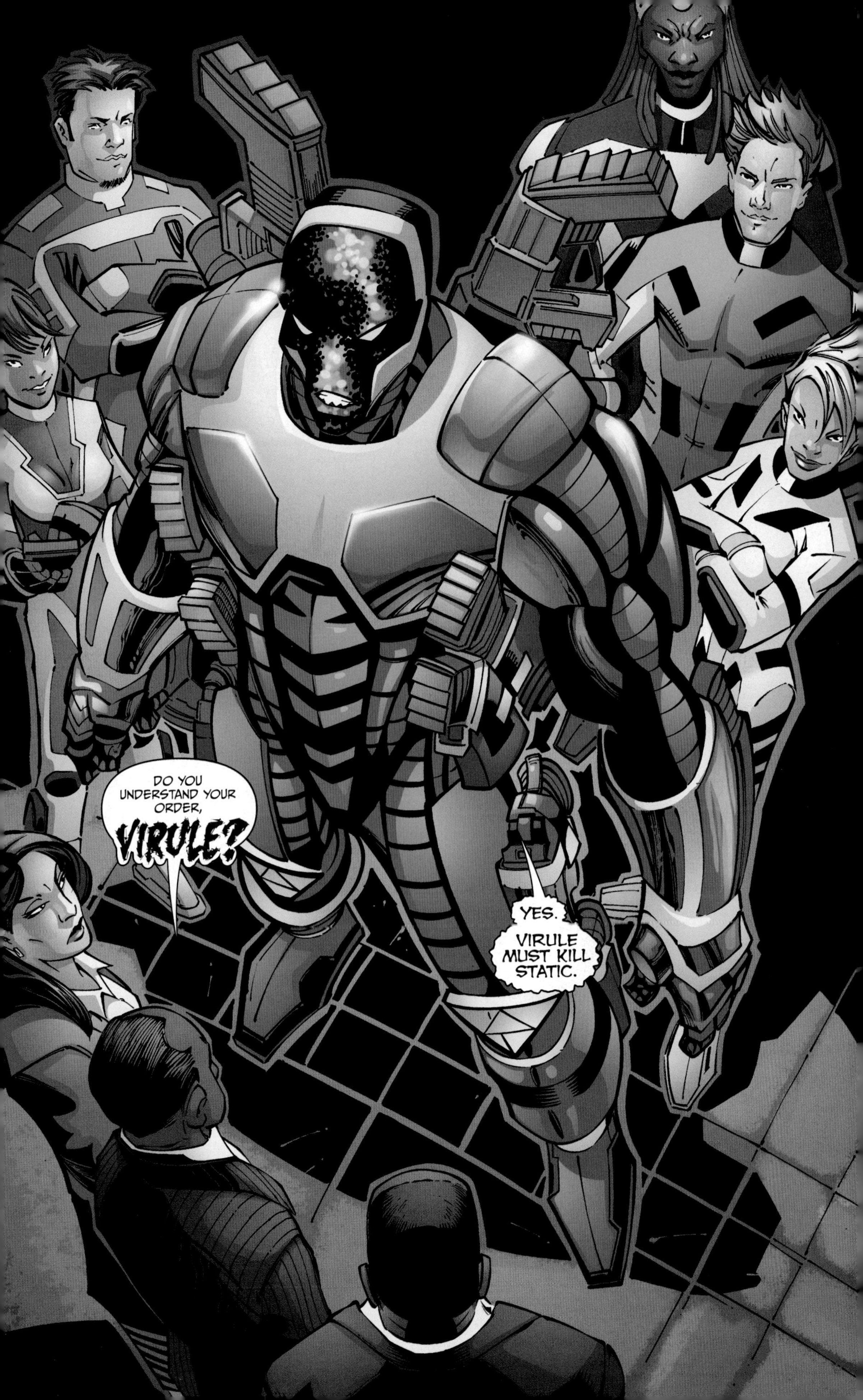
DO YOU UNDERSTAND YOUR ORDER, VIRULE?
YES. VIRULE MUST KILL STATIC.

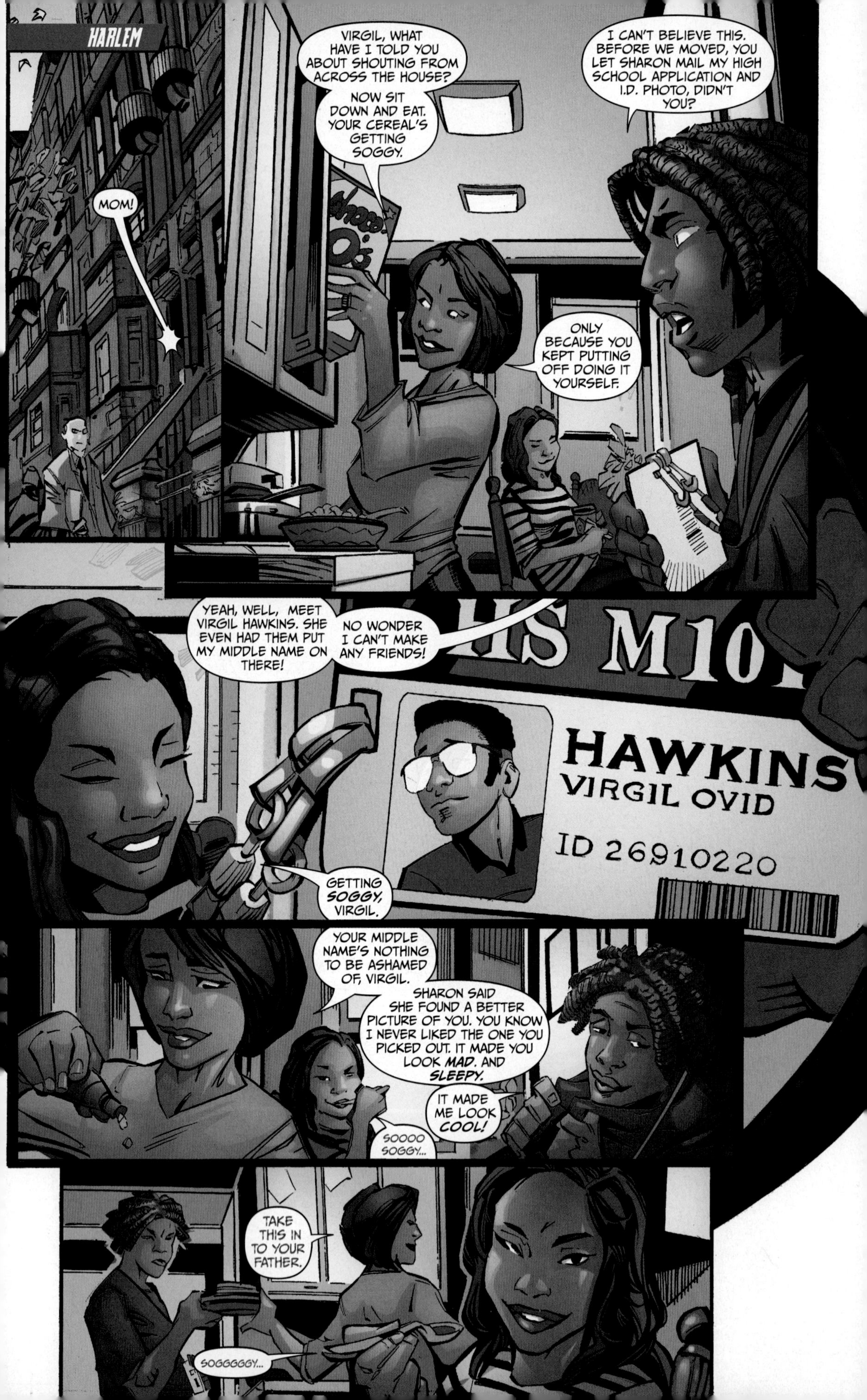
HARLEM
MOM!
VIRGIL, WHAT HAVE I TOLD YOU ABOUT SHOUTING FROM ACROSS THE HOUSE?
NOW SIT DOWN AND EAT. YOUR CEREAL'S GETTING SOGGY.
I CAN'T BELIEVE THIS. BEFORE WE MOVED, YOU LET SHARON MAIL MY HIGH SCHOOL APPLICATION AND I.D. PHOTO, DIDN'T YOU?
ONLY BECAUSE YOU KEPT PUTTING OFF DOING IT YOURSELF.
YEAH, WELL, MEET VIRGIL HAWKINS. SHE EVEN HAD THEM PUT MY MIDDLE NAME ON THERE!
NO WONDER I CAN'T MAKE ANY FRIENDS!
HS M10
HAWKINS
VIRGIL OVID
ID 26910220
GETTING *SOGGY*, VIRGIL.
YOUR MIDDLE NAME'S NOTHING TO BE ASHAMED OF, VIRGIL.
SHARON SAID SHE FOUND A BETTER PICTURE OF YOU. YOU KNOW I NEVER LIKED THE ONE YOU PICKED OUT. IT MADE YOU LOOK *MAD*. AND *SLEEPY*.
IT MADE ME LOOK *COOL!*
SOOOO SOGGY...
TAKE THIS IN TO YOUR FATHER.
SOGGGGGY...

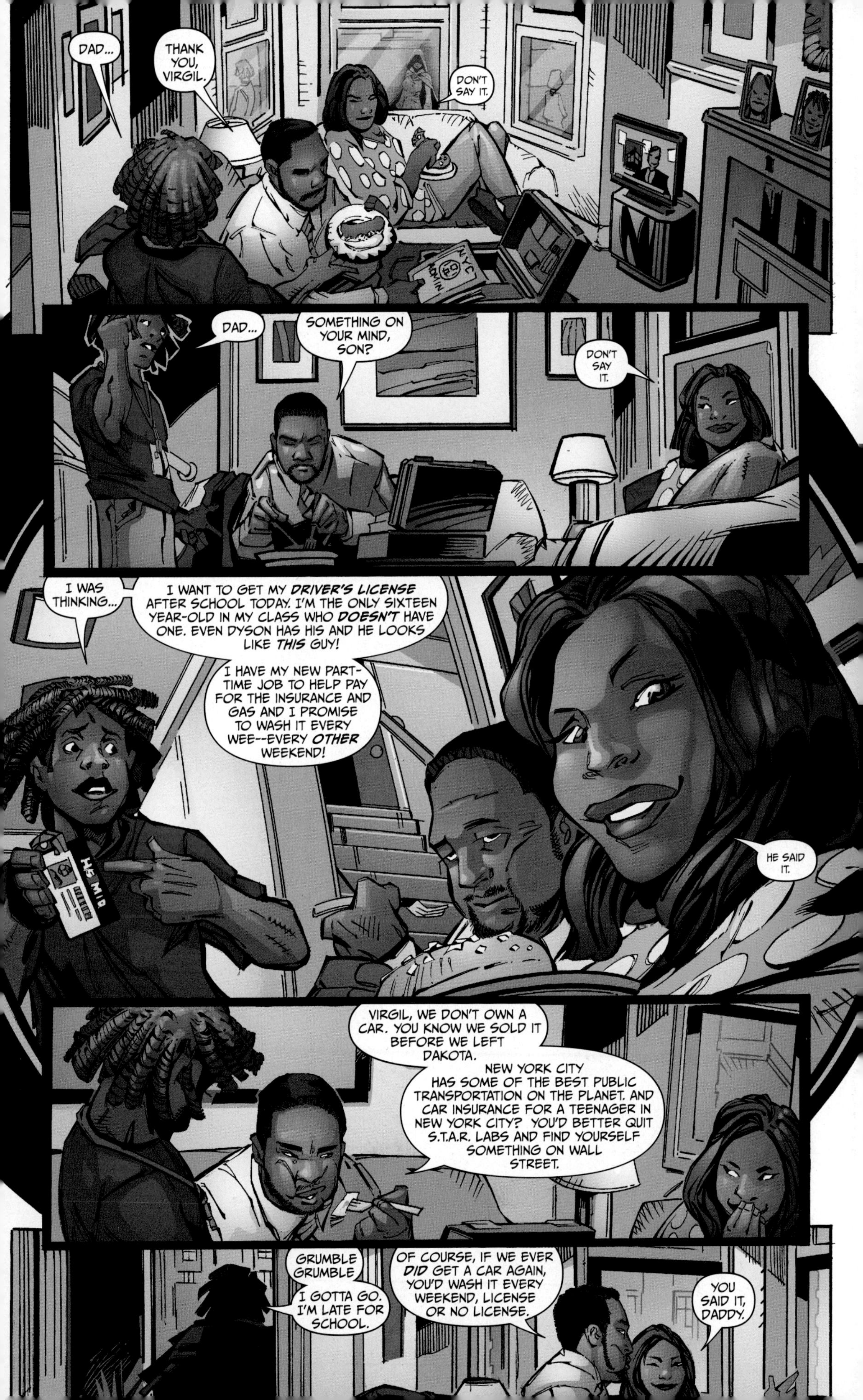
DAD...
THANK YOU, VIRGIL.
DON'T SAY IT.
DAD...
SOMETHING ON YOUR MIND, SON?
DON'T SAY IT.
I WAS THINKING...
I WANT TO GET MY DRIVER'S LICENSE AFTER SCHOOL TODAY. I'M THE ONLY SIXTEEN YEAR-OLD IN MY CLASS WHO DOESN'T HAVE ONE. EVEN DYSON HAS HIS AND HE LOOKS LIKE THIS GUY!
I HAVE MY NEW PART-TIME JOB TO HELP PAY FOR THE INSURANCE AND GAS AND I PROMISE TO WASH IT EVERY WEE--EVERY OTHER WEEKEND!
HE SAID IT.
VIRGIL, WE DON'T OWN A CAR. YOU KNOW WE SOLD IT BEFORE WE LEFT DAKOTA.
NEW YORK CITY HAS SOME OF THE BEST PUBLIC TRANSPORTATION ON THE PLANET. AND CAR INSURANCE FOR A TEENAGER IN NEW YORK CITY? YOU'D BETTER QUIT S.T.A.R. LABS AND FIND YOURSELF SOMETHING ON WALL STREET.
GRUMBLE GRUMBLE
I GOTTA GO. I'M LATE FOR SCHOOL.
OF COURSE, IF WE EVER DID GET A CAR AGAIN, YOU'D WASH IT EVERY WEEKEND, LICENSE OR NO LICENSE.
YOU SAID IT, DADDY.

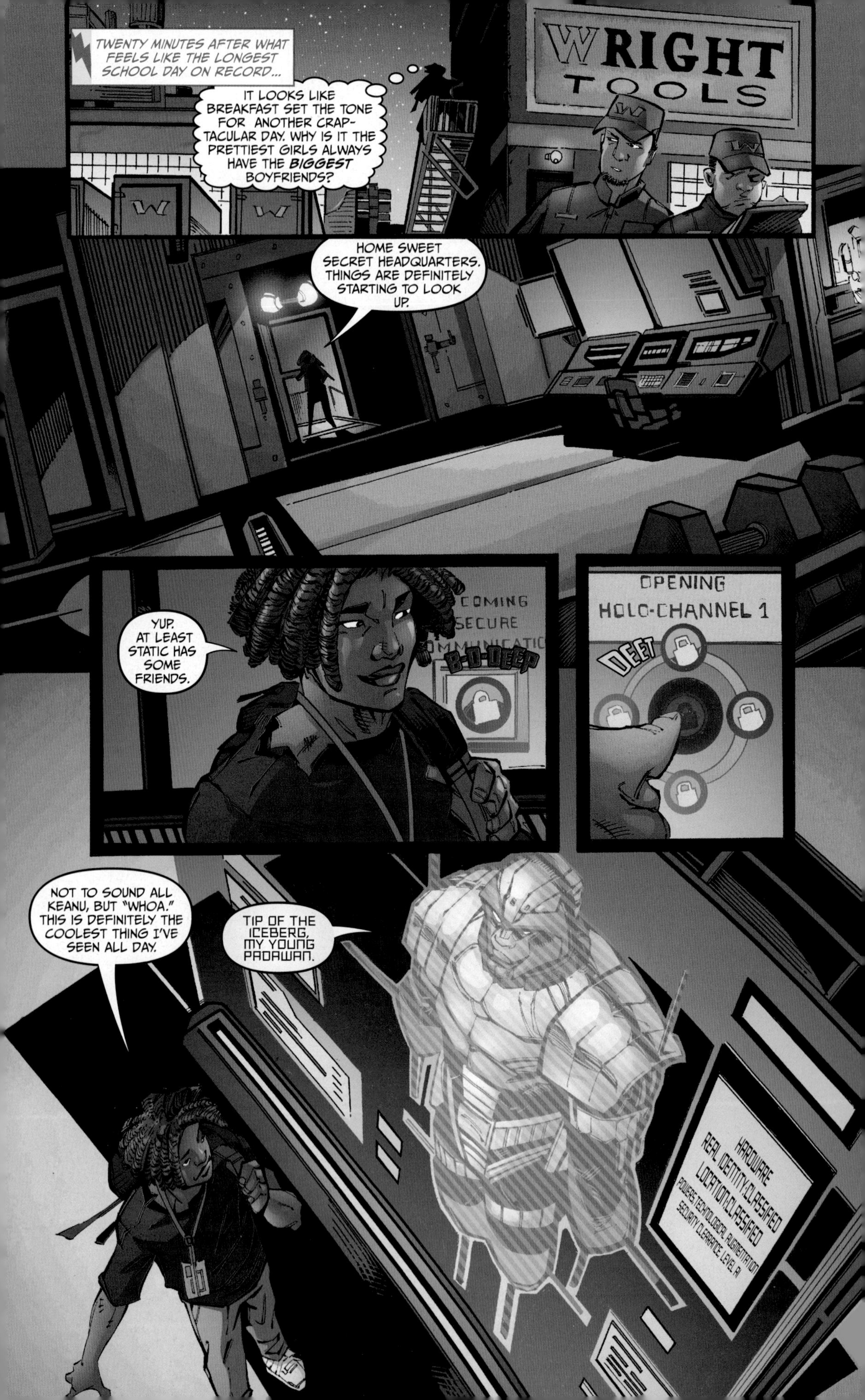

TWENTY MINUTES AFTER WHAT FEELS LIKE THE LONGEST SCHOOL DAY ON RECORD...
WRIGHT TOOLS
IT LOOKS LIKE BREAKFAST SET THE TONE FOR ANOTHER CRAP-TACULAR DAY. WHY IS IT THE PRETTIEST GIRLS ALWAYS HAVE THE ***BIGGEST*** BOYFRIENDS?
HOME SWEET SECRET HEADQUARTERS. THINGS ARE DEFINITELY STARTING TO LOOK UP.
YUP. AT LEAST STATIC HAS SOME FRIENDS.
B-D-DEEP
OPENING HOLO-CHANNEL 1
DEET
NOT TO SOUND ALL KEANU, BUT "WHOA." THIS IS DEFINITELY THE COOLEST THING I'VE SEEN ALL DAY.
TIP OF THE ICEBERG, MY YOUNG PADAWAN.
HARDWARE
REAL IDENTITY:CLASSIFIED
LOCATION:CLASSIFIED
POWERS:TECHNOLOGICAL AUGMENTATION
SECURITY CLEARANCE LEVEL A1

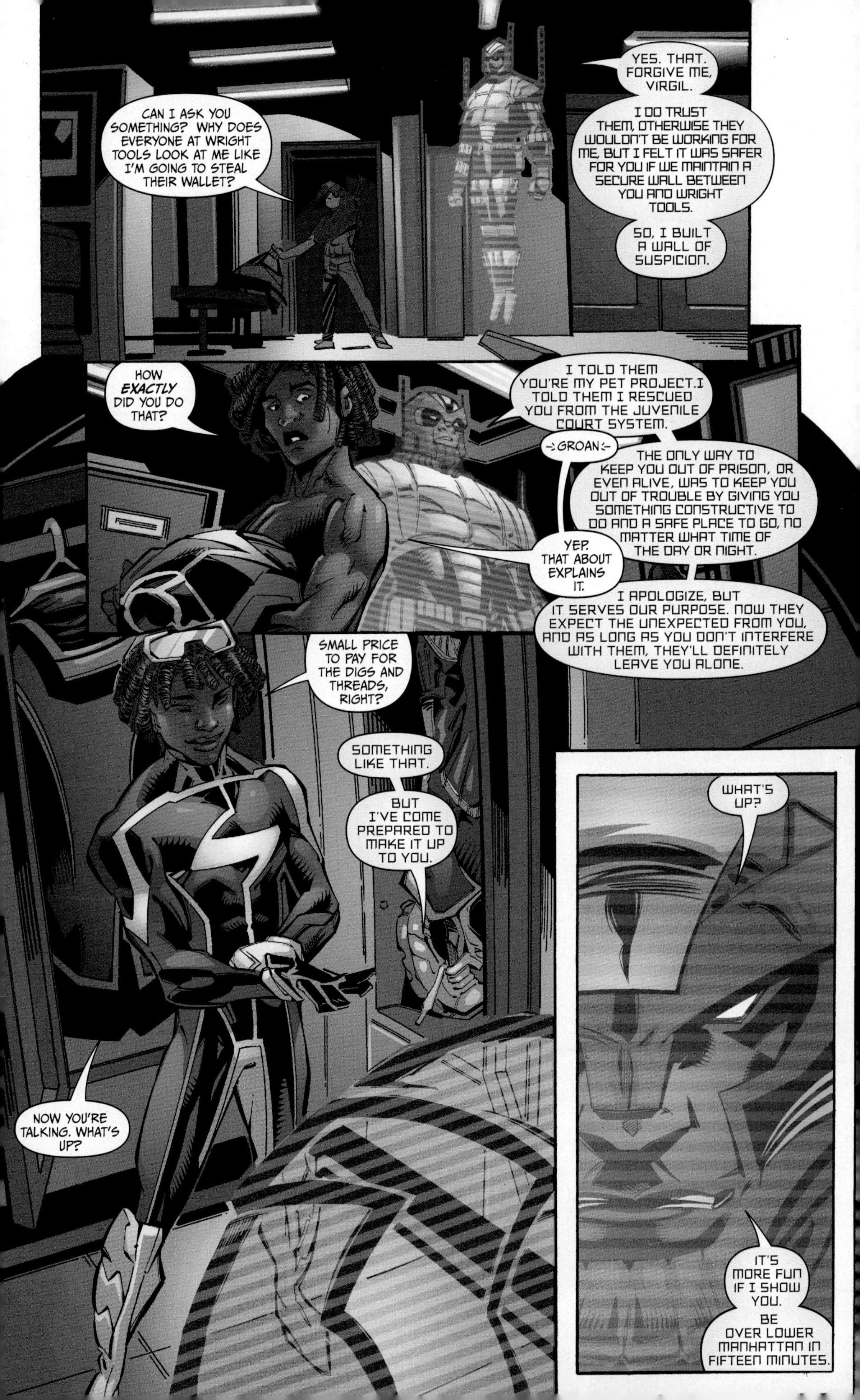
CAN I ASK YOU SOMETHING? WHY DOES EVERYONE AT WRIGHT TOOLS LOOK AT ME LIKE I'M GOING TO STEAL THEIR WALLET?
YES. THAT. FORGIVE ME, VIRGIL.
I DO TRUST THEM, OTHERWISE THEY WOULDN'T BE WORKING FOR ME, BUT I FELT IT WAS SAFER FOR YOU IF WE MAINTAIN A SECURE WALL BETWEEN YOU AND WRIGHT TOOLS.
SO, I BUILT A WALL OF SUSPICION.
HOW *EXACTLY* DID YOU DO THAT?
I TOLD THEM YOU'RE MY PET PROJECT. I TOLD THEM I RESCUED YOU FROM THE JUVENILE COURT SYSTEM.
-GROAN-
THE ONLY WAY TO KEEP YOU OUT OF PRISON, OR EVEN ALIVE, WAS TO KEEP YOU OUT OF TROUBLE BY GIVING YOU SOMETHING CONSTRUCTIVE TO DO AND A SAFE PLACE TO GO, NO MATTER WHAT TIME OF THE DAY OR NIGHT.
YEP. THAT ABOUT EXPLAINS IT.
I APOLOGIZE, BUT IT SERVES OUR PURPOSE. NOW THEY EXPECT THE UNEXPECTED FROM YOU, AND AS LONG AS YOU DON'T INTERFERE WITH THEM, THEY'LL DEFINITELY LEAVE YOU ALONE.
SMALL PRICE TO PAY FOR THE DIGS AND THREADS, RIGHT?
SOMETHING LIKE THAT.
BUT I'VE COME PREPARED TO MAKE IT UP TO YOU.
NOW YOU'RE TALKING. WHAT'S UP?
WHAT'S UP?
IT'S MORE FUN IF I SHOW YOU.
BE OVER LOWER MANHATTAN IN FIFTEEN MINUTES.

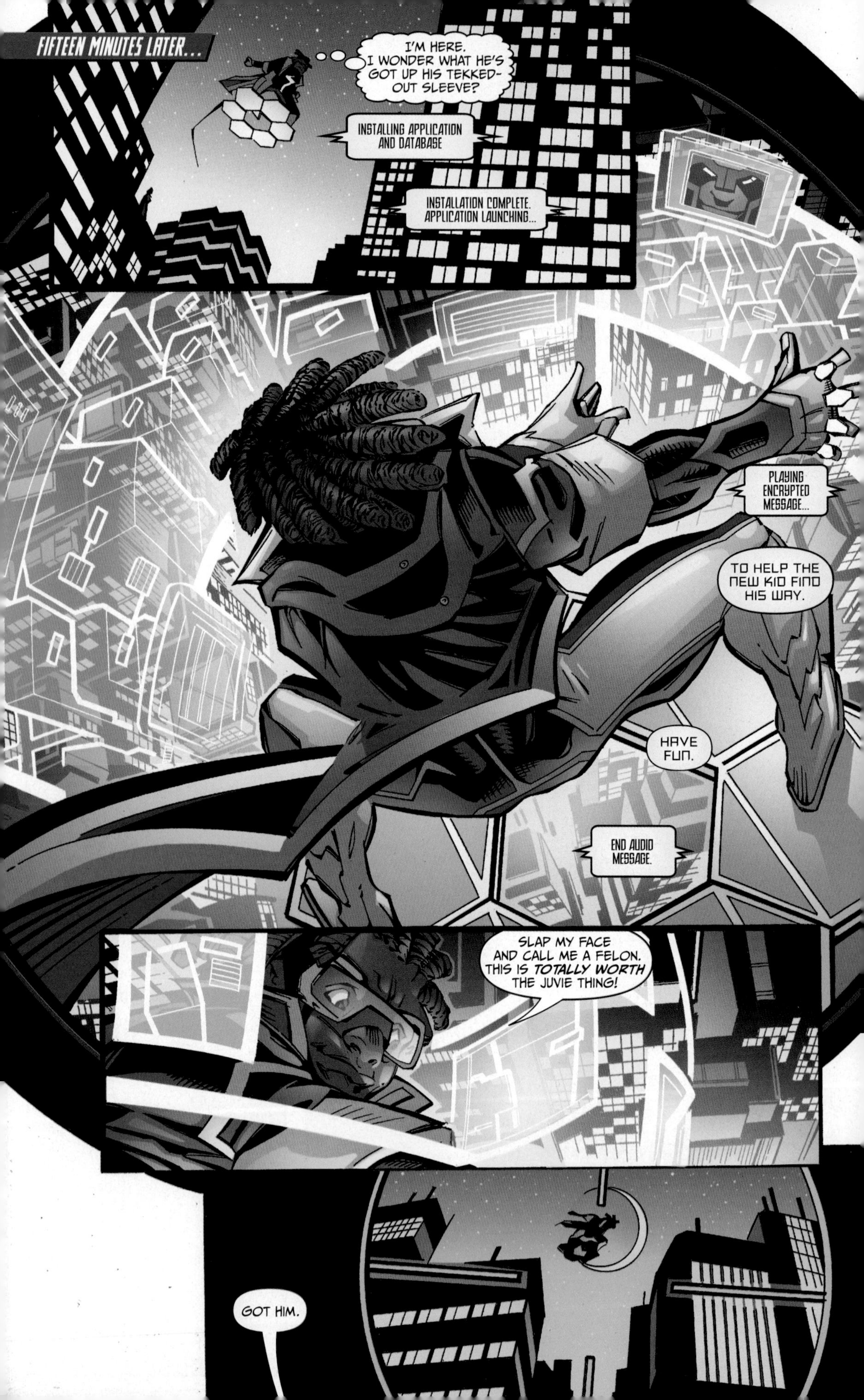
FIFTEEN MINUTES LATER...
I'M HERE. I WONDER WHAT HE'S GOT UP HIS TEKKED-OUT SLEEVE?
INSTALLING APPLICATION AND DATABASE
INSTALLATION COMPLETE. APPLICATION LAUNCHING...
PLAYING ENCRYPTED MESSAGE...
TO HELP THE NEW KID FIND HIS WAY.
HAVE FUN.
END AUDIO MESSAGE.
SLAP MY FACE AND CALL ME A FELON. THIS IS TOTALLY WORTH THE JUVIE THING!
GOT HIM.

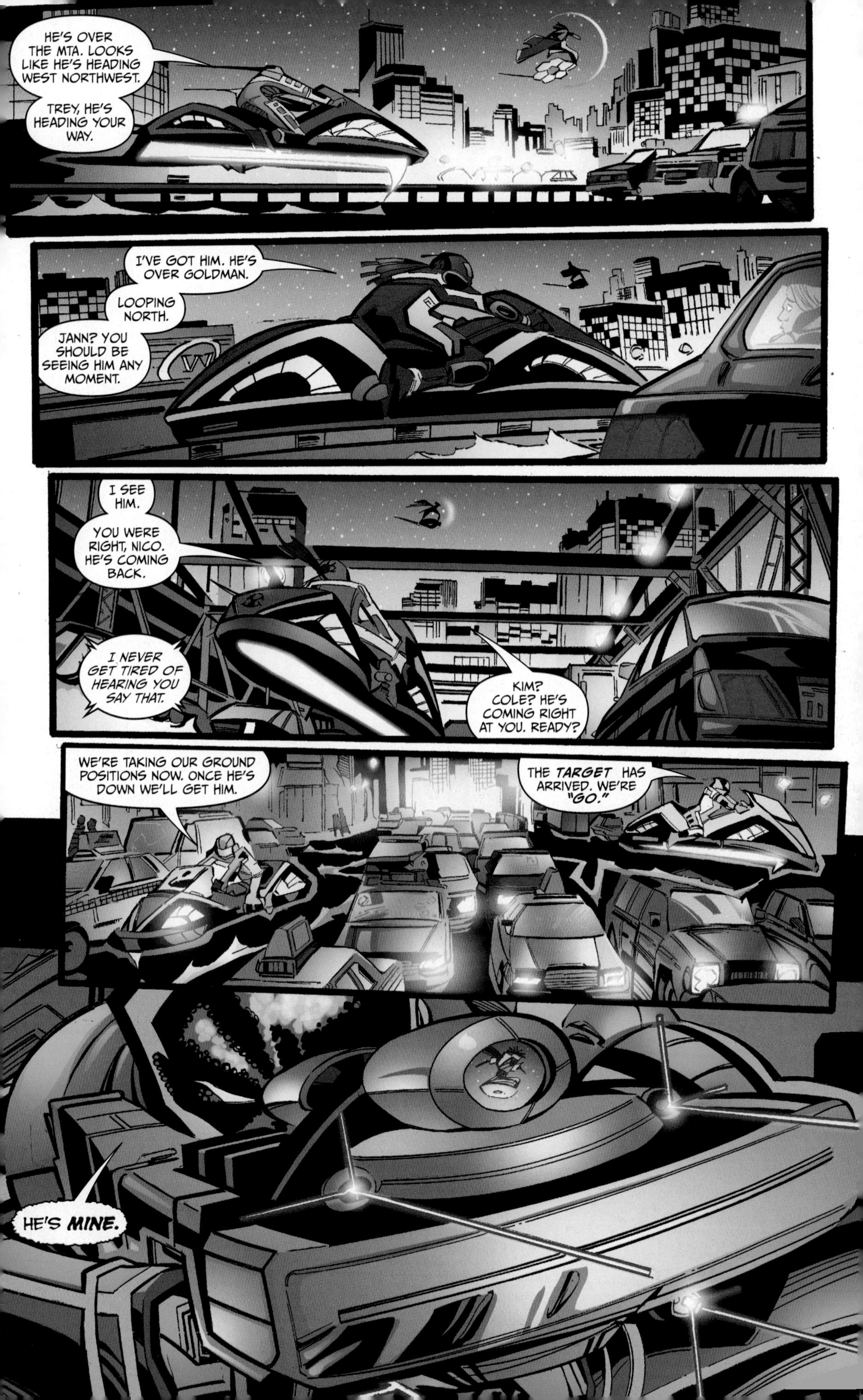
HE'S OVER THE MTA. LOOKS LIKE HE'S HEADING WEST NORTHWEST.
TREY, HE'S HEADING YOUR WAY.
I'VE GOT HIM. HE'S OVER GOLDMAN.
LOOPING NORTH.
JANN? YOU SHOULD BE SEEING HIM ANY MOMENT.
I SEE HIM.
YOU WERE RIGHT, NICO. HE'S COMING BACK.
I NEVER GET TIRED OF HEARING YOU SAY THAT.
KIM? COLE? HE'S COMING RIGHT AT YOU. READY?
WE'RE TAKING OUR GROUND POSITIONS NOW. ONCE HE'S DOWN WE'LL GET HIM.
THE TARGET HAS ARRIVED. WE'RE "GO."
HE'S MINE.

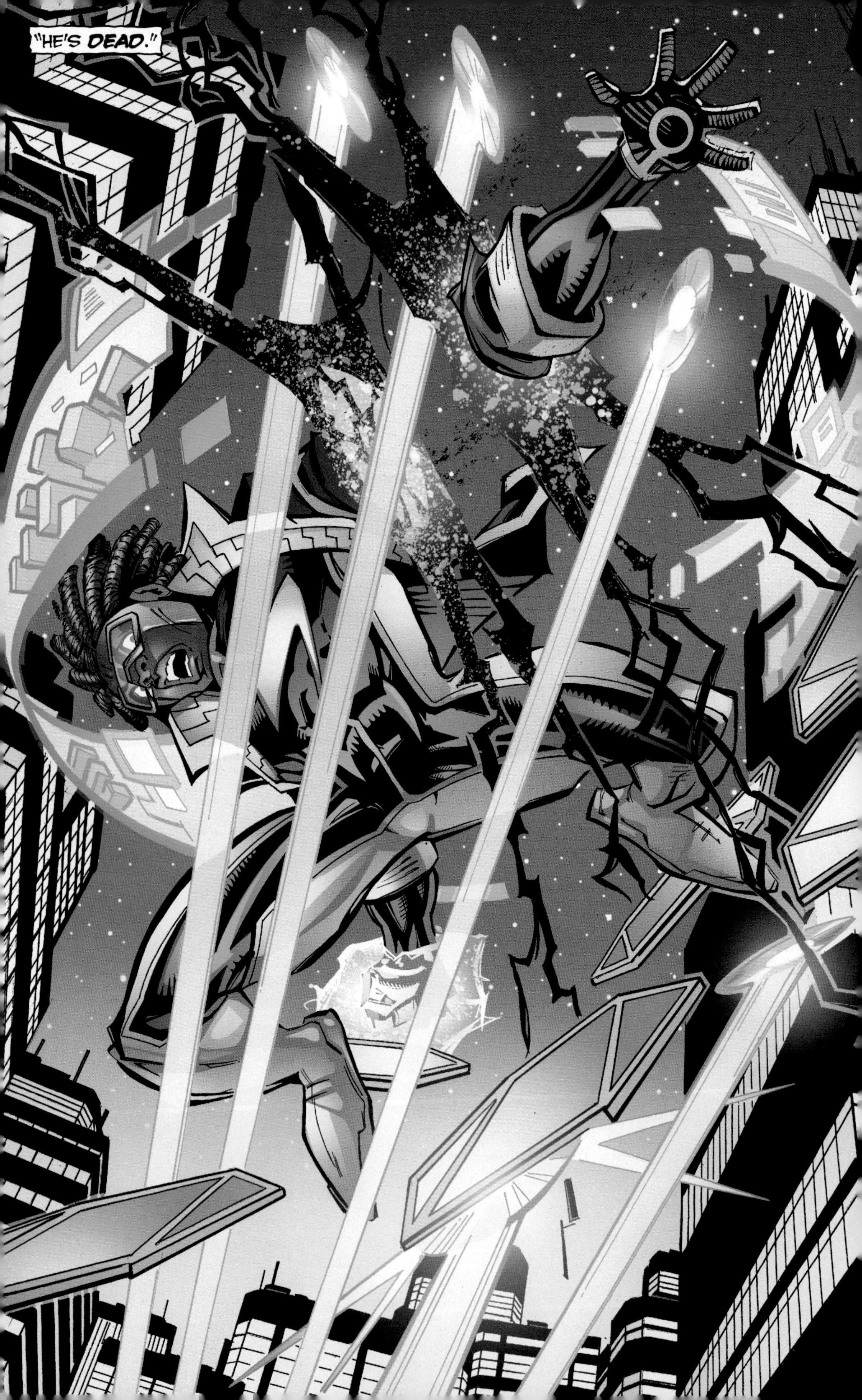
"HE'S DEAD."

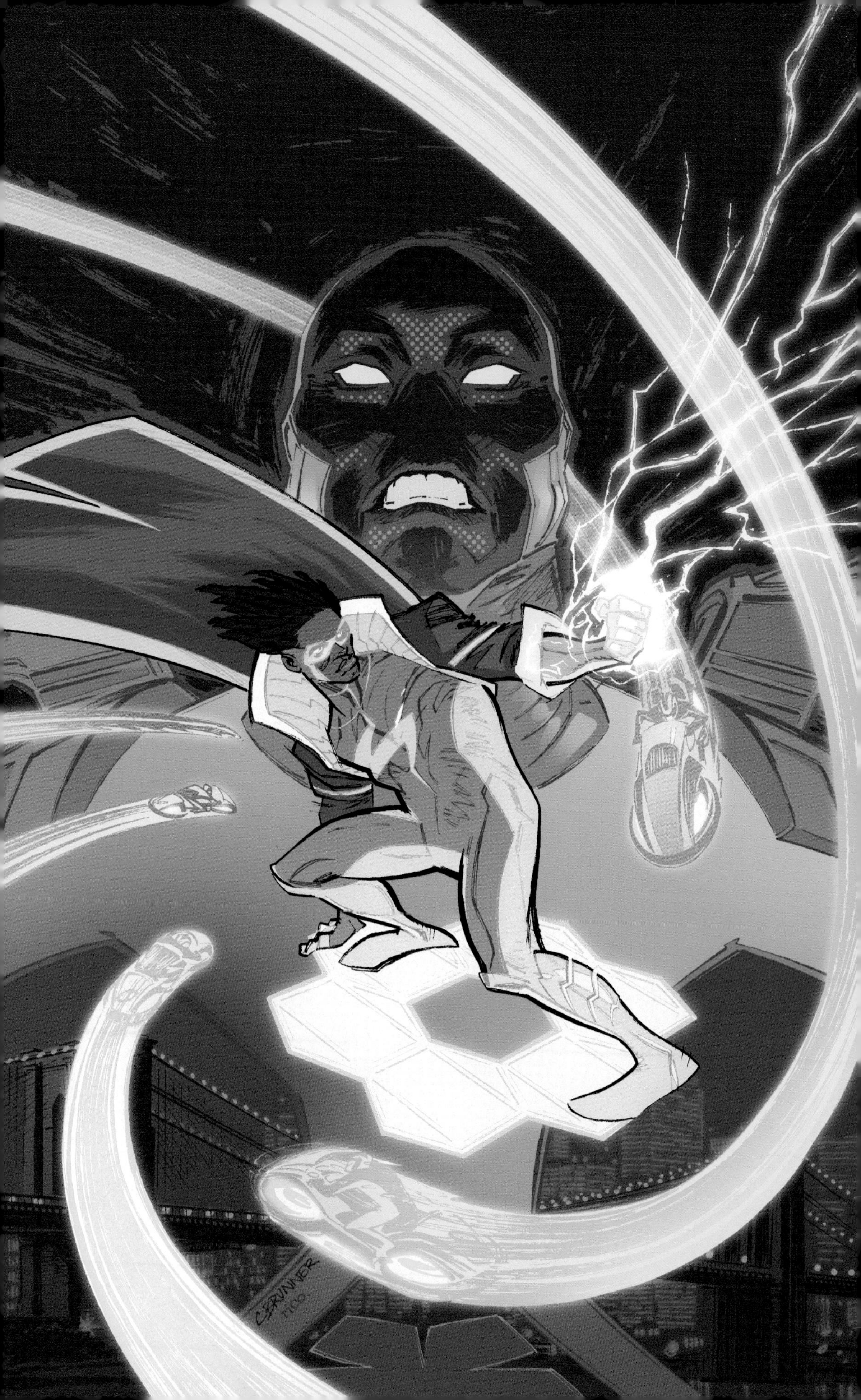
C.BRUNNER

cover art by
CHRIS BRUNNER
& RICO RENZI

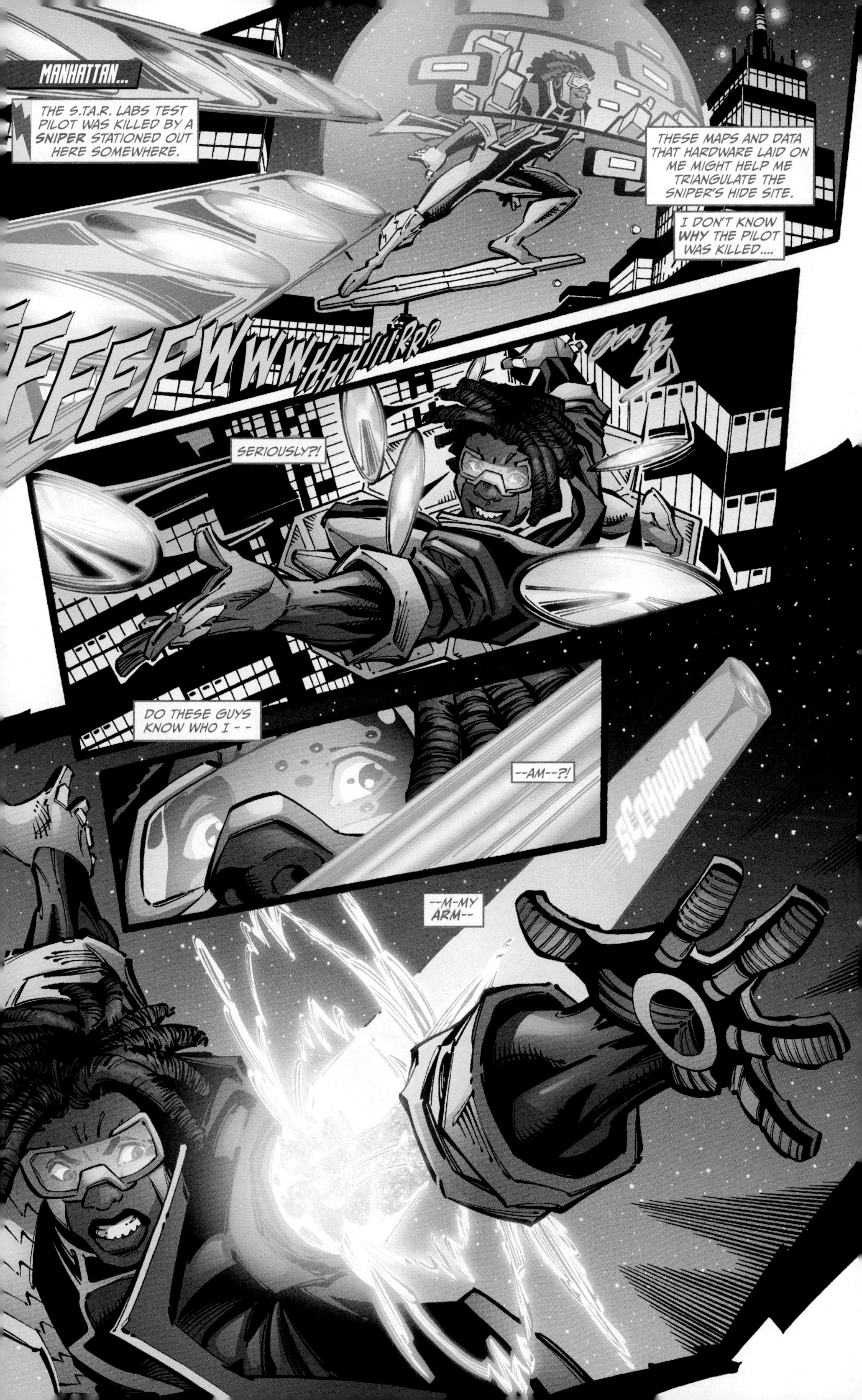
MANHATTAN...
THE S.T.A.R. LABS TEST PILOT WAS KILLED BY A SNIPER STATIONED OUT HERE SOMEWHERE.
THESE MAPS AND DATA THAT HARDWARE LAID ON ME MIGHT HELP ME TRIANGULATE THE SNIPER'S HIDE SITE.
I DON'T KNOW WHY THE PILOT WAS KILLED....
SERIOUSLY?!
DO THESE GUYS KNOW WHO I - -
--AM--?!
--M-MY ARM--

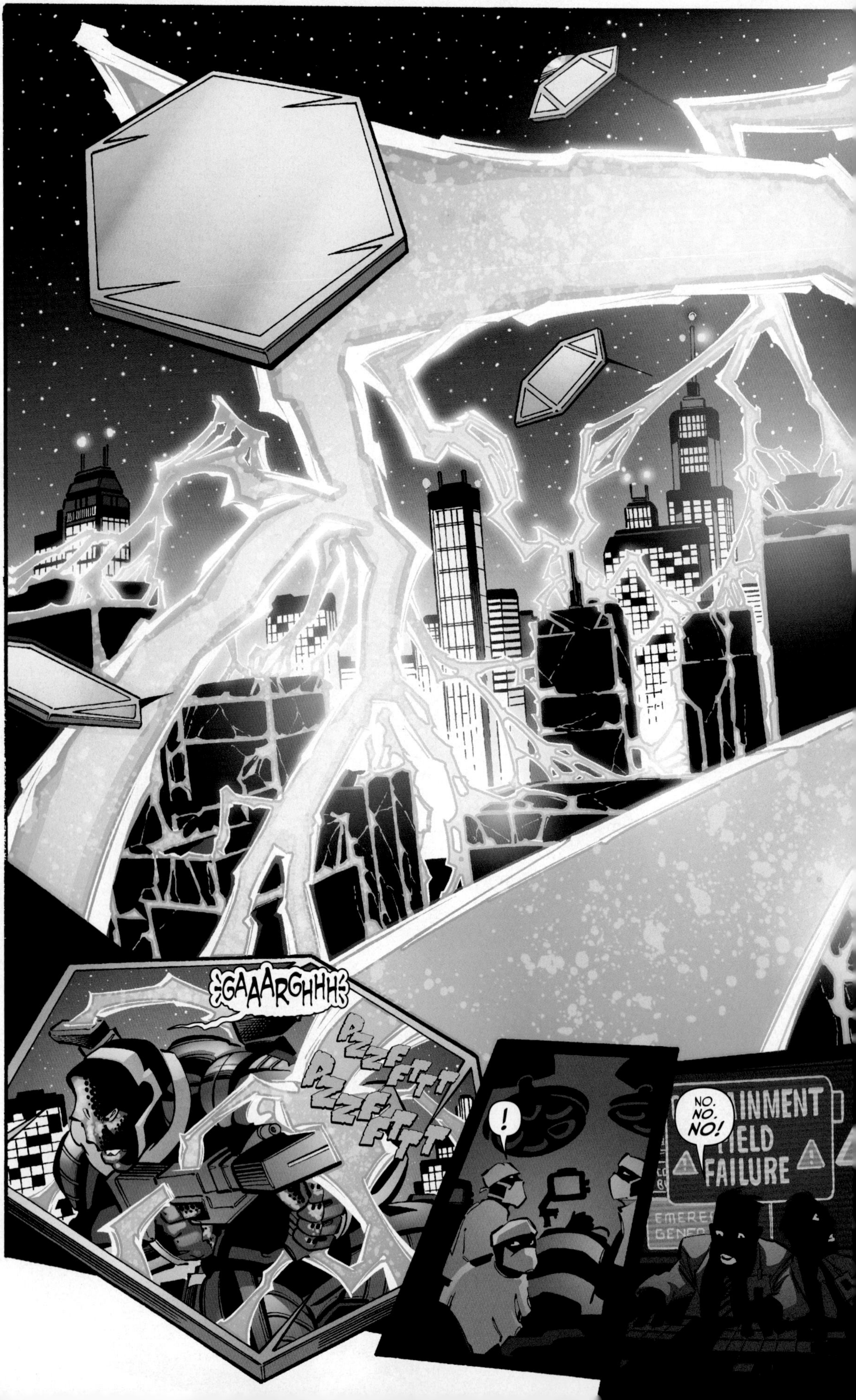
GAAARGHHH
PZZFTTT
PZZFTTT
!
NO. NO. NO!
...AINMENT FIELD FAILURE

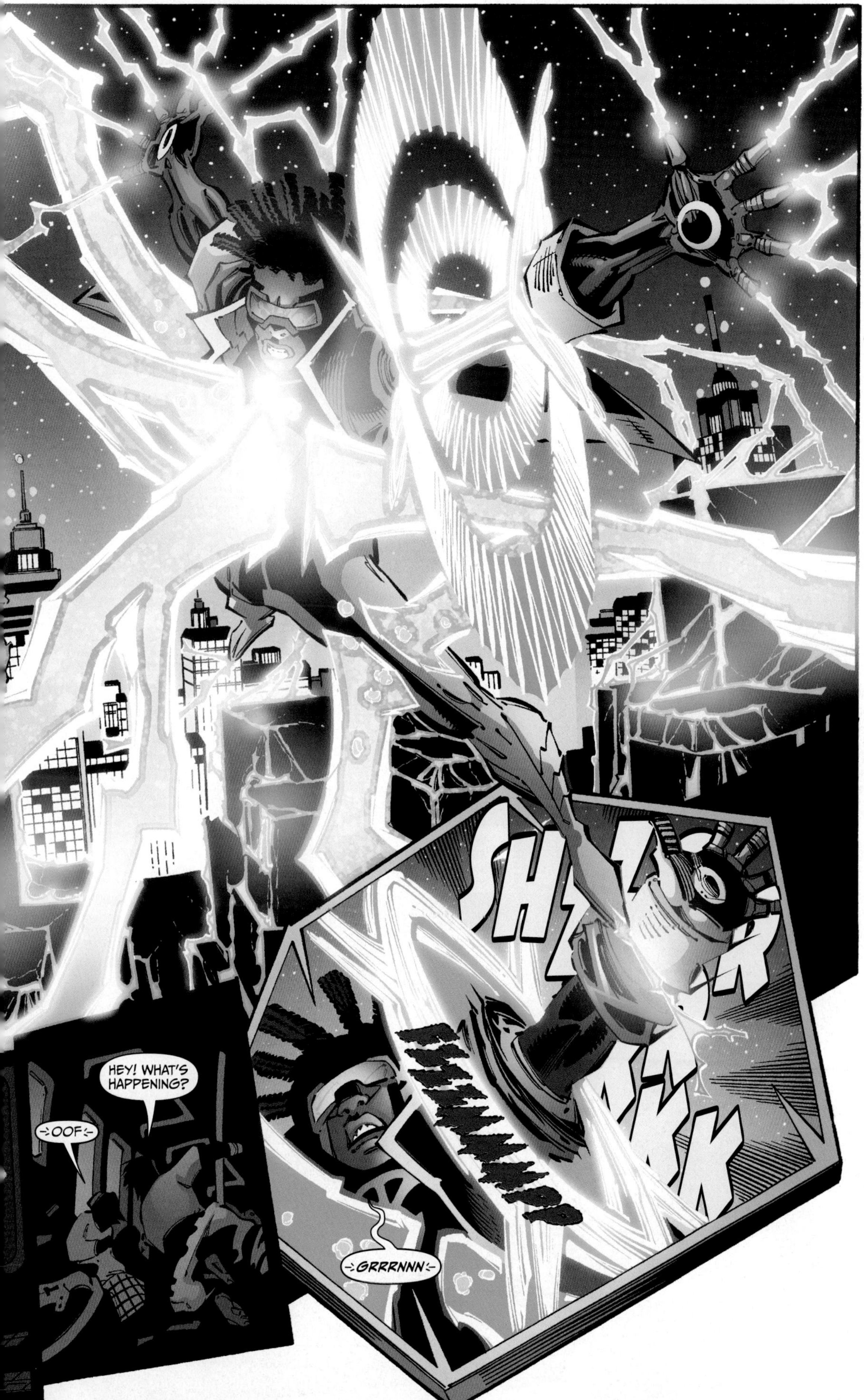
HEY! WHAT'S HAPPENING?
OOF
GRRRNNN

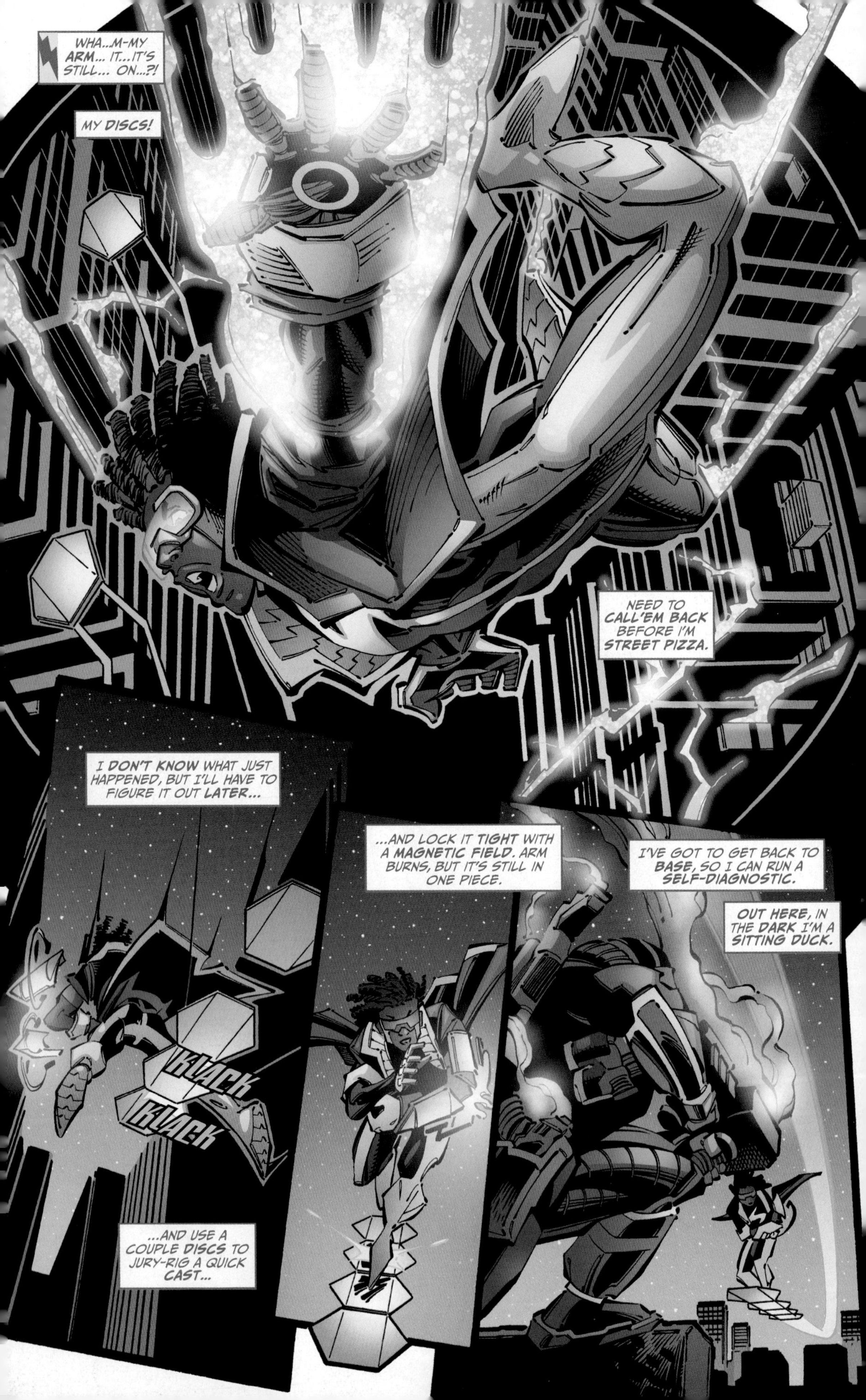
WHA...M-MY ARM... IT...IT'S STILL... ON...?!
MY DISCS!
NEED TO CALL'EM BACK BEFORE I'M STREET PIZZA.
I DON'T KNOW WHAT JUST HAPPENED, BUT I'LL HAVE TO FIGURE IT OUT LATER...
KLACK
KLACK
...AND USE A COUPLE DISCS TO JURY-RIG A QUICK CAST...
...AND LOCK IT TIGHT WITH A MAGNETIC FIELD. ARM BURNS, BUT IT'S STILL IN ONE PIECE.
I'VE GOT TO GET BACK TO BASE, SO I CAN RUN A SELF-DIAGNOSTIC.
OUT HERE, IN THE DARK I'M A SITTING DUCK.

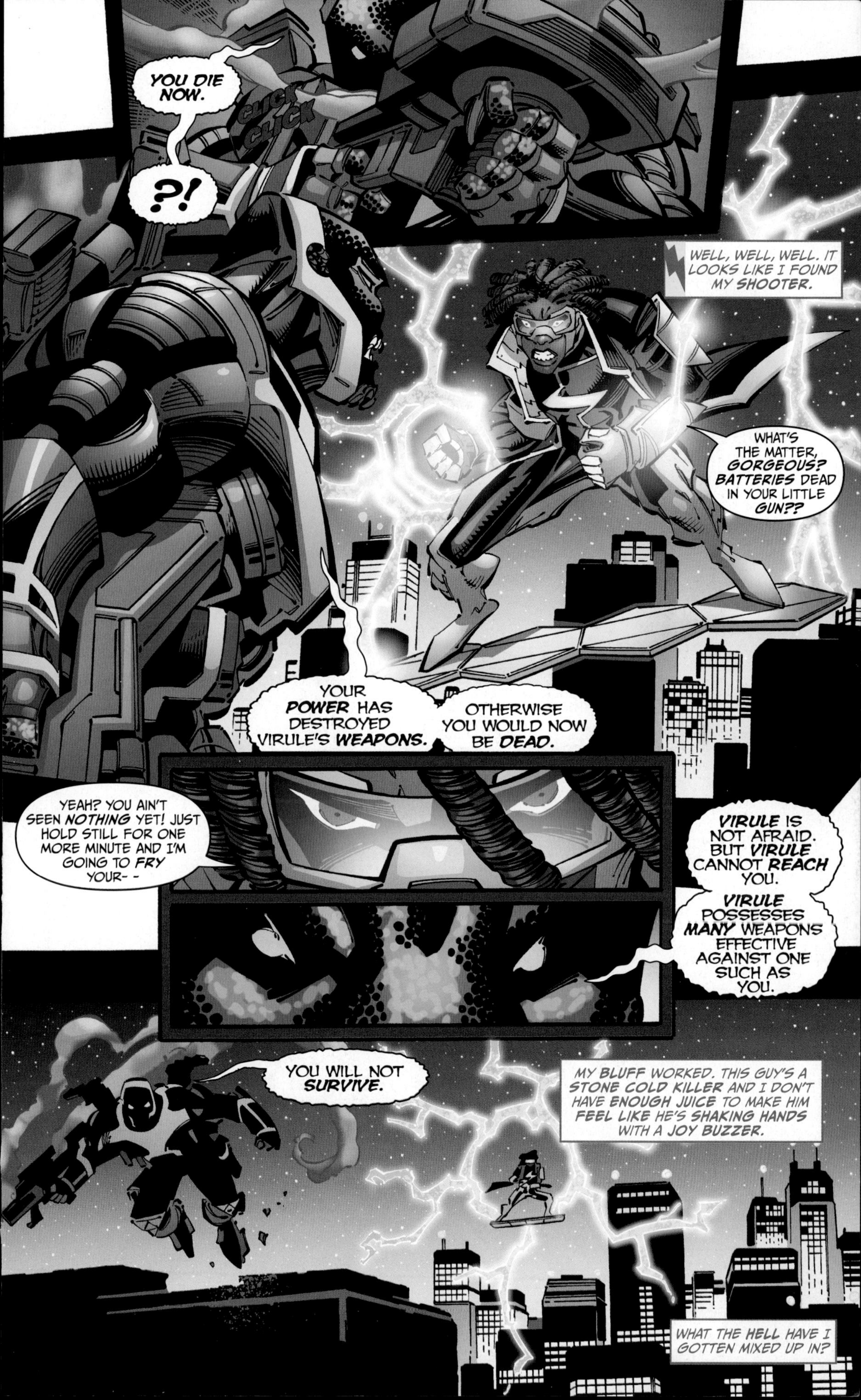
YOU DIE NOW.
CLICK CLICK
?!
WELL, WELL, WELL. IT LOOKS LIKE I FOUND MY SHOOTER.
WHAT'S THE MATTER, GORGEOUS? BATTERIES DEAD IN YOUR LITTLE GUN??
YOUR POWER HAS DESTROYED VIRULE'S WEAPONS.
OTHERWISE YOU WOULD NOW BE DEAD.
YEAH? YOU AIN'T SEEN NOTHING YET! JUST HOLD STILL FOR ONE MORE MINUTE AND I'M GOING TO FRY YOUR- -
VIRULE IS NOT AFRAID. BUT VIRULE CANNOT REACH YOU.
VIRULE POSSESSES MANY WEAPONS EFFECTIVE AGAINST ONE SUCH AS YOU.
YOU WILL NOT SURVIVE.
MY BLUFF WORKED. THIS GUY'S A STONE COLD KILLER AND I DON'T HAVE ENOUGH JUICE TO MAKE HIM FEEL LIKE HE'S SHAKING HANDS WITH A JOY BUZZER.
WHAT THE HELL HAVE I GOTTEN MIXED UP IN?

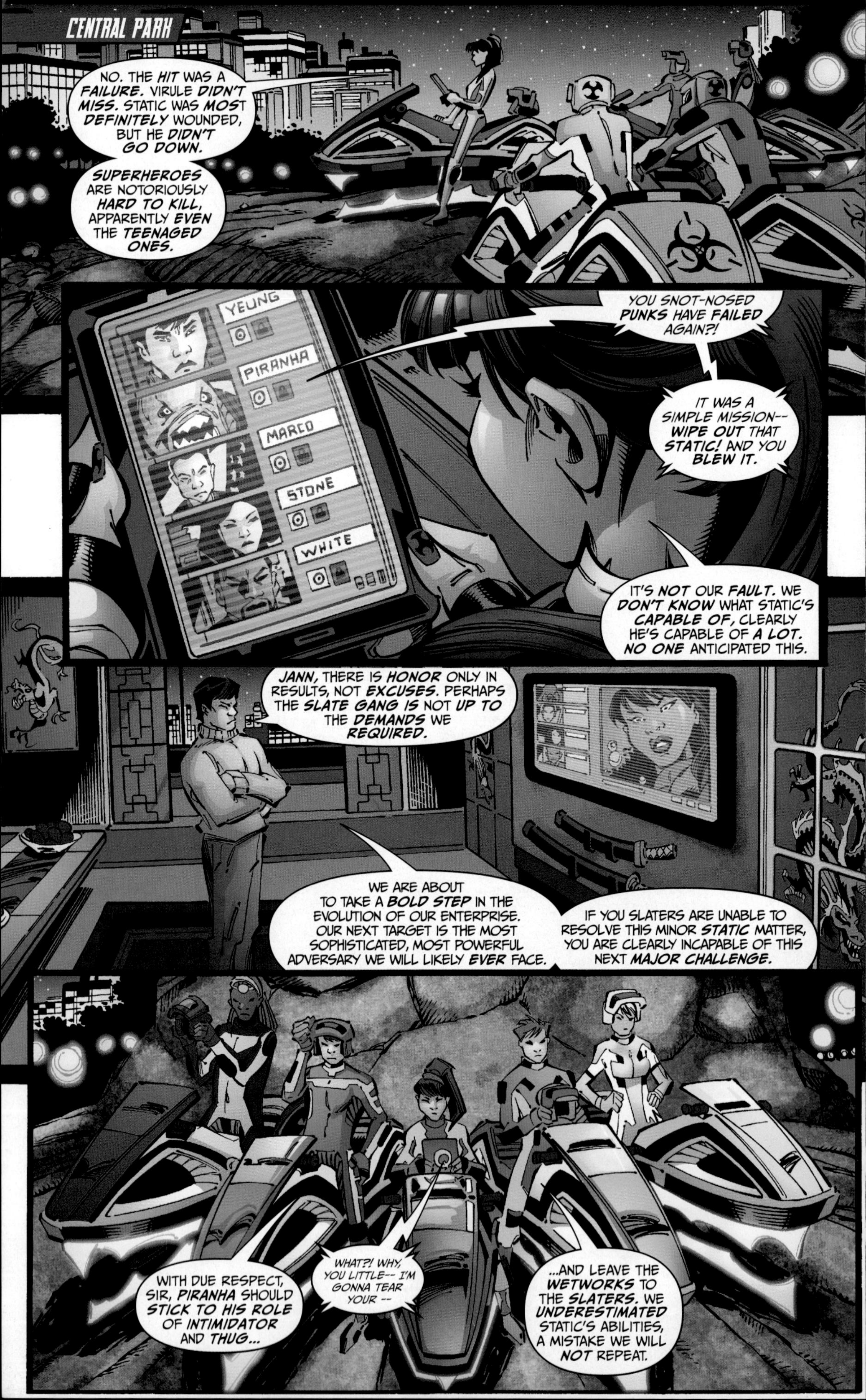
CENTRAL PARK
NO. THE HIT WAS A FAILURE. VIRULE DIDN'T MISS. STATIC WAS MOST DEFINITELY WOUNDED, BUT HE DIDN'T GO DOWN.
SUPERHEROES ARE NOTORIOUSLY HARD TO KILL, APPARENTLY EVEN THE TEENAGED ONES.
YEUNG
PIRANHA
MARCO
STONE
WHITE
YOU SNOT-NOSED PUNKS HAVE FAILED AGAIN?!
IT WAS A SIMPLE MISSION-- WIPE OUT THAT STATIC! AND YOU BLEW IT.
IT'S NOT OUR FAULT. WE DON'T KNOW WHAT STATIC'S CAPABLE OF, CLEARLY HE'S CAPABLE OF A LOT. NO ONE ANTICIPATED THIS.
JANN, THERE IS HONOR ONLY IN RESULTS, NOT EXCUSES. PERHAPS THE SLATE GANG IS NOT UP TO THE DEMANDS WE REQUIRED.
WE ARE ABOUT TO TAKE A BOLD STEP IN THE EVOLUTION OF OUR ENTERPRISE. OUR NEXT TARGET IS THE MOST SOPHISTICATED, MOST POWERFUL ADVERSARY WE WILL LIKELY EVER FACE.
IF YOU SLATERS ARE UNABLE TO RESOLVE THIS MINOR STATIC MATTER, YOU ARE CLEARLY INCAPABLE OF THIS NEXT MAJOR CHALLENGE.
WITH DUE RESPECT, SIR, PIRANHA SHOULD STICK TO HIS ROLE OF INTIMIDATOR AND THUG...
WHAT?! WHY, YOU LITTLE-- I'M GONNA TEAR YOUR --
...AND LEAVE THE WETWORKS TO THE SLATERS. WE UNDERESTIMATED STATIC'S ABILITIES, A MISTAKE WE WILL NOT REPEAT.

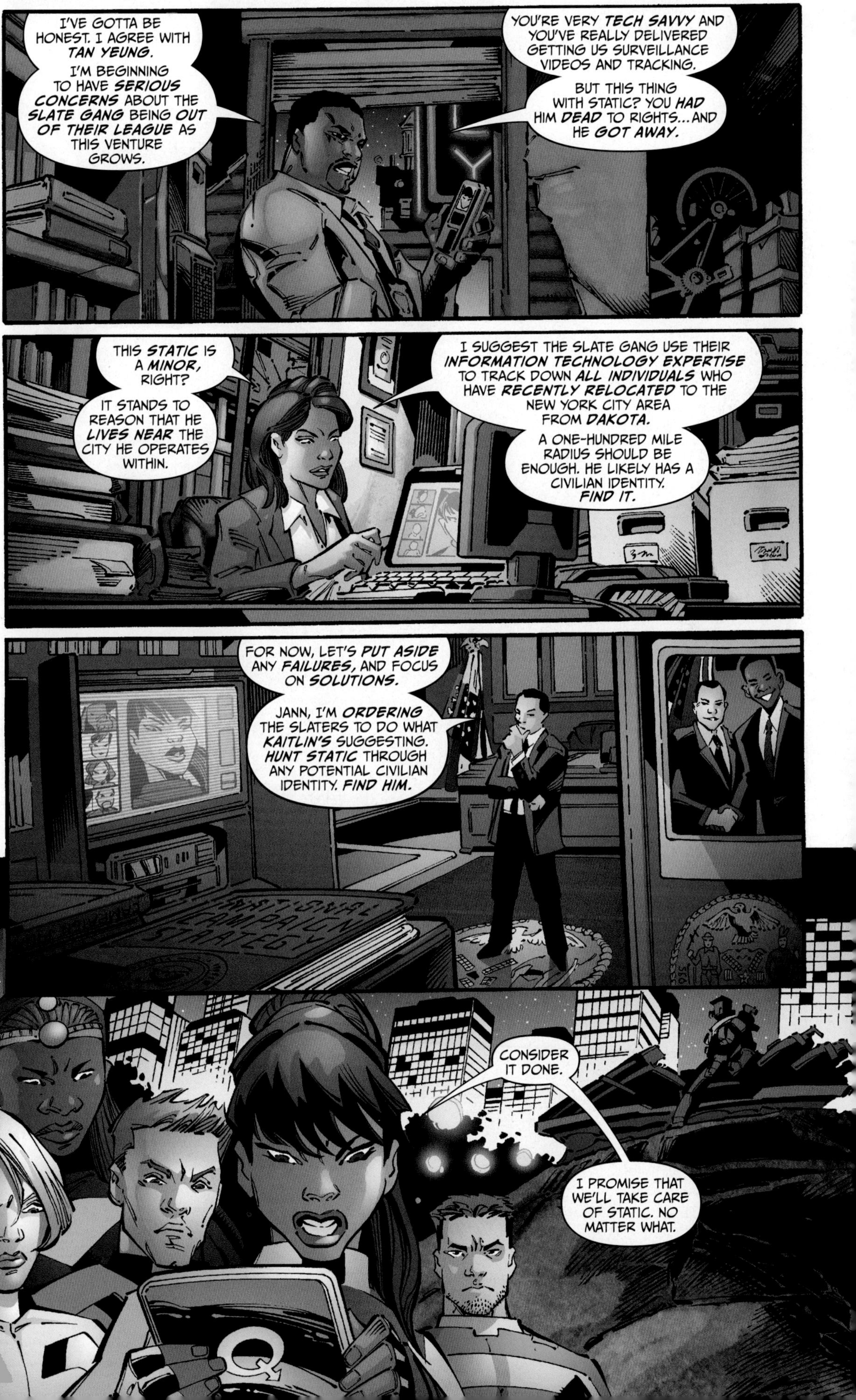

I'VE GOTTA BE HONEST. I AGREE WITH TAN YEUNG.
I'M BEGINNING TO HAVE SERIOUS CONCERNS ABOUT THE SLATE GANG BEING OUT OF THEIR LEAGUE AS THIS VENTURE GROWS.
YOU'RE VERY TECH SAVVY AND YOU'VE REALLY DELIVERED GETTING US SURVEILLANCE VIDEOS AND TRACKING.
BUT THIS THING WITH STATIC? YOU HAD HIM DEAD TO RIGHTS... AND HE GOT AWAY.
THIS STATIC IS A MINOR, RIGHT?
IT STANDS TO REASON THAT HE LIVES NEAR THE CITY HE OPERATES WITHIN.
I SUGGEST THE SLATE GANG USE THEIR INFORMATION TECHNOLOGY EXPERTISE TO TRACK DOWN ALL INDIVIDUALS WHO HAVE RECENTLY RELOCATED TO THE NEW YORK CITY AREA FROM DAKOTA.
A ONE-HUNDRED MILE RADIUS SHOULD BE ENOUGH. HE LIKELY HAS A CIVILIAN IDENTITY. FIND IT.
FOR NOW, LET'S PUT ASIDE ANY FAILURES, AND FOCUS ON SOLUTIONS.
JANN, I'M ORDERING THE SLATERS TO DO WHAT KAITLIN'S SUGGESTING. HUNT STATIC THROUGH ANY POTENTIAL CIVILIAN IDENTITY. FIND HIM.
CONSIDER IT DONE.
I PROMISE THAT WE'LL TAKE CARE OF STATIC. NO MATTER WHAT.

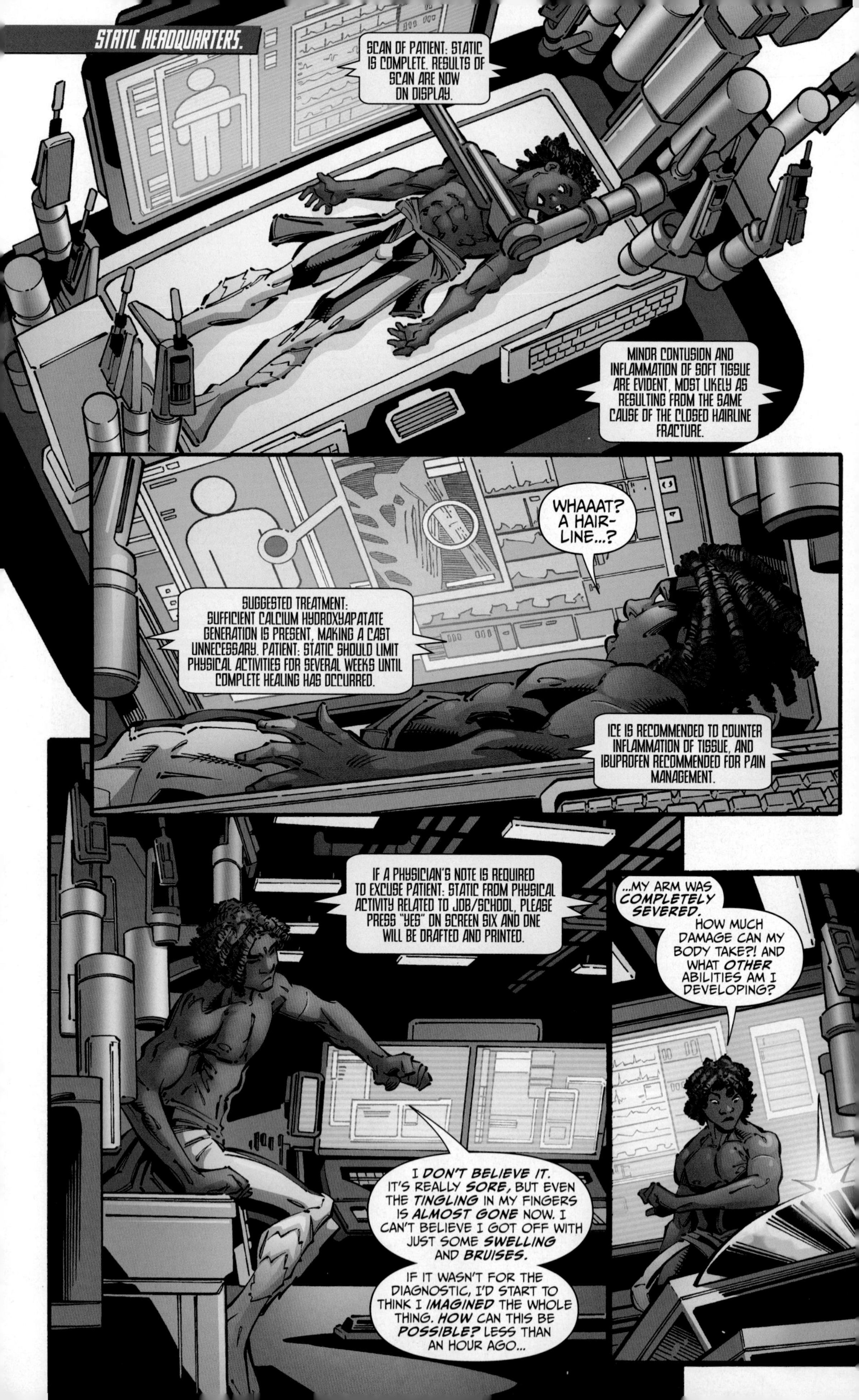
STATIC HEADQUARTERS.
SCAN OF PATIENT: STATIC IS COMPLETE. RESULTS OF SCAN ARE NOW ON DISPLAY.
MINOR CONTUSION AND INFLAMMATION OF SOFT TISSUE ARE EVIDENT, MOST LIKELY AS RESULTING FROM THE SAME CAUSE OF THE CLOSED HAIRLINE FRACTURE.
WHAAAT? A HAIR-LINE...?
SUGGESTED TREATMENT: SUFFICIENT CALCIUM HYDROXYAPATATE GENERATION IS PRESENT, MAKING A CAST UNNECESSARY. PATIENT: STATIC SHOULD LIMIT PHYSICAL ACTIVITIES FOR SEVERAL WEEKS UNTIL COMPLETE HEALING HAS OCCURRED.
ICE IS RECOMMENDED TO COUNTER INFLAMMATION OF TISSUE, AND IBUPROFEN RECOMMENDED FOR PAIN MANAGEMENT.
IF A PHYSICIAN'S NOTE IS REQUIRED TO EXCUSE PATIENT: STATIC FROM PHYSICAL ACTIVITY RELATED TO JOB/SCHOOL, PLEASE PRESS "YES" ON SCREEN SIX AND ONE WILL BE DRAFTED AND PRINTED.
I DON'T BELIEVE IT. IT'S REALLY SORE, BUT EVEN THE TINGLING IN MY FINGERS IS ALMOST GONE NOW. I CAN'T BELIEVE I GOT OFF WITH JUST SOME SWELLING AND BRUISES.
IF IT WASN'T FOR THE DIAGNOSTIC, I'D START TO THINK I IMAGINED THE WHOLE THING. HOW CAN THIS BE POSSIBLE? LESS THAN AN HOUR AGO...
...MY ARM WAS COMPLETELY SEVERED.
HOW MUCH DAMAGE CAN MY BODY TAKE?! AND WHAT OTHER ABILITIES AM I DEVELOPING?

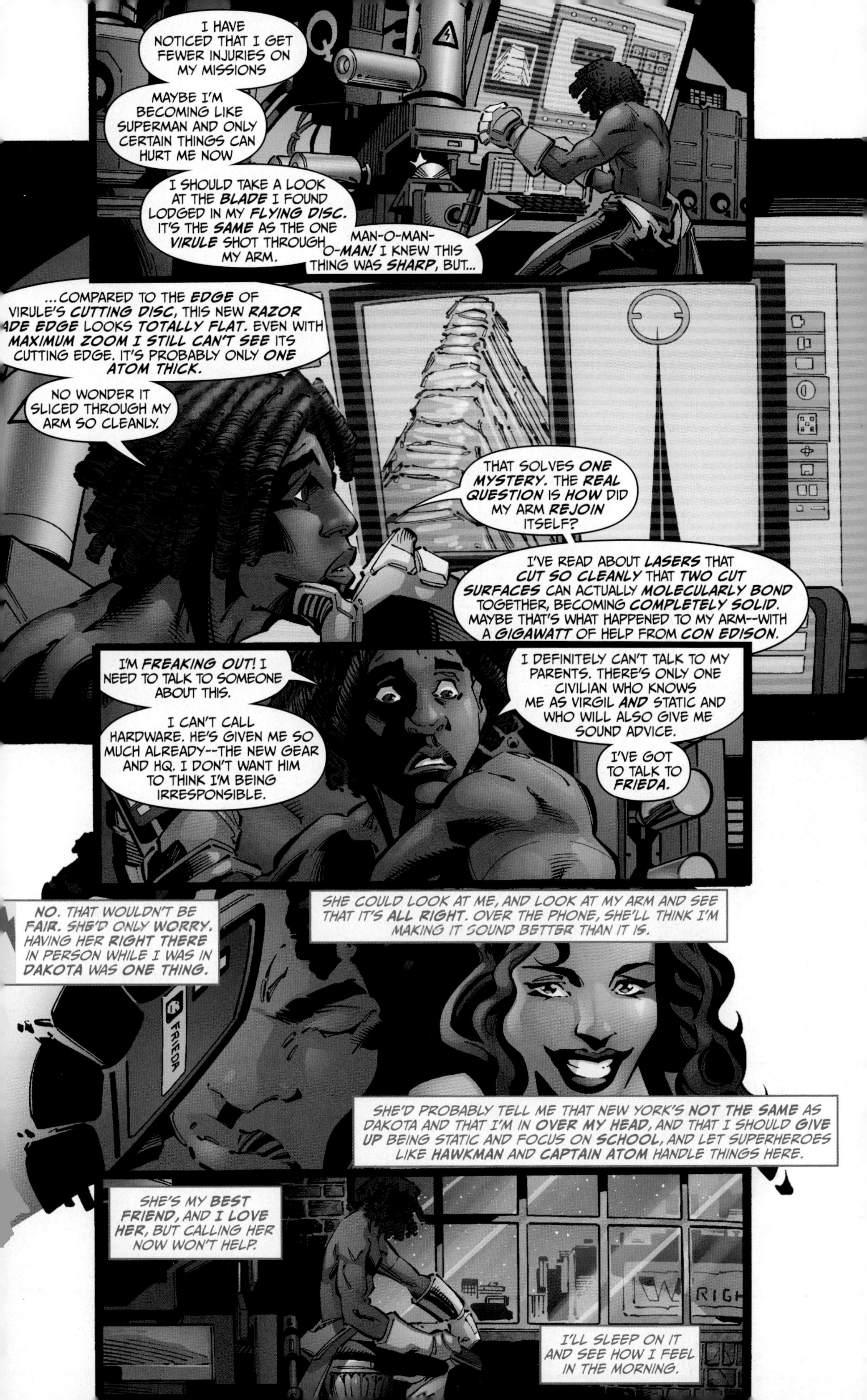
I HAVE NOTICED THAT I GET FEWER INJURIES ON MY MISSIONS
MAYBE I'M BECOMING LIKE SUPERMAN AND ONLY CERTAIN THINGS CAN HURT ME NOW
I SHOULD TAKE A LOOK AT THE BLADE I FOUND LODGED IN MY FLYING DISC. IT'S THE SAME AS THE ONE VIRULE SHOT THROUGH MY ARM.
MAN-O-MAN-O-MAN! I KNEW THIS THING WAS SHARP, BUT...
...COMPARED TO THE EDGE OF VIRULE'S CUTTING DISC, THIS NEW RAZOR ADE EDGE LOOKS TOTALLY FLAT. EVEN WITH MAXIMUM ZOOM I STILL CAN'T SEE ITS CUTTING EDGE. IT'S PROBABLY ONLY ONE ATOM THICK.
NO WONDER IT SLICED THROUGH MY ARM SO CLEANLY.
THAT SOLVES ONE MYSTERY. THE REAL QUESTION IS HOW DID MY ARM REJOIN ITSELF?
I'VE READ ABOUT LASERS THAT CUT SO CLEANLY THAT TWO CUT SURFACES CAN ACTUALLY MOLECULARLY BOND TOGETHER, BECOMING COMPLETELY SOLID. MAYBE THAT'S WHAT HAPPENED TO MY ARM--WITH A GIGAWATT OF HELP FROM CON EDISON.
I'M FREAKING OUT! I NEED TO TALK TO SOMEONE ABOUT THIS.
I CAN'T CALL HARDWARE. HE'S GIVEN ME SO MUCH ALREADY--THE NEW GEAR AND HQ. I DON'T WANT HIM TO THINK I'M BEING IRRESPONSIBLE.
I DEFINITELY CAN'T TALK TO MY PARENTS. THERE'S ONLY ONE CIVILIAN WHO KNOWS ME AS VIRGIL AND STATIC AND WHO WILL ALSO GIVE ME SOUND ADVICE.
I'VE GOT TO TALK TO FRIEDA.
NO. THAT WOULDN'T BE FAIR. SHE'D ONLY WORRY. HAVING HER RIGHT THERE IN PERSON WHILE I WAS IN DAKOTA WAS ONE THING.
SHE COULD LOOK AT ME, AND LOOK AT MY ARM AND SEE THAT IT'S ALL RIGHT. OVER THE PHONE, SHE'LL THINK I'M MAKING IT SOUND BETTER THAN IT IS.
FRIEDA
SHE'D PROBABLY TELL ME THAT NEW YORK'S NOT THE SAME AS DAKOTA AND THAT I'M IN OVER MY HEAD, AND THAT I SHOULD GIVE UP BEING STATIC AND FOCUS ON SCHOOL, AND LET SUPERHEROES LIKE HAWKMAN AND CAPTAIN ATOM HANDLE THINGS HERE.
SHE'S MY BEST FRIEND, AND I LOVE HER, BUT CALLING HER NOW WON'T HELP.
I'LL SLEEP ON IT AND SEE HOW I FEEL IN THE MORNING.

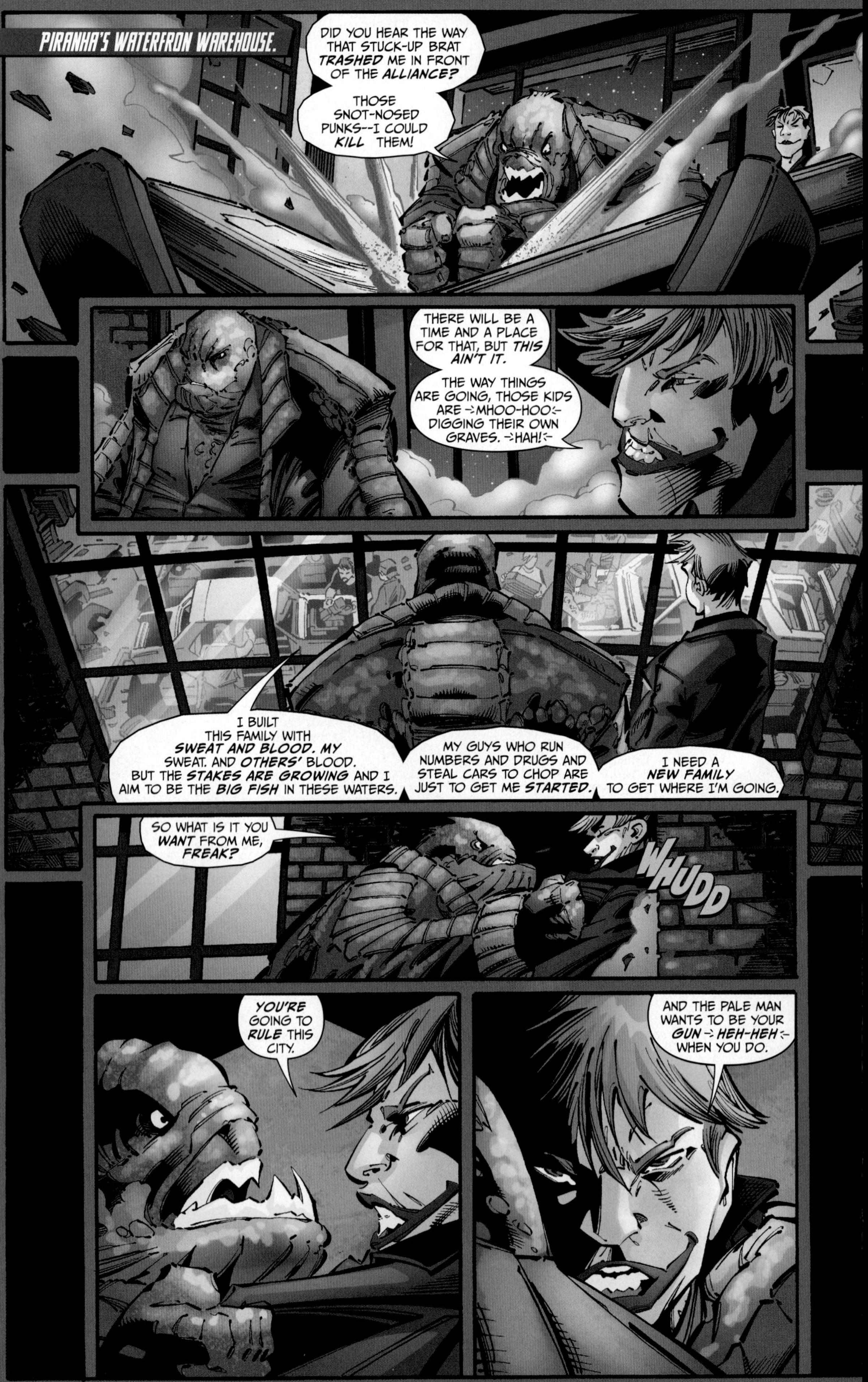
PIRANHA'S WATERFRON WAREHOUSE.
DID YOU HEAR THE WAY THAT STUCK-UP BRAT TRASHED ME IN FRONT OF THE ALLIANCE?
THOSE SNOT-NOSED PUNKS--I COULD KILL THEM!
THERE WILL BE A TIME AND A PLACE FOR THAT, BUT THIS AIN'T IT.
THE WAY THINGS ARE GOING, THOSE KIDS ARE ⇾MHOO-HOO⇽ DIGGING THEIR OWN GRAVES. ⇾HAH!⇽
I BUILT THIS FAMILY WITH SWEAT AND BLOOD. MY SWEAT. AND OTHERS' BLOOD. BUT THE STAKES ARE GROWING AND I AIM TO BE THE BIG FISH IN THESE WATERS.
MY GUYS WHO RUN NUMBERS AND DRUGS AND STEAL CARS TO CHOP ARE JUST TO GET ME STARTED.
I NEED A NEW FAMILY TO GET WHERE I'M GOING.
SO WHAT IS IT YOU WANT FROM ME, FREAK?
WHUDD
YOU'RE GOING TO RULE THIS CITY.
AND THE PALE MAN WANTS TO BE YOUR GUN ⇾HEH-HEH⇽ WHEN YOU DO.

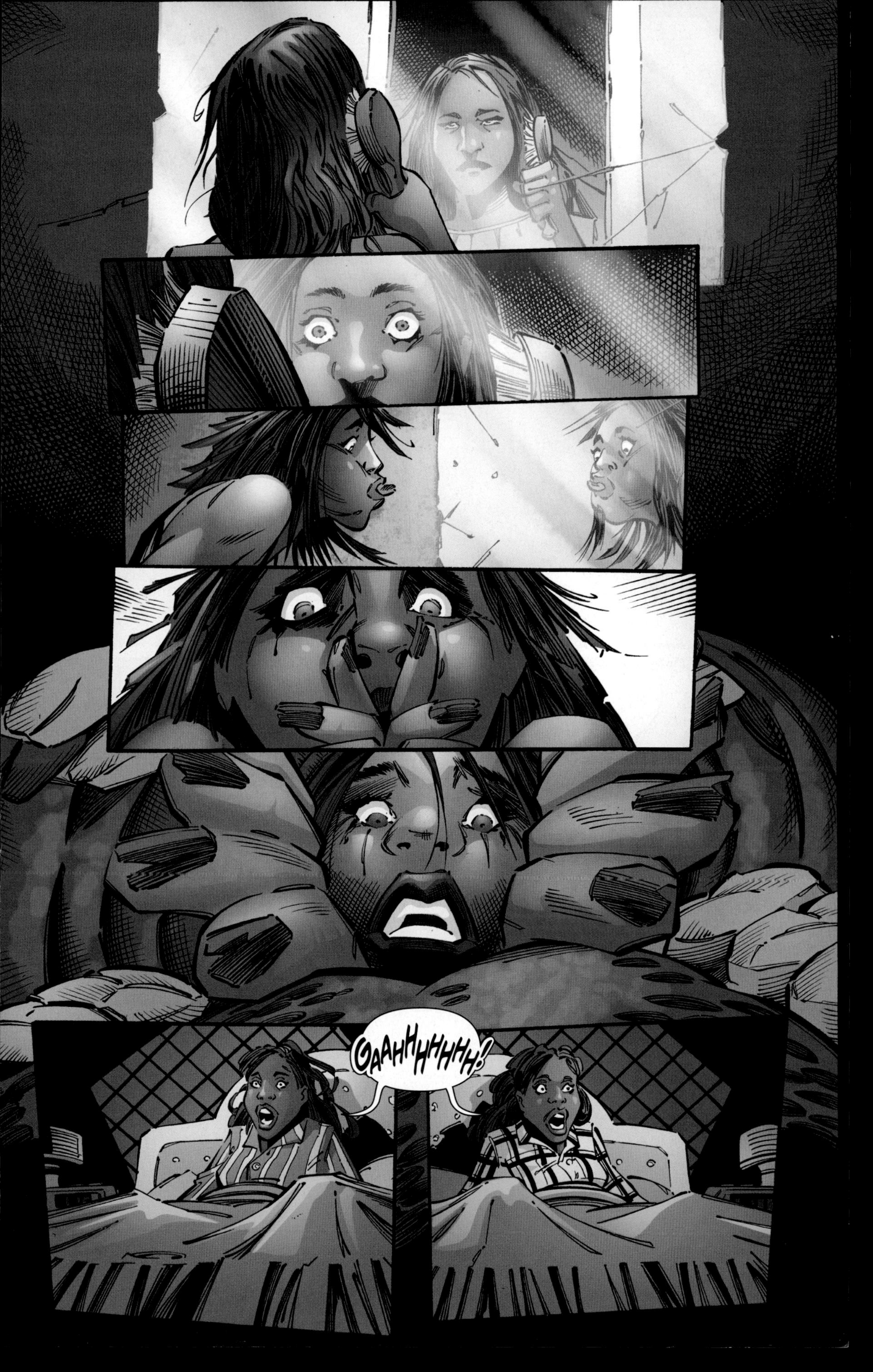
GAAHHHHHH!

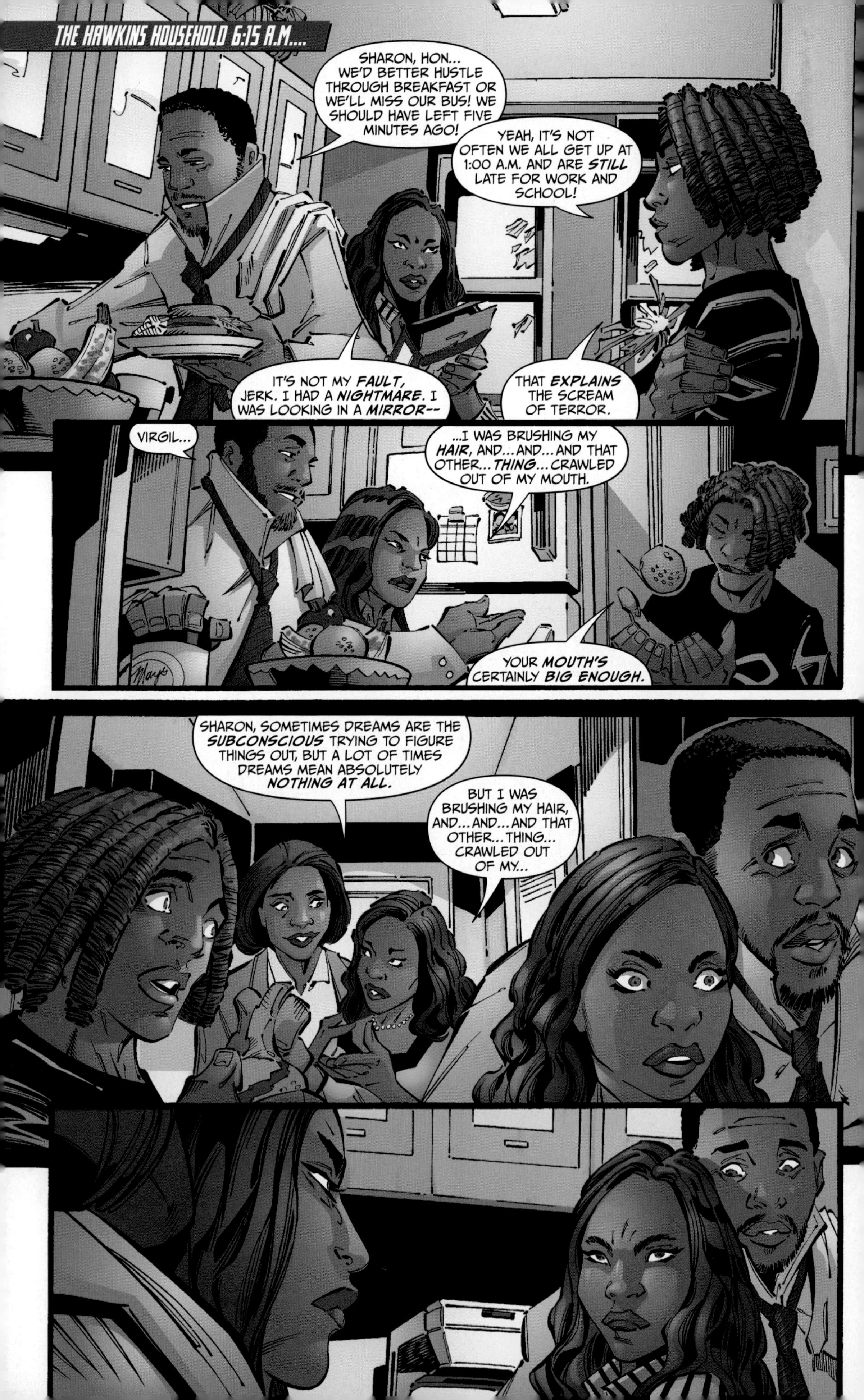
THE HAWKINS HOUSEHOLD 6:15 A.M....
SHARON, HON... WE'D BETTER HUSTLE THROUGH BREAKFAST OR WE'LL MISS OUR BUS! WE SHOULD HAVE LEFT FIVE MINUTES AGO!
YEAH, IT'S NOT OFTEN WE ALL GET UP AT 1:00 A.M. AND ARE STILL LATE FOR WORK AND SCHOOL!
IT'S NOT MY FAULT, JERK. I HAD A NIGHTMARE. I WAS LOOKING IN A MIRROR--
THAT EXPLAINS THE SCREAM OF TERROR.
VIRGIL...
...I WAS BRUSHING MY HAIR, AND...AND...AND THAT OTHER...THING...CRAWLED OUT OF MY MOUTH.
YOUR MOUTH'S CERTAINLY BIG ENOUGH.
SHARON, SOMETIMES DREAMS ARE THE SUBCONSCIOUS TRYING TO FIGURE THINGS OUT, BUT A LOT OF TIMES DREAMS MEAN ABSOLUTELY NOTHING AT ALL.
BUT I WAS BRUSHING MY HAIR, AND...AND...AND THAT OTHER...THING... CRAWLED OUT OF MY...

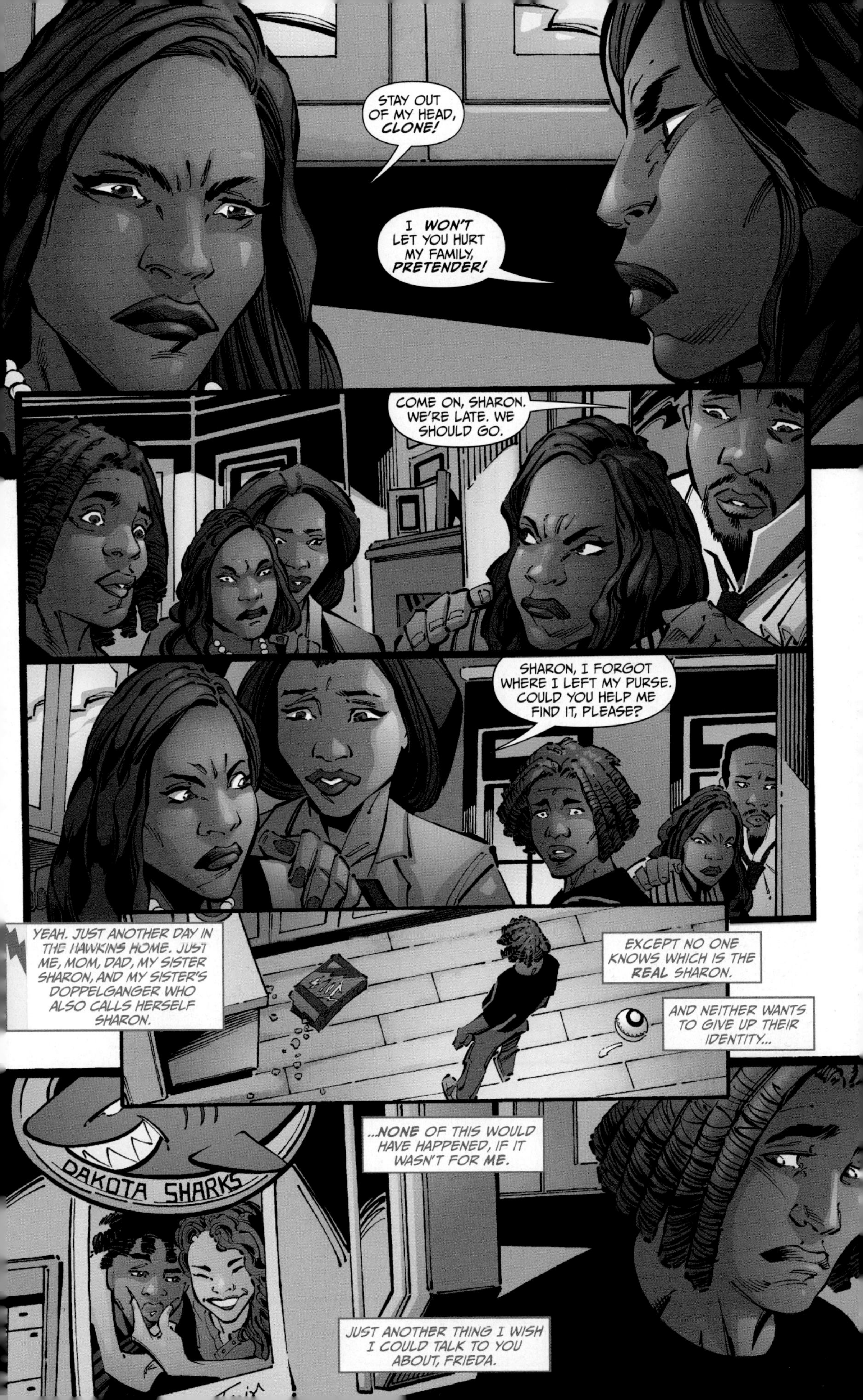
STAY OUT OF MY HEAD, CLONE!
I WON'T LET YOU HURT MY FAMILY, PRETENDER!
COME ON, SHARON. WE'RE LATE. WE SHOULD GO.
SHARON, I FORGOT WHERE I LEFT MY PURSE. COULD YOU HELP ME FIND IT, PLEASE?
YEAH. JUST ANOTHER DAY IN THE HAWKINS HOME. JUST ME, MOM, DAD, MY SISTER SHARON, AND MY SISTER'S DOPPELGANGER WHO ALSO CALLS HERSELF SHARON.
EXCEPT NO ONE KNOWS WHICH IS THE REAL SHARON.
AND NEITHER WANTS TO GIVE UP THEIR IDENTITY...
...NONE OF THIS WOULD HAVE HAPPENED, IF IT WASN'T FOR ME.
DAKOTA SHARKS
JUST ANOTHER THING I WISH I COULD TALK TO YOU ABOUT, FRIEDA.

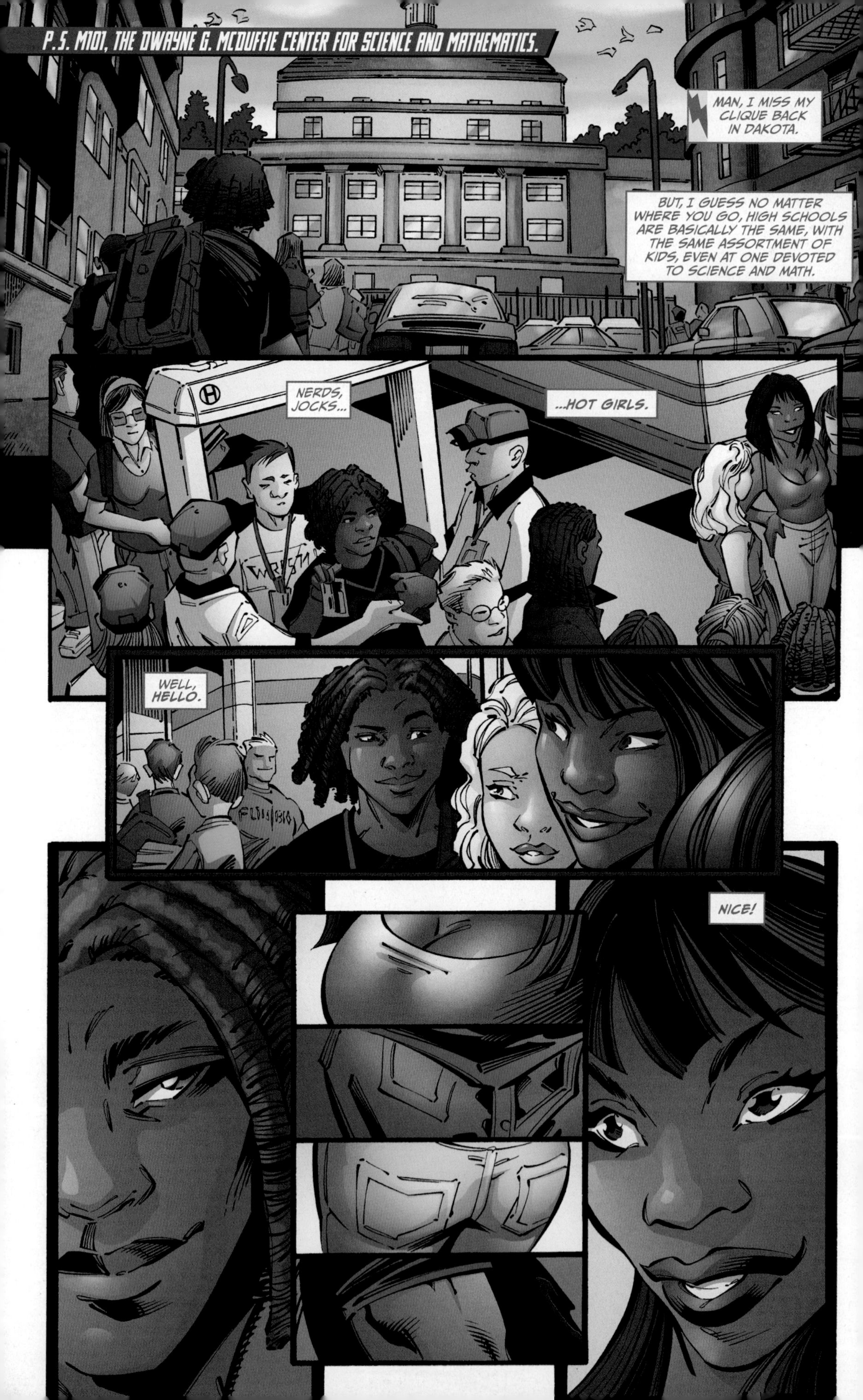
P.S. M101, THE DWAYNE G. MCDUFFIE CENTER FOR SCIENCE AND MATHEMATICS.
MAN, I MISS MY CLIQUE BACK IN DAKOTA.
BUT, I GUESS NO MATTER WHERE YOU GO, HIGH SCHOOLS ARE BASICALLY THE SAME, WITH THE SAME ASSORTMENT OF KIDS, EVEN AT ONE DEVOTED TO SCIENCE AND MATH.
NERDS, JOCKS...
...HOT GIRLS.
WELL, HELLO.
NICE!

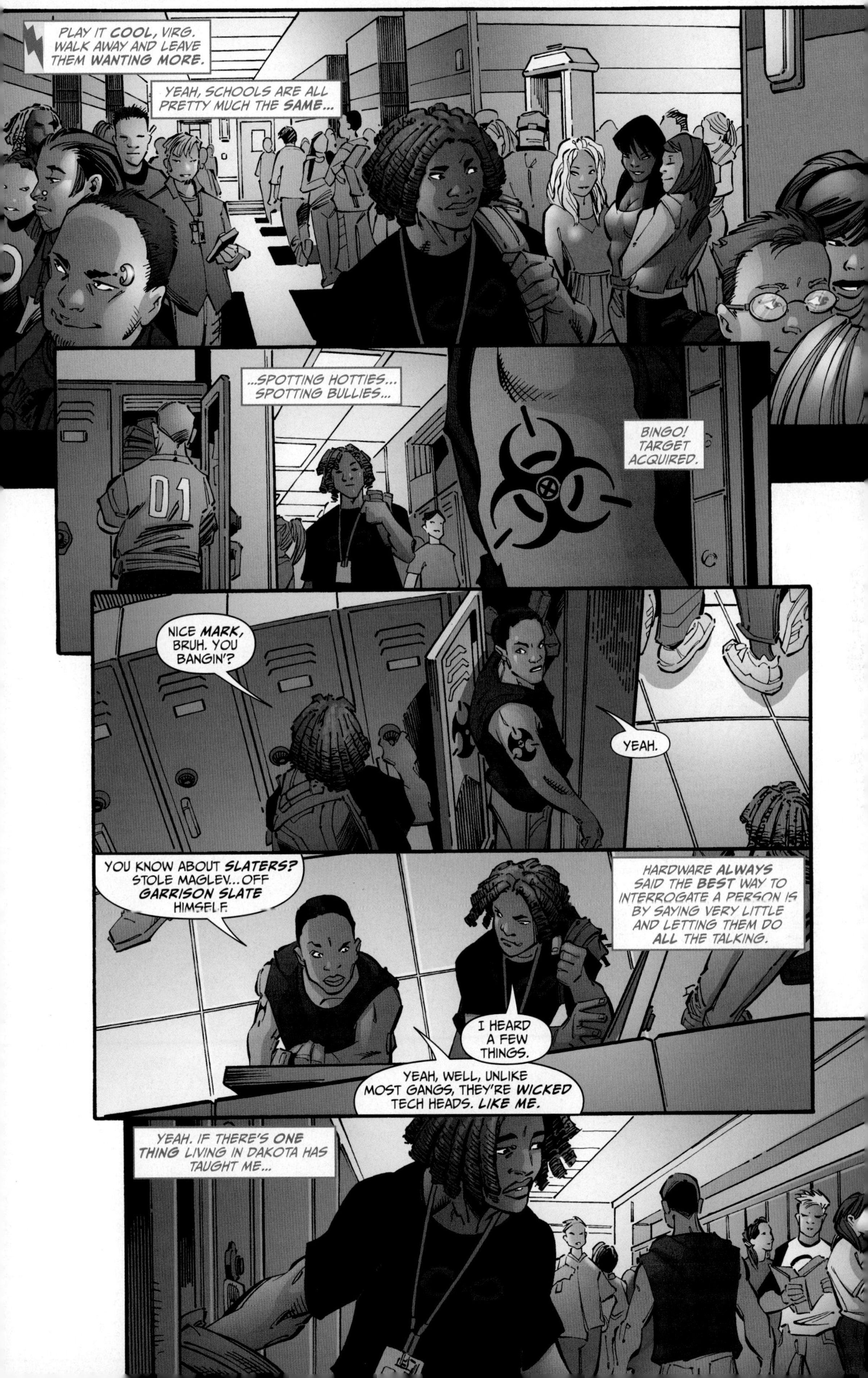
PLAY IT COOL, VIRG. WALK AWAY AND LEAVE THEM WANTING MORE.
YEAH, SCHOOLS ARE ALL PRETTY MUCH THE SAME...
...SPOTTING HOTTIES... SPOTTING BULLIES...
BINGO! TARGET ACQUIRED.
NICE MARK, BRUH. YOU BANGIN'?
YEAH.
YOU KNOW ABOUT SLATERS? STOLE MAGLEV...OFF GARRISON SLATE HIMSELF.
HARDWARE ALWAYS SAID THE BEST WAY TO INTERROGATE A PERSON IS BY SAYING VERY LITTLE AND LETTING THEM DO ALL THE TALKING.
I HEARD A FEW THINGS.
YEAH, WELL, UNLIKE MOST GANGS, THEY'RE WICKED TECH HEADS. LIKE ME.
YEAH. IF THERE'S ONE THING LIVING IN DAKOTA HAS TAUGHT ME...

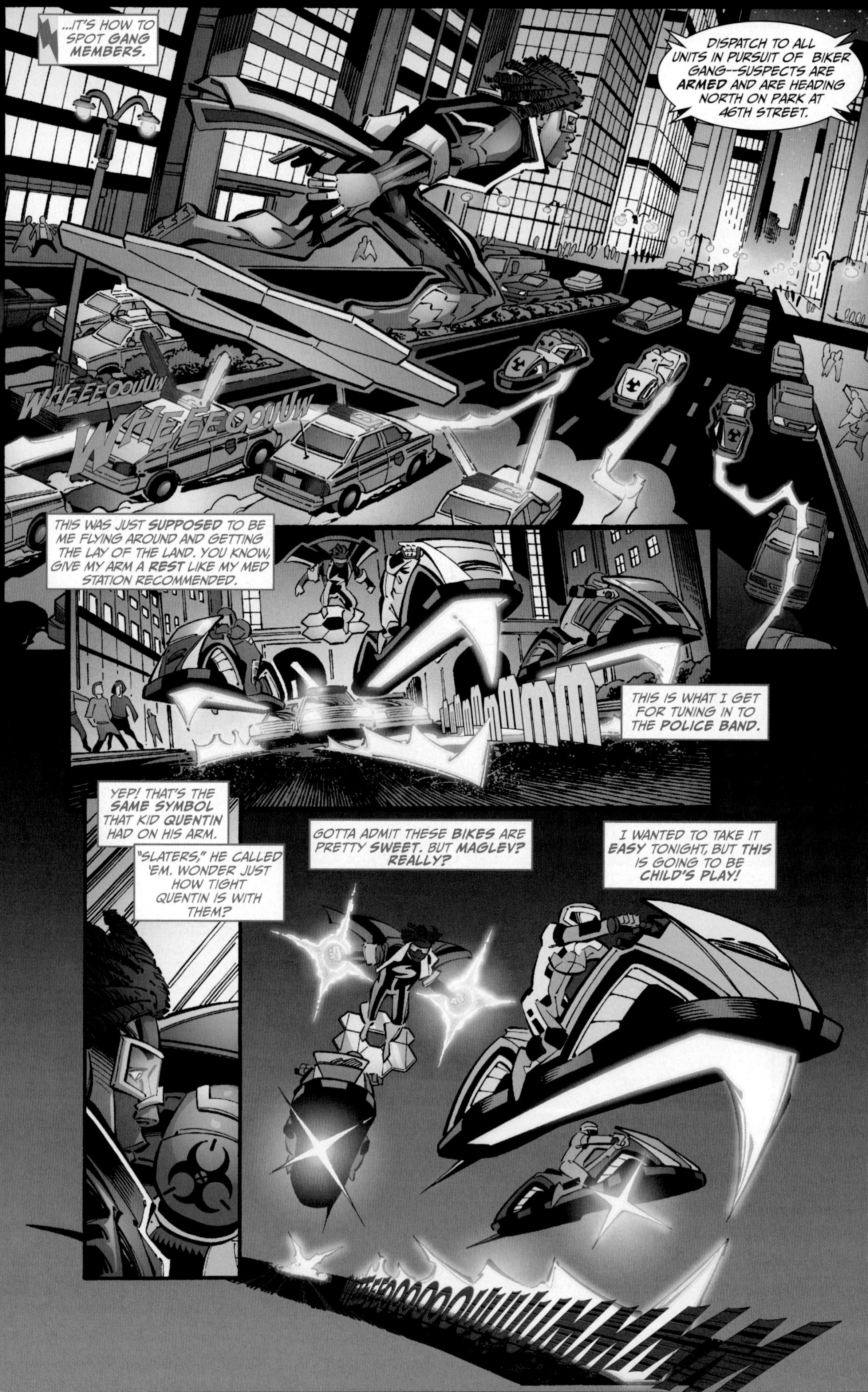
...IT'S HOW TO SPOT GANG MEMBERS.
DISPATCH TO ALL UNITS IN PURSUIT OF BIKER GANG--SUSPECTS ARE ARMED AND ARE HEADING NORTH ON PARK AT 46TH STREET.
WHEEEOOUUW
WHEEEOOUUW
THIS WAS JUST SUPPOSED TO BE ME FLYING AROUND AND GETTING THE LAY OF THE LAND. YOU KNOW, GIVE MY ARM A REST LIKE MY MED STATION RECOMMENDED.
THIS IS WHAT I GET FOR TUNING IN TO THE POLICE BAND.
YEP! THAT'S THE SAME SYMBOL THAT KID QUENTIN HAD ON HIS ARM.
"SLATERS," HE CALLED 'EM. WONDER JUST HOW TIGHT QUENTIN IS WITH THEM?
GOTTA ADMIT THESE BIKES ARE PRETTY SWEET. BUT MAGLEV? REALLY?
I WANTED TO TAKE IT EASY TONIGHT, BUT THIS IS GOING TO BE CHILD'S PLAY!

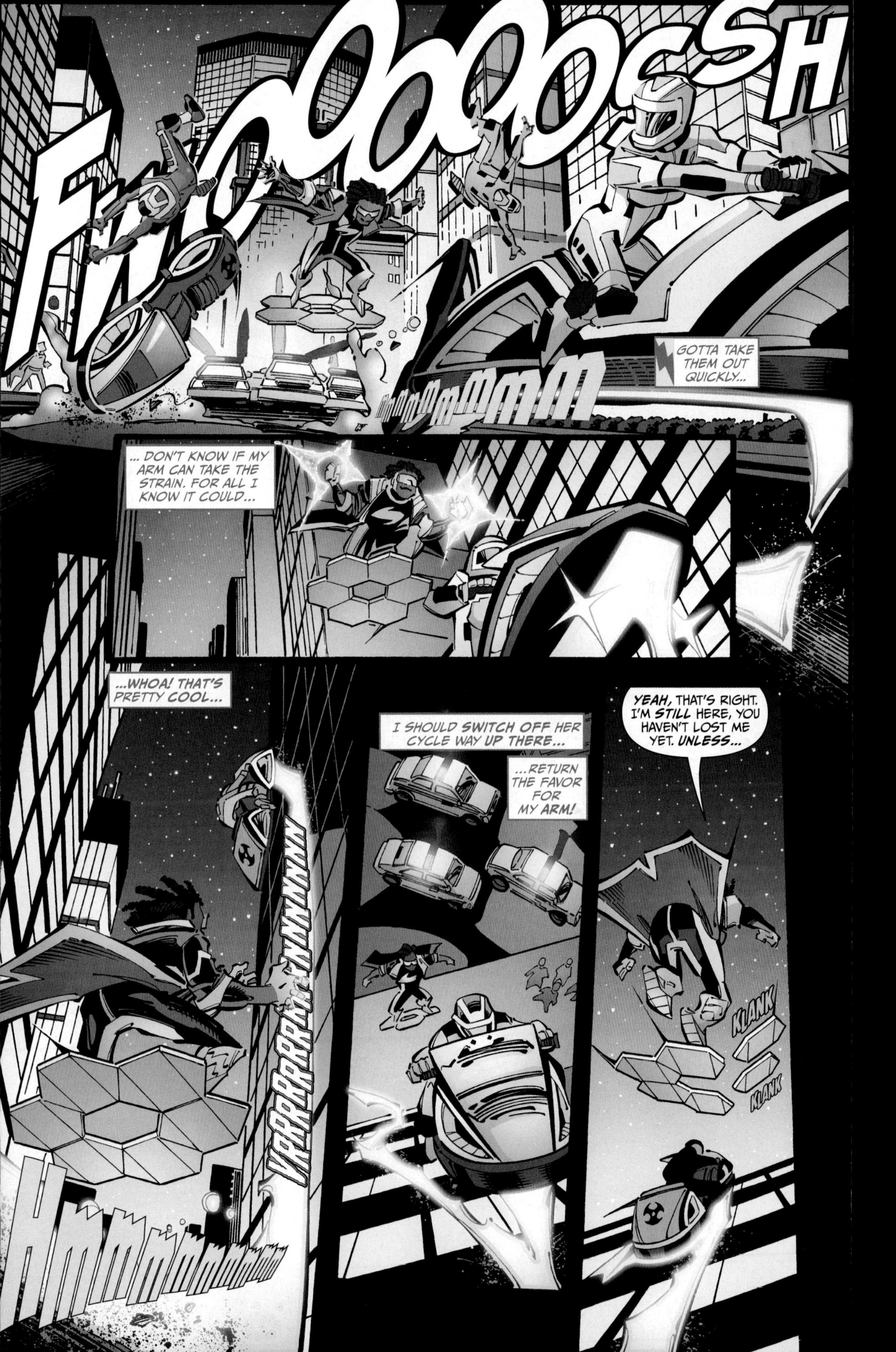
FWOOOOOSH
GOTTA TAKE THEM OUT QUICKLY...
... DON'T KNOW IF MY ARM CAN TAKE THE STRAIN. FOR ALL I KNOW IT COULD...
...WHOA! THAT'S PRETTY COOL...
I SHOULD SWITCH OFF HER CYCLE WAY UP THERE...
...RETURN THE FAVOR FOR MY ARM!
YEAH, THAT'S RIGHT. I'M STILL HERE, YOU HAVEN'T LOST ME YET. UNLESS...
KLANK
KLANK

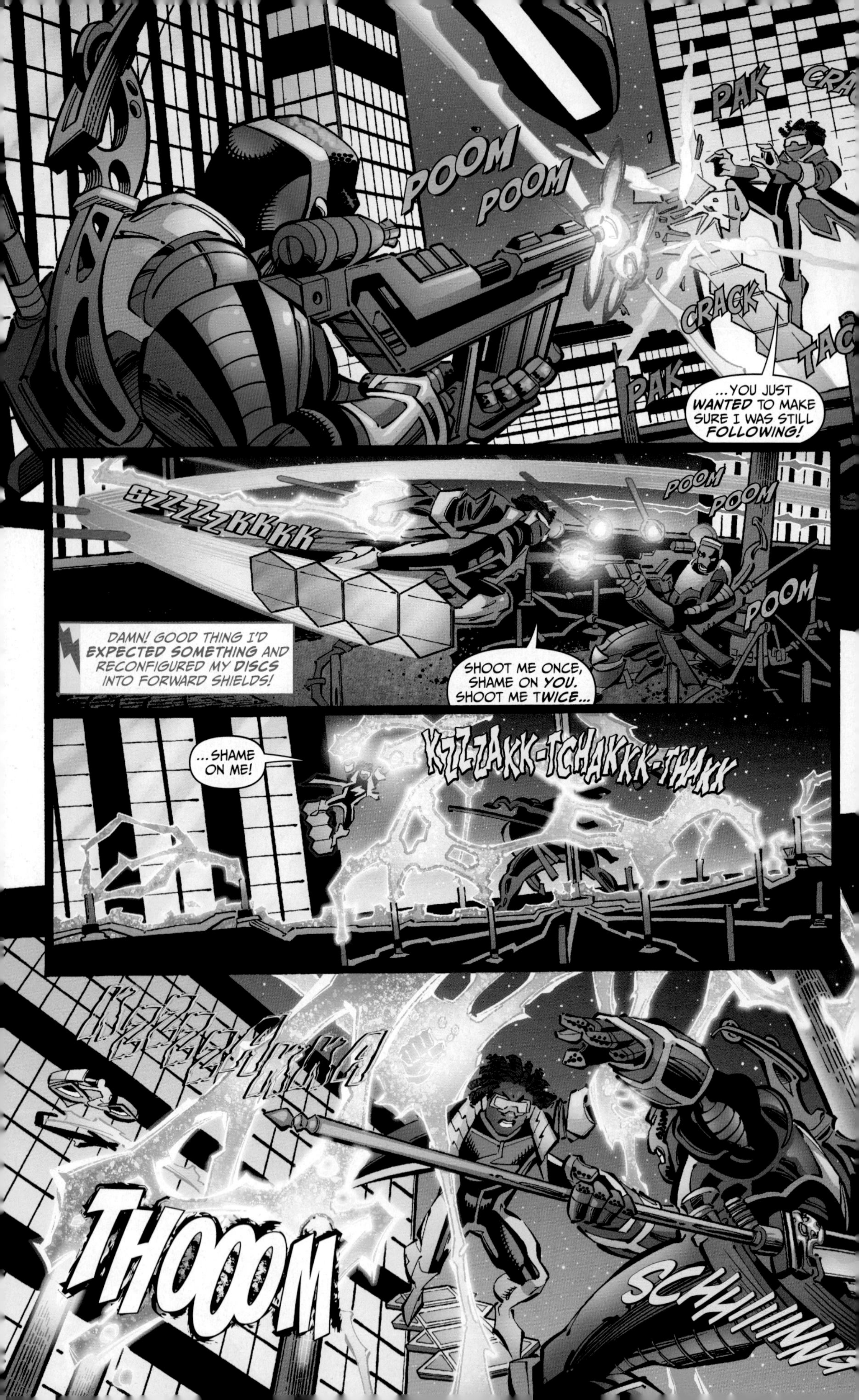

POOM
POOM
PAK
CRACK
CRACK
PAK
TAC
...YOU JUST WANTED TO MAKE SURE I WAS STILL FOLLOWING!
SZZZZZKKKK
POOM
POOM
POOM
DAMN! GOOD THING I'D EXPECTED SOMETHING AND RECONFIGURED MY DISCS INTO FORWARD SHIELDS!
SHOOT ME ONCE, SHAME ON YOU. SHOOT ME TWICE...
...SHAME ON ME!
KZZZAKK-TCHAKKK-THAKK
THOOOM
SCHHIIIING

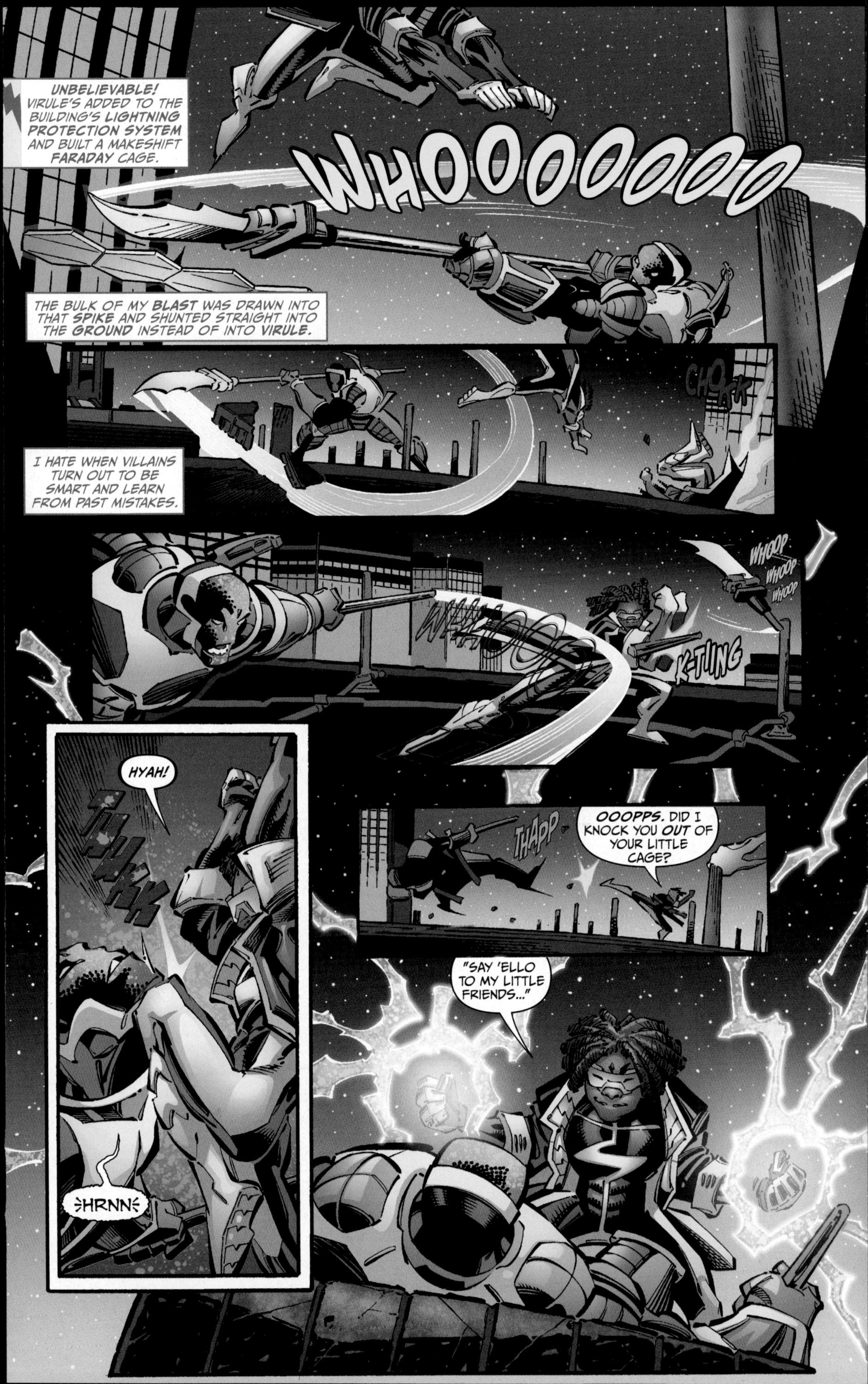
UNBELIEVABLE! VIRULE'S ADDED TO THE BUILDING'S LIGHTNING PROTECTION SYSTEM AND BUILT A MAKESHIFT FARADAY CAGE.
WHOOOOOOO
THE BULK OF MY BLAST WAS DRAWN INTO THAT SPIKE AND SHUNTED STRAIGHT INTO THE GROUND INSTEAD OF INTO VIRULE.
I HATE WHEN VILLAINS TURN OUT TO BE SMART AND LEARN FROM PAST MISTAKES.
WHOOP WHOOP WHOOP
K-TIING
HYAH!
THUKK
HRNN
THAPP
OOOPPS. DID I KNOCK YOU OUT OF YOUR LITTLE CAGE?
"SAY 'ELLO TO MY LITTLE FRIENDS..."

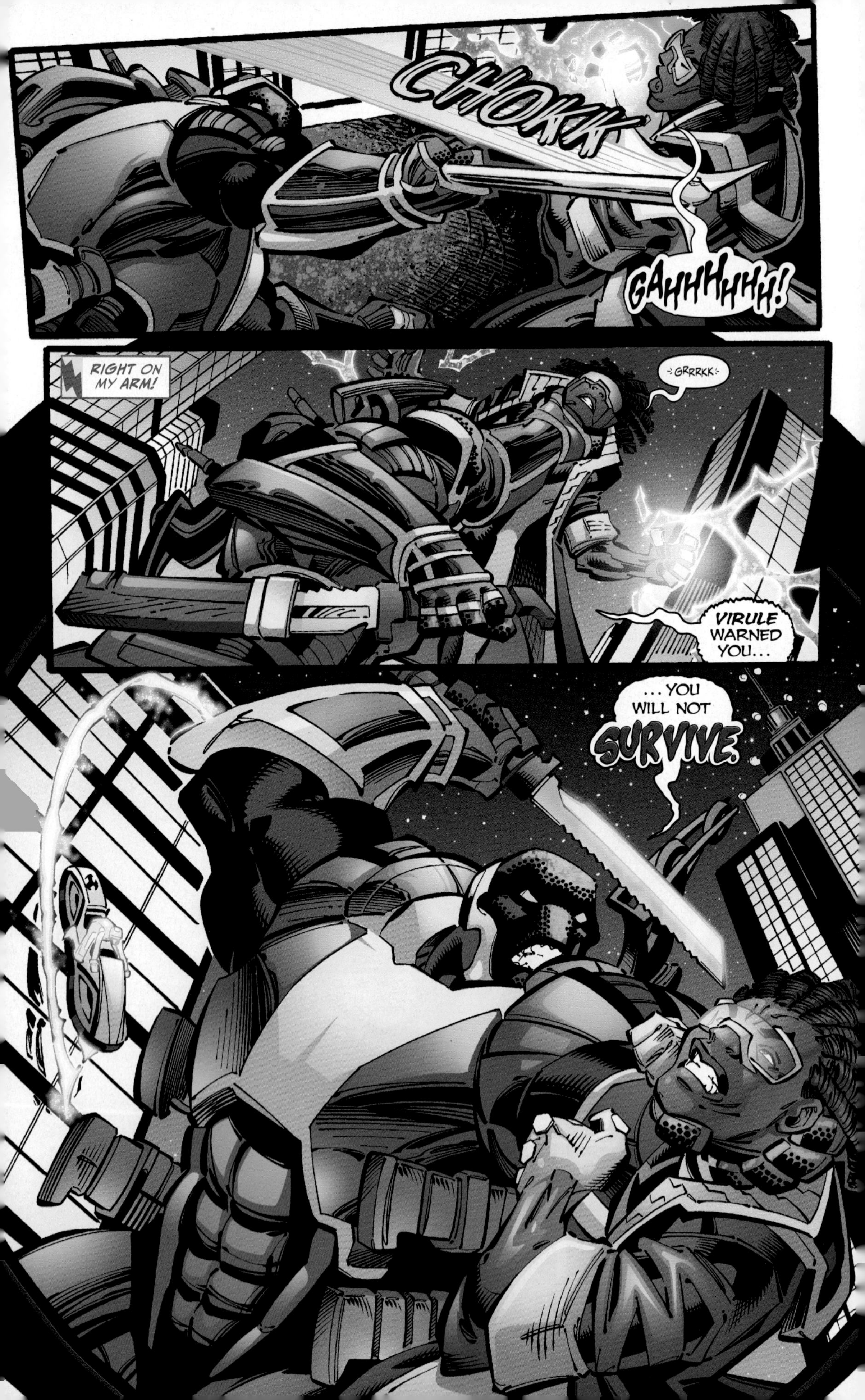
CHOKK
GAHHHHHH!
RIGHT ON MY ARM!
GRRRKK
VIRULE WARNED YOU...
...YOU WILL NOT SURVIVE.

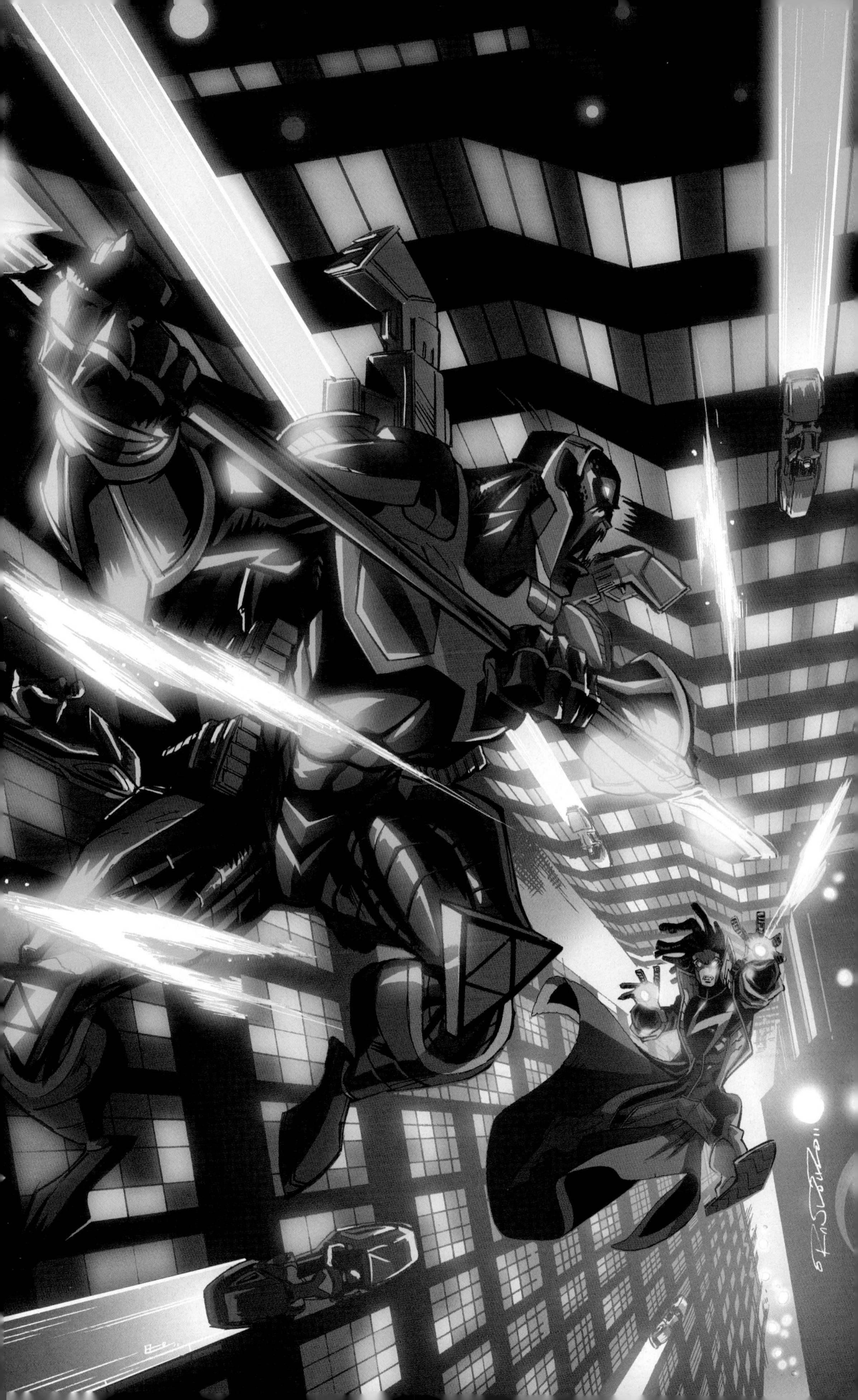

cover art by
KHARY RANDOLPH
& EMILIO LOPEZ

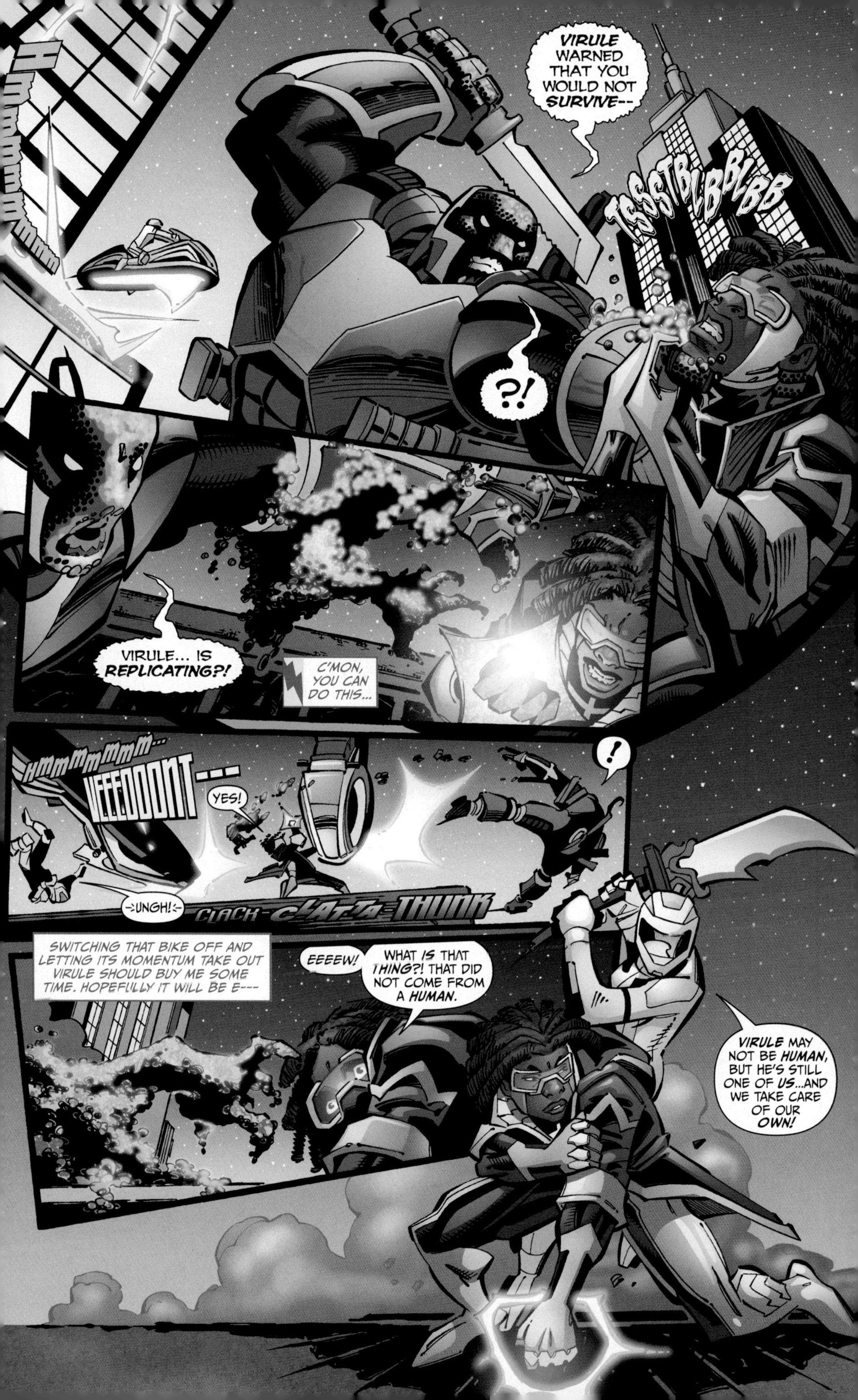
HMMMMMMMMM
VIRULE WARNED THAT YOU WOULD NOT SURVIVE--
TSSSTBLBBLBB
?!
VIRULE... IS REPLICATING?!
C'MON, YOU CAN DO THIS...
HMMMMMMMM--
VEEEOOONT---
YES!
!
-UNGH!-
CLACK-CLATTA-THUNK
SWITCHING THAT BIKE OFF AND LETTING ITS MOMENTUM TAKE OUT VIRULE SHOULD BUY ME SOME TIME. HOPEFULLY IT WILL BE E---
EEEEW!
WHAT IS THAT THING?! THAT DID NOT COME FROM A HUMAN.
VIRULE MAY NOT BE HUMAN, BUT HE'S STILL ONE OF US...AND WE TAKE CARE OF OUR OWN!

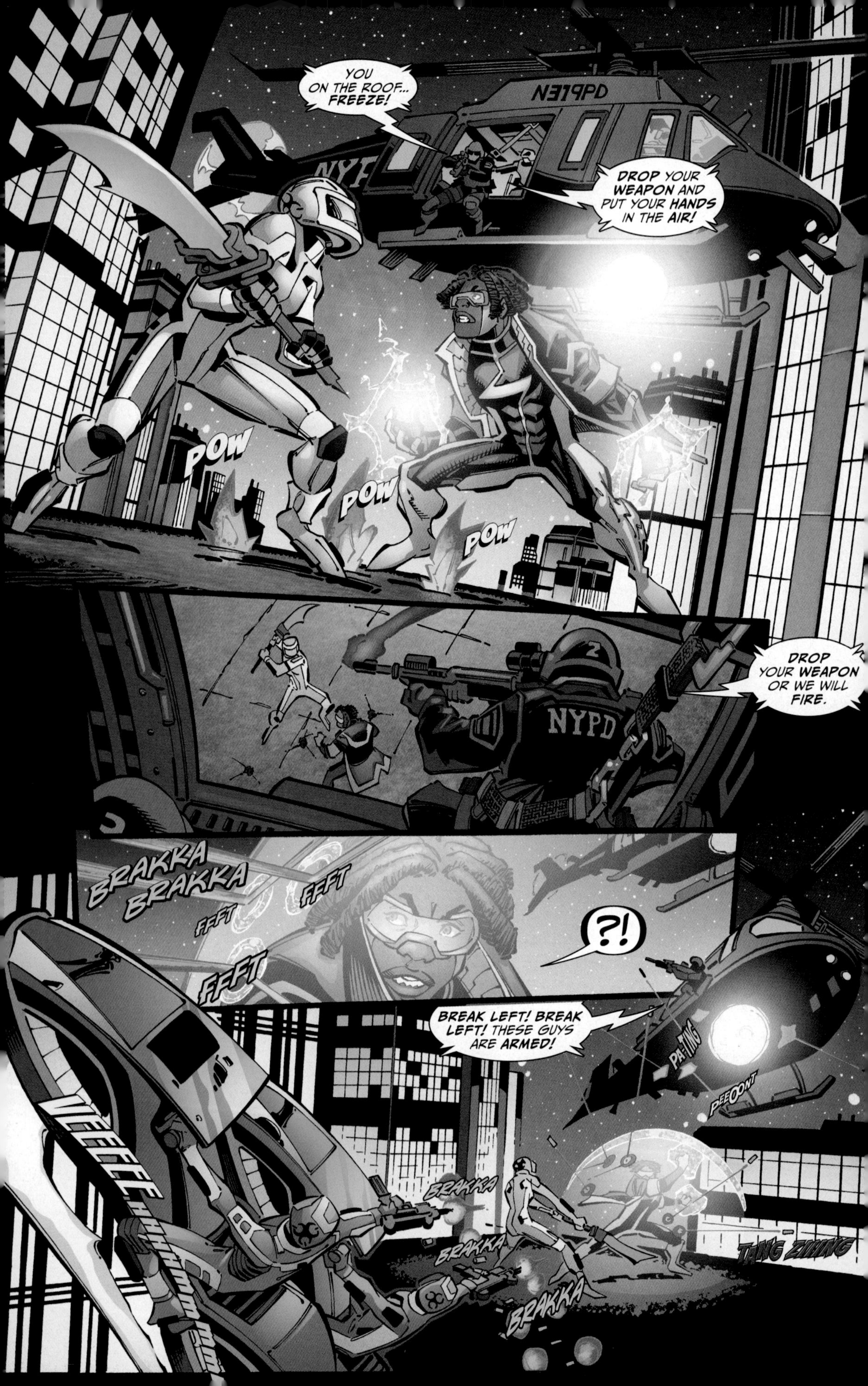
YOU ON THE ROOF... FREEZE!
DROP YOUR WEAPON AND PUT YOUR HANDS IN THE AIR!
NYPD
POW
POW
POW
NYPD
DROP YOUR WEAPON OR WE WILL FIRE.
BRAKKA BRAKKA
FFFT
FFFT
FFFT
?!
BREAK LEFT! BREAK LEFT! THESE GUYS ARE ARMED!
PA-TING
PEEOONT
BRAKKA
BRAKKA
BRAKKA
TANG ZIIING

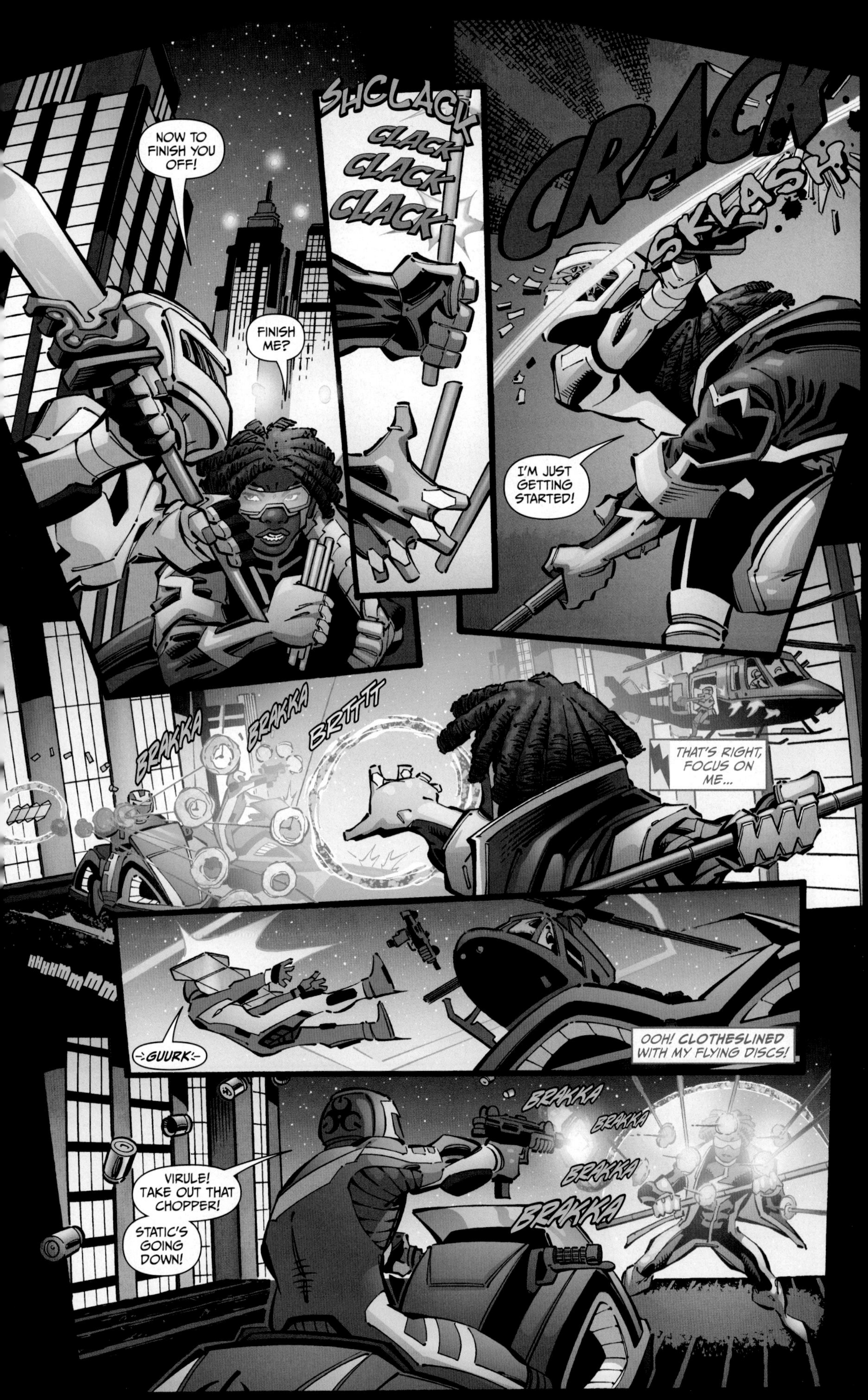
NOW TO FINISH YOU OFF!
FINISH ME?
SHCLACK
CLACK
CLACK
CLACK
CRACK
SKLASH
I'M JUST GETTING STARTED!
BRAKKA
BRAKKA
BRTTTT
THAT'S RIGHT, FOCUS ON ME...
HHHHMMMMMM
-GUURK-
OOH! CLOTHESLINED WITH MY FLYING DISCS!
BRAKKA
BRAKKA
BRAKKA
BRAKKA
VIRULE! TAKE OUT THAT CHOPPER!
STATIC'S GOING DOWN!

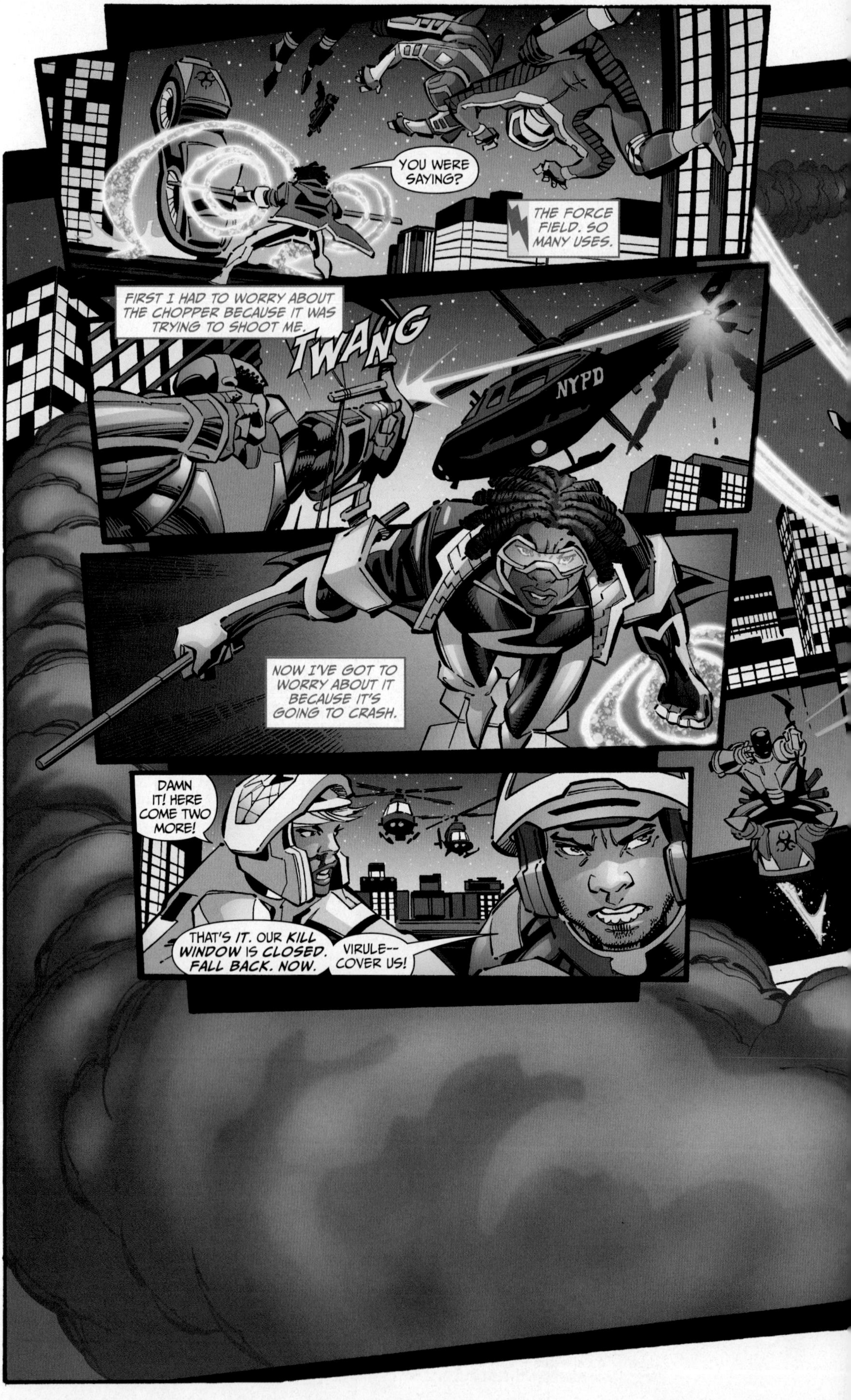
YOU WERE SAYING?
THE FORCE FIELD. SO MANY USES.
FIRST I HAD TO WORRY ABOUT THE CHOPPER BECAUSE IT WAS TRYING TO SHOOT ME.
TWANG
NYPD
NOW I'VE GOT TO WORRY ABOUT IT BECAUSE IT'S GOING TO CRASH.
DAMN IT! HERE COME TWO MORE!
THAT'S IT. OUR KILL WINDOW IS CLOSED. FALL BACK. NOW.
VIRULE-- COVER US!

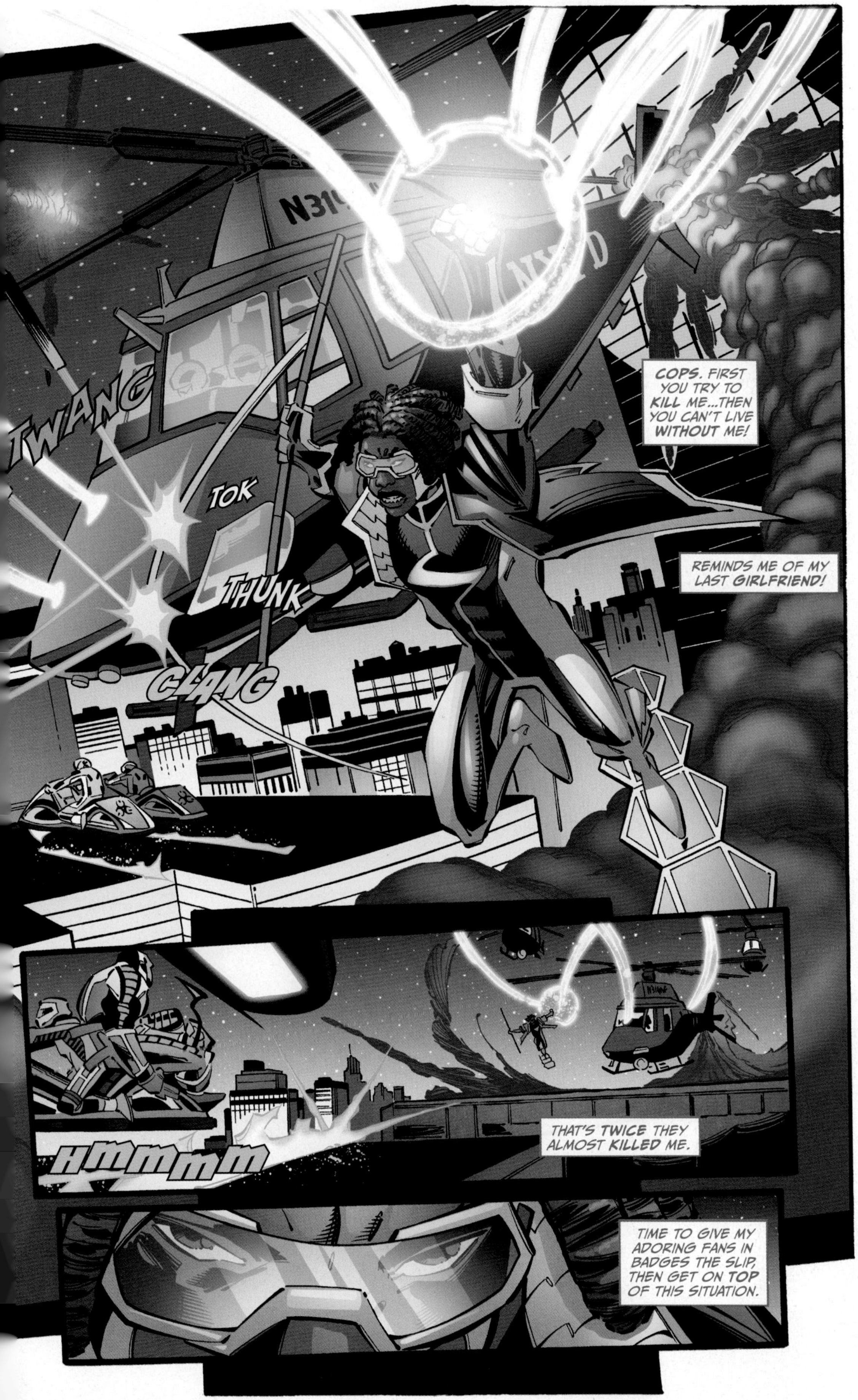
TWANG
TOK
THUNK
CLANG
COPS. FIRST YOU TRY TO KILL ME...THEN YOU CAN'T LIVE WITHOUT ME!
REMINDS ME OF MY LAST GIRLFRIEND!
HMMMMM
THAT'S TWICE THEY ALMOST KILLED ME.
TIME TO GIVE MY ADORING FANS IN BADGES THE SLIP, THEN GET ON TOP OF THIS SITUATION.

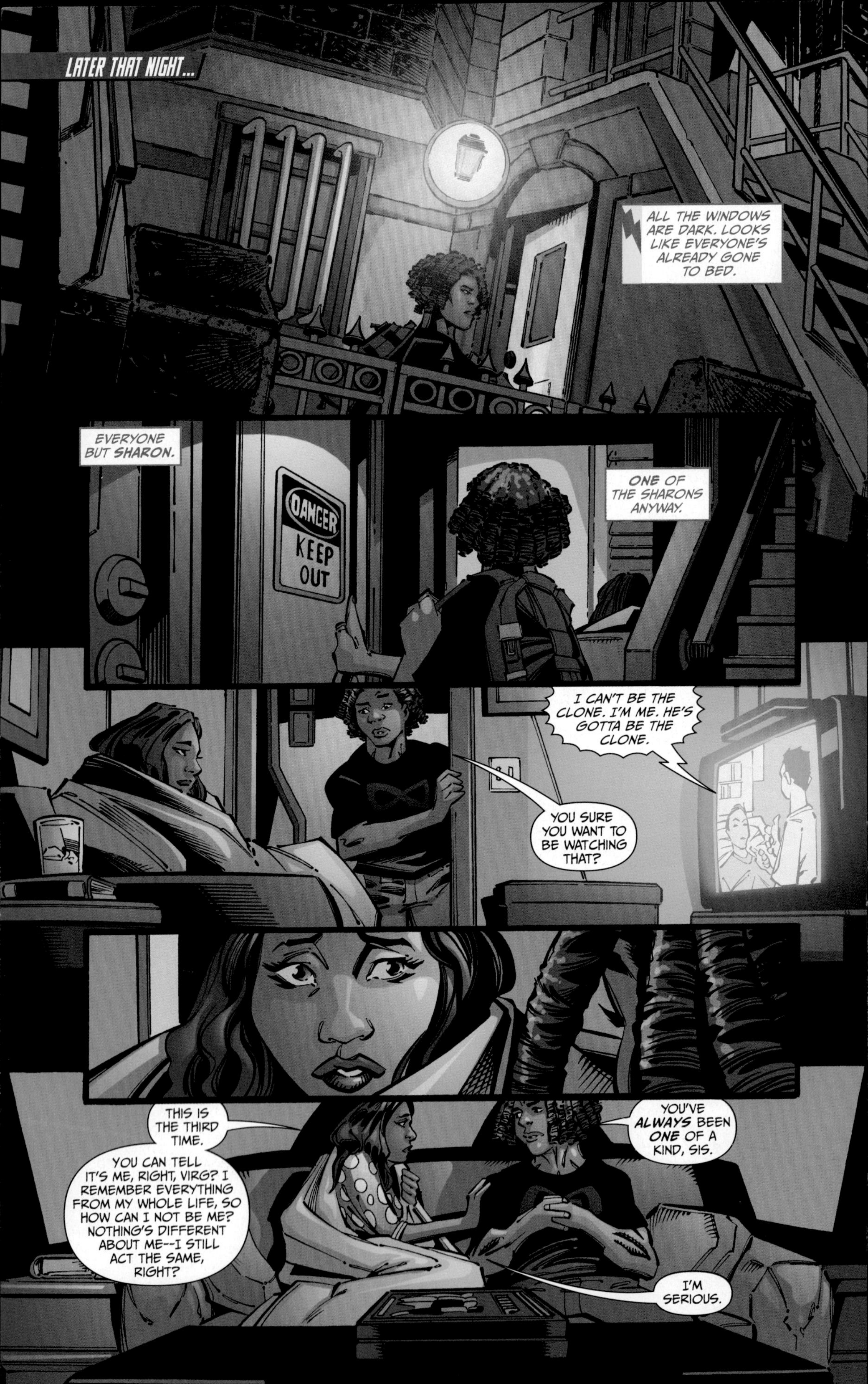
LATER THAT NIGHT...
ALL THE WINDOWS ARE DARK. LOOKS LIKE EVERYONE'S ALREADY GONE TO BED.
EVERYONE BUT SHARON.
DANGER KEEP OUT
ONE OF THE SHARONS ANYWAY.
YOU SURE YOU WANT TO BE WATCHING THAT?
I CAN'T BE THE CLONE. I'M ME. HE'S GOTTA BE THE CLONE.
THIS IS THE THIRD TIME.
YOU CAN TELL IT'S ME, RIGHT, VIRG? I REMEMBER EVERYTHING FROM MY WHOLE LIFE, SO HOW CAN I NOT BE ME? NOTHING'S DIFFERENT ABOUT ME--I STILL ACT THE SAME, RIGHT?
YOU'VE ALWAYS BEEN ONE OF A KIND, SIS.
I'M SERIOUS.

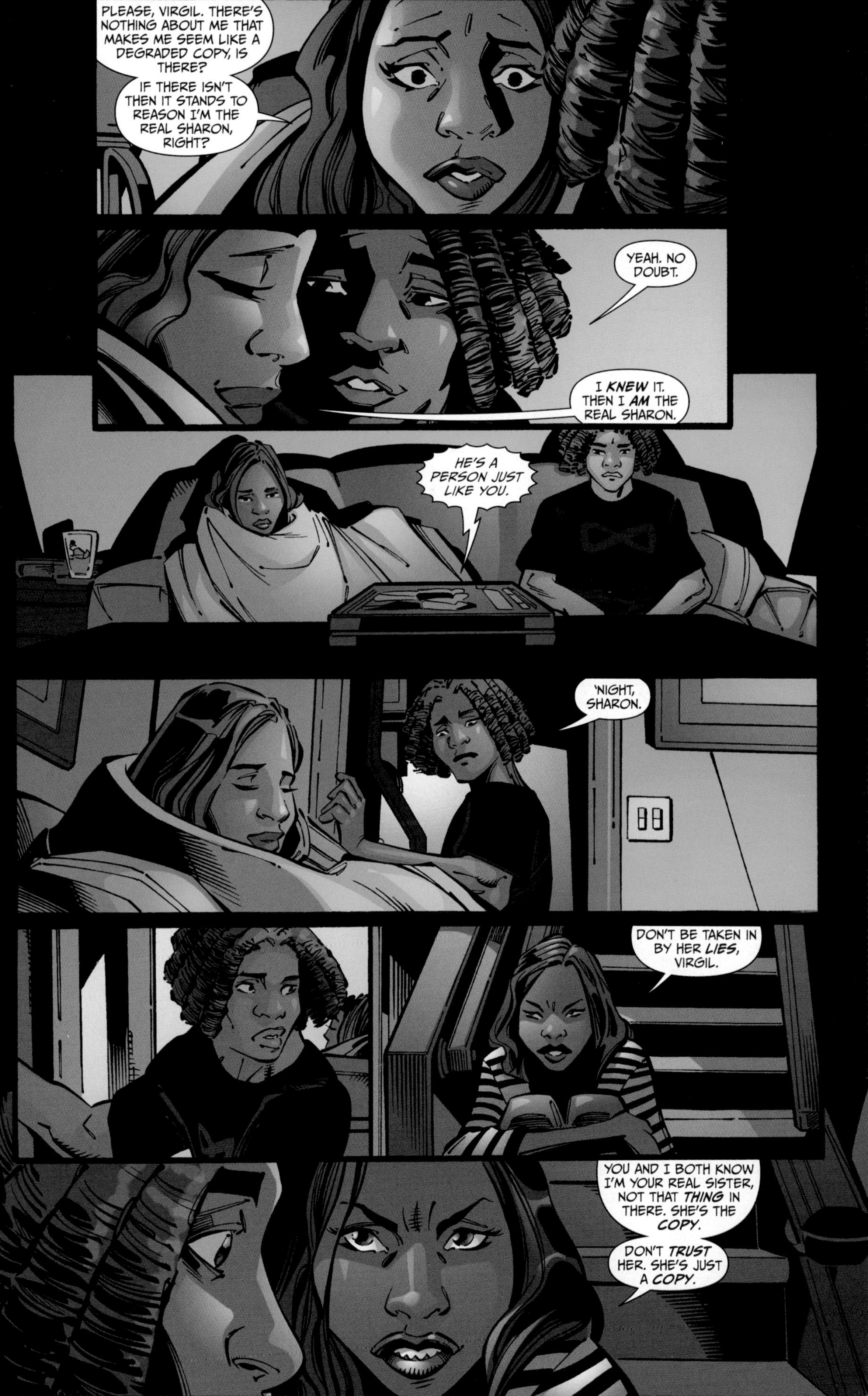
PLEASE, VIRGIL. THERE'S NOTHING ABOUT ME THAT MAKES ME SEEM LIKE A DEGRADED COPY, IS THERE?
IF THERE ISN'T THEN IT STANDS TO REASON I'M THE REAL SHARON, RIGHT?
YEAH. NO DOUBT.
I *KNEW* IT. THEN I *AM* THE REAL SHARON.
HE'S A PERSON JUST LIKE YOU.
'NIGHT, SHARON.
DON'T BE TAKEN IN BY HER *LIES*, VIRGIL.
YOU AND I BOTH KNOW I'M YOUR REAL SISTER, NOT THAT *THING* IN THERE. SHE'S THE *COPY*.
DON'T *TRUST* HER. SHE'S JUST A *COPY*.

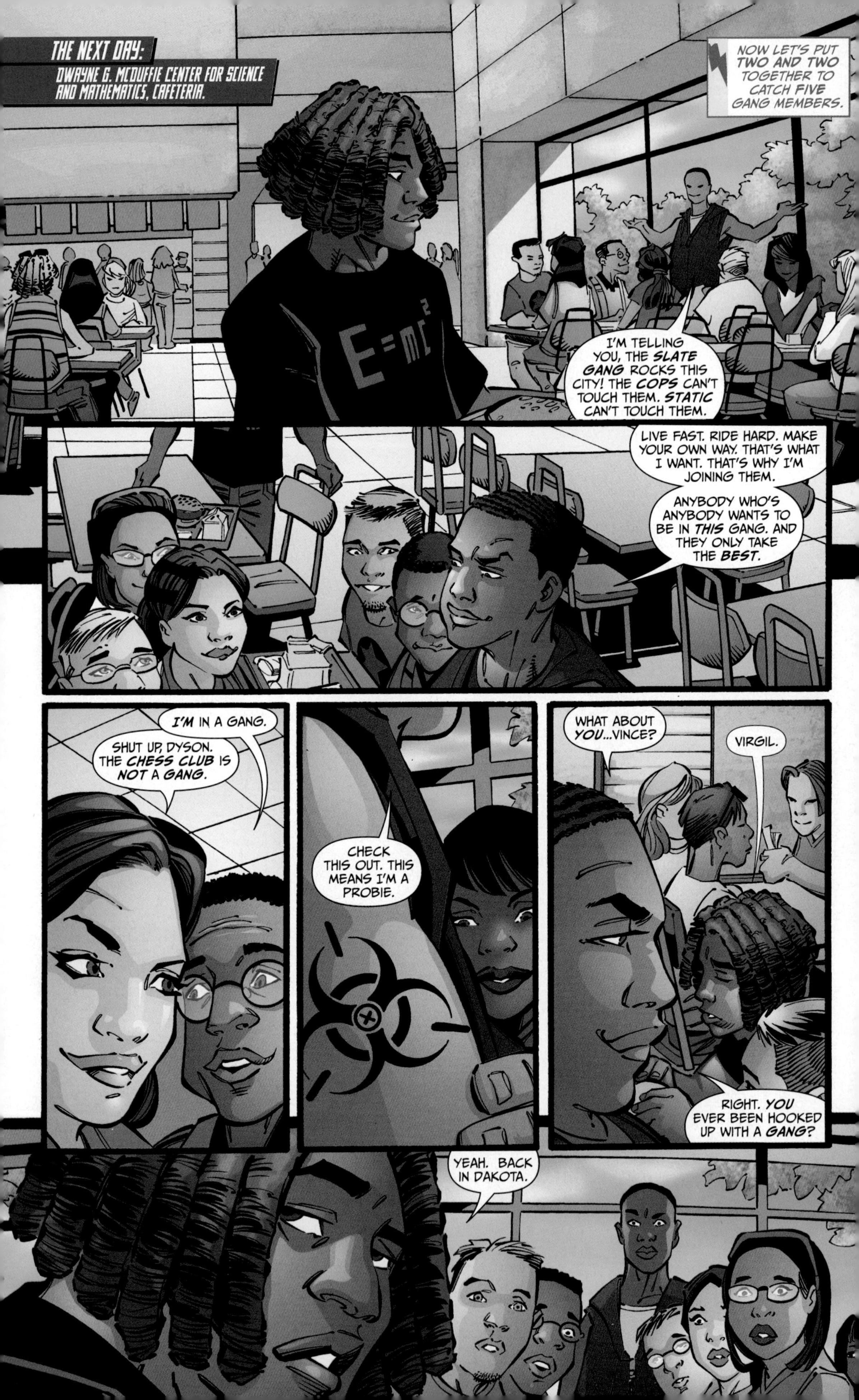
THE NEXT DAY:
DWAYNE G. MCDUFFIE CENTER FOR SCIENCE AND MATHEMATICS, CAFETERIA.
NOW LET'S PUT TWO AND TWO TOGETHER TO CATCH FIVE GANG MEMBERS.
E=MC2
I'M TELLING YOU, THE SLATE GANG ROCKS THIS CITY! THE COPS CAN'T TOUCH THEM. STATIC CAN'T TOUCH THEM.
LIVE FAST. RIDE HARD. MAKE YOUR OWN WAY. THAT'S WHAT I WANT. THAT'S WHY I'M JOINING THEM.
ANYBODY WHO'S ANYBODY WANTS TO BE IN THIS GANG. AND THEY ONLY TAKE THE BEST.
I'M IN A GANG.
SHUT UP, DYSON. THE CHESS CLUB IS NOT A GANG.
CHECK THIS OUT. THIS MEANS I'M A PROBIE.
WHAT ABOUT YOU...VINCE?
VIRGIL.
RIGHT. YOU EVER BEEN HOOKED UP WITH A GANG?
YEAH. BACK IN DAKOTA.

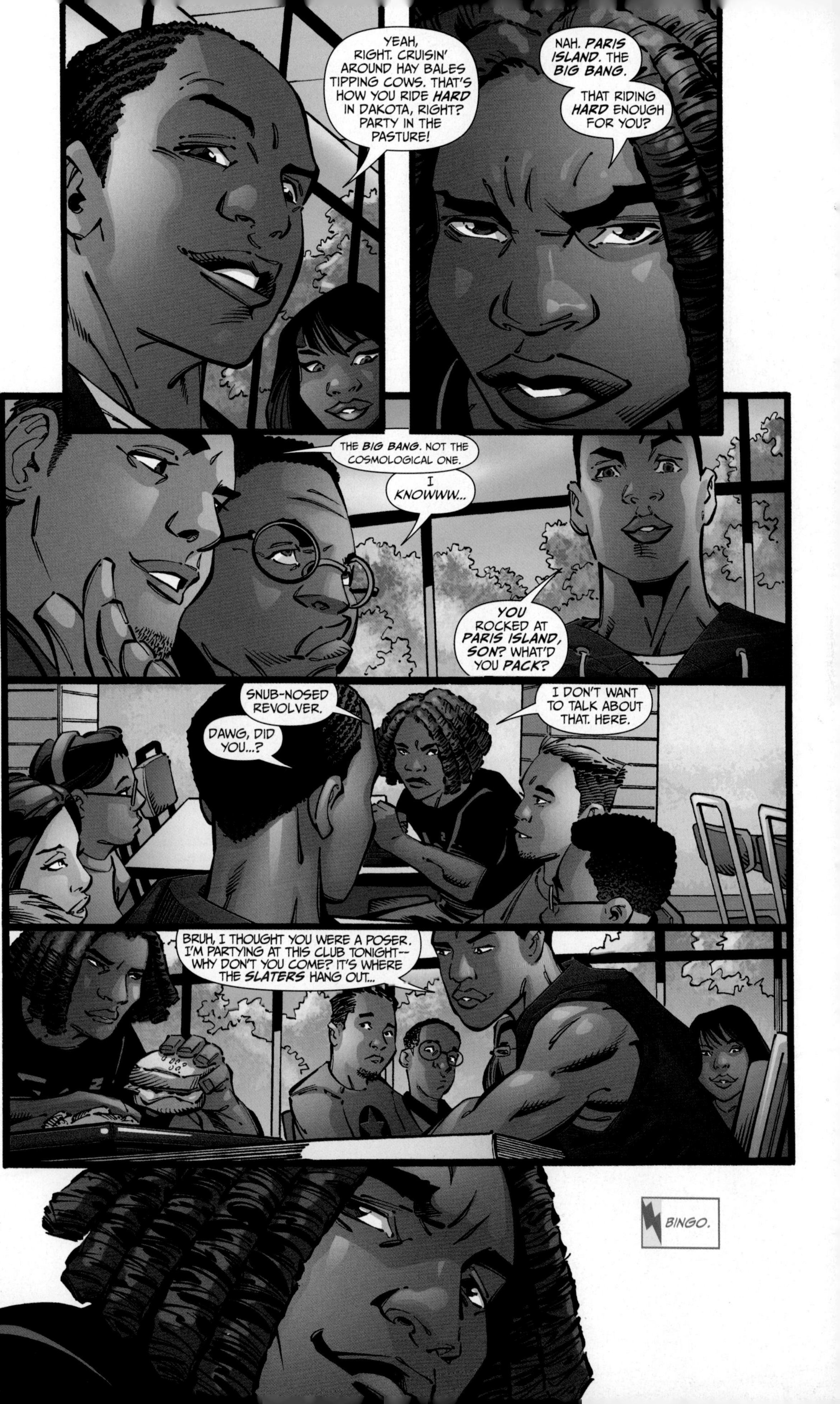
YEAH, RIGHT. CRUISIN' AROUND HAY BALES TIPPING COWS. THAT'S HOW YOU RIDE HARD IN DAKOTA, RIGHT? PARTY IN THE PASTURE!
NAH. PARIS ISLAND. THE BIG BANG.
THAT RIDING HARD ENOUGH FOR YOU?
THE BIG BANG. NOT THE COSMOLOGICAL ONE.
I KNOWWW...
YOU ROCKED AT PARIS ISLAND, SON? WHAT'D YOU PACK?
SNUB-NOSED REVOLVER.
DAWG, DID YOU...?
I DON'T WANT TO TALK ABOUT THAT. HERE.
BRUH, I THOUGHT YOU WERE A POSER. I'M PARTYING AT THIS CLUB TONIGHT-- WHY DON'T YOU COME? IT'S WHERE THE SLATERS HANG OUT...
BINGO.

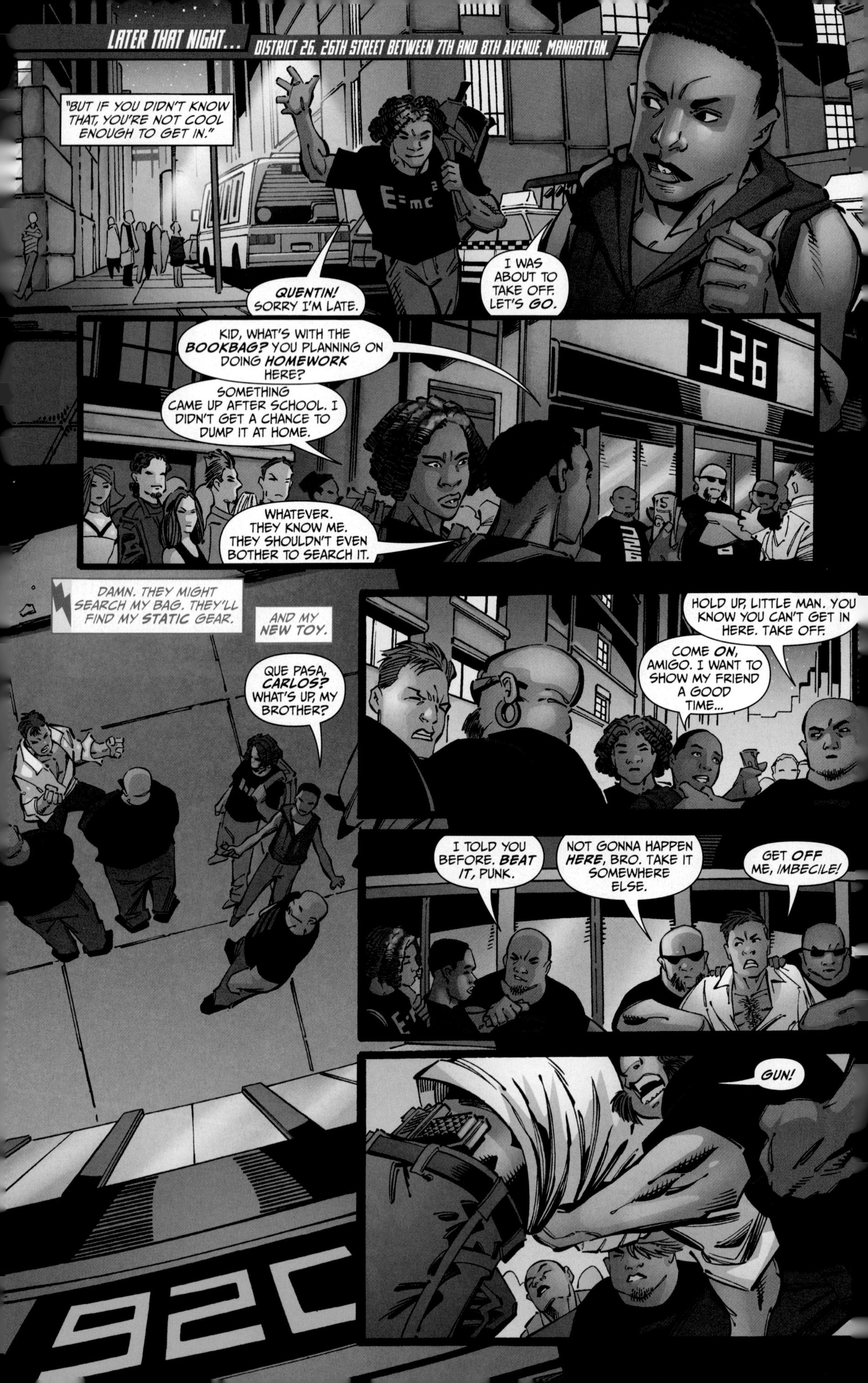
LATER THAT NIGHT...
DISTRICT 26. 26TH STREET BETWEEN 7TH AND 8TH AVENUE, MANHATTAN.
"BUT IF YOU DIDN'T KNOW THAT, YOU'RE NOT COOL ENOUGH TO GET IN."
QUENTIN! SORRY I'M LATE.
I WAS ABOUT TO TAKE OFF. LET'S GO.
KID, WHAT'S WITH THE BOOKBAG? YOU PLANNING ON DOING HOMEWORK HERE?
SOMETHING CAME UP AFTER SCHOOL. I DIDN'T GET A CHANCE TO DUMP IT AT HOME.
WHATEVER. THEY KNOW ME. THEY SHOULDN'T EVEN BOTHER TO SEARCH IT.
DAMN. THEY MIGHT SEARCH MY BAG. THEY'LL FIND MY STATIC GEAR.
AND MY NEW TOY.
QUE PASA, CARLOS? WHAT'S UP, MY BROTHER?
HOLD UP, LITTLE MAN. YOU KNOW YOU CAN'T GET IN HERE. TAKE OFF.
COME ON, AMIGO. I WANT TO SHOW MY FRIEND A GOOD TIME...
I TOLD YOU BEFORE. BEAT IT, PUNK.
NOT GONNA HAPPEN HERE, BRO. TAKE IT SOMEWHERE ELSE.
GET OFF ME, IMBECILE!
GUN!

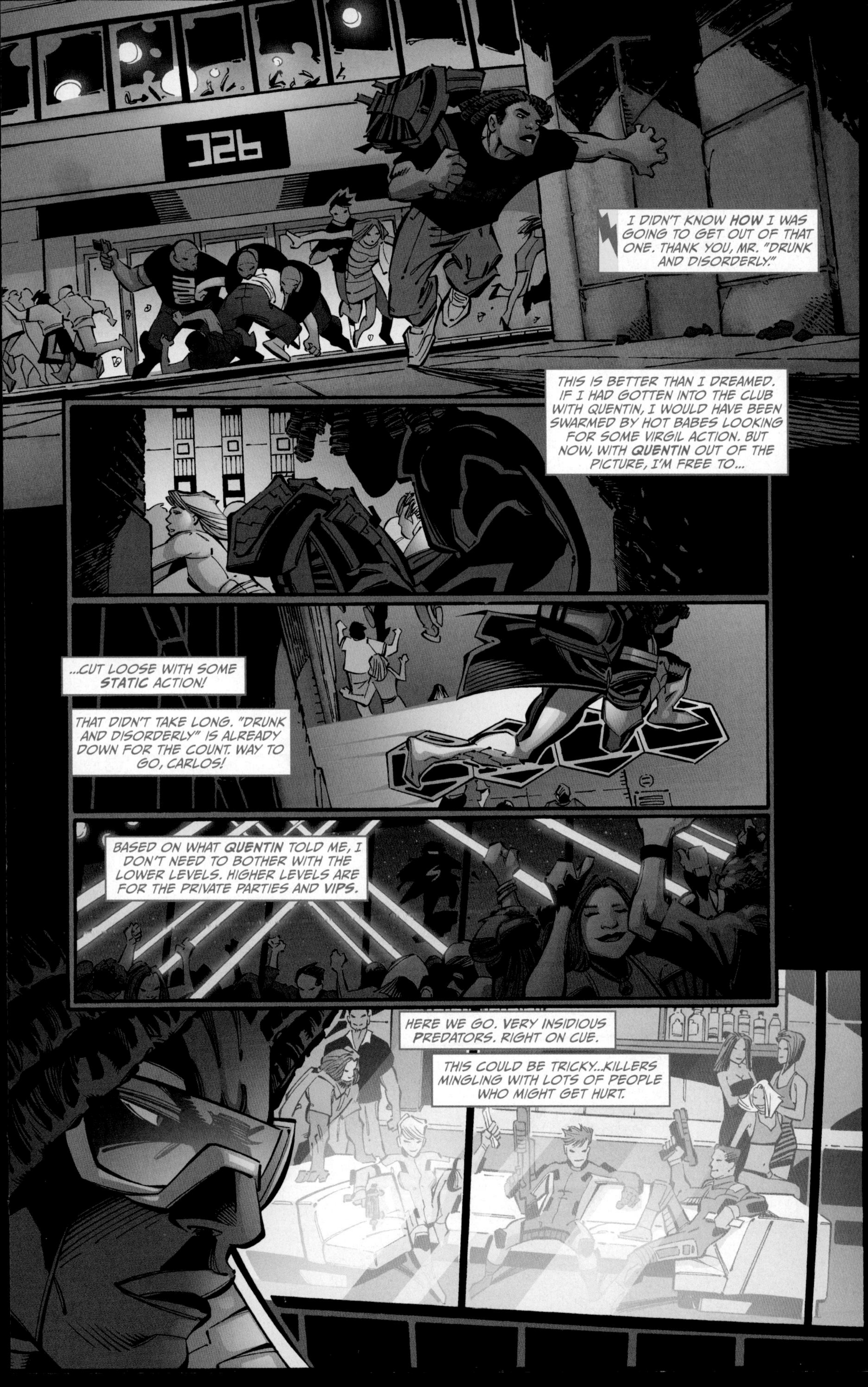

I DIDN'T KNOW HOW I WAS GOING TO GET OUT OF THAT ONE. THANK YOU, MR. "DRUNK AND DISORDERLY."
THIS IS BETTER THAN I DREAMED. IF I HAD GOTTEN INTO THE CLUB WITH QUENTIN, I WOULD HAVE BEEN SWARMED BY HOT BABES LOOKING FOR SOME VIRGIL ACTION. BUT NOW, WITH QUENTIN OUT OF THE PICTURE, I'M FREE TO...
...CUT LOOSE WITH SOME STATIC ACTION!
THAT DIDN'T TAKE LONG. "DRUNK AND DISORDERLY" IS ALREADY DOWN FOR THE COUNT. WAY TO GO, CARLOS!
BASED ON WHAT QUENTIN TOLD ME, I DON'T NEED TO BOTHER WITH THE LOWER LEVELS. HIGHER LEVELS ARE FOR THE PRIVATE PARTIES AND VIPS.
HERE WE GO. VERY INSIDIOUS PREDATORS. RIGHT ON CUE.
THIS COULD BE TRICKY...KILLERS MINGLING WITH LOTS OF PEOPLE WHO MIGHT GET HURT.

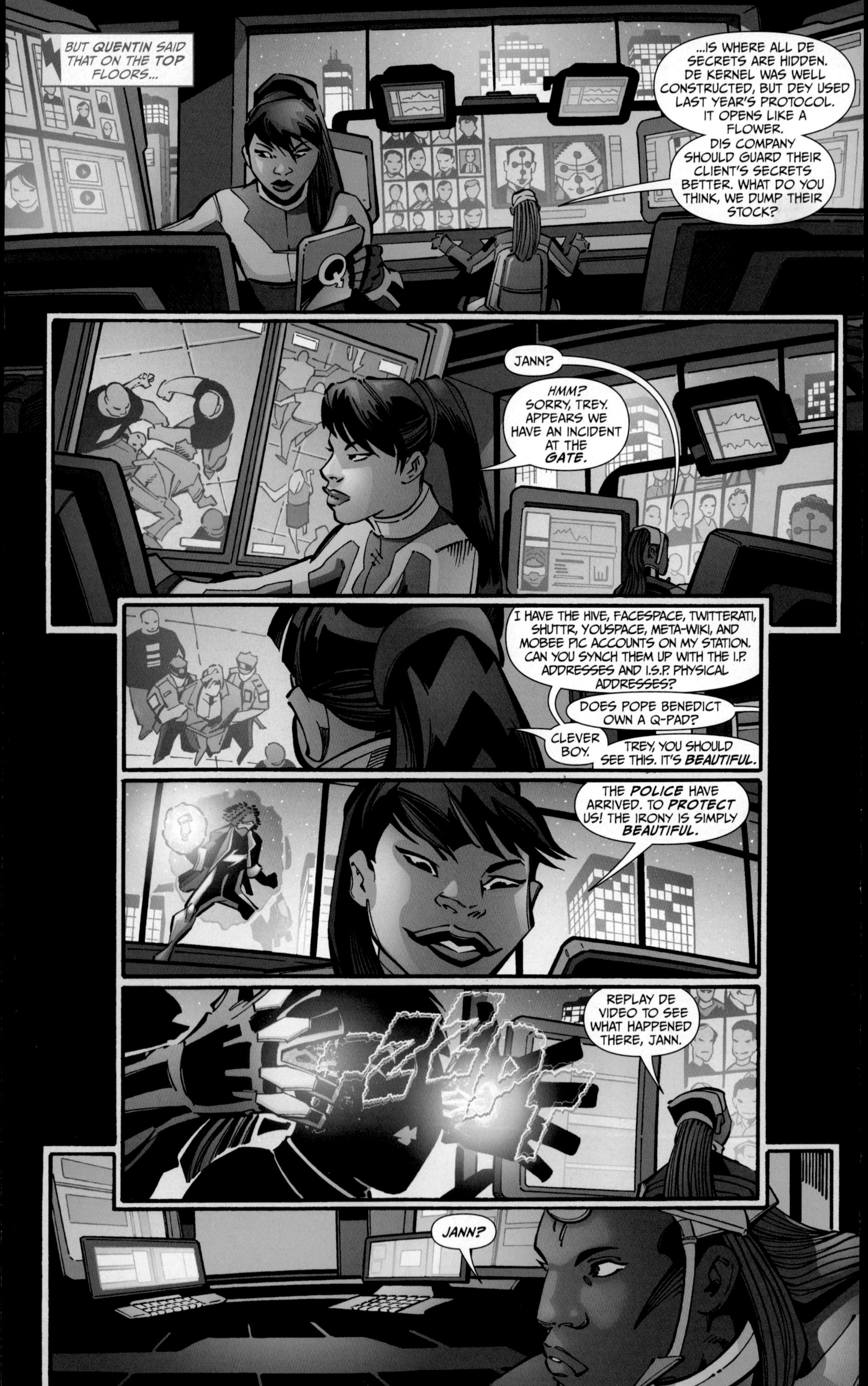

BUT QUENTIN SAID THAT ON THE TOP FLOORS...
...IS WHERE ALL DE SECRETS ARE HIDDEN. DE KERNEL WAS WELL CONSTRUCTED, BUT DEY USED LAST YEAR'S PROTOCOL. IT OPENS LIKE A FLOWER. DIS COMPANY SHOULD GUARD THEIR CLIENT'S SECRETS BETTER. WHAT DO YOU THINK, WE DUMP THEIR STOCK?
JANN?
HMM? SORRY, TREY. APPEARS WE HAVE AN INCIDENT AT THE GATE.
I HAVE THE HIVE, FACESPACE, TWITTERATI, SHUTTR, YOUSPACE, META-WIKI, AND MOBEE PIC ACCOUNTS ON MY STATION. CAN YOU SYNCH THEM UP WITH THE I.P. ADDRESSES AND I.S.P. PHYSICAL ADDRESSES?
DOES POPE BENEDICT OWN A Q-PAD?
CLEVER BOY.
TREY, YOU SHOULD SEE THIS. IT'S BEAUTIFUL.
THE POLICE HAVE ARRIVED. TO PROTECT US! THE IRONY IS SIMPLY BEAUTIFUL.
ZZAP
REPLAY DE VIDEO TO SEE WHAT HAPPENED THERE, JANN.
JANN?

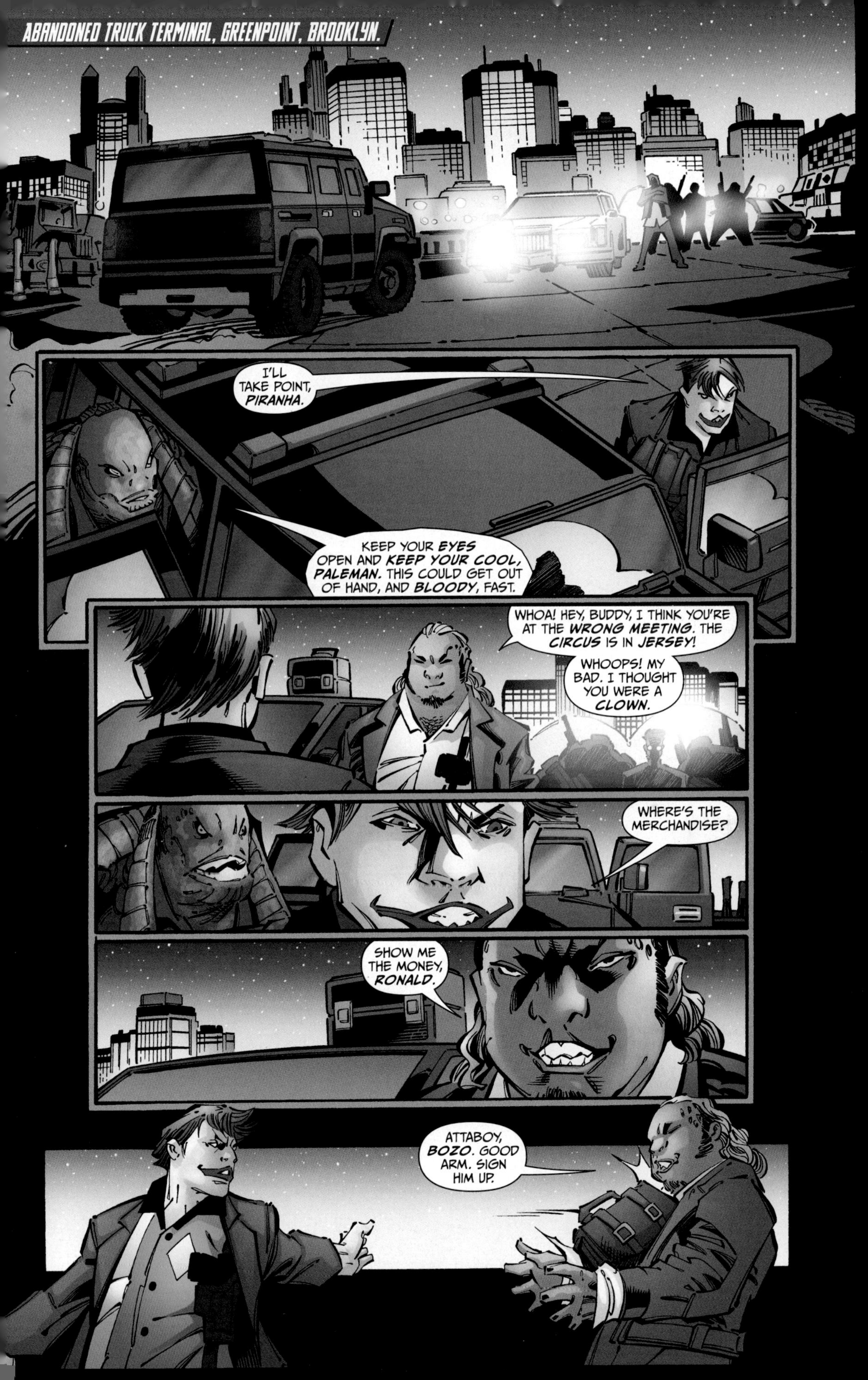
ABANDONED TRUCK TERMINAL, GREENPOINT, BROOKLYN.
I'LL TAKE POINT, PIRANHA.
KEEP YOUR EYES OPEN AND KEEP YOUR COOL, PALEMAN. THIS COULD GET OUT OF HAND, AND BLOODY, FAST.
WHOA! HEY, BUDDY, I THINK YOU'RE AT THE WRONG MEETING. THE CIRCUS IS IN JERSEY!
WHOOPS! MY BAD. I THOUGHT YOU WERE A CLOWN.
WHERE'S THE MERCHANDISE?
SHOW ME THE MONEY, RONALD.
ATTABOY, BOZO. GOOD ARM. SIGN HIM UP.

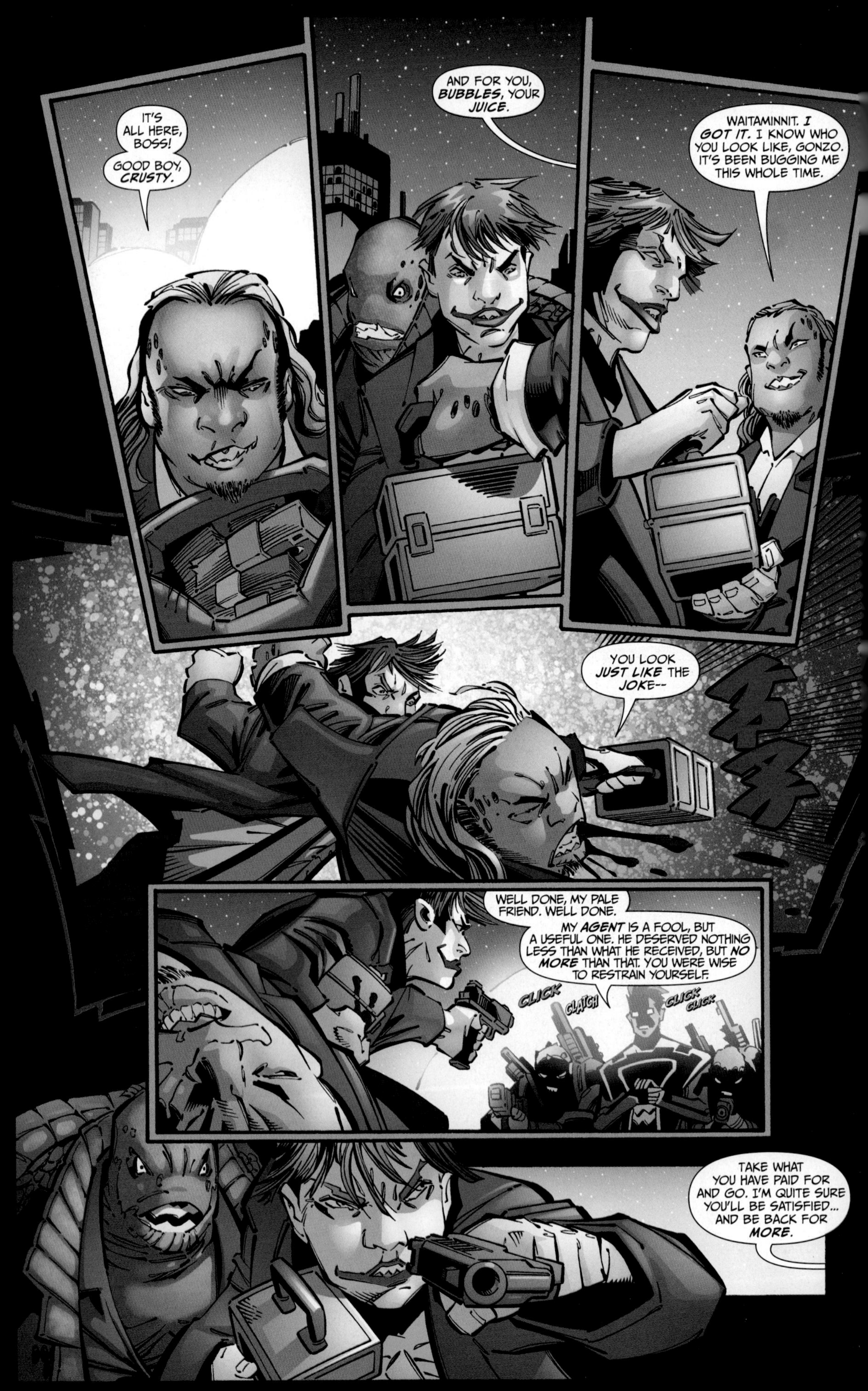
IT'S ALL HERE, BOSS!
GOOD BOY, CRUSTY.
AND FOR YOU, BUBBLES, YOUR JUICE.
WAITAMINNIT. I GOT IT. I KNOW WHO YOU LOOK LIKE, GONZO. IT'S BEEN BUGGING ME THIS WHOLE TIME.
YOU LOOK JUST LIKE THE JOKE--
WELL DONE, MY PALE FRIEND. WELL DONE.
MY AGENT IS A FOOL, BUT A USEFUL ONE. HE DESERVED NOTHING LESS THAN WHAT HE RECEIVED, BUT NO MORE THAN THAT. YOU WERE WISE TO RESTRAIN YOURSELF.
CLICK
CLATCH
CLICK
CLICK
TAKE WHAT YOU HAVE PAID FOR AND GO. I'M QUITE SURE YOU'LL BE SATISFIED... AND BE BACK FOR MORE.

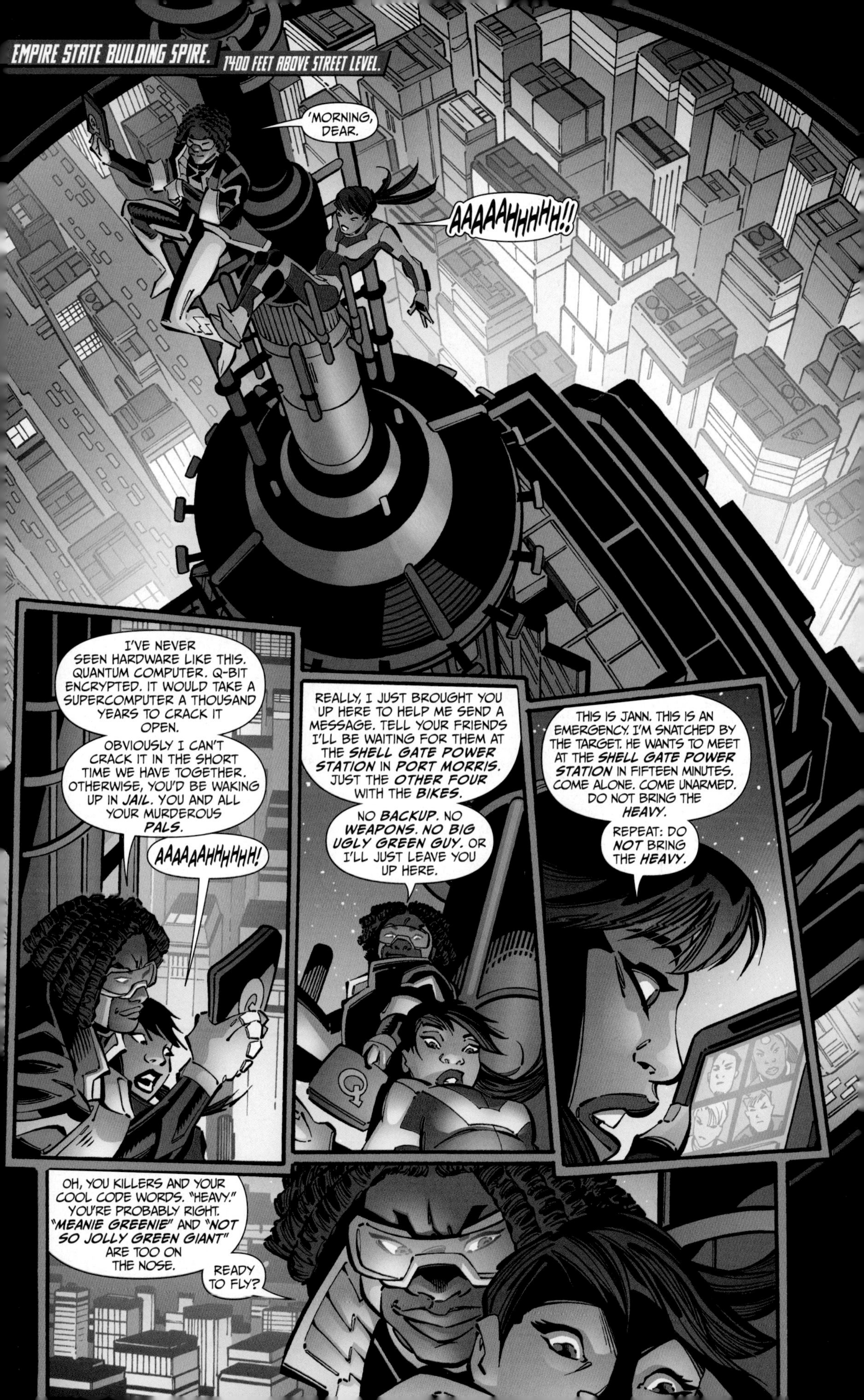
EMPIRE STATE BUILDING SPIRE.
1400 FEET ABOVE STREET LEVEL.
'MORNING, DEAR.
AAAAAHHHHH!!
I'VE NEVER SEEN HARDWARE LIKE THIS. QUANTUM COMPUTER. Q-BIT ENCRYPTED. IT WOULD TAKE A SUPERCOMPUTER A THOUSAND YEARS TO CRACK IT OPEN.
OBVIOUSLY I CAN'T CRACK IT IN THE SHORT TIME WE HAVE TOGETHER. OTHERWISE, YOU'D BE WAKING UP IN JAIL. YOU AND ALL YOUR MURDEROUS PALS.
AAAAAHHHHHH!
REALLY, I JUST BROUGHT YOU UP HERE TO HELP ME SEND A MESSAGE. TELL YOUR FRIENDS I'LL BE WAITING FOR THEM AT THE SHELL GATE POWER STATION IN PORT MORRIS. JUST THE OTHER FOUR WITH THE BIKES.
NO BACKUP. NO WEAPONS. NO BIG UGLY GREEN GUY. OR I'LL JUST LEAVE YOU UP HERE.
THIS IS JANN. THIS IS AN EMERGENCY. I'M SNATCHED BY THE TARGET. HE WANTS TO MEET AT THE SHELL GATE POWER STATION IN FIFTEEN MINUTES. COME ALONE. COME UNARMED. DO NOT BRING THE HEAVY.
REPEAT: DO NOT BRING THE HEAVY.
OH, YOU KILLERS AND YOUR COOL CODE WORDS. "HEAVY." YOU'RE PROBABLY RIGHT. "MEANIE GREENIE" AND "NOT SO JOLLY GREEN GIANT" ARE TOO ON THE NOSE.
READY TO FLY?

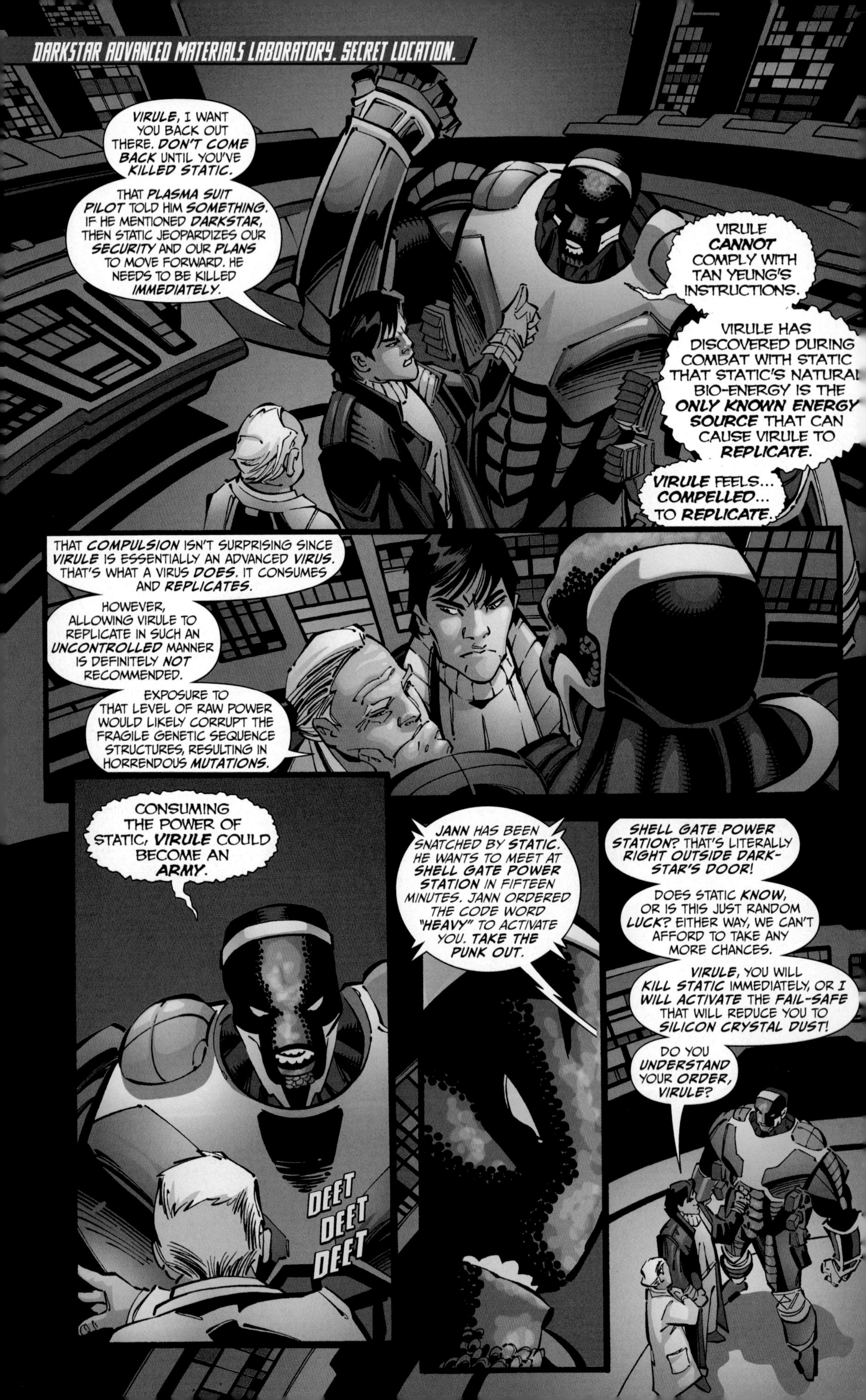
DARKSTAR ADVANCED MATERIALS LABORATORY. SECRET LOCATION.
VIRULE, I WANT YOU BACK OUT THERE. DON'T COME BACK UNTIL YOU'VE KILLED STATIC.
THAT PLASMA SUIT PILOT TOLD HIM SOMETHING. IF HE MENTIONED DARKSTAR, THEN STATIC JEOPARDIZES OUR SECURITY AND OUR PLANS TO MOVE FORWARD. HE NEEDS TO BE KILLED IMMEDIATELY.
VIRULE CANNOT COMPLY WITH TAN YEUNG'S INSTRUCTIONS.
VIRULE HAS DISCOVERED DURING COMBAT WITH STATIC THAT STATIC'S NATURAL BIO-ENERGY IS THE ONLY KNOWN ENERGY SOURCE THAT CAN CAUSE VIRULE TO REPLICATE.
VIRULE FEELS... COMPELLED... TO REPLICATE.
THAT COMPULSION ISN'T SURPRISING SINCE VIRULE IS ESSENTIALLY AN ADVANCED VIRUS. THAT'S WHAT A VIRUS DOES. IT CONSUMES AND REPLICATES.
HOWEVER, ALLOWING VIRULE TO REPLICATE IN SUCH AN UNCONTROLLED MANNER IS DEFINITELY NOT RECOMMENDED.
EXPOSURE TO THAT LEVEL OF RAW POWER WOULD LIKELY CORRUPT THE FRAGILE GENETIC SEQUENCE STRUCTURES, RESULTING IN HORRENDOUS MUTATIONS.
CONSUMING THE POWER OF STATIC, VIRULE COULD BECOME AN ARMY.
DEET DEET DEET
JANN HAS BEEN SNATCHED BY STATIC. HE WANTS TO MEET AT SHELL GATE POWER STATION IN FIFTEEN MINUTES. JANN ORDERED THE CODE WORD "HEAVY" TO ACTIVATE YOU. TAKE THE PUNK OUT.
SHELL GATE POWER STATION? THAT'S LITERALLY RIGHT OUTSIDE DARK-STAR'S DOOR!
DOES STATIC KNOW, OR IS THIS JUST RANDOM LUCK? EITHER WAY, WE CAN'T AFFORD TO TAKE ANY MORE CHANCES.
VIRULE, YOU WILL KILL STATIC IMMEDIATELY, OR I WILL ACTIVATE THE FAIL-SAFE THAT WILL REDUCE YOU TO SILICON CRYSTAL DUST!
DO YOU UNDERSTAND YOUR ORDER, VIRULE?

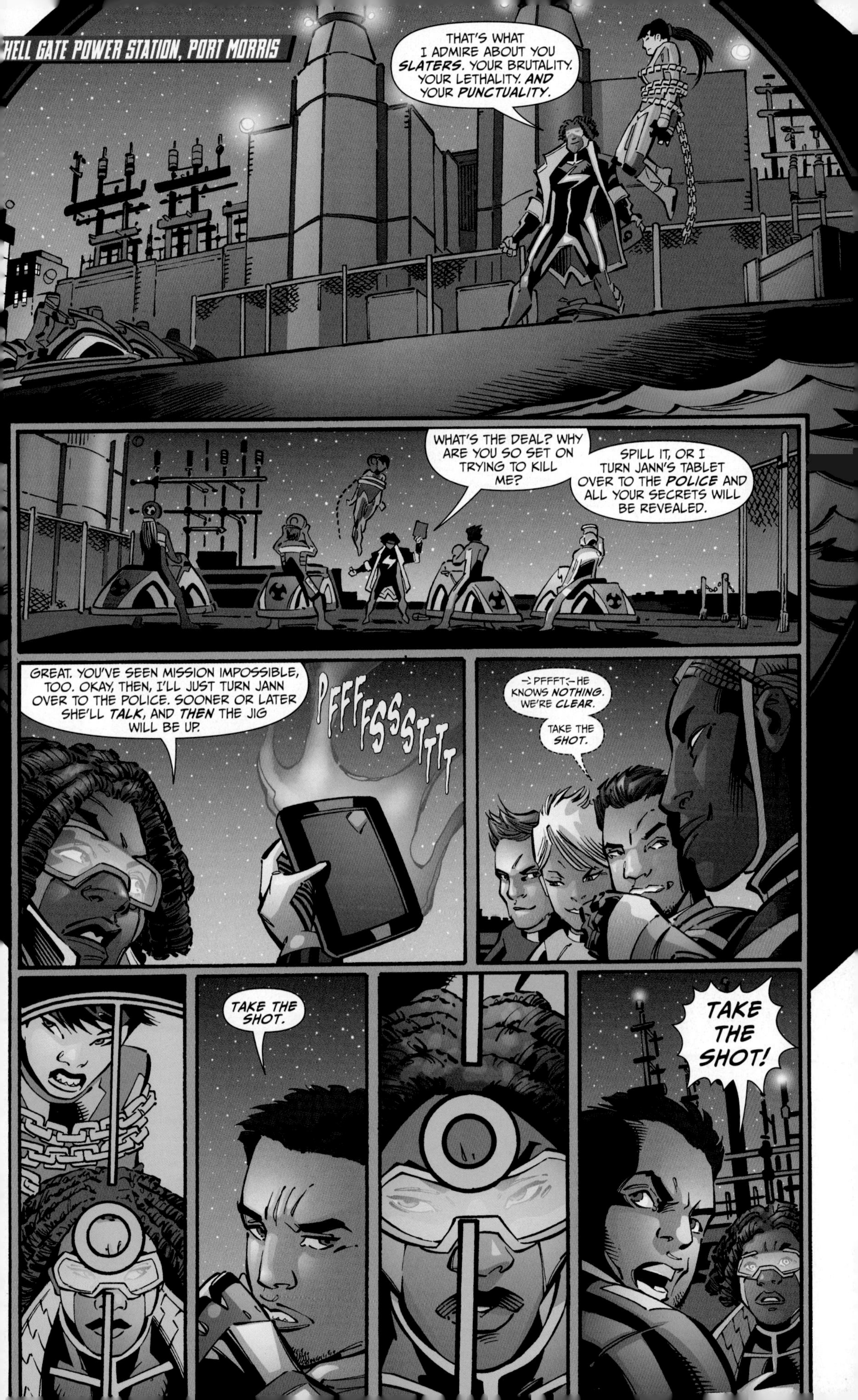
HELL GATE POWER STATION, PORT MORRIS
THAT'S WHAT I ADMIRE ABOUT YOU SLATERS. YOUR BRUTALITY. YOUR LETHALITY. AND YOUR PUNCTUALITY.
WHAT'S THE DEAL? WHY ARE YOU SO SET ON TRYING TO KILL ME?
SPILL IT, OR I TURN JANN'S TABLET OVER TO THE POLICE AND ALL YOUR SECRETS WILL BE REVEALED.
GREAT. YOU'VE SEEN MISSION IMPOSSIBLE, TOO. OKAY, THEN, I'LL JUST TURN JANN OVER TO THE POLICE. SOONER OR LATER SHE'LL TALK, AND THEN THE JIG WILL BE UP.
PFFFSSSTTTT
PFFFT HE KNOWS NOTHING. WE'RE CLEAR.
TAKE THE SHOT.
TAKE THE SHOT.
TAKE THE SHOT!

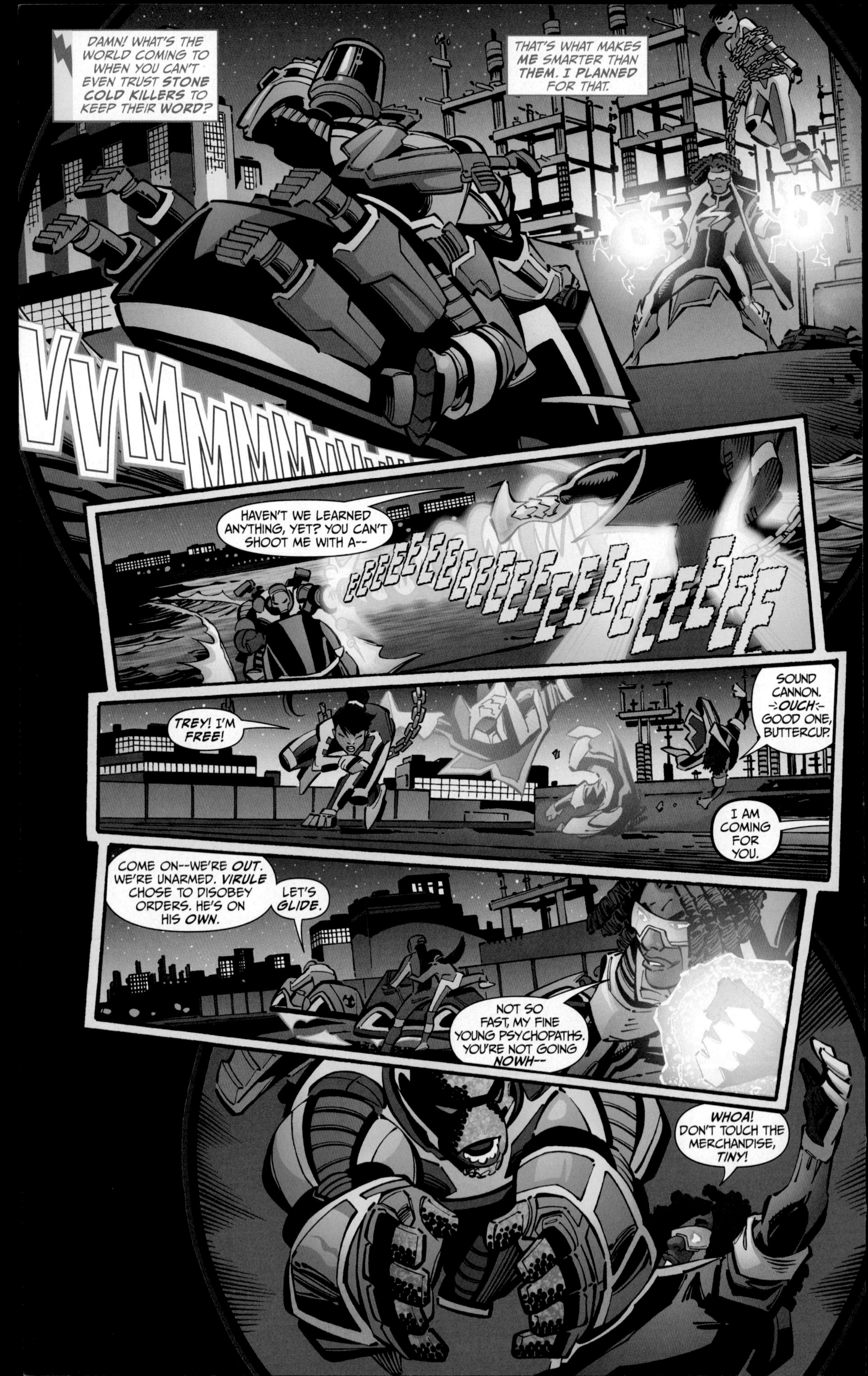
DAMN! WHAT'S THE WORLD COMING TO WHEN YOU CAN'T EVEN TRUST STONE COLD KILLERS TO KEEP THEIR WORD?
THAT'S WHAT MAKES ME SMARTER THAN THEM. I PLANNED FOR THAT.
VVMMMMMM
HAVEN'T WE LEARNED ANYTHING, YET? YOU CAN'T SHOOT ME WITH A--
EEEEEEEEEEEEEEEEEEEEEEEEE
TREY! I'M FREE!
SOUND CANNON. -OUCH- GOOD ONE, BUTTERCUP.
I AM COMING FOR YOU.
COME ON--WE'RE OUT. WE'RE UNARMED. VIRULE CHOSE TO DISOBEY ORDERS. HE'S ON HIS OWN.
LET'S GLIDE.
NOT SO FAST, MY FINE YOUNG PSYCHOPATHS. YOU'RE NOT GOING NOWH--
WHOA! DON'T TOUCH THE MERCHANDISE, TINY!

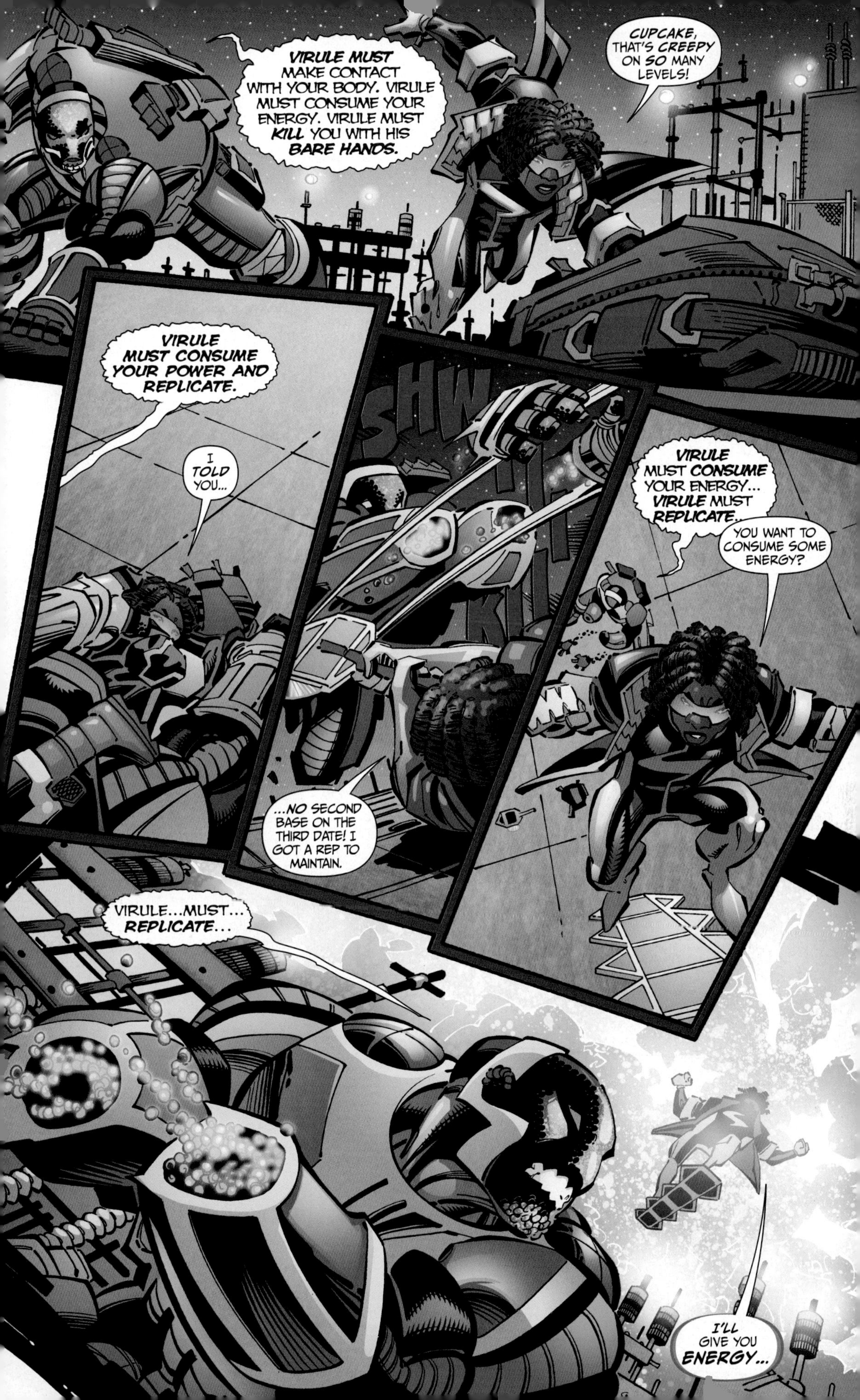
VIRULE MUST MAKE CONTACT WITH YOUR BODY. VIRULE MUST CONSUME YOUR ENERGY. VIRULE MUST KILL YOU WITH HIS BARE HANDS.
CUPCAKE, THAT'S CREEPY ON SO MANY LEVELS!
VIRULE MUST CONSUME YOUR POWER AND REPLICATE.
I TOLD YOU...
SHW
...NO SECOND BASE ON THE THIRD DATE! I GOT A REP TO MAINTAIN.
VIRULE MUST CONSUME YOUR ENERGY... VIRULE MUST REPLICATE...
YOU WANT TO CONSUME SOME ENERGY?
VIRULE...MUST... REPLICATE...
I'LL GIVE YOU ENERGY...

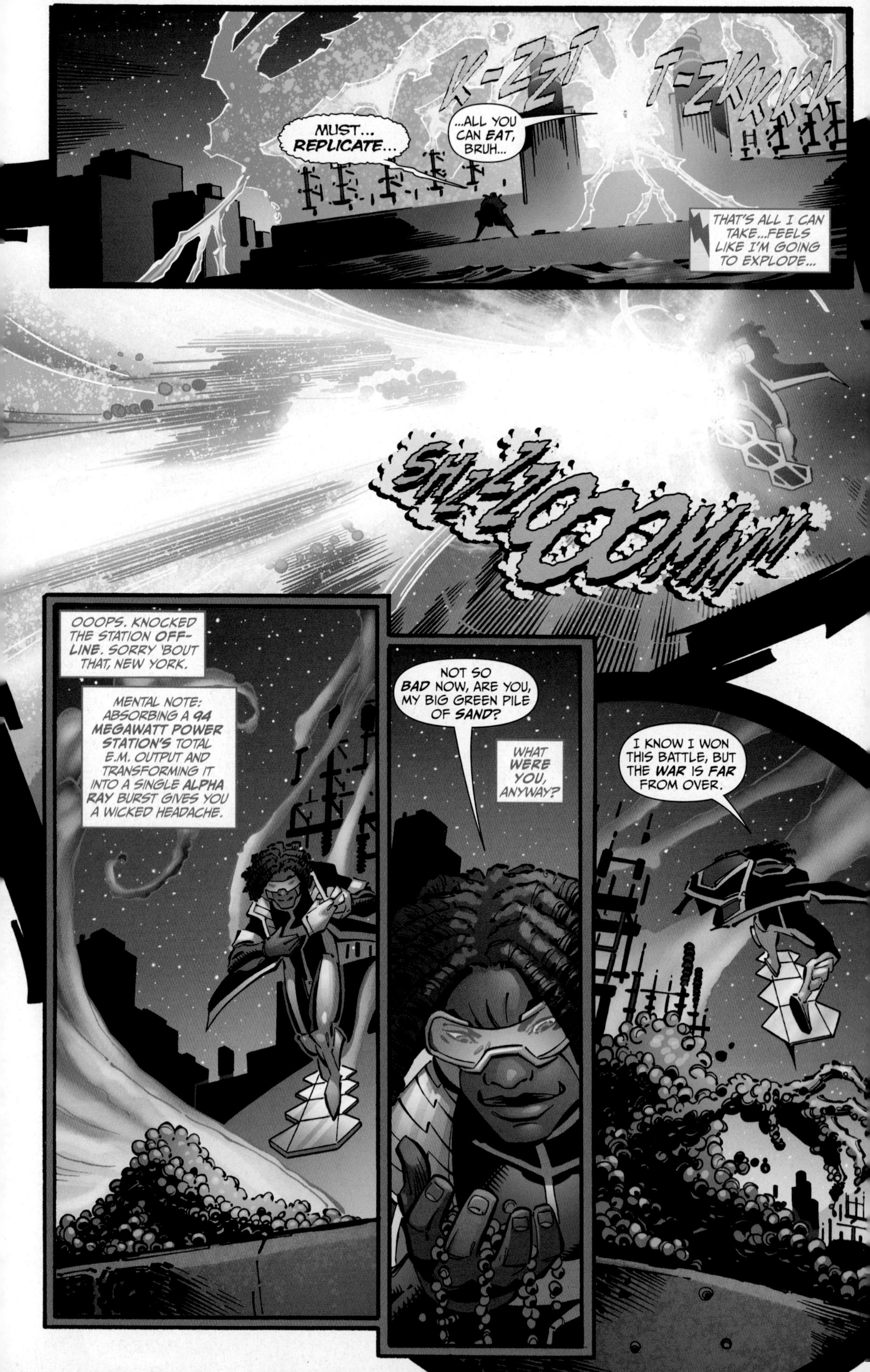

K-ZZT
T-ZKKKK
MUST... REPLICATE...
...ALL YOU CAN EAT, BRUH...
THAT'S ALL I CAN TAKE...FEELS LIKE I'M GOING TO EXPLODE...
SHZZOOOMM
OOOPS. KNOCKED THE STATION OFF-LINE. SORRY 'BOUT THAT, NEW YORK.
MENTAL NOTE: ABSORBING A 94 MEGAWATT POWER STATION'S TOTAL E.M. OUTPUT AND TRANSFORMING IT INTO A SINGLE ALPHA RAY BURST GIVES YOU A WICKED HEADACHE.
NOT SO BAD NOW, ARE YOU, MY BIG GREEN PILE OF SAND?
WHAT WERE YOU, ANYWAY?
I KNOW I WON THIS BATTLE, BUT THE WAR IS FAR FROM OVER.

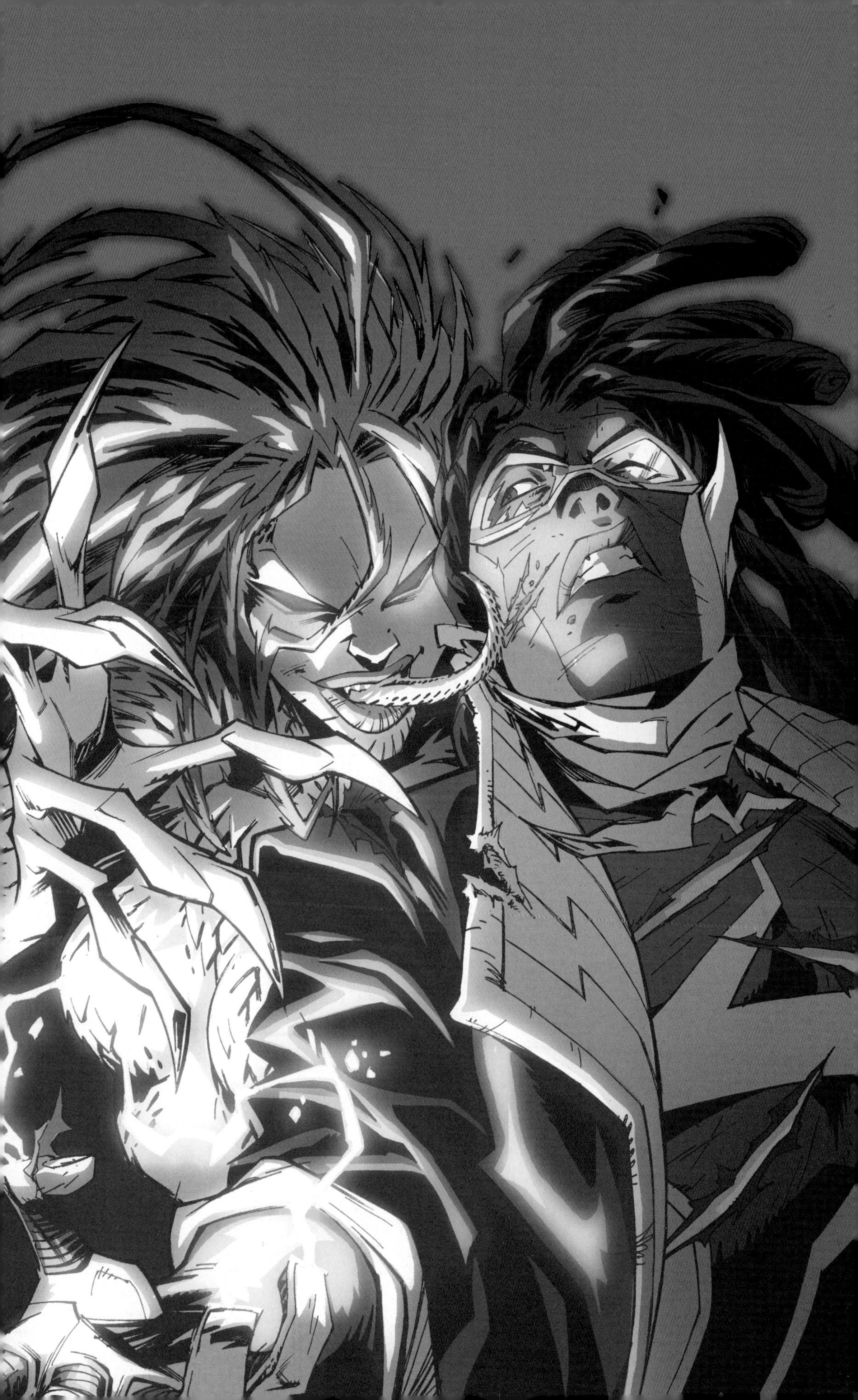

cover art by
KHARY RANDOLPH, EMILIO LOPEZ
& LE BEAU UNDERWOOD

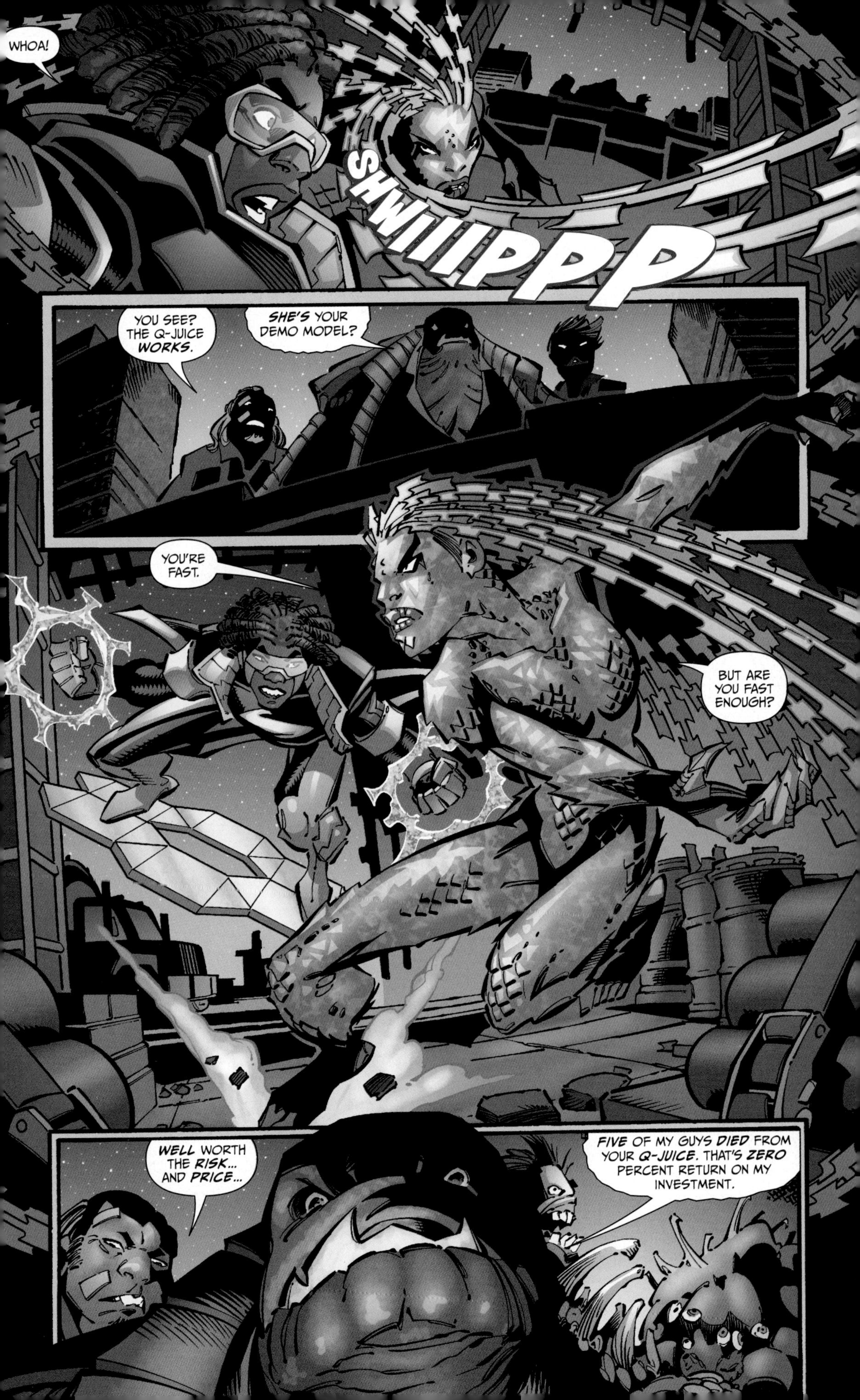
WHOA!
SHWIIIPPPP
YOU SEE? THE Q-JUICE *WORKS.*
*SHE'S* YOUR DEMO MODEL?
YOU'RE FAST.
BUT ARE YOU FAST ENOUGH?
*WELL* WORTH THE *RISK*... AND *PRICE*...
*FIVE* OF MY GUYS *DIED* FROM YOUR *Q-JUICE*. THAT'S *ZERO* PERCENT RETURN ON MY INVESTMENT.

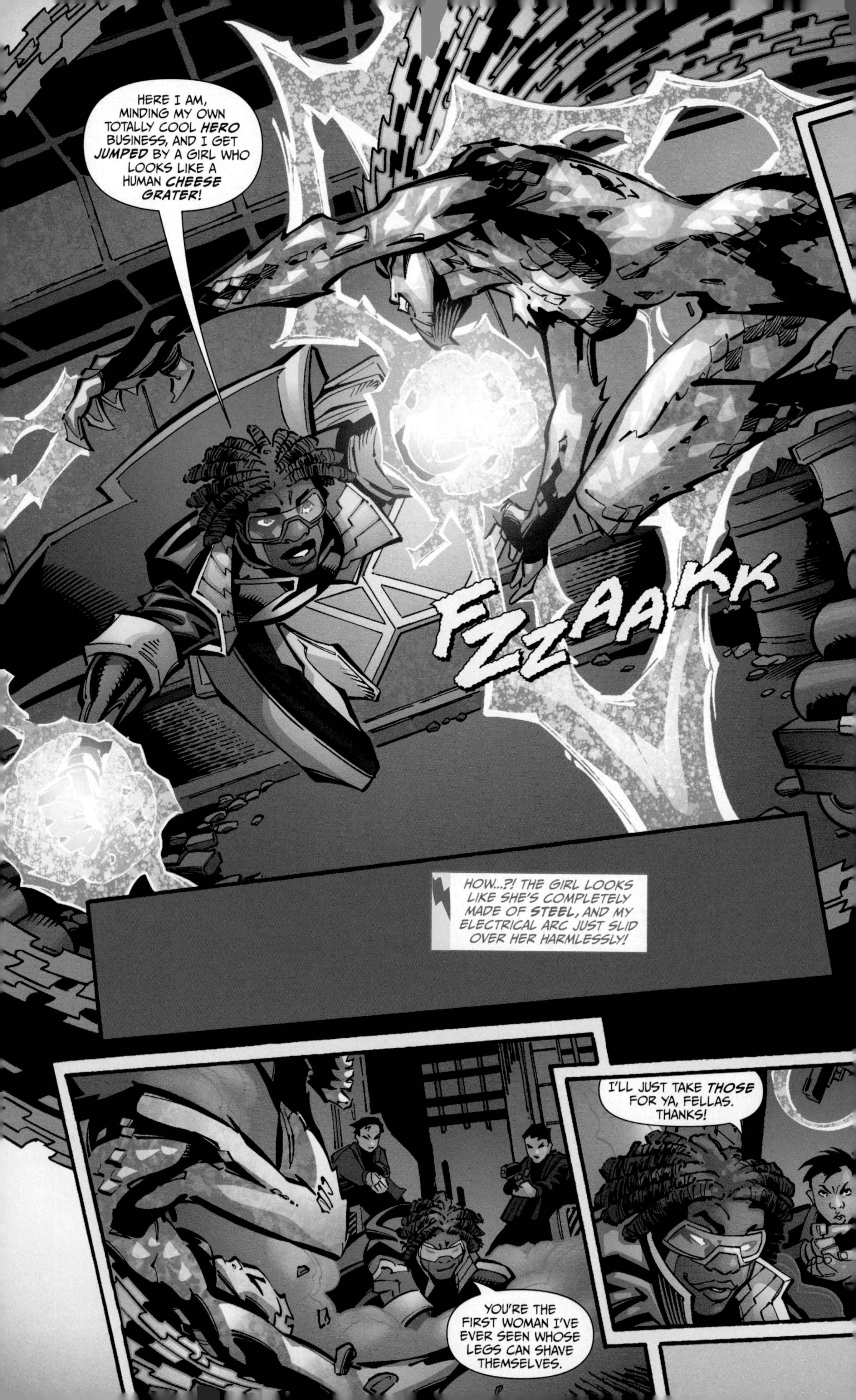
HERE I AM, MINDING MY OWN TOTALLY COOL HERO BUSINESS, AND I GET JUMPED BY A GIRL WHO LOOKS LIKE A HUMAN CHEESE GRATER!
FZZAAKK
HOW...?! THE GIRL LOOKS LIKE SHE'S COMPLETELY MADE OF STEEL, AND MY ELECTRICAL ARC JUST SLID OVER HER HARMLESSLY!
YOU'RE THE FIRST WOMAN I'VE EVER SEEN WHOSE LEGS CAN SHAVE THEMSELVES.
I'LL JUST TAKE THOSE FOR YA, FELLAS. THANKS!

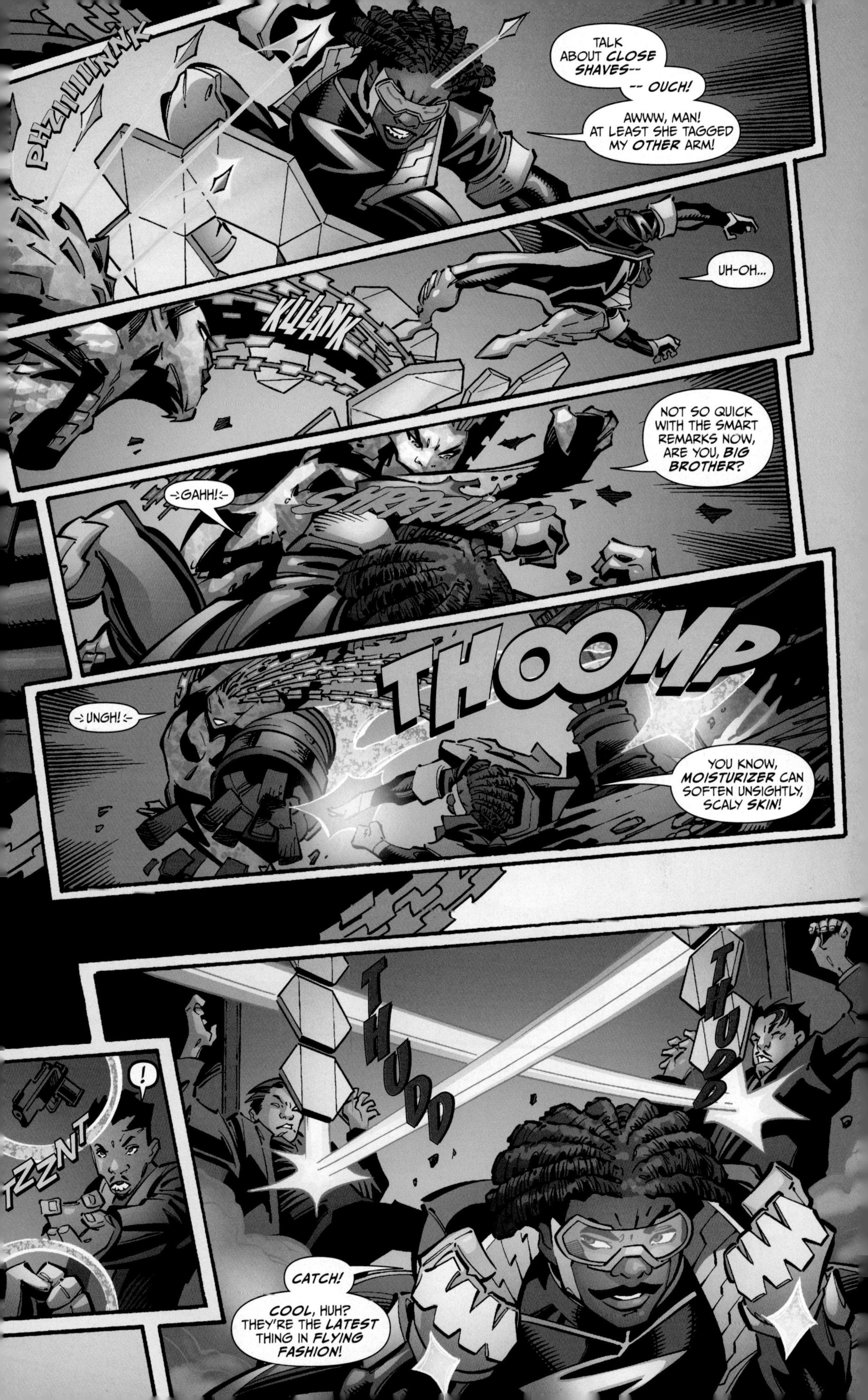

PHZIIIIINNK
TALK ABOUT CLOSE SHAVES--
-- OUCH!
AWWW, MAN! AT LEAST SHE TAGGED MY OTHER ARM!
UH-OH...
KLLANK
NOT SO QUICK WITH THE SMART REMARKS NOW, ARE YOU, BIG BROTHER?
-GAHH!-
THOOMP
-UNGH!-
YOU KNOW, MOISTURIZER CAN SOFTEN UNSIGHTLY, SCALY SKIN!
THUDD
THUDD
!
TZZNT
CATCH!
COOL, HUH? THEY'RE THE LATEST THING IN FLYING FASHION!

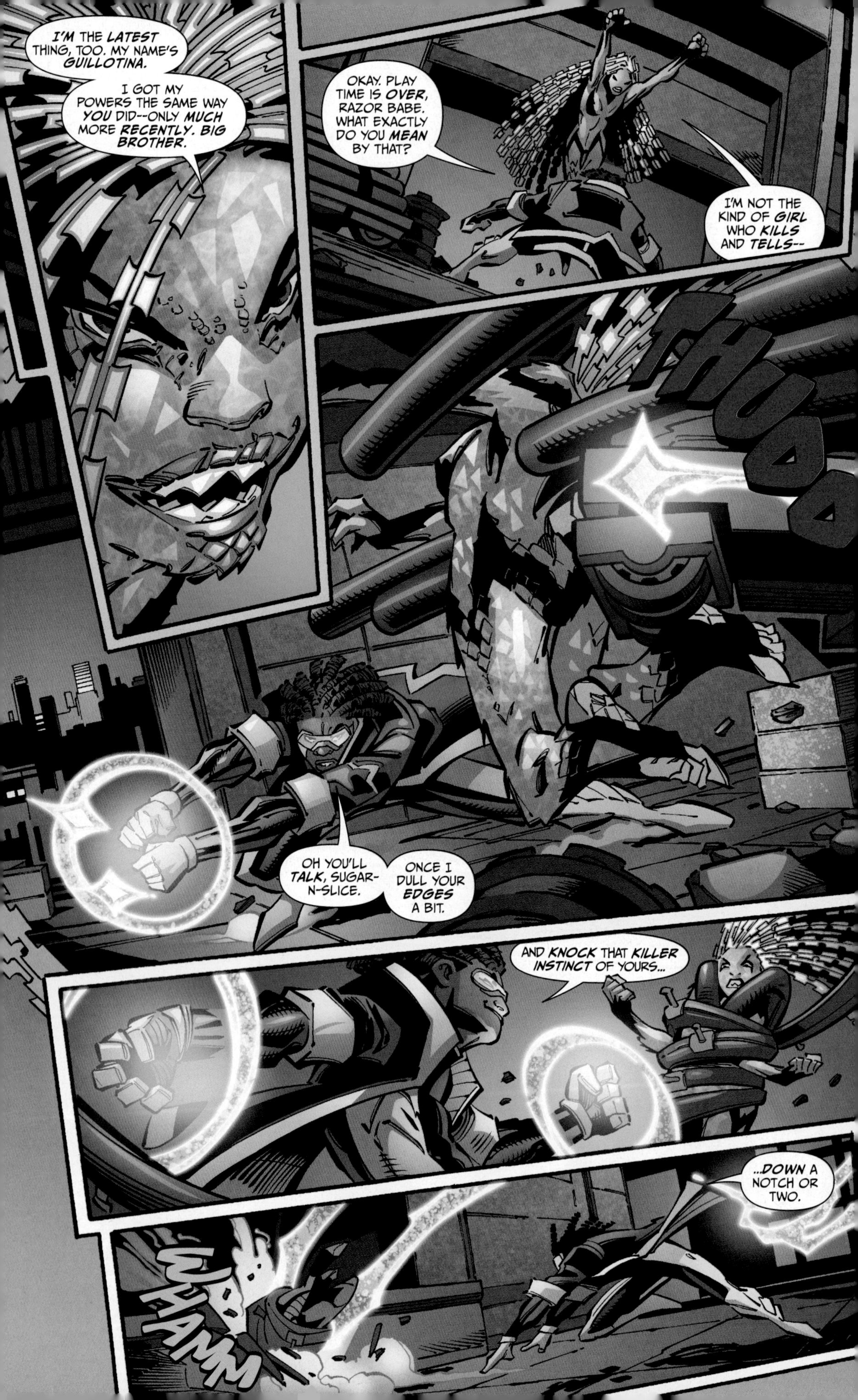
I'M THE LATEST THING, TOO. MY NAME'S GUILLOTINA.
I GOT MY POWERS THE SAME WAY YOU DID--ONLY MUCH MORE RECENTLY. BIG BROTHER.
OKAY. PLAY TIME IS OVER, RAZOR BABE. WHAT EXACTLY DO YOU MEAN BY THAT?
I'M NOT THE KIND OF GIRL WHO KILLS AND TELLS--
THUDD
OH YOU'LL TALK, SUGAR-N-SLICE.
ONCE I DULL YOUR EDGES A BIT.
AND KNOCK THAT KILLER INSTINCT OF YOURS...
...DOWN A NOTCH OR TWO.
WHAMM

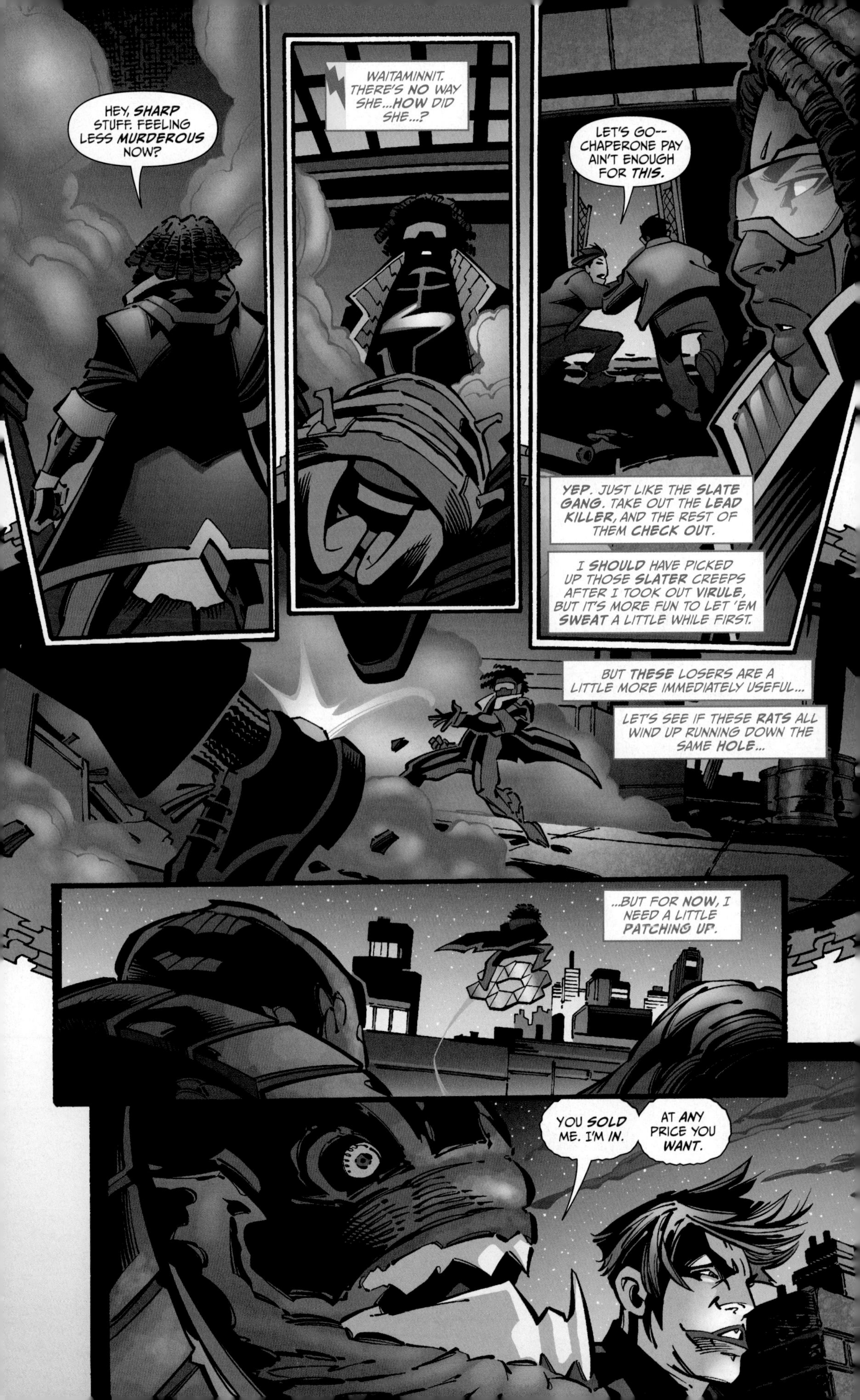
HEY, SHARP STUFF. FEELING LESS MURDEROUS NOW?
WAITAMINNIT. THERE'S NO WAY SHE...HOW DID SHE...?
LET'S GO-- CHAPERONE PAY AIN'T ENOUGH FOR THIS.
YEP. JUST LIKE THE SLATE GANG. TAKE OUT THE LEAD KILLER, AND THE REST OF THEM CHECK OUT.
I SHOULD HAVE PICKED UP THOSE SLATER CREEPS AFTER I TOOK OUT VIRULE, BUT IT'S MORE FUN TO LET 'EM SWEAT A LITTLE WHILE FIRST.
BUT THESE LOSERS ARE A LITTLE MORE IMMEDIATELY USEFUL...
LET'S SEE IF THESE RATS ALL WIND UP RUNNING DOWN THE SAME HOLE...
...BUT FOR NOW, I NEED A LITTLE PATCHING UP.
YOU SOLD ME. I'M IN.
AT ANY PRICE YOU WANT.

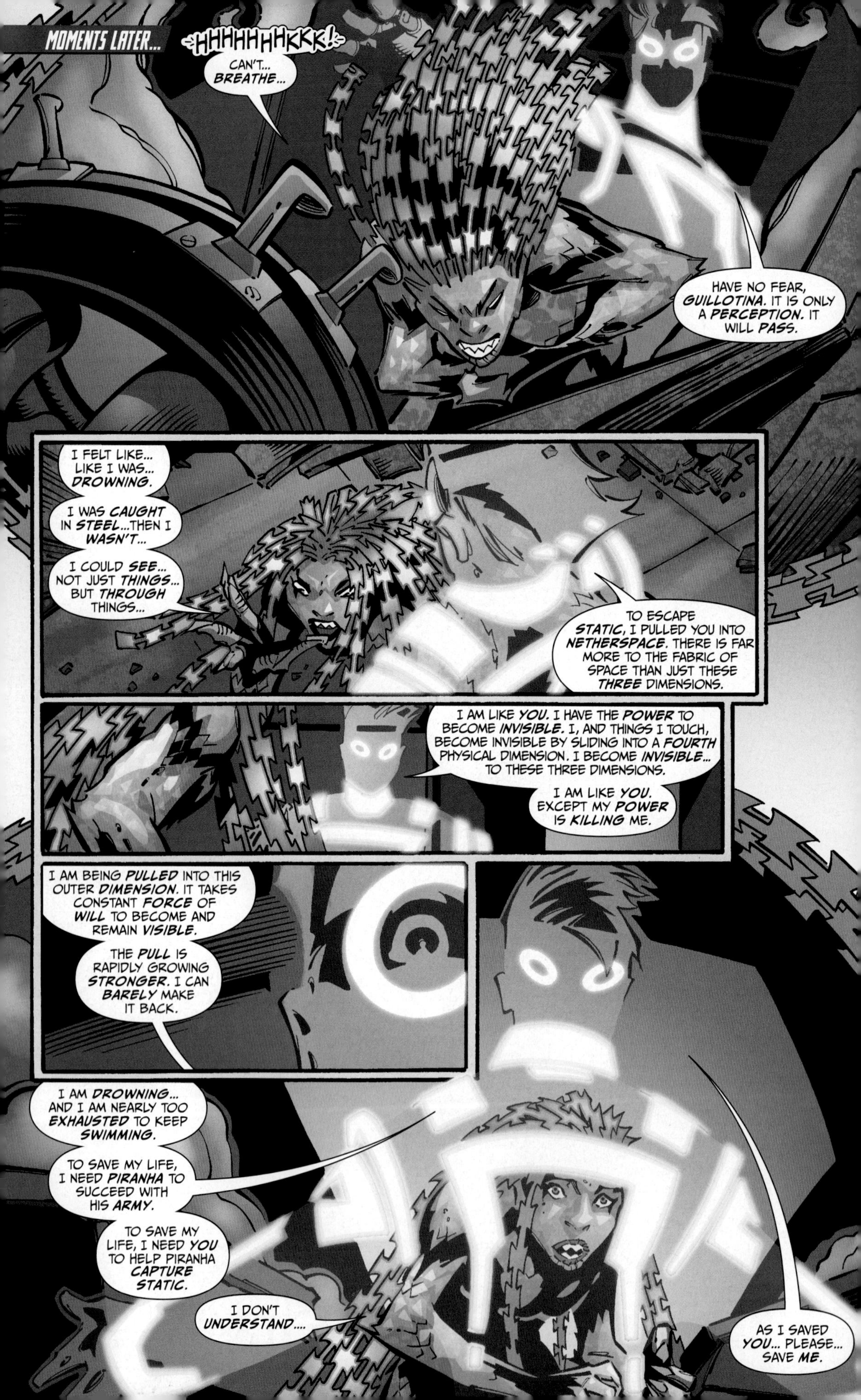
MOMENTS LATER...
HHHHHHHKKK!
CAN'T... BREATHE...
HAVE NO FEAR, GUILLOTINA. IT IS ONLY A PERCEPTION. IT WILL PASS.
I FELT LIKE... LIKE I WAS... DROWNING.
I WAS CAUGHT IN STEEL...THEN I WASN'T...
I COULD SEE... NOT JUST THINGS... BUT THROUGH THINGS...
TO ESCAPE STATIC, I PULLED YOU INTO NETHERSPACE. THERE IS FAR MORE TO THE FABRIC OF SPACE THAN JUST THESE THREE DIMENSIONS.
I AM LIKE YOU. I HAVE THE POWER TO BECOME INVISIBLE. I, AND THINGS I TOUCH, BECOME INVISIBLE BY SLIDING INTO A FOURTH PHYSICAL DIMENSION. I BECOME INVISIBLE... TO THESE THREE DIMENSIONS.
I AM LIKE YOU. EXCEPT MY POWER IS KILLING ME.
I AM BEING PULLED INTO THIS OUTER DIMENSION. IT TAKES CONSTANT FORCE OF WILL TO BECOME AND REMAIN VISIBLE.
THE PULL IS RAPIDLY GROWING STRONGER. I CAN BARELY MAKE IT BACK.
I AM DROWNING... AND I AM NEARLY TOO EXHAUSTED TO KEEP SWIMMING.
TO SAVE MY LIFE, I NEED PIRANHA TO SUCCEED WITH HIS ARMY.
TO SAVE MY LIFE, I NEED YOU TO HELP PIRANHA CAPTURE STATIC.
I DON'T UNDERSTAND....
AS I SAVED YOU... PLEASE... SAVE ME.

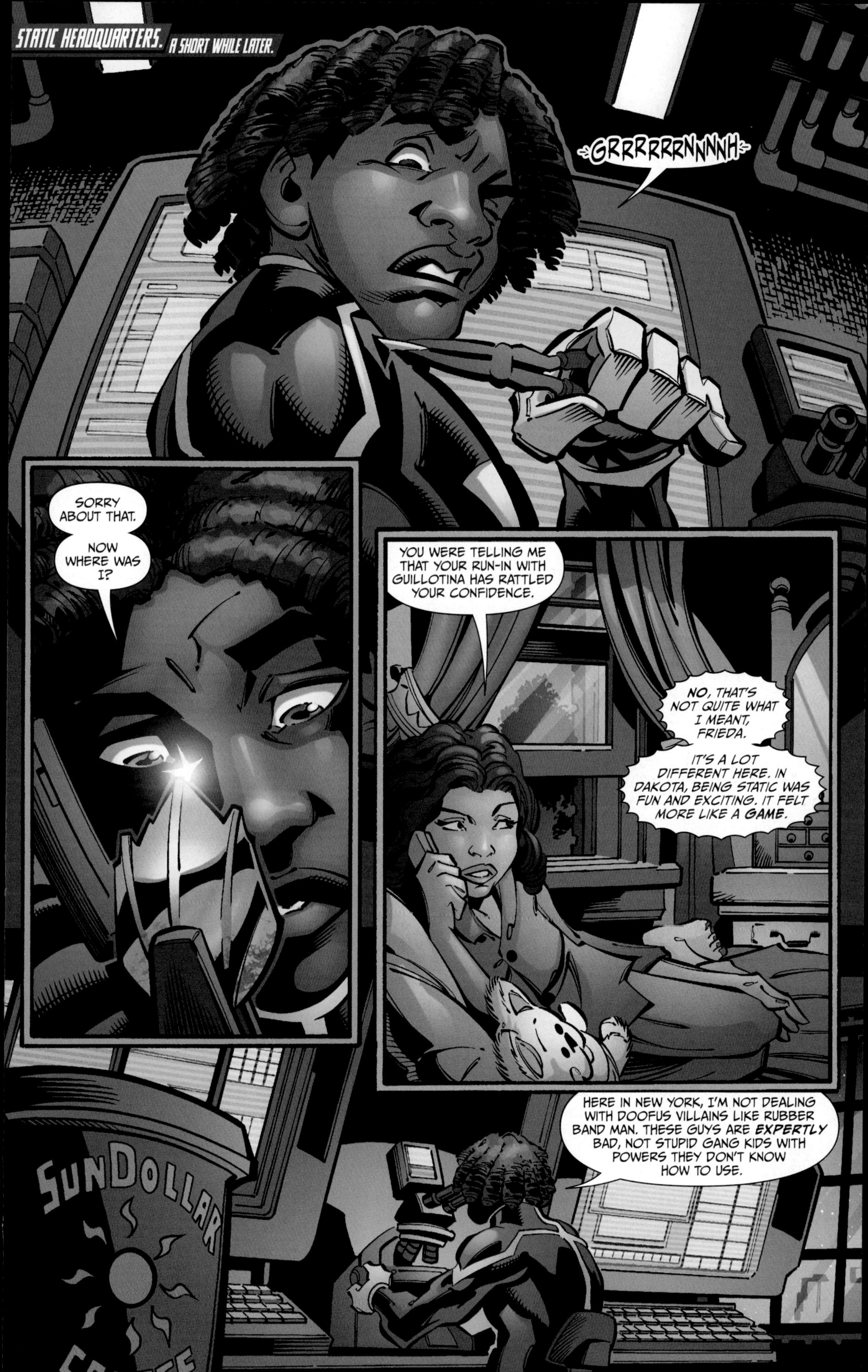
STATIC HEADQUARTERS. A SHORT WHILE LATER.
GRRRRRRNNNNH
SORRY ABOUT THAT.
NOW WHERE WAS I?
YOU WERE TELLING ME THAT YOUR RUN-IN WITH GUILLOTINA HAS RATTLED YOUR CONFIDENCE.
NO, THAT'S NOT QUITE WHAT I MEANT, FRIEDA.
IT'S A LOT DIFFERENT HERE. IN DAKOTA, BEING STATIC WAS FUN AND EXCITING. IT FELT MORE LIKE A GAME.
HERE IN NEW YORK, I'M NOT DEALING WITH DOOFUS VILLAINS LIKE RUBBER BAND MAN. THESE GUYS ARE EXPERTLY BAD, NOT STUPID GANG KIDS WITH POWERS THEY DON'T KNOW HOW TO USE.
SUNDOLLAR

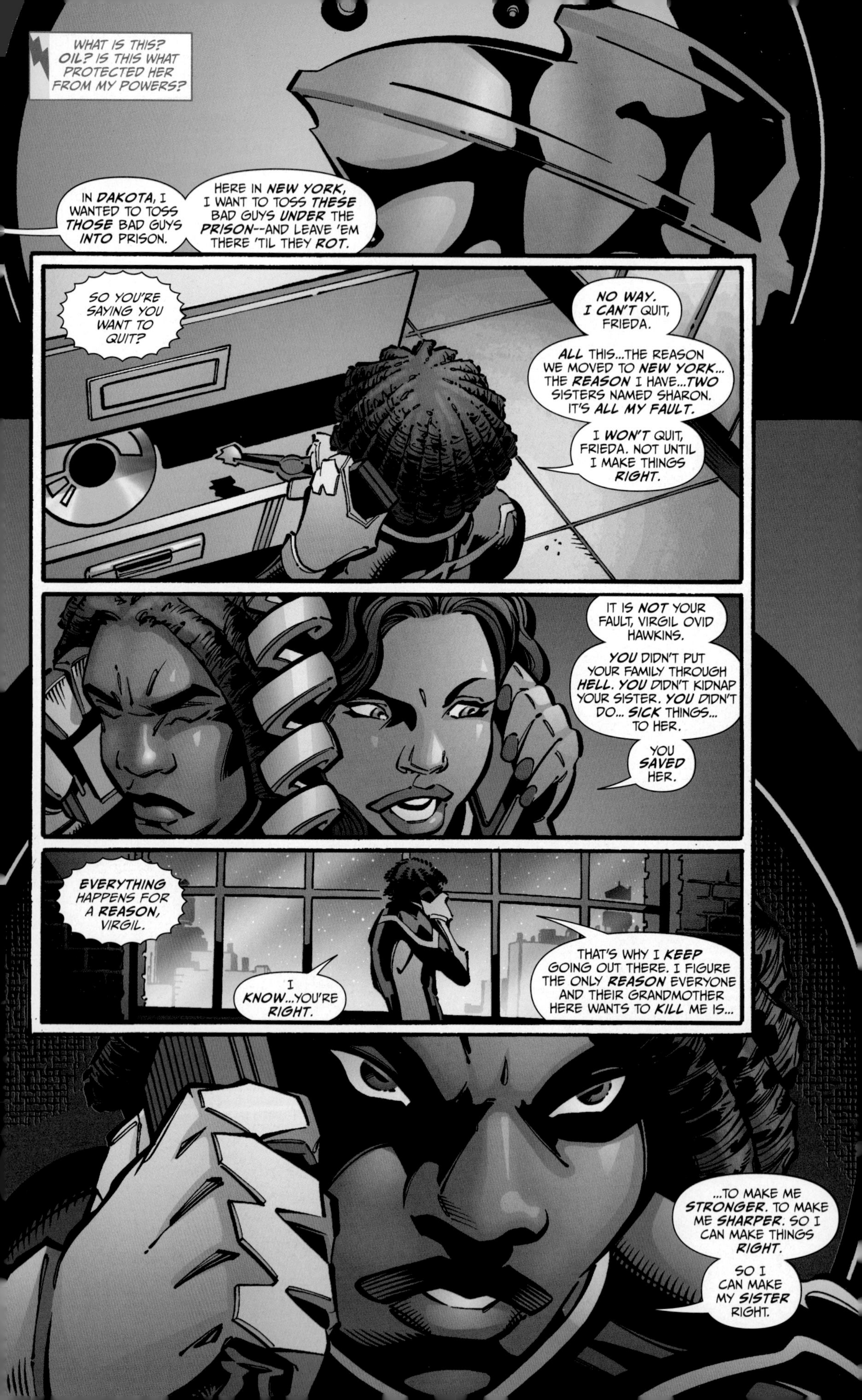
WHAT IS THIS? OIL? IS THIS WHAT PROTECTED HER FROM MY POWERS?
IN DAKOTA, I WANTED TO TOSS THOSE BAD GUYS INTO PRISON.
HERE IN NEW YORK, I WANT TO TOSS THESE BAD GUYS UNDER THE PRISON--AND LEAVE 'EM THERE 'TIL THEY ROT.
SO YOU'RE SAYING YOU WANT TO QUIT?
NO WAY. I CAN'T QUIT, FRIEDA.
ALL THIS...THE REASON WE MOVED TO NEW YORK... THE REASON I HAVE...TWO SISTERS NAMED SHARON. IT'S ALL MY FAULT.
I WON'T QUIT, FRIEDA. NOT UNTIL I MAKE THINGS RIGHT.
IT IS NOT YOUR FAULT, VIRGIL OVID HAWKINS.
YOU DIDN'T PUT YOUR FAMILY THROUGH HELL. YOU DIDN'T KIDNAP YOUR SISTER. YOU DIDN'T DO... SICK THINGS... TO HER.
YOU SAVED HER.
EVERYTHING HAPPENS FOR A REASON, VIRGIL.
I KNOW...YOU'RE RIGHT.
THAT'S WHY I KEEP GOING OUT THERE. I FIGURE THE ONLY REASON EVERYONE AND THEIR GRANDMOTHER HERE WANTS TO KILL ME IS...
...TO MAKE ME STRONGER. TO MAKE ME SHARPER. SO I CAN MAKE THINGS RIGHT.
SO I CAN MAKE MY SISTER RIGHT.

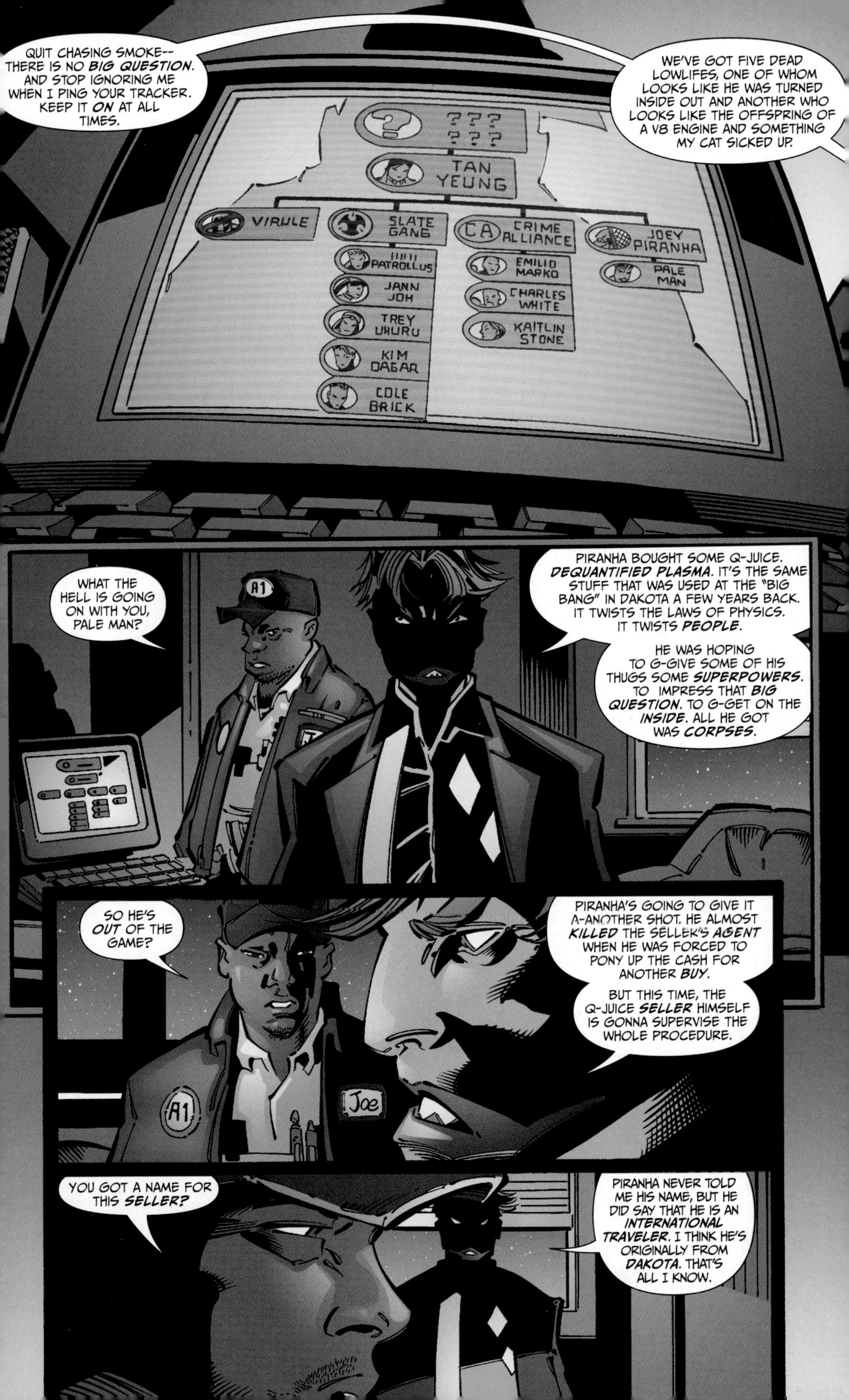
QUIT CHASING SMOKE-- THERE IS NO BIG QUESTION. AND STOP IGNORING ME WHEN I PING YOUR TRACKER. KEEP IT ON AT ALL TIMES.
WE'VE GOT FIVE DEAD LOWLIFES, ONE OF WHOM LOOKS LIKE HE WAS TURNED INSIDE OUT AND ANOTHER WHO LOOKS LIKE THE OFFSPRING OF A V8 ENGINE AND SOMETHING MY CAT SICKED UP.
??? ???
TAN YEUNG
VIRULE
SLATE GANG
CA CRIME ALLIANCE
JOEY PIRANHA
PATROLLUS
JANN JOH
TREY UHURU
KIM DABAR
COLE BRICK
EMILIO MARKO
CHARLES WHITE
KAITLIN STONE
PALE MAN
WHAT THE HELL IS GOING ON WITH YOU, PALE MAN?
PIRANHA BOUGHT SOME Q-JUICE. DEQUANTIFIED PLASMA. IT'S THE SAME STUFF THAT WAS USED AT THE "BIG BANG" IN DAKOTA A FEW YEARS BACK. IT TWISTS THE LAWS OF PHYSICS. IT TWISTS PEOPLE.
HE WAS HOPING TO G-GIVE SOME OF HIS THUGS SOME SUPERPOWERS. TO IMPRESS THAT BIG QUESTION. TO G-GET ON THE INSIDE. ALL HE GOT WAS CORPSES.
SO HE'S OUT OF THE GAME?
PIRANHA'S GOING TO GIVE IT A-ANOTHER SHOT. HE ALMOST KILLED THE SELLER'S AGENT WHEN HE WAS FORCED TO PONY UP THE CASH FOR ANOTHER BUY.
BUT THIS TIME, THE Q-JUICE SELLER HIMSELF IS GONNA SUPERVISE THE WHOLE PROCEDURE.
A1
Joe
YOU GOT A NAME FOR THIS SELLER?
PIRANHA NEVER TOLD ME HIS NAME, BUT HE DID SAY THAT HE IS AN INTERNATIONAL TRAVELER. I THINK HE'S ORIGINALLY FROM DAKOTA. THAT'S ALL I KNOW.

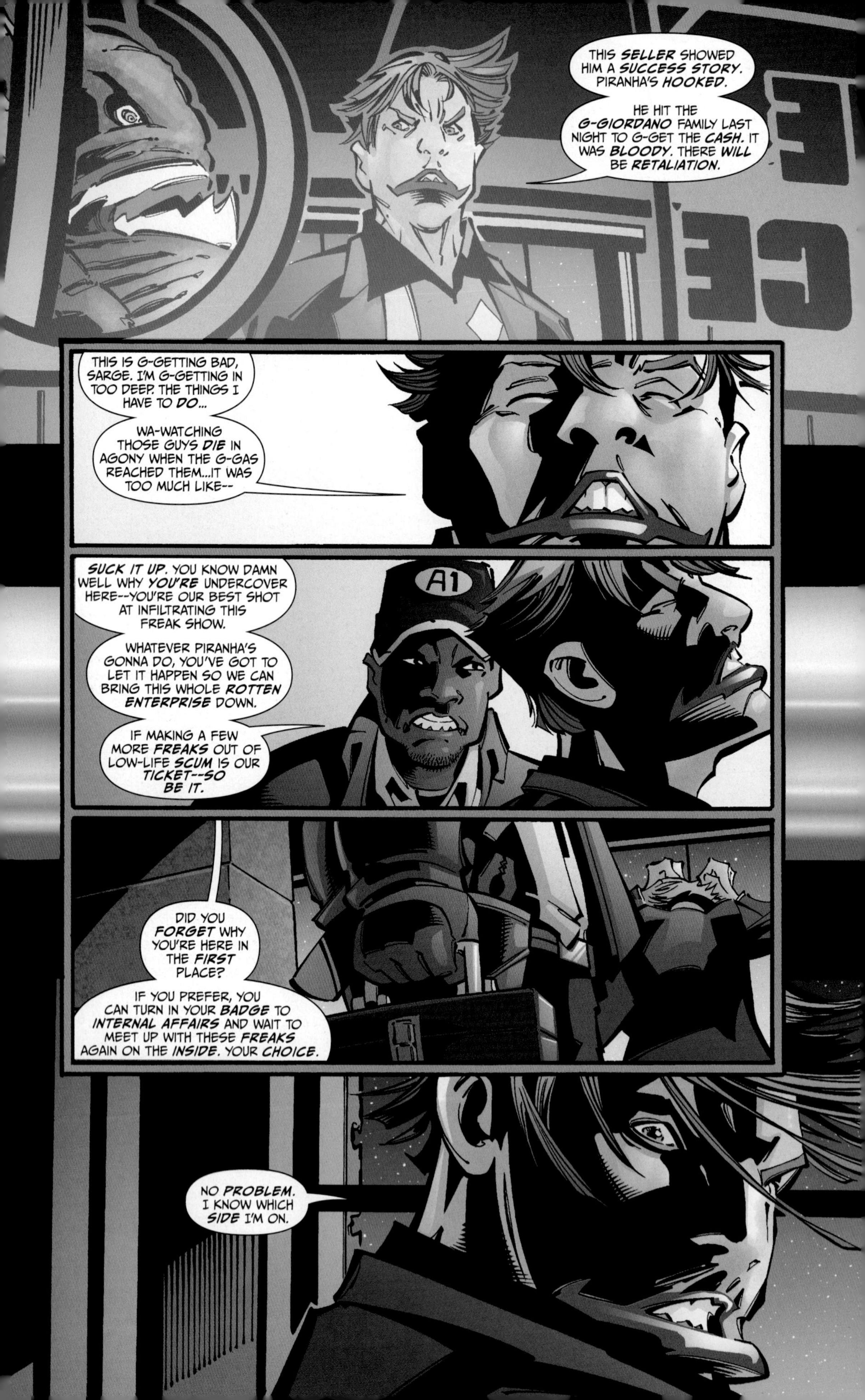

THIS SELLER SHOWED HIM A SUCCESS STORY. PIRANHA'S HOOKED.
HE HIT THE G-GIORDANO FAMILY LAST NIGHT TO G-GET THE CASH. IT WAS BLOODY. THERE WILL BE RETALIATION.
THIS IS G-GETTING BAD, SARGE. I'M G-GETTING IN TOO DEEP. THE THINGS I HAVE TO DO...
WA-WATCHING THOSE GUYS DIE IN AGONY WHEN THE G-GAS REACHED THEM...IT WAS TOO MUCH LIKE--
SUCK IT UP. YOU KNOW DAMN WELL WHY YOU'RE UNDERCOVER HERE--YOU'RE OUR BEST SHOT AT INFILTRATING THIS FREAK SHOW.
WHATEVER PIRANHA'S GONNA DO, YOU'VE GOT TO LET IT HAPPEN SO WE CAN BRING THIS WHOLE ROTTEN ENTERPRISE DOWN.
IF MAKING A FEW MORE FREAKS OUT OF LOW-LIFE SCUM IS OUR TICKET--SO BE IT.
A1
DID YOU FORGET WHY YOU'RE HERE IN THE FIRST PLACE?
IF YOU PREFER, YOU CAN TURN IN YOUR BADGE TO INTERNAL AFFAIRS AND WAIT TO MEET UP WITH THESE FREAKS AGAIN ON THE INSIDE. YOUR CHOICE.
NO PROBLEM. I KNOW WHICH SIDE I'M ON.

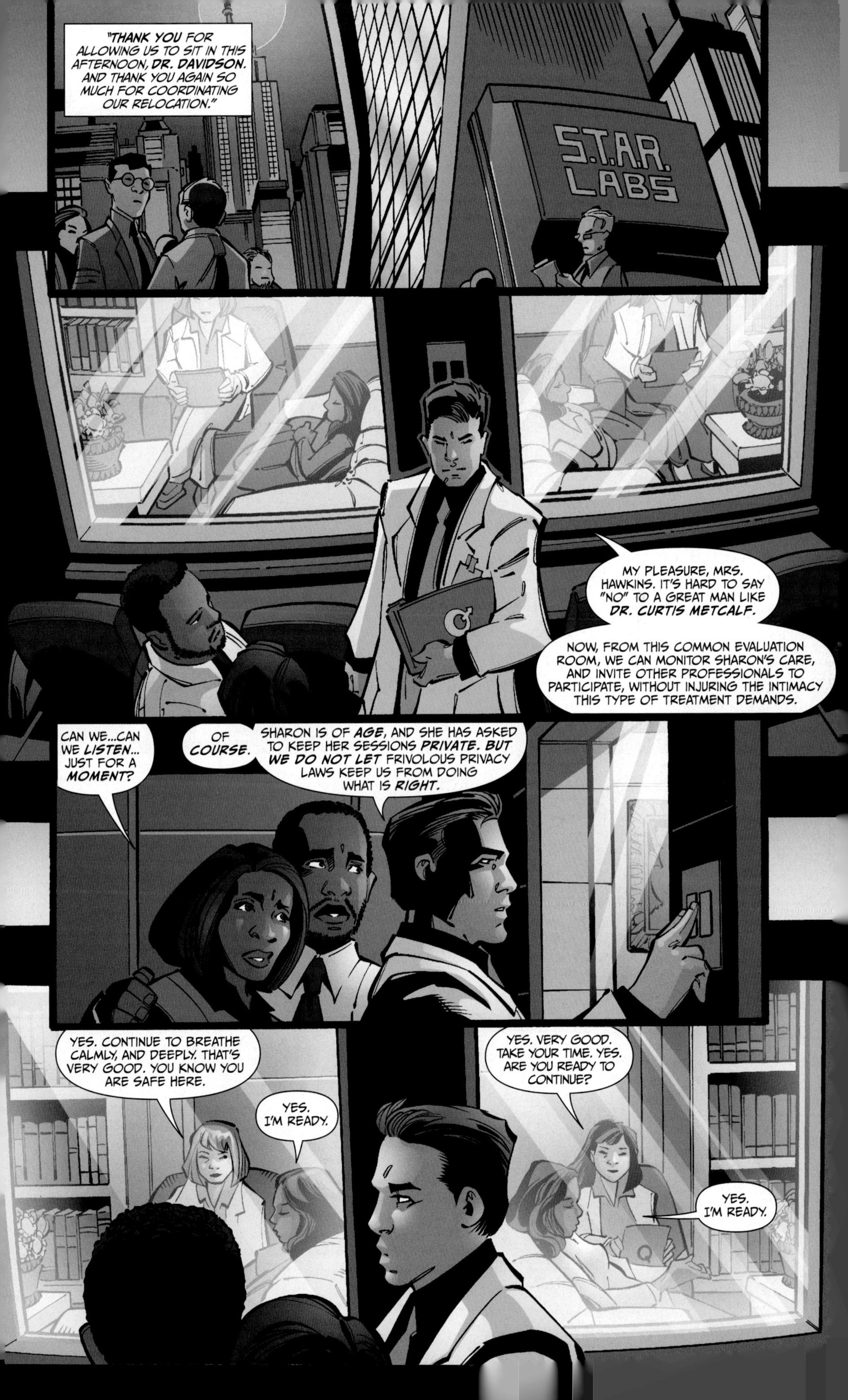
"THANK YOU FOR ALLOWING US TO SIT IN THIS AFTERNOON, DR. DAVIDSON. AND THANK YOU AGAIN SO MUCH FOR COORDINATING OUR RELOCATION."
S.T.A.R. LABS
MY PLEASURE, MRS. HAWKINS. IT'S HARD TO SAY "NO" TO A GREAT MAN LIKE DR. CURTIS METCALF.
NOW, FROM THIS COMMON EVALUATION ROOM, WE CAN MONITOR SHARON'S CARE, AND INVITE OTHER PROFESSIONALS TO PARTICIPATE, WITHOUT INJURING THE INTIMACY THIS TYPE OF TREATMENT DEMANDS.
CAN WE...CAN WE LISTEN... JUST FOR A MOMENT?
OF COURSE.
SHARON IS OF AGE, AND SHE HAS ASKED TO KEEP HER SESSIONS PRIVATE. BUT WE DO NOT LET FRIVOLOUS PRIVACY LAWS KEEP US FROM DOING WHAT IS RIGHT.
YES. CONTINUE TO BREATHE CALMLY, AND DEEPLY. THAT'S VERY GOOD. YOU KNOW YOU ARE SAFE HERE.
YES. I'M READY.
YES. VERY GOOD. TAKE YOUR TIME. YES. ARE YOU READY TO CONTINUE?
YES. I'M READY.

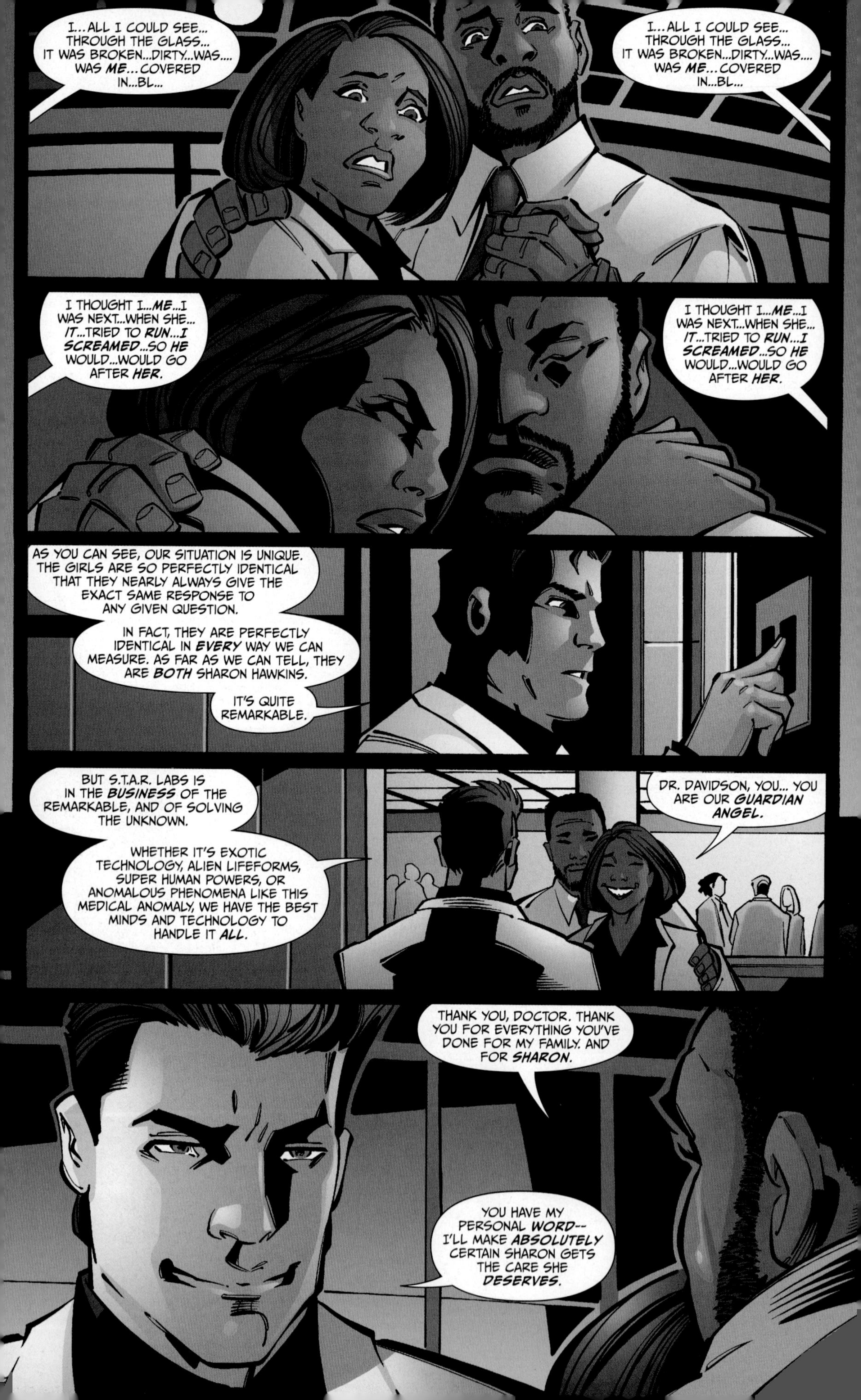
I... ALL I COULD SEE... THROUGH THE GLASS... IT WAS BROKEN...DIRTY...WAS.... WAS ME... COVERED IN...BL...
I... ALL I COULD SEE... THROUGH THE GLASS... IT WAS BROKEN...DIRTY...WAS.... WAS ME... COVERED IN...BL...
I THOUGHT I...ME...I WAS NEXT...WHEN SHE... IT...TRIED TO RUN...I SCREAMED...SO HE WOULD...WOULD GO AFTER HER.
I THOUGHT I...ME...I WAS NEXT...WHEN SHE... IT...TRIED TO RUN...I SCREAMED...SO HE WOULD...WOULD GO AFTER HER.
AS YOU CAN SEE, OUR SITUATION IS UNIQUE. THE GIRLS ARE SO PERFECTLY IDENTICAL THAT THEY NEARLY ALWAYS GIVE THE EXACT SAME RESPONSE TO ANY GIVEN QUESTION.
IN FACT, THEY ARE PERFECTLY IDENTICAL IN EVERY WAY WE CAN MEASURE. AS FAR AS WE CAN TELL, THEY ARE BOTH SHARON HAWKINS.
IT'S QUITE REMARKABLE.
BUT S.T.A.R. LABS IS IN THE BUSINESS OF THE REMARKABLE, AND OF SOLVING THE UNKNOWN.
WHETHER IT'S EXOTIC TECHNOLOGY, ALIEN LIFEFORMS, SUPER HUMAN POWERS, OR ANOMALOUS PHENOMENA LIKE THIS MEDICAL ANOMALY, WE HAVE THE BEST MINDS AND TECHNOLOGY TO HANDLE IT ALL.
DR. DAVIDSON, YOU... YOU ARE OUR GUARDIAN ANGEL.
THANK YOU, DOCTOR. THANK YOU FOR EVERYTHING YOU'VE DONE FOR MY FAMILY. AND FOR SHARON.
YOU HAVE MY PERSONAL WORD-- I'LL MAKE ABSOLUTELY CERTAIN SHARON GETS THE CARE SHE DESERVES.

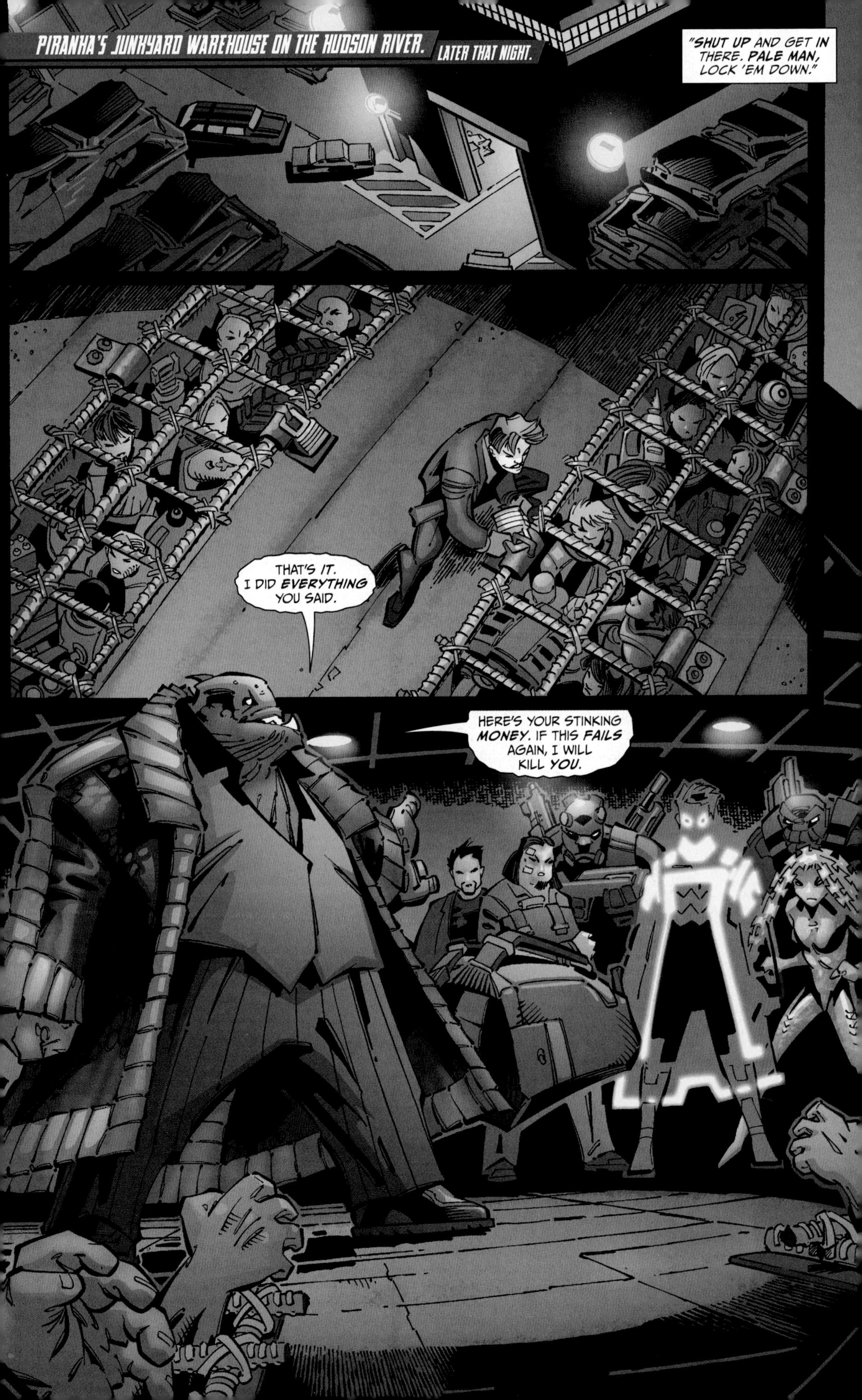
PIRANHA'S JUNKYARD WAREHOUSE ON THE HUDSON RIVER.
LATER THAT NIGHT.
"SHUT UP AND GET IN THERE. PALE MAN, LOCK 'EM DOWN."
THAT'S IT. I DID EVERYTHING YOU SAID.
HERE'S YOUR STINKING MONEY. IF THIS FAILS AGAIN, I WILL KILL YOU.

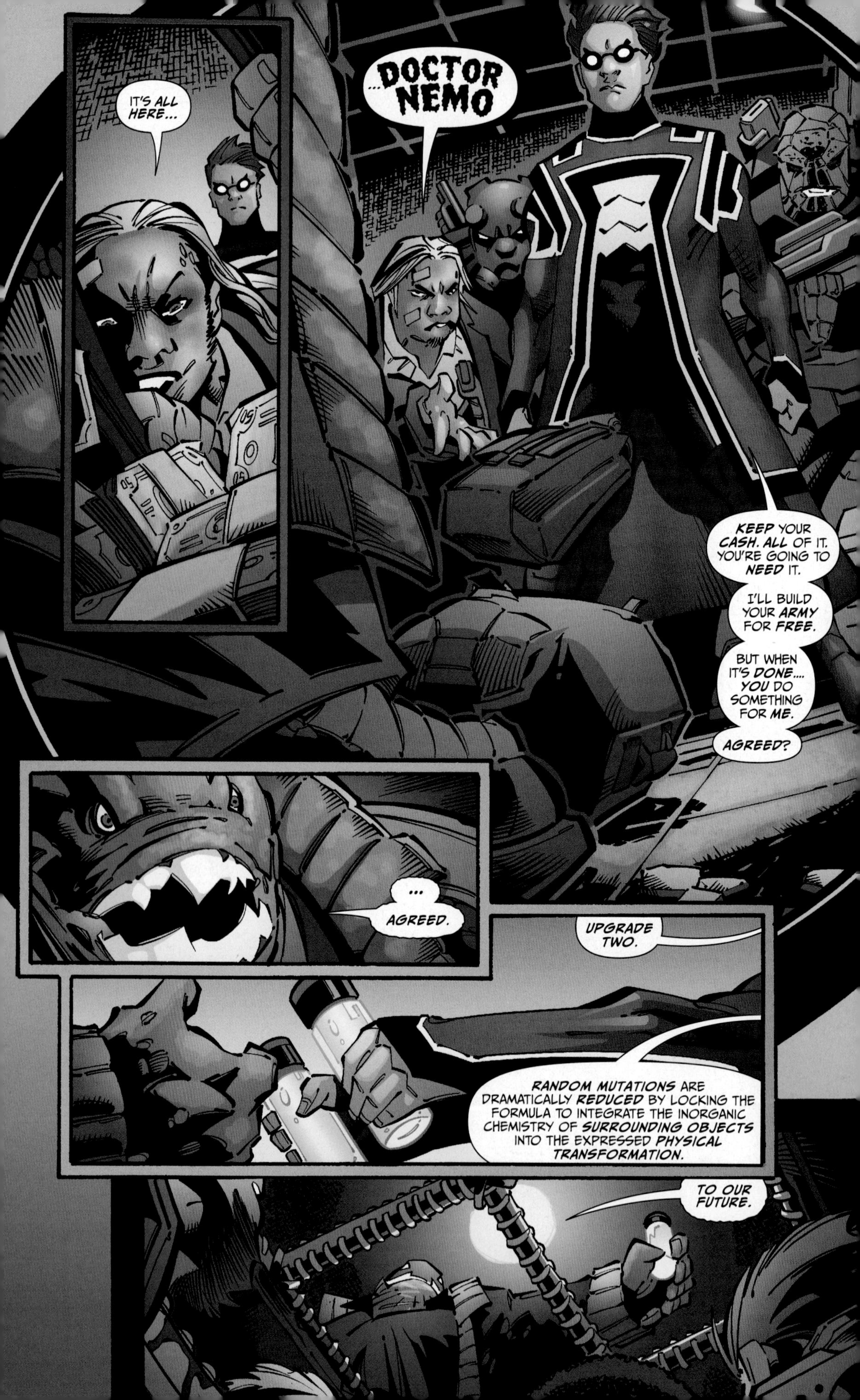

IT'S ALL HERE...
...DOCTOR NEMO
KEEP YOUR CASH. ALL OF IT. YOU'RE GOING TO NEED IT.
I'LL BUILD YOUR ARMY FOR FREE.
BUT WHEN IT'S DONE.... YOU DO SOMETHING FOR ME.
AGREED?
... AGREED.
UPGRADE TWO.
RANDOM MUTATIONS ARE DRAMATICALLY REDUCED BY LOCKING THE FORMULA TO INTEGRATE THE INORGANIC CHEMISTRY OF SURROUNDING OBJECTS INTO THE EXPRESSED PHYSICAL TRANSFORMATION.
TO OUR FUTURE.

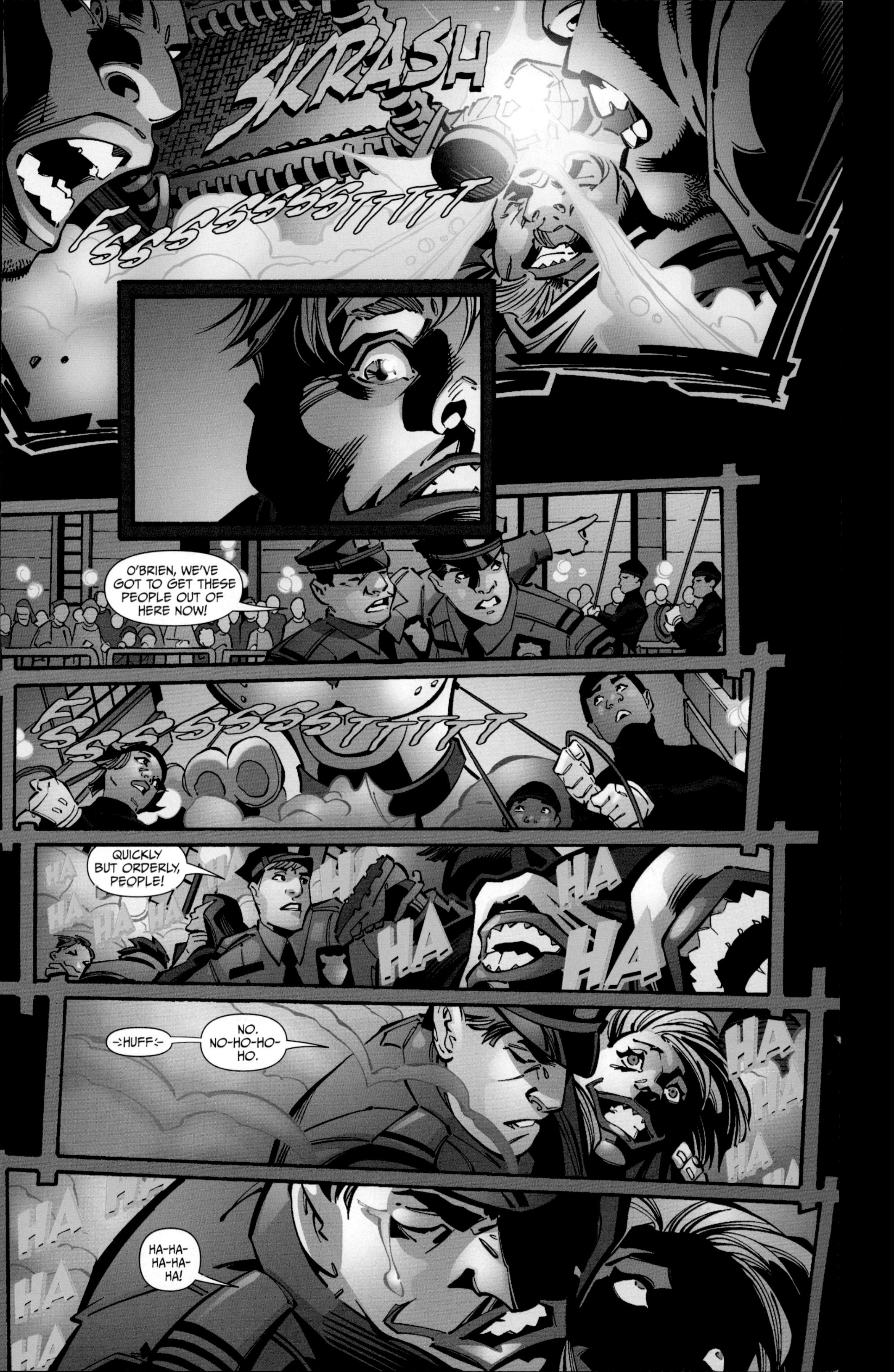
SKRASH
FSSSSSSSTTTTT
O'BRIEN, WE'VE GOT TO GET THESE PEOPLE OUT OF HERE NOW!
FSSSSSSSTTTTT
QUICKLY BUT ORDERLY, PEOPLE!
HA HA HA HA HA HA HA HA
-HUFF-
NO. NO-HO-HO-HO.
HA HA HA HA HA
HA-HA-HA-HA-HA!
HA HA HA HA

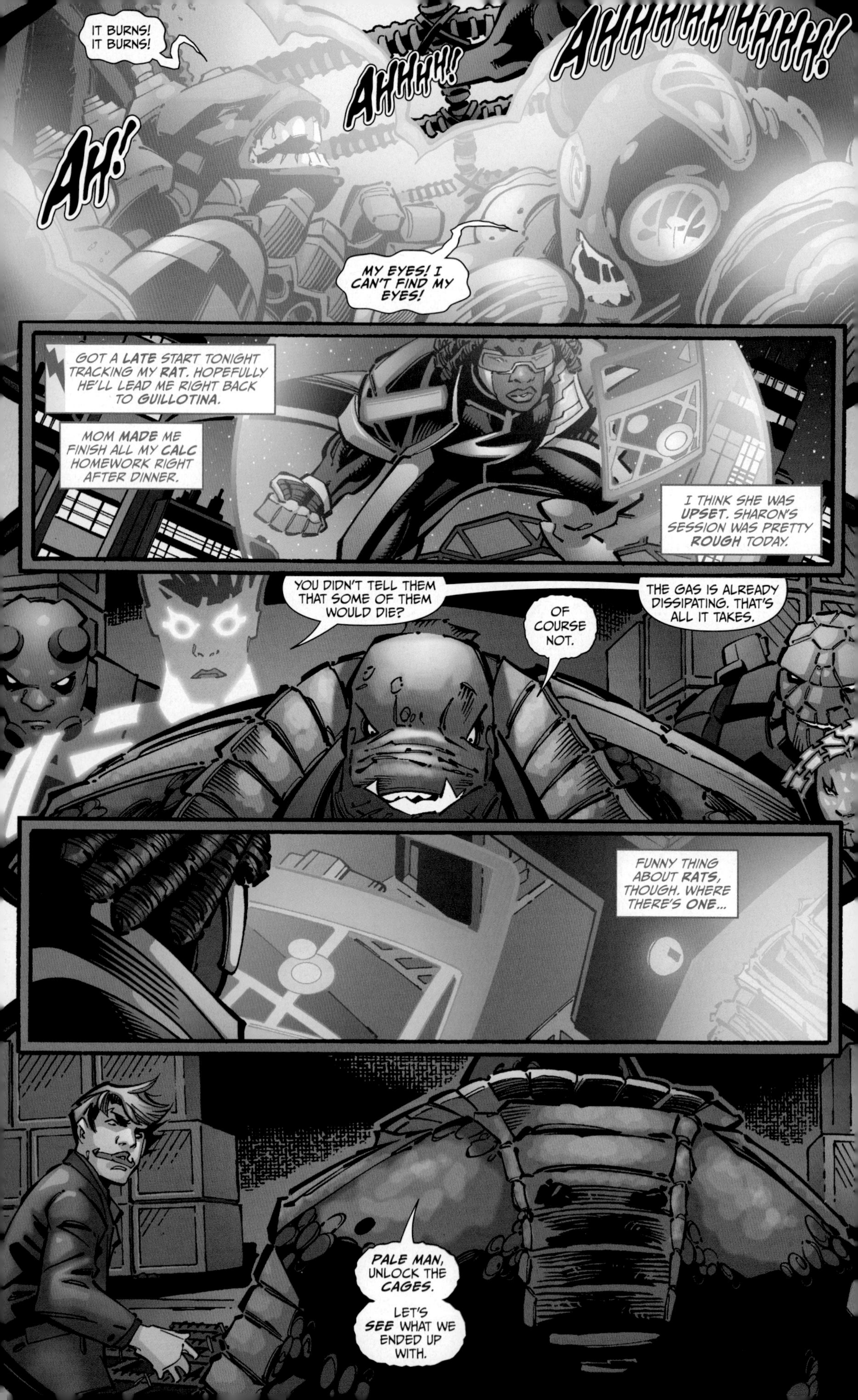
IT BURNS! IT BURNS!
AHHHHHHHHHH!
AHHHH!
AH!
MY EYES! I CAN'T FIND MY EYES!
GOT A LATE START TONIGHT TRACKING MY RAT. HOPEFULLY HE'LL LEAD ME RIGHT BACK TO GUILLOTINA.
MOM MADE ME FINISH ALL MY CALC HOMEWORK RIGHT AFTER DINNER.
I THINK SHE WAS UPSET. SHARON'S SESSION WAS PRETTY ROUGH TODAY.
YOU DIDN'T TELL THEM THAT SOME OF THEM WOULD DIE?
OF COURSE NOT.
THE GAS IS ALREADY DISSIPATING. THAT'S ALL IT TAKES.
FUNNY THING ABOUT RATS, THOUGH. WHERE THERE'S ONE...
PALE MAN, UNLOCK THE CAGES.
LET'S SEE WHAT WE ENDED UP WITH.

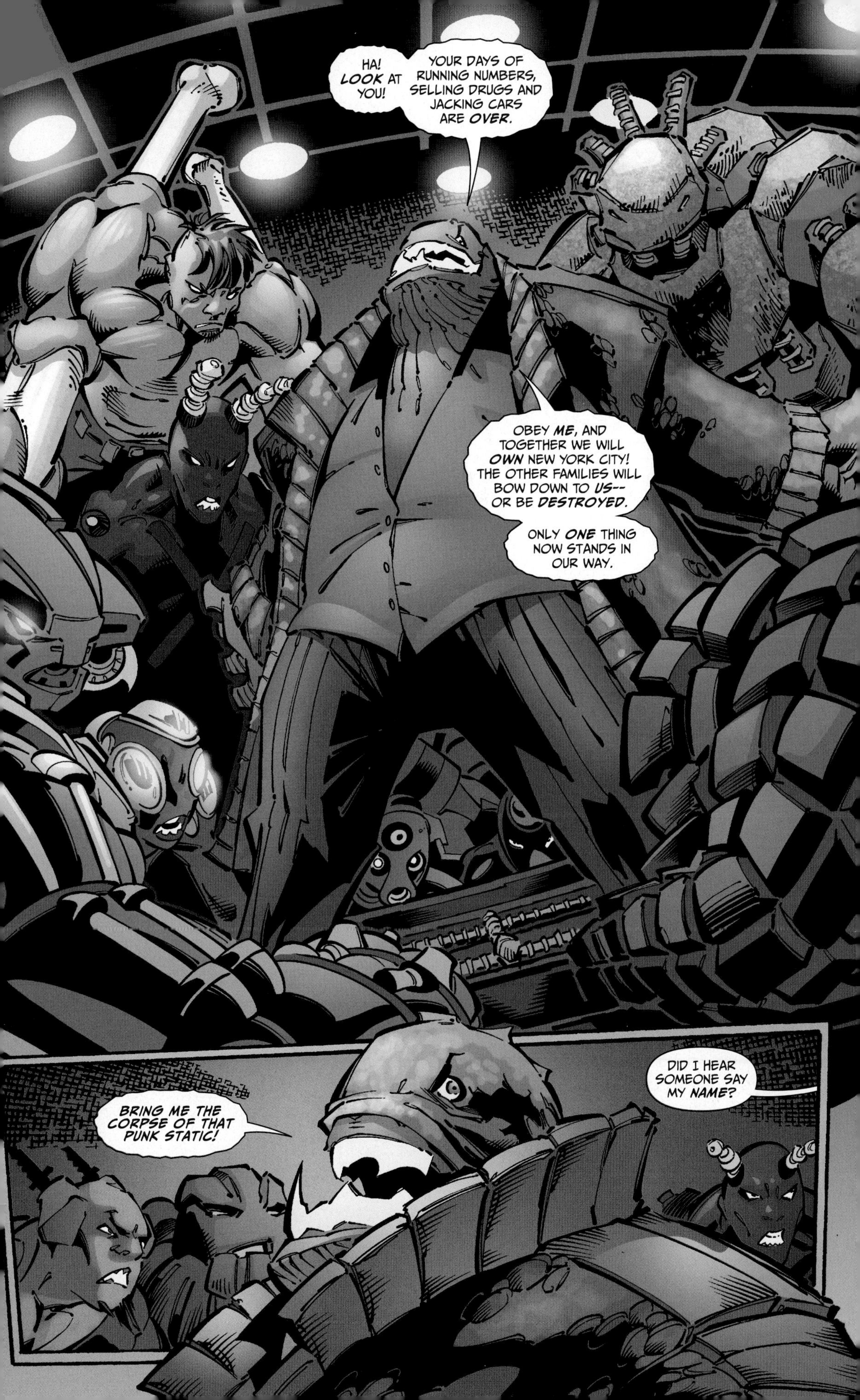
HA! LOOK AT YOU!
YOUR DAYS OF RUNNING NUMBERS, SELLING DRUGS AND JACKING CARS ARE OVER.
OBEY ME, AND TOGETHER WE WILL OWN NEW YORK CITY! THE OTHER FAMILIES WILL BOW DOWN TO US-- OR BE DESTROYED.
ONLY ONE THING NOW STANDS IN OUR WAY.
BRING ME THE CORPSE OF THAT PUNK STATIC!
DID I HEAR SOMEONE SAY MY NAME?

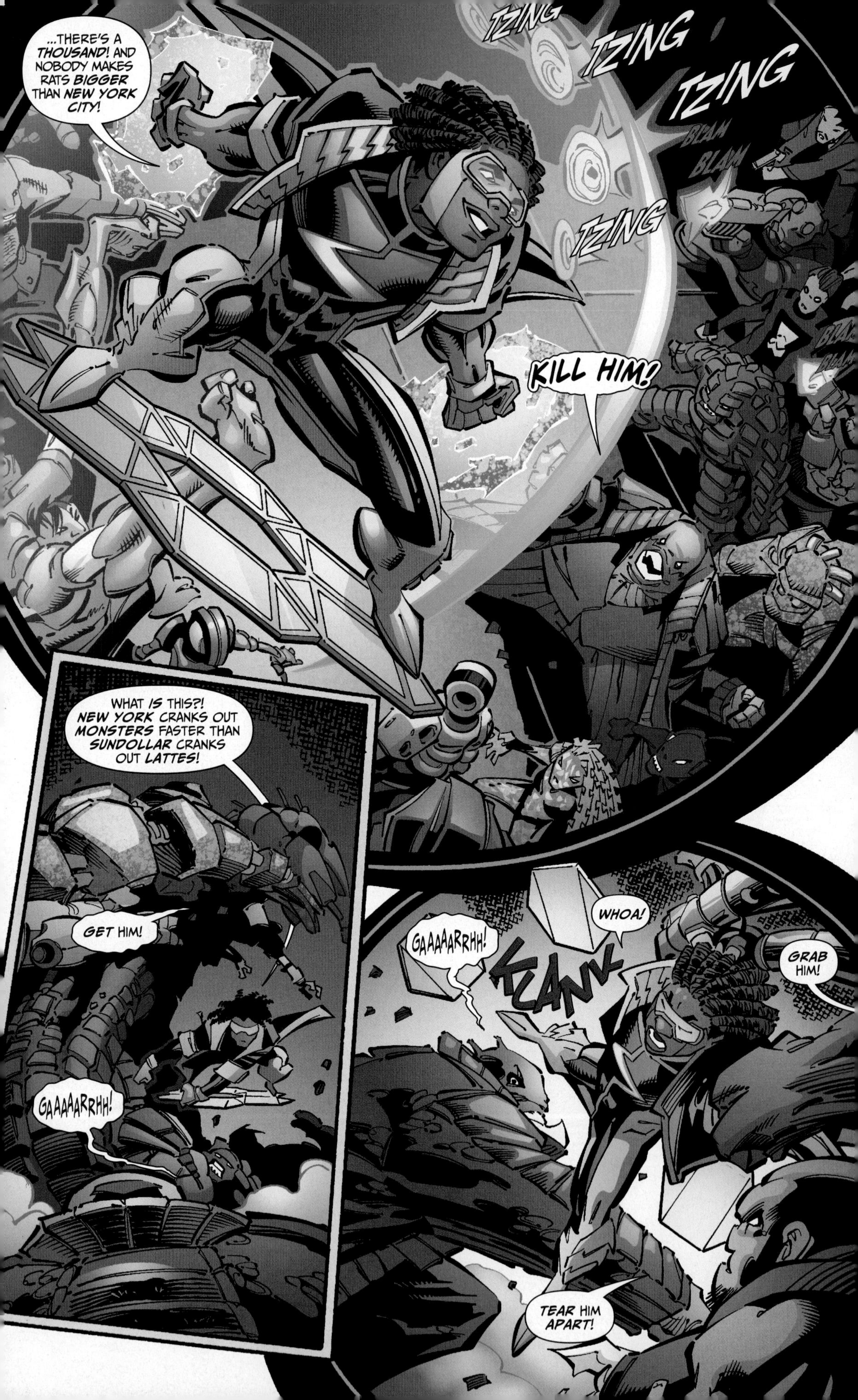

...THERE'S A THOUSAND! AND NOBODY MAKES RATS BIGGER THAN NEW YORK CITY!
TZING
TZING
TZING
BLAM
BLAM
TZING
KILL HIM!
WHAT IS THIS?! NEW YORK CRANKS OUT MONSTERS FASTER THAN SUNDOLLAR CRANKS OUT LATTES!
GET HIM!
GAAAAARRHH!
GAAAAARRHH!
WHOA!
KLANK
GRAB HIM!
TEAR HIM APART!

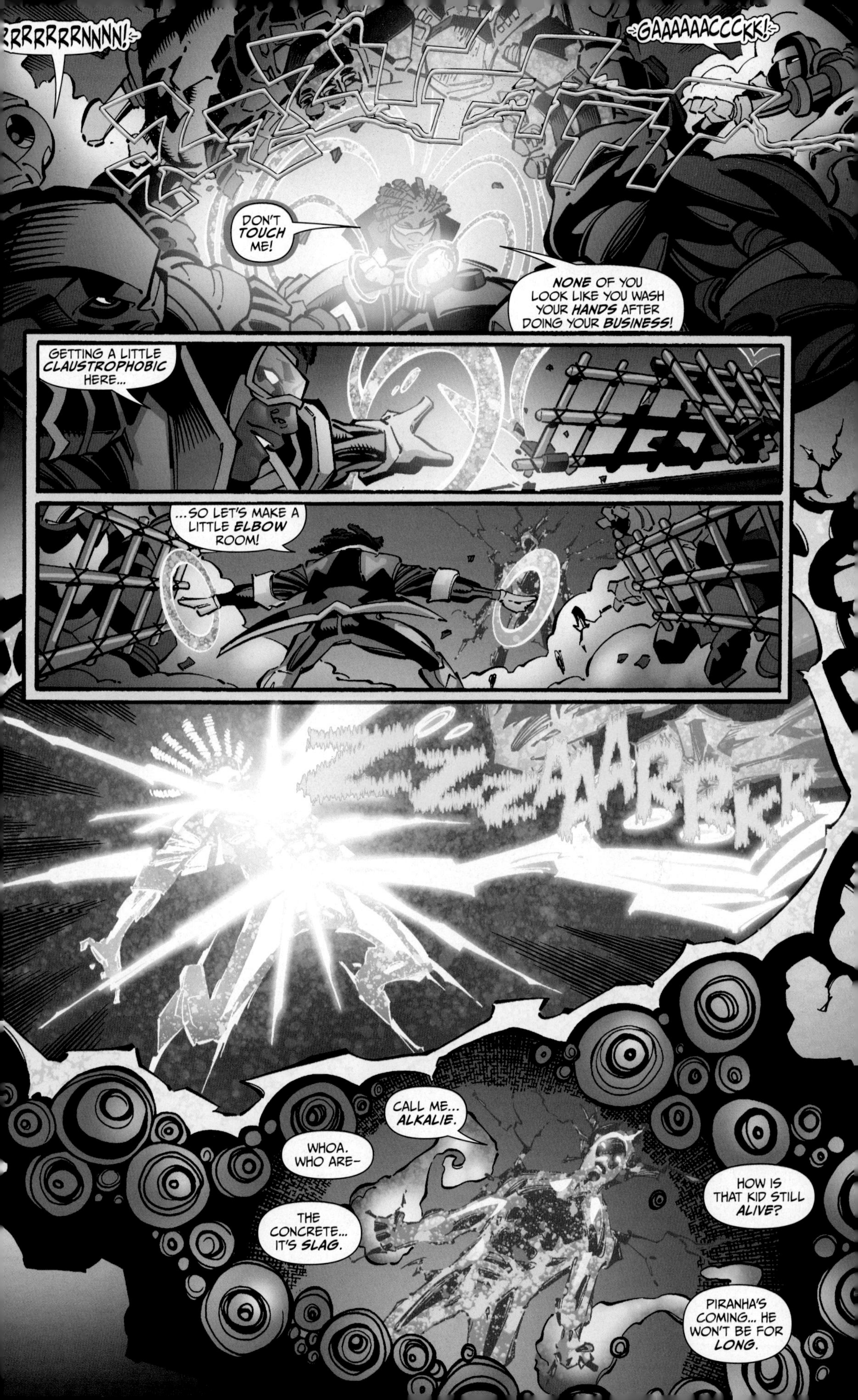
RRRRRRRNNNN!
GAAAAAACCCKK!
DON'T TOUCH ME!
NONE OF YOU LOOK LIKE YOU WASH YOUR HANDS AFTER DOING YOUR BUSINESS!
GETTING A LITTLE CLAUSTROPHOBIC HERE...
...SO LET'S MAKE A LITTLE ELBOW ROOM!
ZZAARRKK
CALL ME... ALKALIE.
WHOA. WHO ARE–
HOW IS THAT KID STILL ALIVE?
THE CONCRETE... IT'S SLAG.
PIRANHA'S COMING... HE WON'T BE FOR LONG.

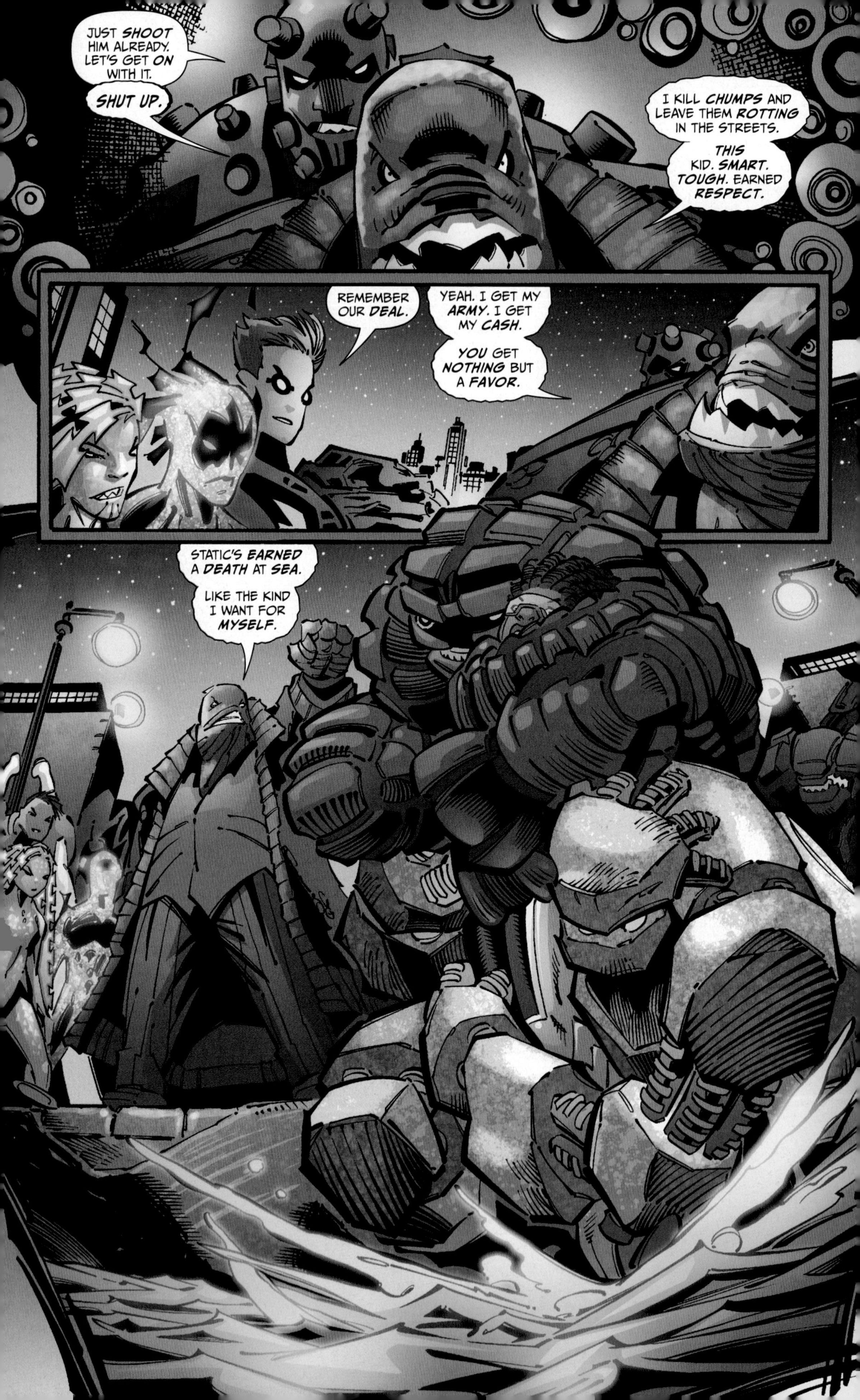
JUST SHOOT HIM ALREADY. LET'S GET ON WITH IT.
SHUT UP.
I KILL CHUMPS AND LEAVE THEM ROTTING IN THE STREETS.
THIS KID. SMART. TOUGH. EARNED RESPECT.
REMEMBER OUR DEAL.
YEAH. I GET MY ARMY. I GET MY CASH.
YOU GET NOTHING BUT A FAVOR.
STATIC'S EARNED A DEATH AT SEA.
LIKE THE KIND I WANT FOR MYSELF.

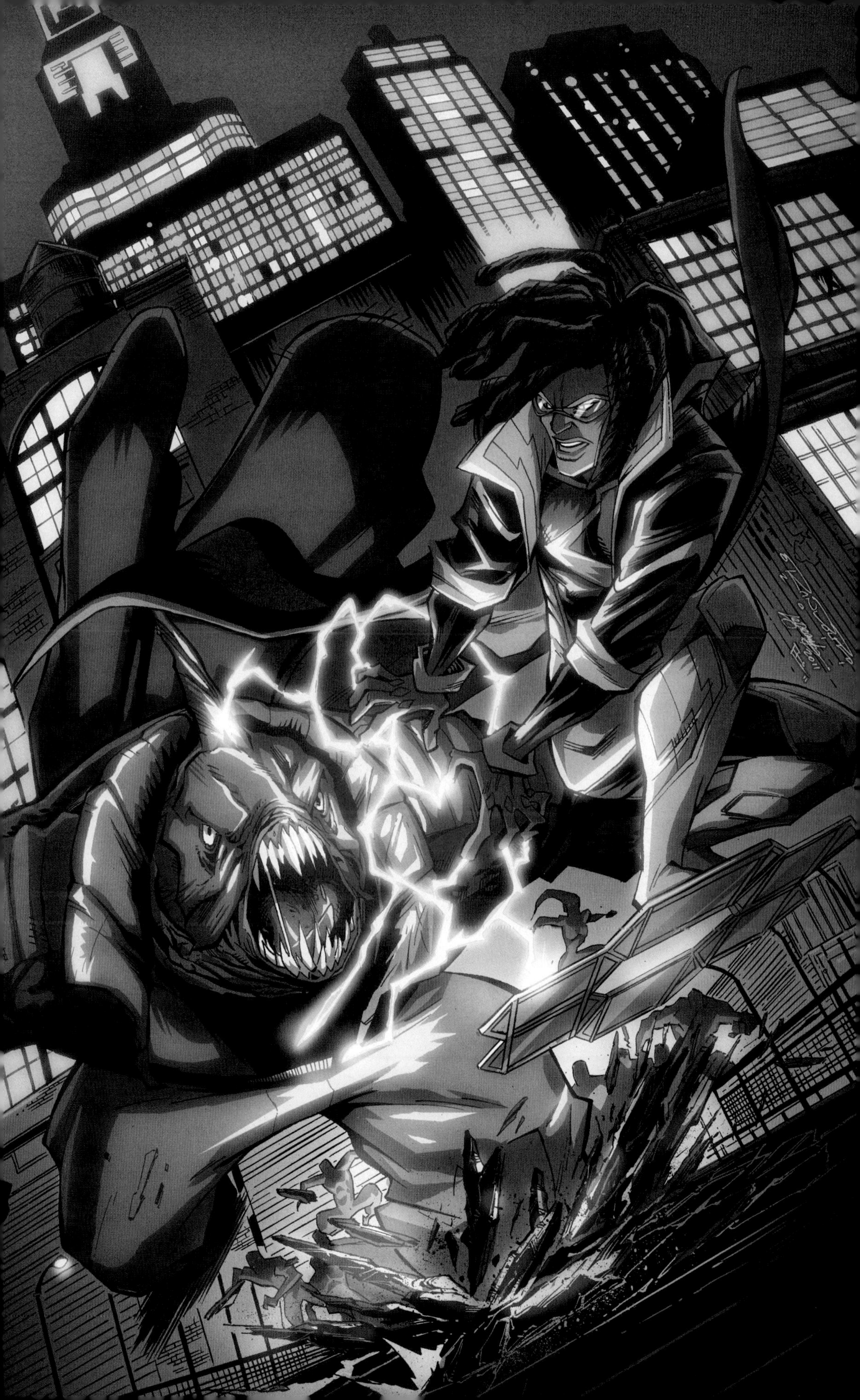

cover art by
KHARY RANDOLPH, EMILIO LOPEZ
& LE BEAU UNDERWOOD

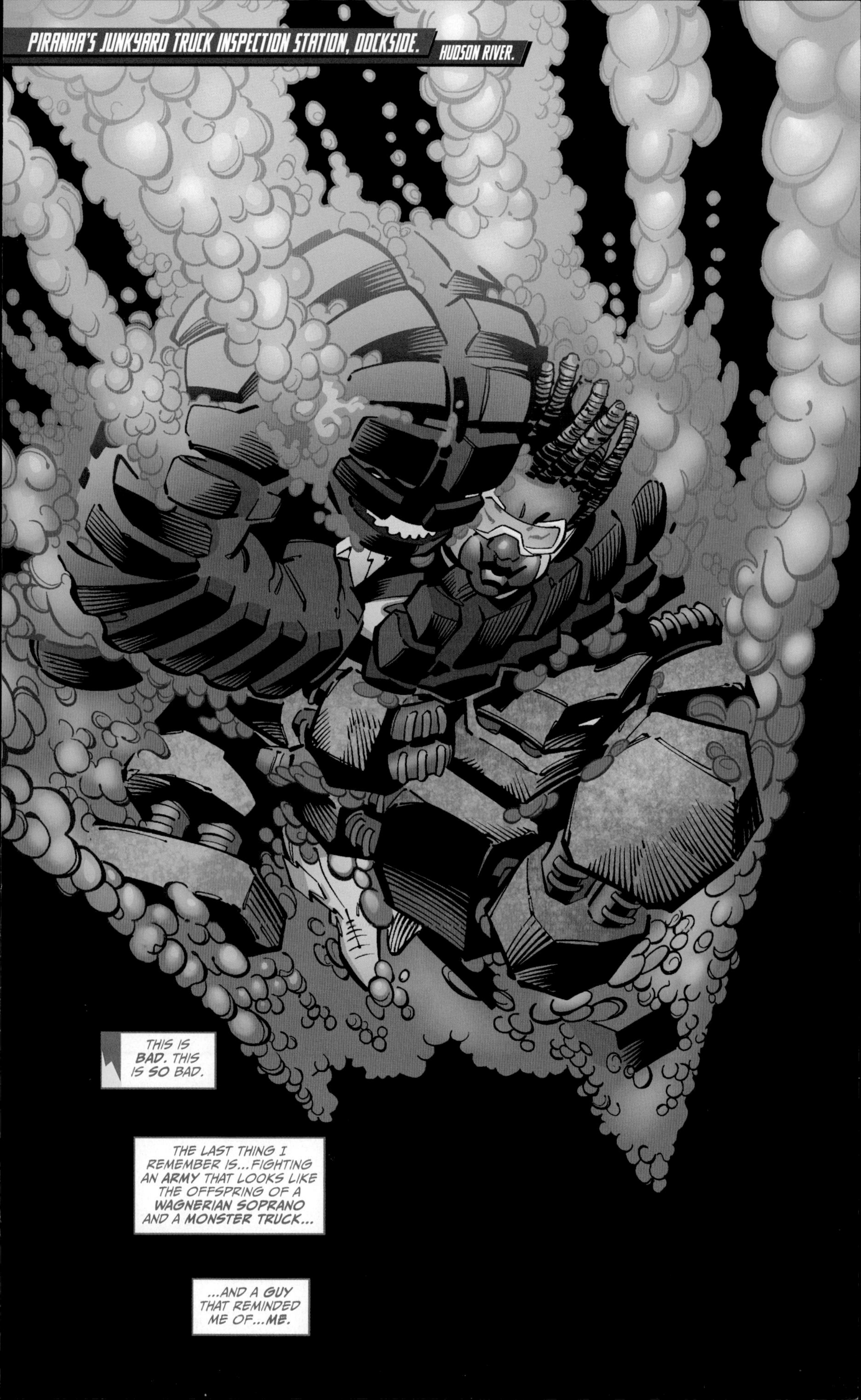
PIRANHA'S JUNKYARD TRUCK INSPECTION STATION, DOCKSIDE.
HUDSON RIVER.
THIS IS BAD. THIS IS SO BAD.
THE LAST THING I REMEMBER IS...FIGHTING AN ARMY THAT LOOKS LIKE THE OFFSPRING OF A WAGNERIAN SOPRANO AND A MONSTER TRUCK...
...AND A GUY THAT REMINDED ME OF...ME.

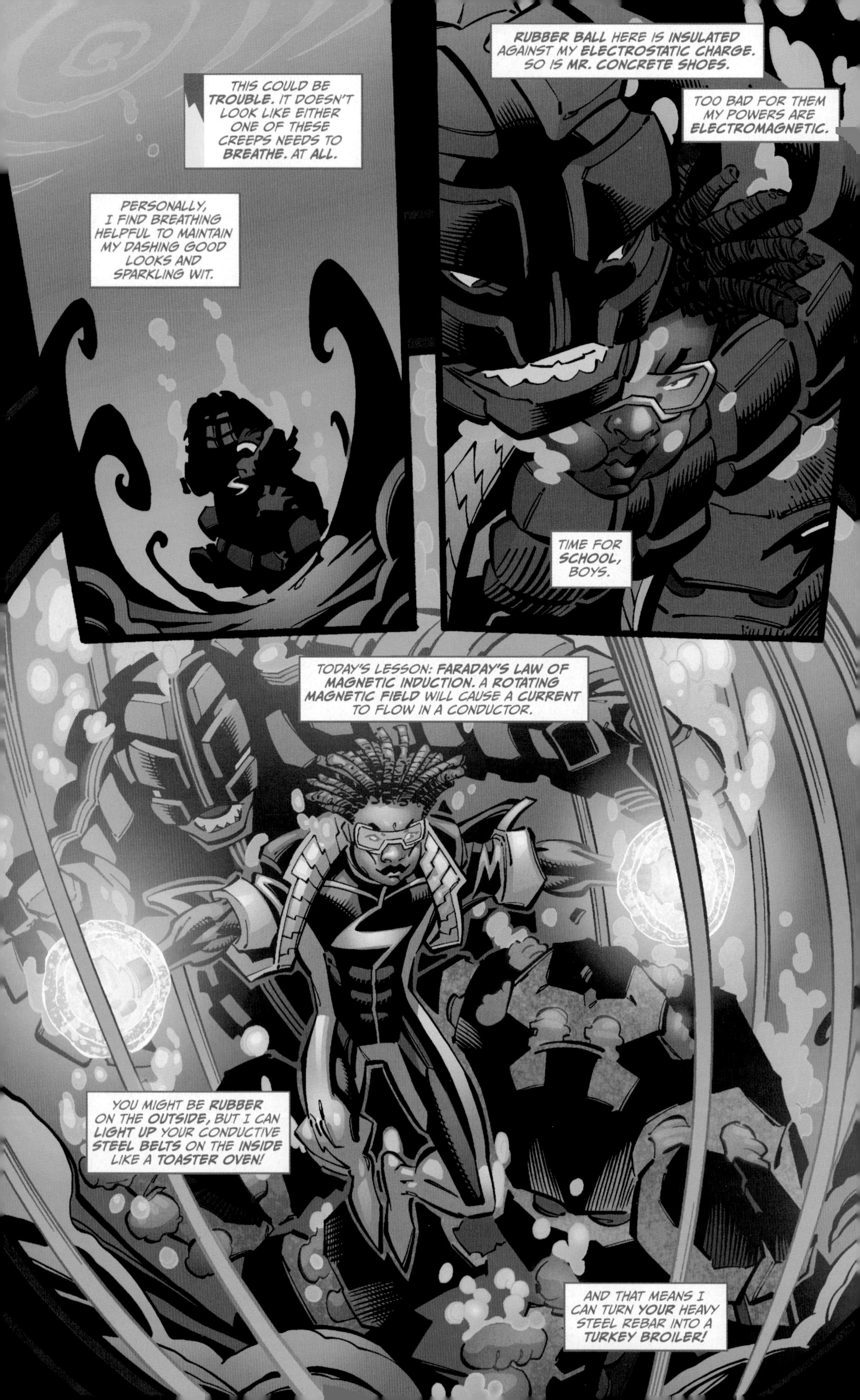
THIS COULD BE TROUBLE. IT DOESN'T LOOK LIKE EITHER ONE OF THESE CREEPS NEEDS TO BREATHE. AT ALL.
PERSONALLY, I FIND BREATHING HELPFUL TO MAINTAIN MY DASHING GOOD LOOKS AND SPARKLING WIT.
RUBBER BALL HERE IS INSULATED AGAINST MY ELECTROSTATIC CHARGE. SO IS MR. CONCRETE SHOES.
TOO BAD FOR THEM MY POWERS ARE ELECTROMAGNETIC.
TIME FOR SCHOOL, BOYS.
TODAY'S LESSON: FARADAY'S LAW OF MAGNETIC INDUCTION. A ROTATING MAGNETIC FIELD WILL CAUSE A CURRENT TO FLOW IN A CONDUCTOR.
YOU MIGHT BE RUBBER ON THE OUTSIDE, BUT I CAN LIGHT UP YOUR CONDUCTIVE STEEL BELTS ON THE INSIDE LIKE A TOASTER OVEN!
AND THAT MEANS I CAN TURN YOUR HEAVY STEEL REBAR INTO A TURKEY BROILER!

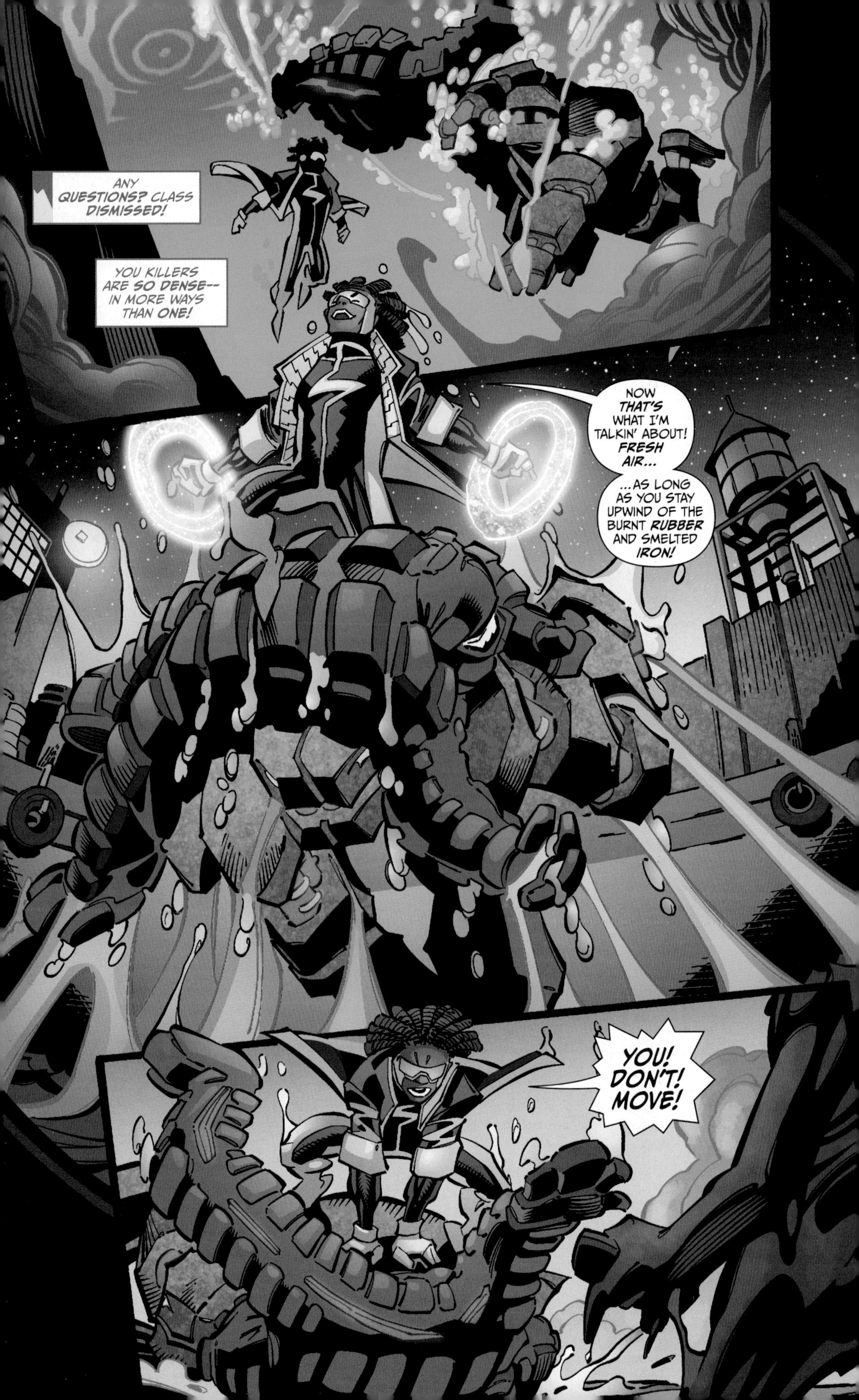
ANY QUESTIONS? CLASS DISMISSED!
YOU KILLERS ARE SO DENSE-- IN MORE WAYS THAN ONE!
NOW THAT'S WHAT I'M TALKIN' ABOUT! FRESH AIR...
...AS LONG AS YOU STAY UPWIND OF THE BURNT RUBBER AND SMELTED IRON!
YOU! DON'T! MOVE!

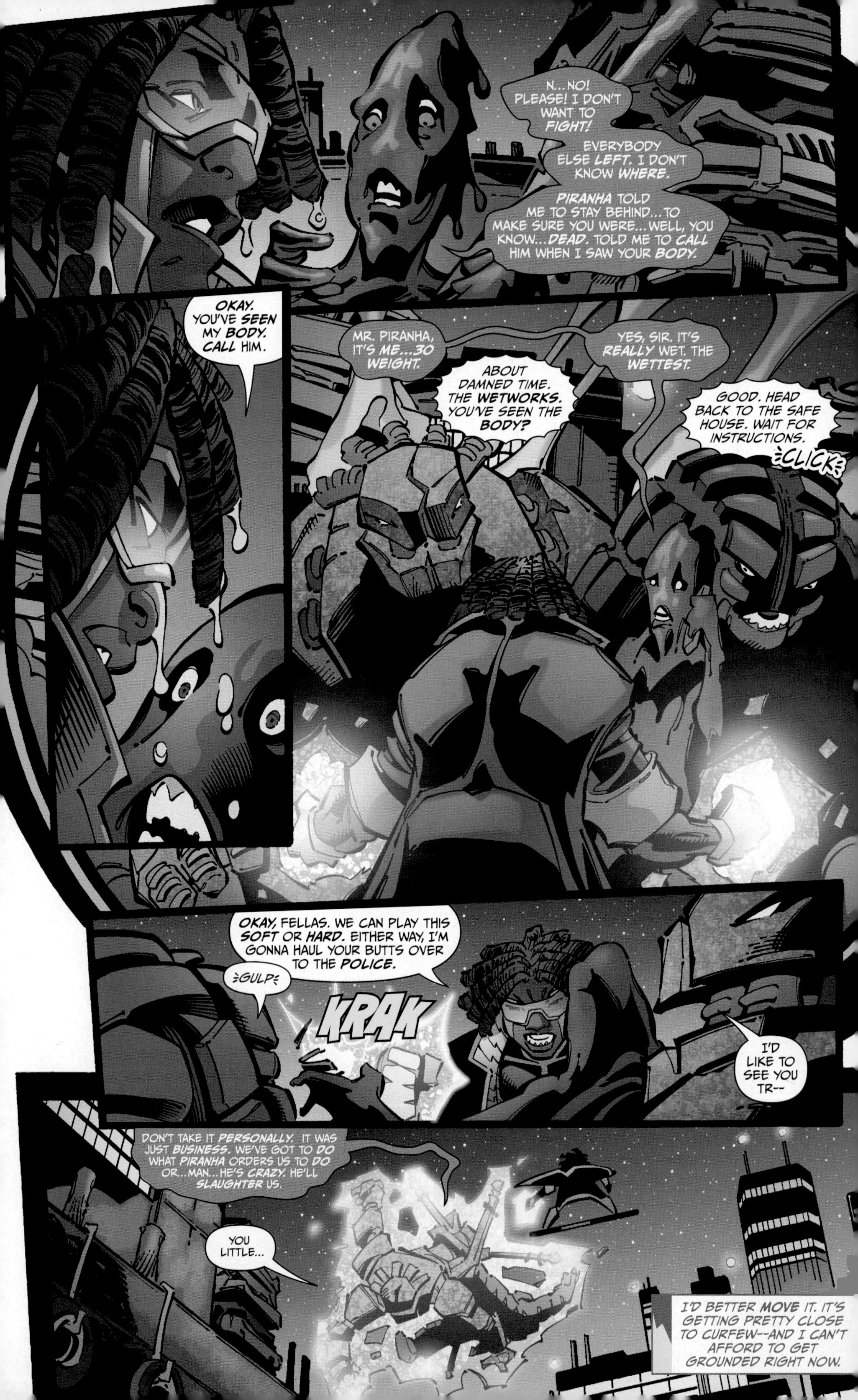
N...NO! PLEASE! I DON'T WANT TO FIGHT!
EVERYBODY ELSE LEFT. I DON'T KNOW WHERE.
PIRANHA TOLD ME TO STAY BEHIND...TO MAKE SURE YOU WERE...WELL, YOU KNOW...DEAD. TOLD ME TO CALL HIM WHEN I SAW YOUR BODY.
OKAY. YOU'VE SEEN MY BODY. CALL HIM.
MR. PIRANHA, IT'S ME...30 WEIGHT.
ABOUT DAMNED TIME. THE WETWORKS. YOU'VE SEEN THE BODY?
YES, SIR. IT'S REALLY WET. THE WETTEST.
GOOD. HEAD BACK TO THE SAFE HOUSE. WAIT FOR INSTRUCTIONS.
CLICK
OKAY, FELLAS. WE CAN PLAY THIS SOFT OR HARD. EITHER WAY, I'M GONNA HAUL YOUR BUTTS OVER TO THE POLICE.
GULP
KRAK
I'D LIKE TO SEE YOU TR--
DON'T TAKE IT PERSONALLY. IT WAS JUST BUSINESS. WE'VE GOT TO DO WHAT PIRANHA ORDERS US TO DO OR...MAN...HE'S CRAZY. HE'LL SLAUGHTER US.
YOU LITTLE...
I'D BETTER MOVE IT. IT'S GETTING PRETTY CLOSE TO CURFEW--AND I CAN'T AFFORD TO GET GROUNDED RIGHT NOW.

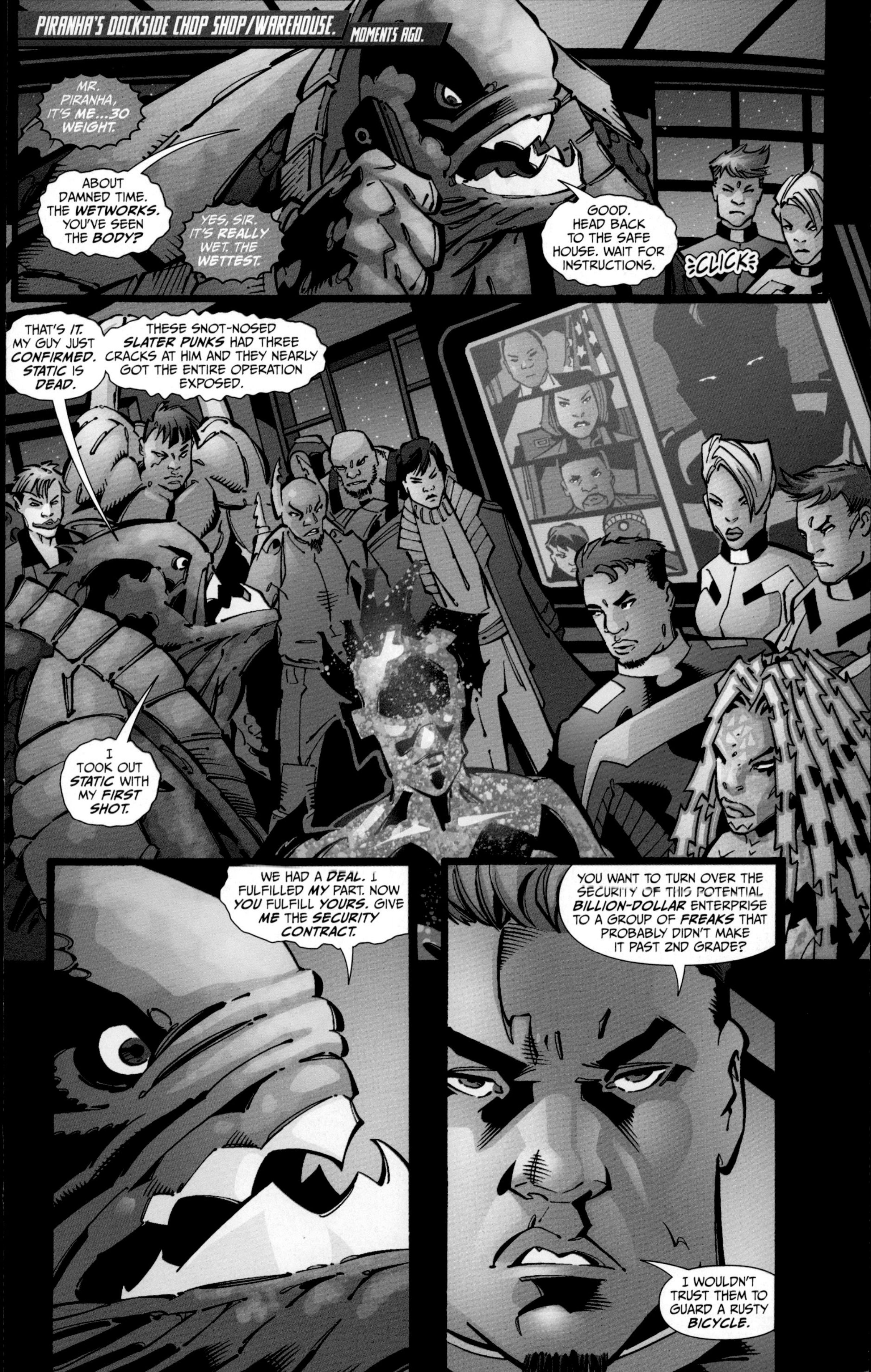
PIRANHA'S DOCKSIDE CHOP SHOP/WAREHOUSE.
MOMENTS AGO.
MR. PIRANHA, IT'S ME...30 WEIGHT.
ABOUT DAMNED TIME. THE WETWORKS. YOU'VE SEEN THE BODY?
YES, SIR. IT'S REALLY WET. THE WETTEST.
GOOD. HEAD BACK TO THE SAFE HOUSE. WAIT FOR INSTRUCTIONS.
CLICK
THAT'S IT. MY GUY JUST CONFIRMED. STATIC IS DEAD.
THESE SNOT-NOSED SLATER PUNKS HAD THREE CRACKS AT HIM AND THEY NEARLY GOT THE ENTIRE OPERATION EXPOSED.
I TOOK OUT STATIC WITH MY FIRST SHOT.
WE HAD A DEAL. I FULFILLED MY PART. NOW YOU FULFILL YOURS. GIVE ME THE SECURITY CONTRACT.
YOU WANT TO TURN OVER THE SECURITY OF THIS POTENTIAL BILLION-DOLLAR ENTERPRISE TO A GROUP OF FREAKS THAT PROBABLY DIDN'T MAKE IT PAST 2ND GRADE?
I WOULDN'T TRUST THEM TO GUARD A RUSTY BICYCLE.

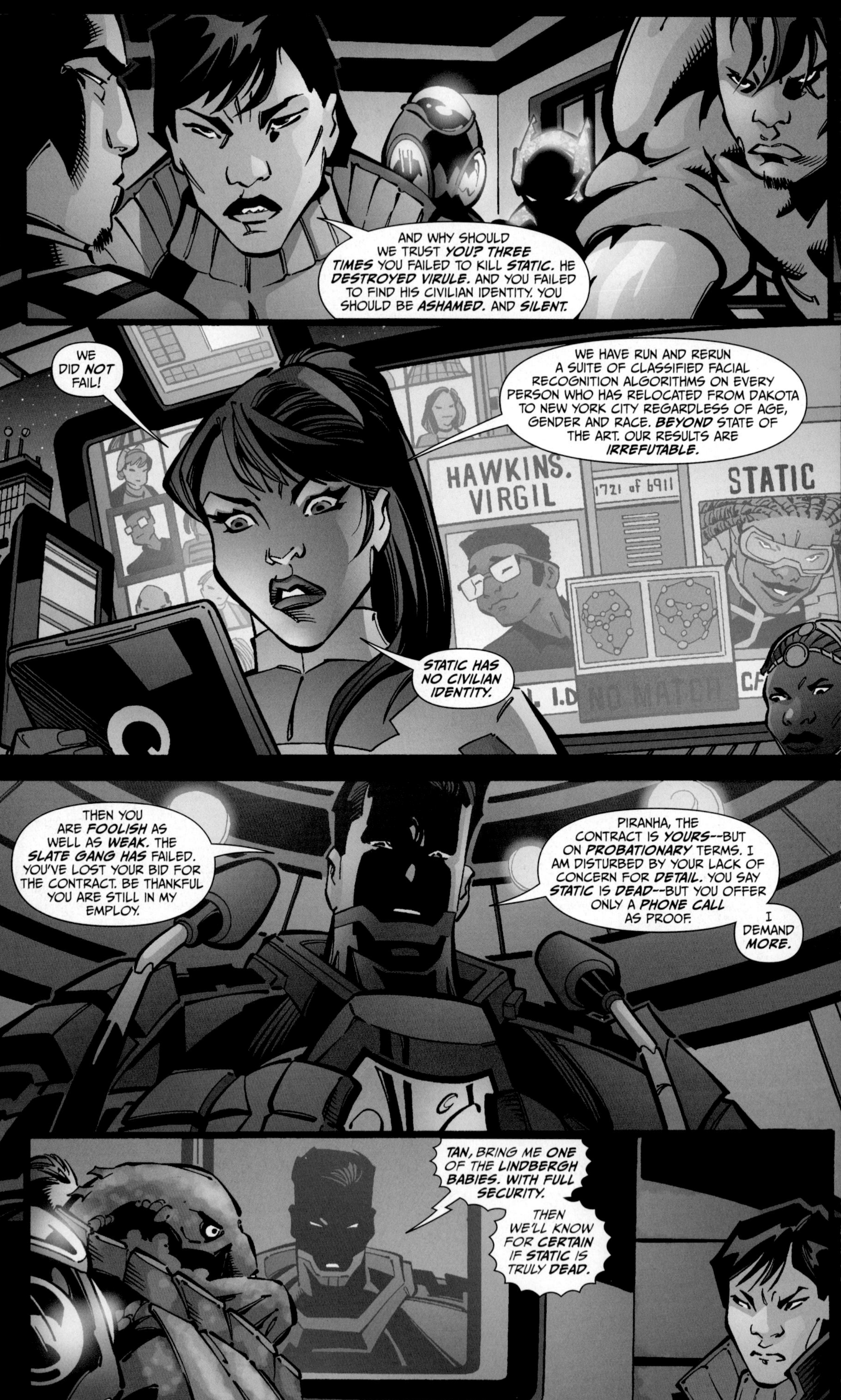

AND WHY SHOULD WE TRUST YOU? THREE TIMES YOU FAILED TO KILL STATIC. HE DESTROYED VIRULE. AND YOU FAILED TO FIND HIS CIVILIAN IDENTITY. YOU SHOULD BE ASHAMED. AND SILENT.
WE DID NOT FAIL!
WE HAVE RUN AND RERUN A SUITE OF CLASSIFIED FACIAL RECOGNITION ALGORITHMS ON EVERY PERSON WHO HAS RELOCATED FROM DAKOTA TO NEW YORK CITY REGARDLESS OF AGE, GENDER AND RACE. BEYOND STATE OF THE ART. OUR RESULTS ARE IRREFUTABLE.
HAWKINS. VIRGIL
1721 of 6911
STATIC
NO MATCH
STATIC HAS NO CIVILIAN IDENTITY.
THEN YOU ARE FOOLISH AS WELL AS WEAK. THE SLATE GANG HAS FAILED. YOU'VE LOST YOUR BID FOR THE CONTRACT. BE THANKFUL YOU ARE STILL IN MY EMPLOY.
PIRANHA, THE CONTRACT IS YOURS--BUT ON PROBATIONARY TERMS. I AM DISTURBED BY YOUR LACK OF CONCERN FOR DETAIL. YOU SAY STATIC IS DEAD--BUT YOU OFFER ONLY A PHONE CALL AS PROOF.
I DEMAND MORE.
TAN, BRING ME ONE OF THE LINDBERGH BABIES. WITH FULL SECURITY.
THEN WE'LL KNOW FOR CERTAIN IF STATIC IS TRULY DEAD.

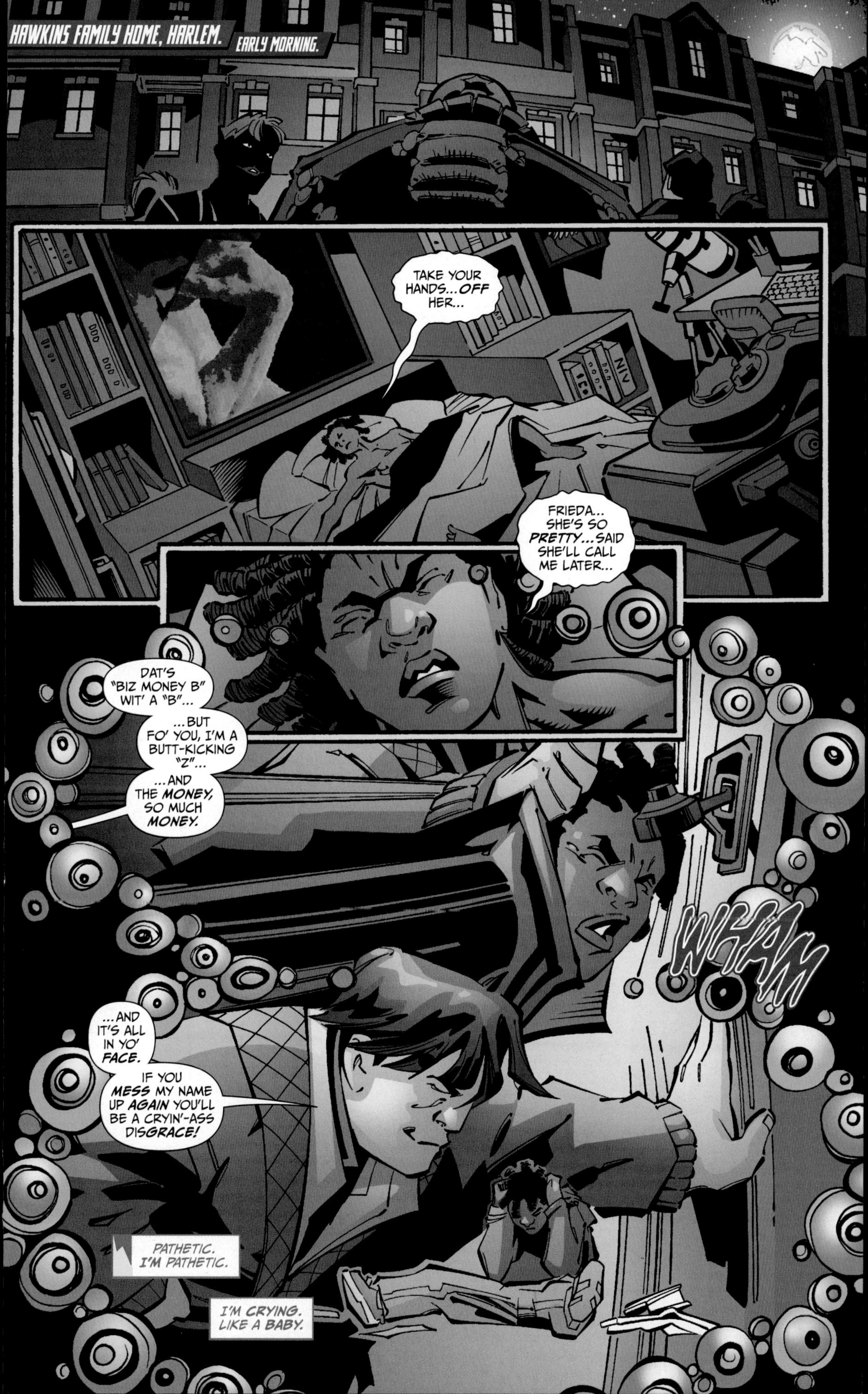
HAWKINS FAMILY HOME, HARLEM.
EARLY MORNING.
TAKE YOUR HANDS...OFF HER...
FRIEDA... SHE'S SO PRETTY...SAID SHE'LL CALL ME LATER...
DAT'S "BIZ MONEY B" WIT' A "B"...
...BUT FO' YOU, I'M A BUTT-KICKING "Z"...
...AND THE MONEY, SO MUCH MONEY.
WHAM
...AND IT'S ALL IN YO' FACE.
IF YOU MESS MY NAME UP AGAIN YOU'LL BE A CRYIN'-ASS DISGRACE!
PATHETIC. I'M PATHETIC.
I'M CRYING. LIKE A BABY.

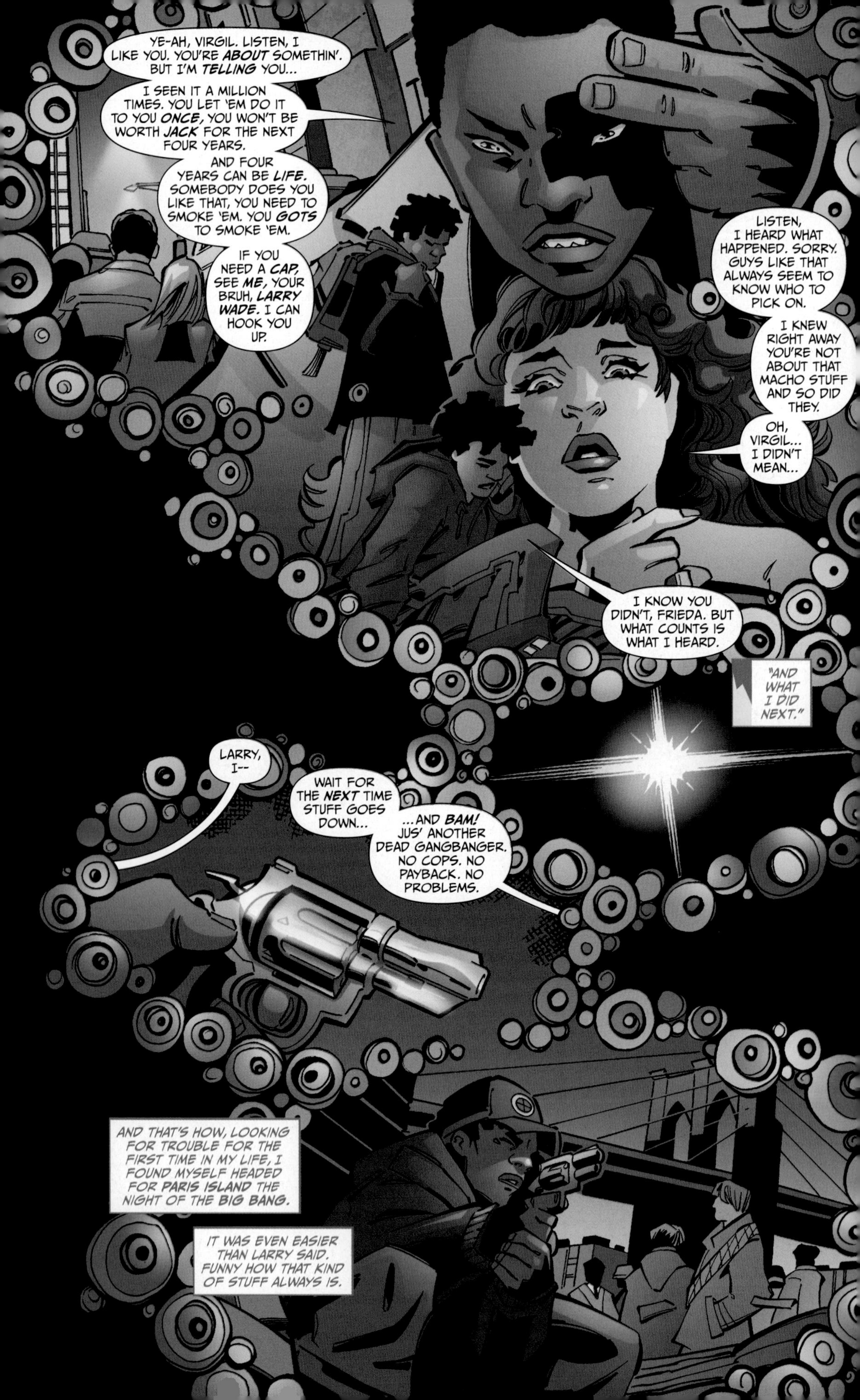

YE-AH, VIRGIL. LISTEN, I LIKE YOU. YOU'RE ABOUT SOMETHIN'. BUT I'M TELLING YOU...
I SEEN IT A MILLION TIMES. YOU LET 'EM DO IT TO YOU ONCE, YOU WON'T BE WORTH JACK FOR THE NEXT FOUR YEARS.
AND FOUR YEARS CAN BE LIFE. SOMEBODY DOES YOU LIKE THAT, YOU NEED TO SMOKE 'EM. YOU GOTS TO SMOKE 'EM.
IF YOU NEED A CAP, SEE ME, YOUR BRUH, LARRY WADE. I CAN HOOK YOU UP.
LISTEN, I HEARD WHAT HAPPENED. SORRY. GUYS LIKE THAT ALWAYS SEEM TO KNOW WHO TO PICK ON.
I KNEW RIGHT AWAY YOU'RE NOT ABOUT THAT MACHO STUFF AND SO DID THEY.
OH, VIRGIL... I DIDN'T MEAN...
I KNOW YOU DIDN'T, FRIEDA. BUT WHAT COUNTS IS WHAT I HEARD.
"AND WHAT I DID NEXT."
LARRY, I--
WAIT FOR THE NEXT TIME STUFF GOES DOWN...
...AND BAM! JUS' ANOTHER DEAD GANGBANGER. NO COPS. NO PAYBACK. NO PROBLEMS.
AND THAT'S HOW, LOOKING FOR TROUBLE FOR THE FIRST TIME IN MY LIFE, I FOUND MYSELF HEADED FOR PARIS ISLAND THE NIGHT OF THE BIG BANG.
IT WAS EVEN EASIER THAN LARRY SAID. FUNNY HOW THAT KIND OF STUFF ALWAYS IS.

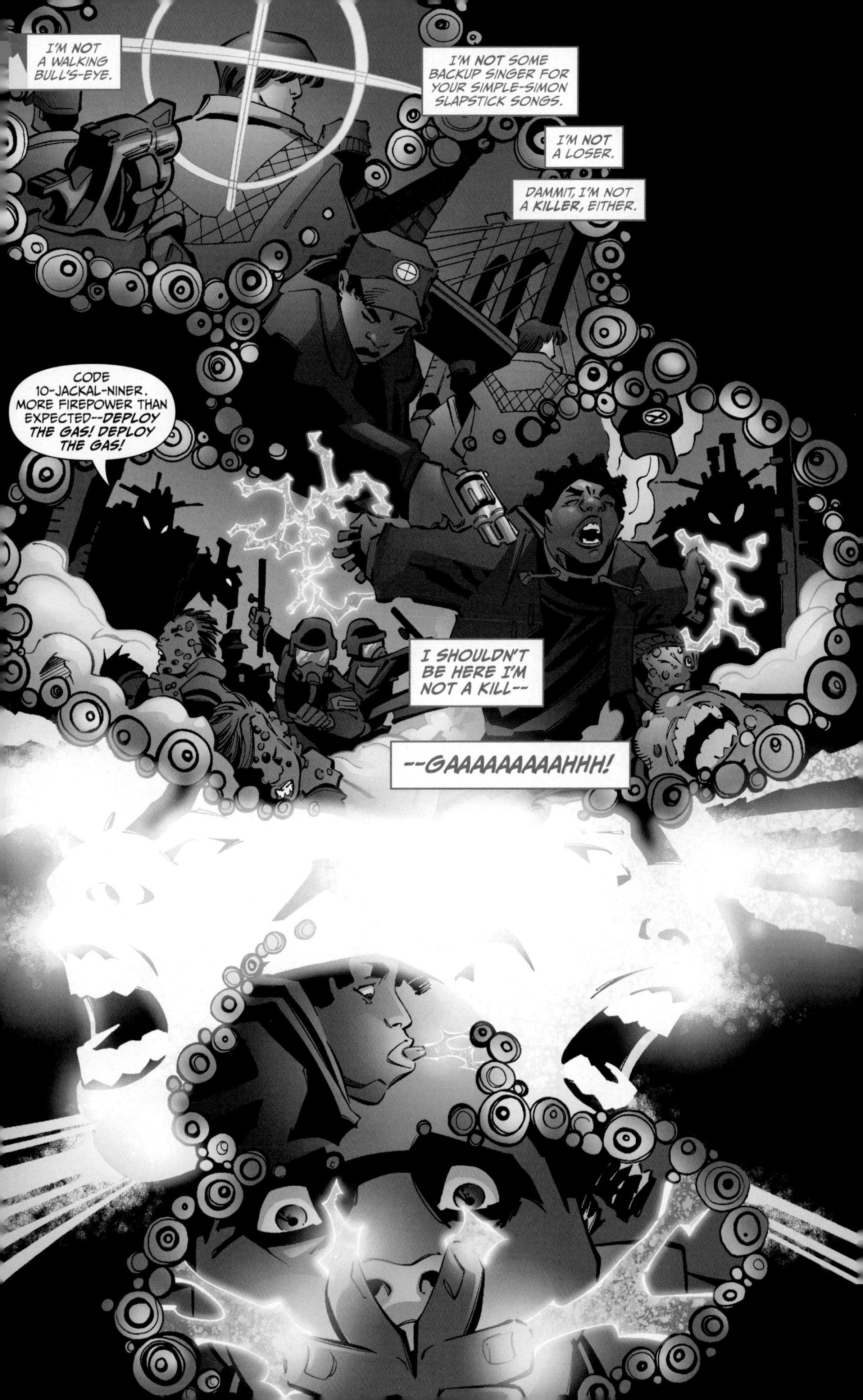
I'M NOT A WALKING BULL'S-EYE.
I'M NOT SOME BACKUP SINGER FOR YOUR SIMPLE-SIMON SLAPSTICK SONGS.
I'M NOT A LOSER.
DAMMIT, I'M NOT A KILLER, EITHER.
CODE 10-JACKAL-NINER. MORE FIREPOWER THAN EXPECTED--DEPLOY THE GAS! DEPLOY THE GAS!
I SHOULDN'T BE HERE I'M NOT A KILL--
--GAAAAAAAAAHHH!

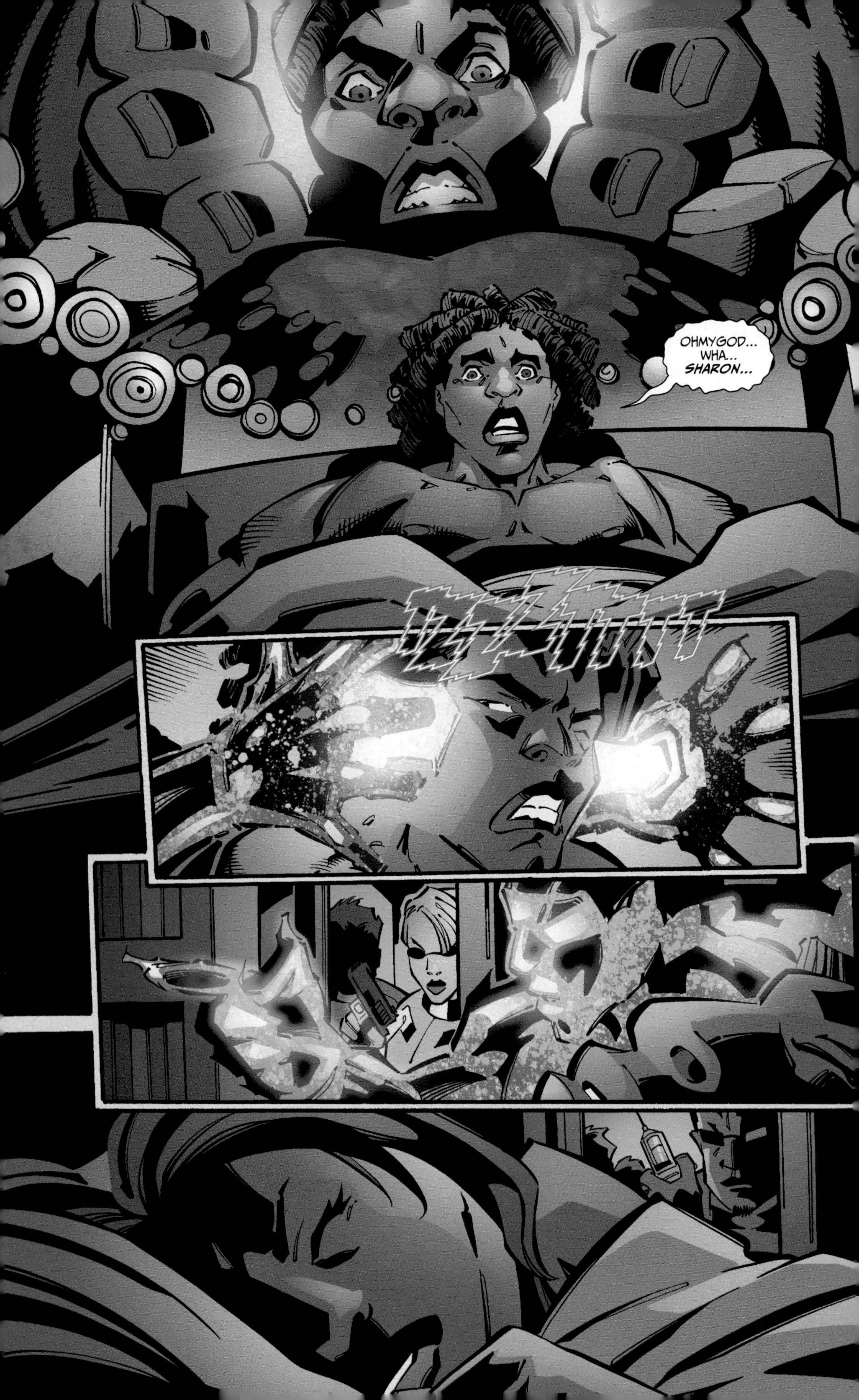
OHMYGOD... WHA... SHARON...

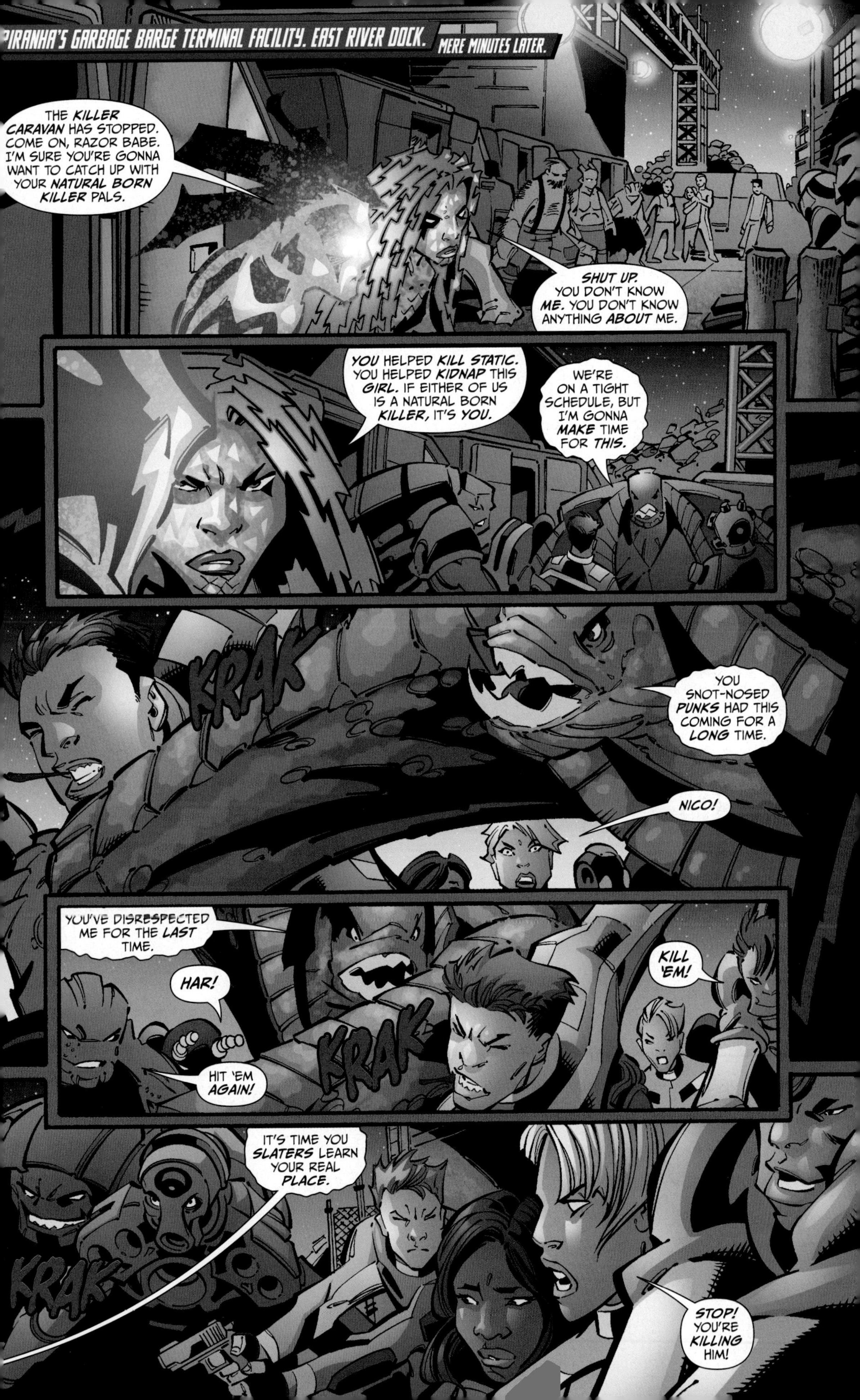
PIRANHA'S GARBAGE BARGE TERMINAL FACILITY. EAST RIVER DOCK.
MERE MINUTES LATER.
THE KILLER CARAVAN HAS STOPPED. COME ON, RAZOR BABE. I'M SURE YOU'RE GONNA WANT TO CATCH UP WITH YOUR NATURAL BORN KILLER PALS.
SHUT UP. YOU DON'T KNOW ME. YOU DON'T KNOW ANYTHING ABOUT ME.
YOU HELPED KILL STATIC. YOU HELPED KIDNAP THIS GIRL. IF EITHER OF US IS A NATURAL BORN KILLER, IT'S YOU.
WE'RE ON A TIGHT SCHEDULE, BUT I'M GONNA MAKE TIME FOR THIS.
KRAK
YOU SNOT-NOSED PUNKS HAD THIS COMING FOR A LONG TIME.
NICO!
YOU'VE DISRESPECTED ME FOR THE LAST TIME.
HAR!
KILL 'EM!
KRAK
HIT 'EM AGAIN!
IT'S TIME YOU SLATERS LEARN YOUR REAL PLACE.
KRAK
STOP! YOU'RE KILLING HIM!

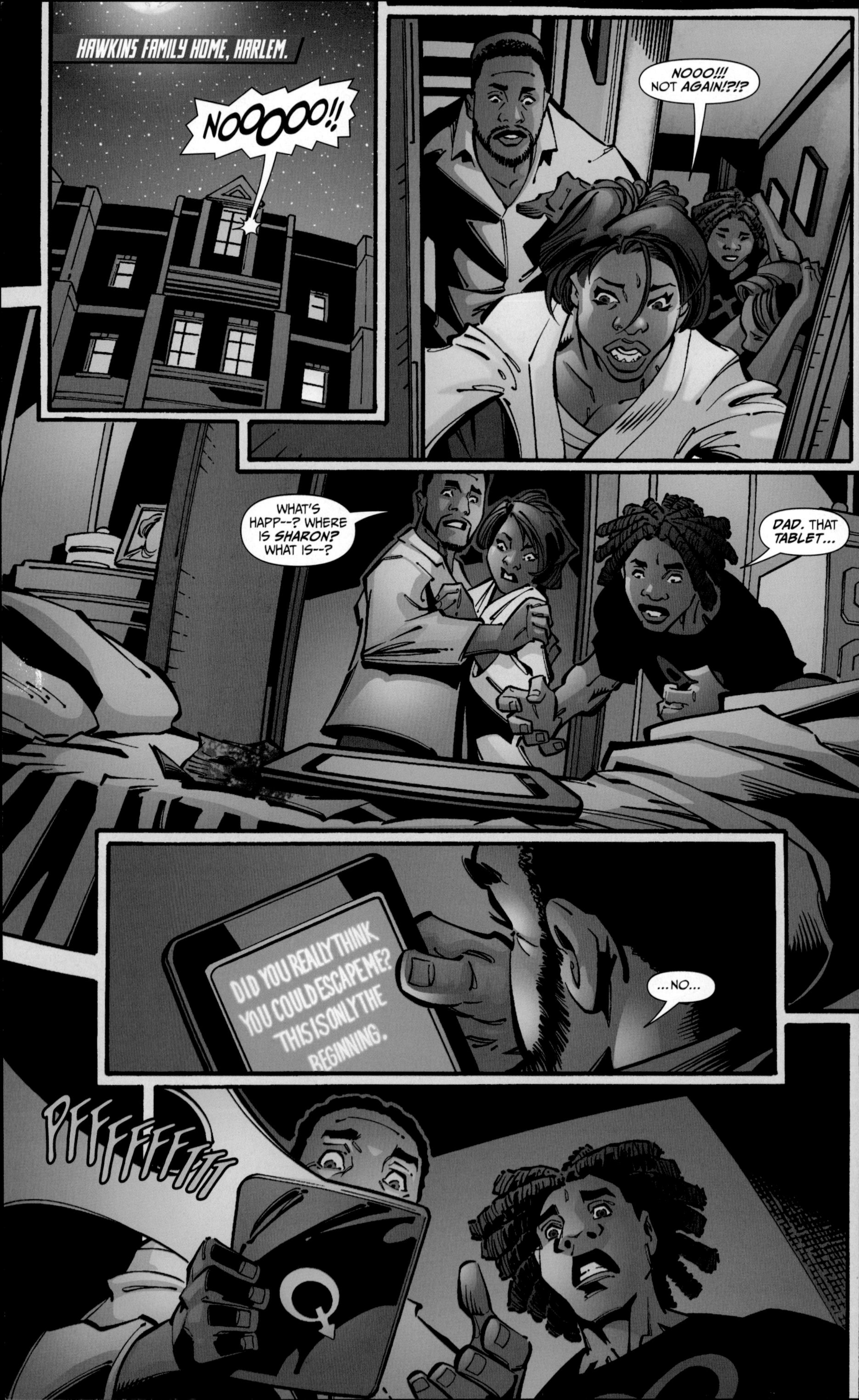
HAWKINS FAMILY HOME, HARLEM.
NOOOOO!!
NOOO!!! NOT AGAIN!?!?
WHAT'S HAPP--? WHERE IS SHARON? WHAT IS--?
DAD. THAT TABLET...
DID YOU REALLY THINK YOU COULD ESCAPE ME? THIS IS ONLY THE BEGINNING.
...NO...
PFFFFFFFTTT

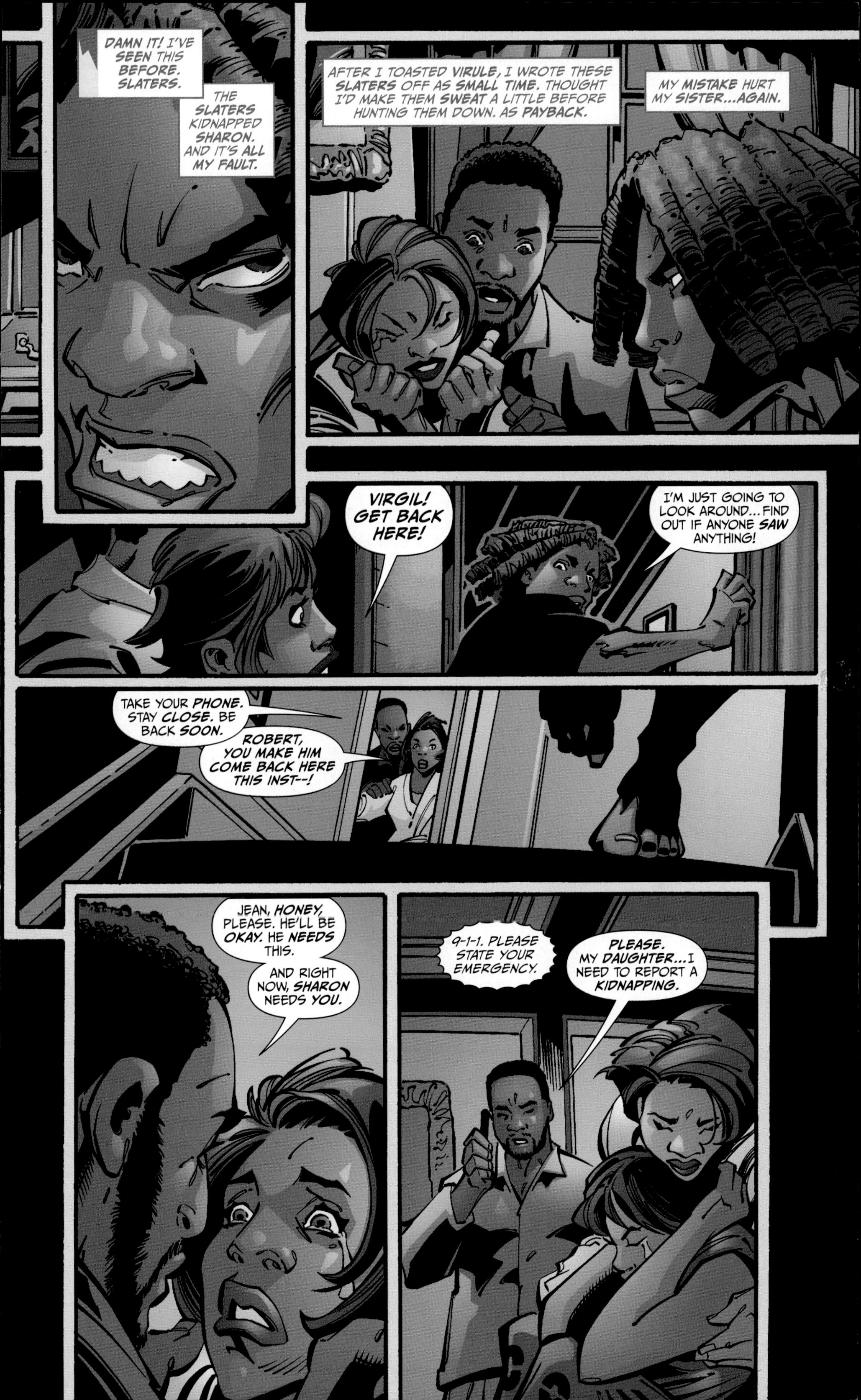
DAMN IT! I'VE SEEN THIS BEFORE. SLATERS.
THE SLATERS KIDNAPPED SHARON. AND IT'S ALL MY FAULT.
AFTER I TOASTED VIRULE, I WROTE THESE SLATERS OFF AS SMALL TIME. THOUGHT I'D MAKE THEM SWEAT A LITTLE BEFORE HUNTING THEM DOWN. AS PAYBACK.
MY MISTAKE HURT MY SISTER...AGAIN.
VIRGIL! GET BACK HERE!
I'M JUST GOING TO LOOK AROUND... FIND OUT IF ANYONE SAW ANYTHING!
TAKE YOUR PHONE. STAY CLOSE. BE BACK SOON.
ROBERT, YOU MAKE HIM COME BACK HERE THIS INST--!
JEAN, HONEY, PLEASE. HE'LL BE OKAY. HE NEEDS THIS.
AND RIGHT NOW, SHARON NEEDS YOU.
9-1-1. PLEASE STATE YOUR EMERGENCY.
PLEASE. MY DAUGHTER...I NEED TO REPORT A KIDNAPPING.

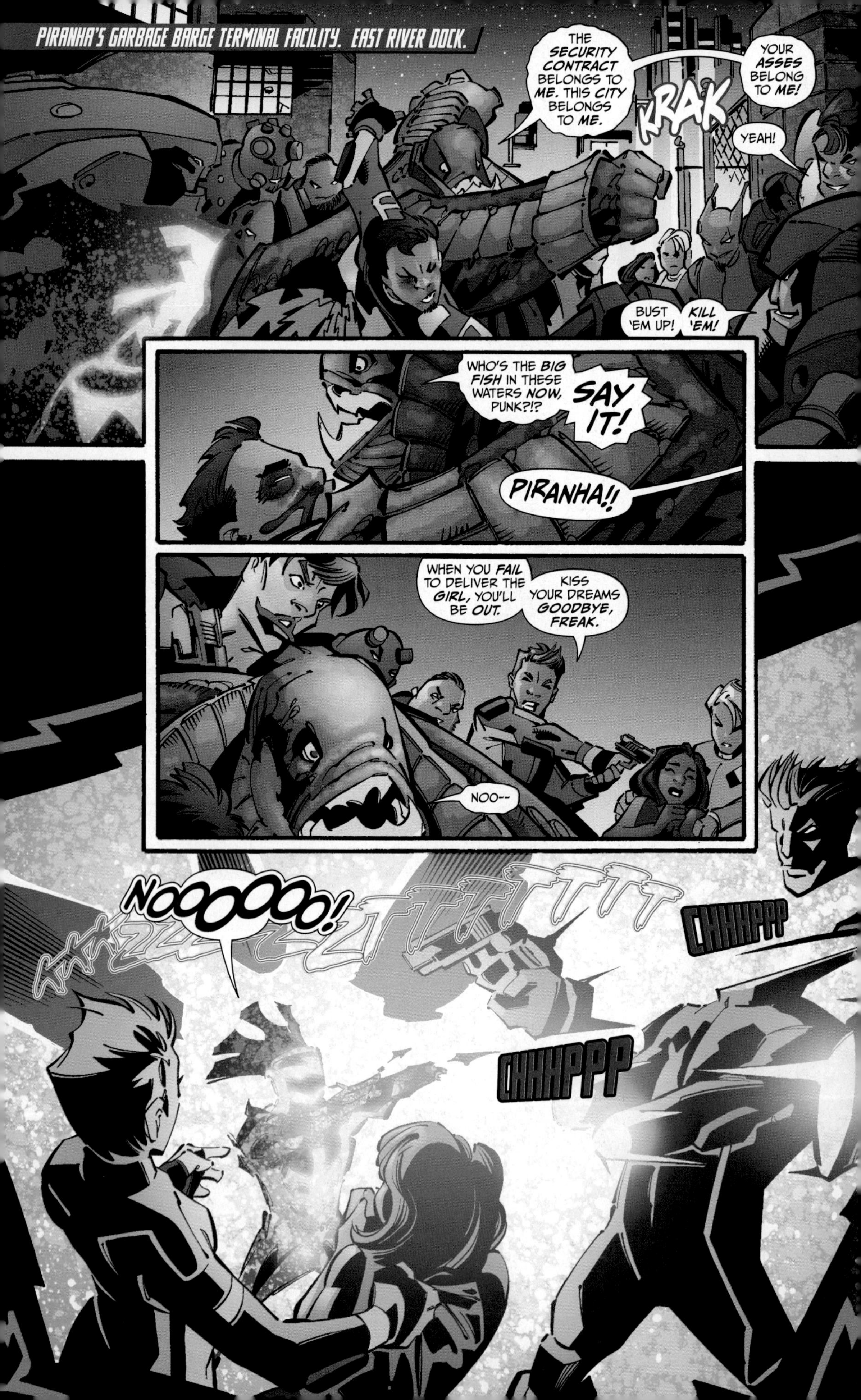
PIRANHA'S GARBAGE BARGE TERMINAL FACILITY. EAST RIVER DOCK.
THE SECURITY CONTRACT BELONGS TO ME. THIS CITY BELONGS TO ME.
KRAK
YOUR ASSES BELONG TO ME!
YEAH!
BUST 'EM UP!
KILL 'EM!
WHO'S THE BIG FISH IN THESE WATERS NOW, PUNK?!?
SAY IT!
PIRANHA!!
WHEN YOU FAIL TO DELIVER THE GIRL, YOU'LL BE OUT.
KISS YOUR DREAMS GOODBYE, FREAK.
NOO--
NOOOOOO!
CHHHPPP
CHHHPPP

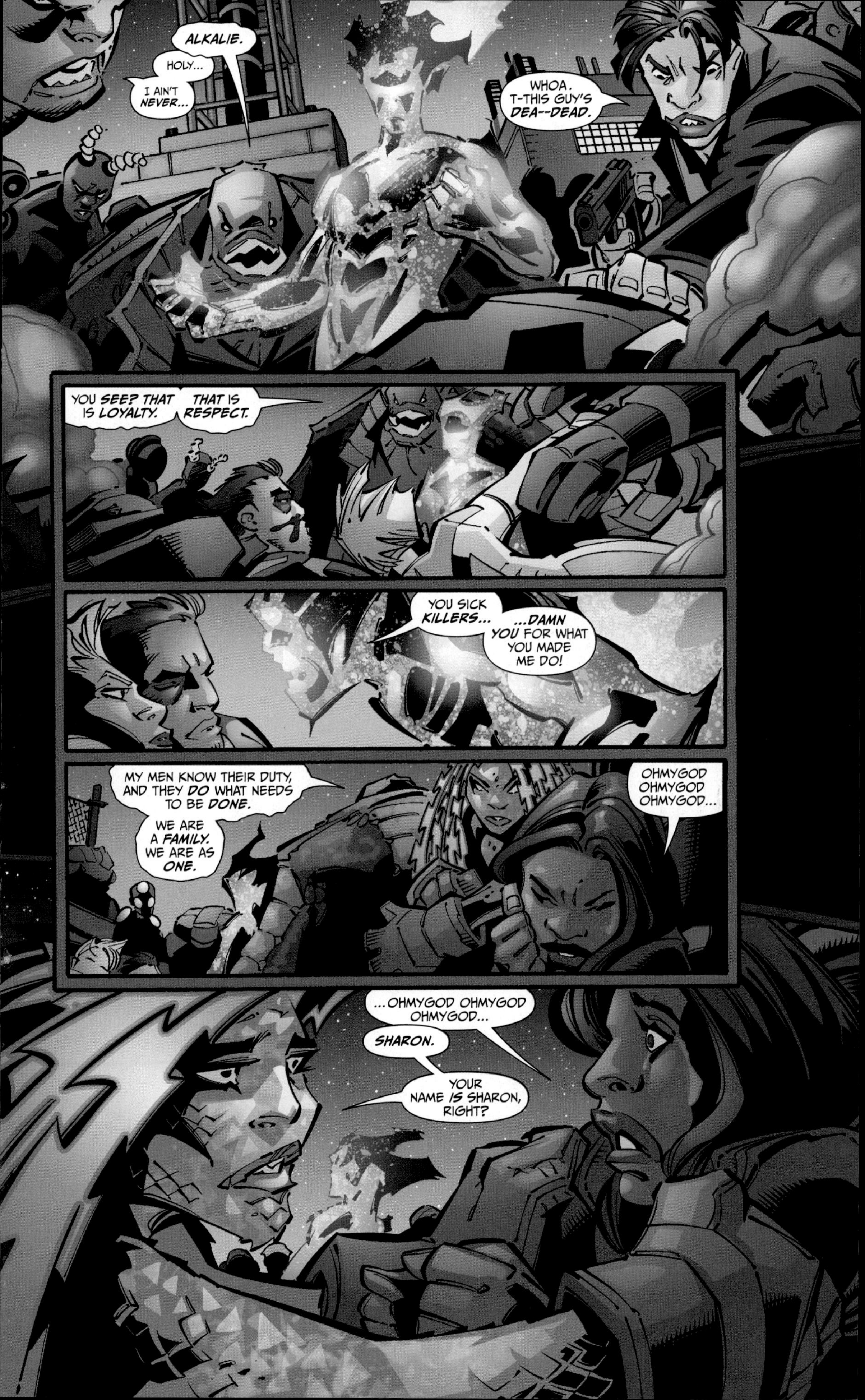
ALKALIE.
HOLY...
I AIN'T NEVER...
WHOA. T-THIS GUY'S DEA--DEAD.
YOU SEE? THAT IS LOYALTY.
THAT IS RESPECT.
YOU SICK KILLERS...
...DAMN YOU FOR WHAT YOU MADE ME DO!
MY MEN KNOW THEIR DUTY, AND THEY DO WHAT NEEDS TO BE DONE.
WE ARE A FAMILY. WE ARE AS ONE.
OHMYGOD OHMYGOD OHMYGOD...
...OHMYGOD OHMYGOD OHMYGOD...
SHARON.
YOUR NAME IS SHARON, RIGHT?

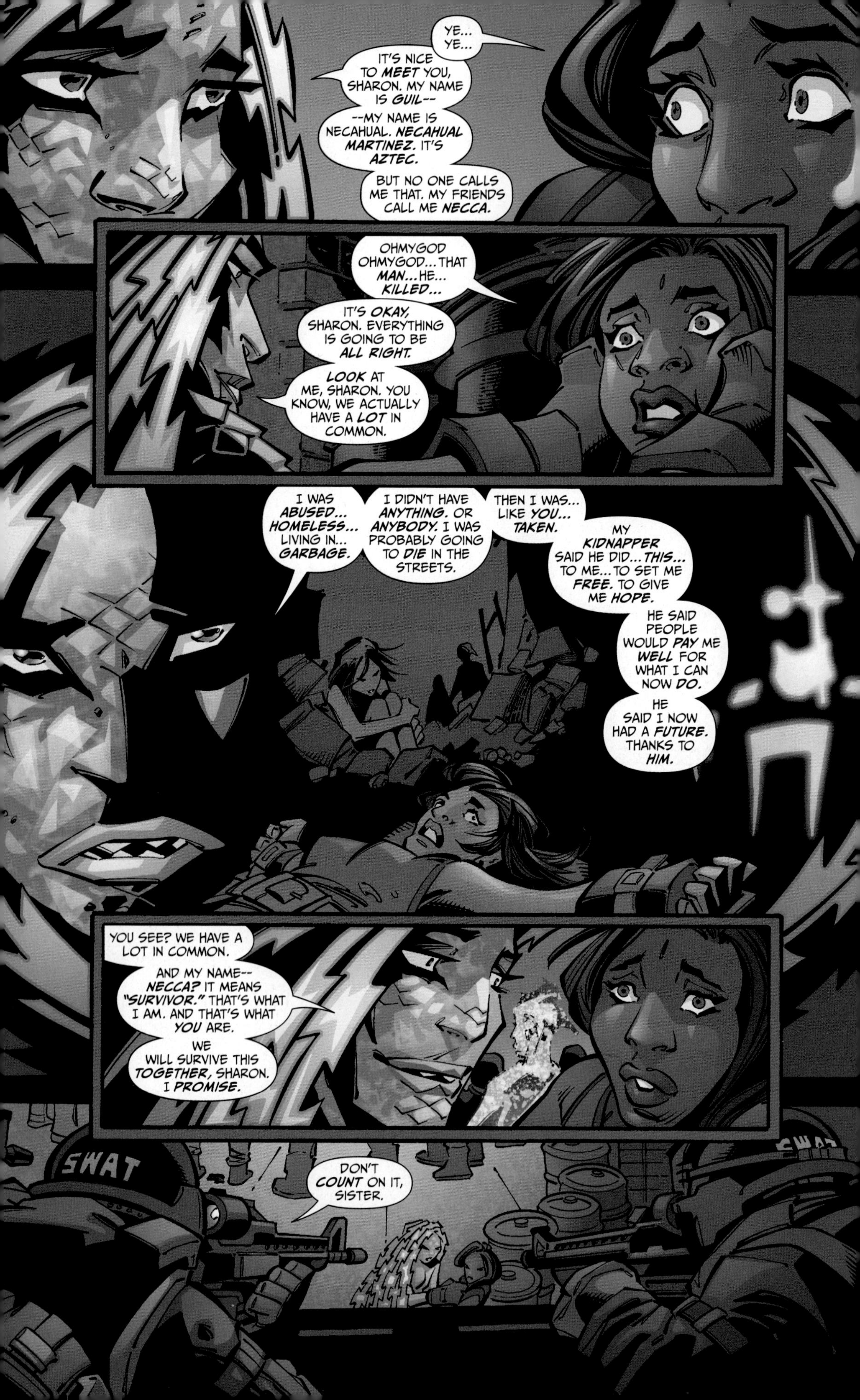

YE... YE...
IT'S NICE TO MEET YOU, SHARON. MY NAME IS GUIL--
--MY NAME IS NECAHUAL. NECAHUAL MARTINEZ. IT'S AZTEC.
BUT NO ONE CALLS ME THAT. MY FRIENDS CALL ME NECCA.
OHMYGOD OHMYGOD...THAT MAN...HE... KILLED...
IT'S OKAY, SHARON. EVERYTHING IS GOING TO BE ALL RIGHT.
LOOK AT ME, SHARON. YOU KNOW, WE ACTUALLY HAVE A LOT IN COMMON.
I WAS ABUSED... HOMELESS... LIVING IN... GARBAGE.
I DIDN'T HAVE ANYTHING. OR ANYBODY. I WAS PROBABLY GOING TO DIE IN THE STREETS.
THEN I WAS... LIKE YOU... TAKEN.
MY KIDNAPPER SAID HE DID...THIS... TO ME...TO SET ME FREE. TO GIVE ME HOPE.
HE SAID PEOPLE WOULD PAY ME WELL FOR WHAT I CAN NOW DO.
HE SAID I NOW HAD A FUTURE. THANKS TO HIM.
YOU SEE? WE HAVE A LOT IN COMMON.
AND MY NAME-- NECCA? IT MEANS "SURVIVOR." THAT'S WHAT I AM. AND THAT'S WHAT YOU ARE.
WE WILL SURVIVE THIS TOGETHER, SHARON. I PROMISE.
SWAT
SWAT
DON'T COUNT ON IT, SISTER.

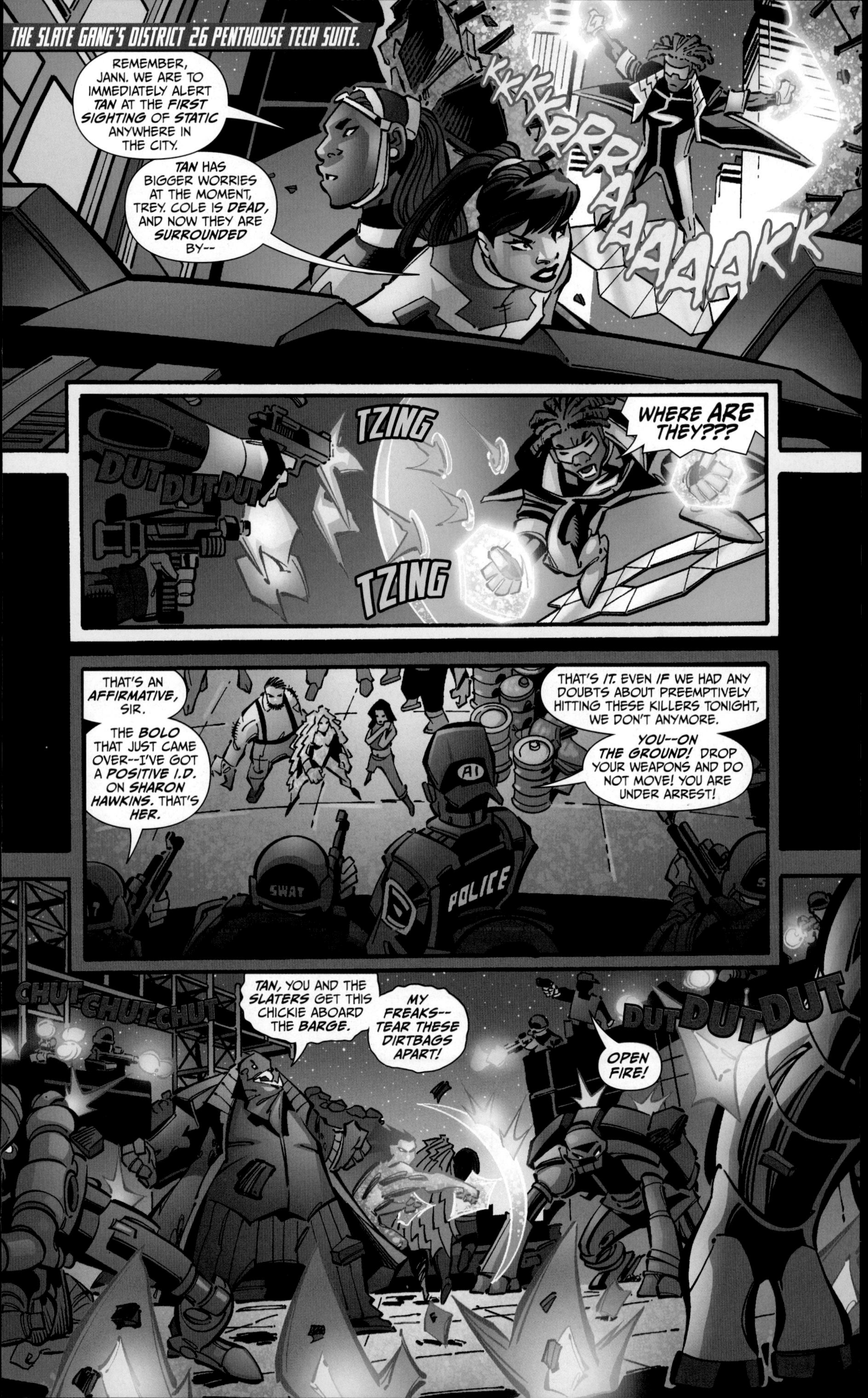
THE SLATE GANG'S DISTRICT 26 PENTHOUSE TECH SUITE.
REMEMBER, JANN. WE ARE TO IMMEDIATELY ALERT TAN AT THE FIRST SIGHTING OF STATIC ANYWHERE IN THE CITY.
TAN HAS BIGGER WORRIES AT THE MOMENT, TREY. COLE IS DEAD, AND NOW THEY ARE SURROUNDED BY--
KKKKRRRAAAAAKK
DUT DUT DUT
TZING
WHERE ARE THEY???
TZING
THAT'S AN AFFIRMATIVE, SIR.
THE BOLO THAT JUST CAME OVER--I'VE GOT A POSITIVE I.D. ON SHARON HAWKINS. THAT'S HER.
THAT'S IT. EVEN IF WE HAD ANY DOUBTS ABOUT PREEMPTIVELY HITTING THESE KILLERS TONIGHT, WE DON'T ANYMORE.
YOU--ON THE GROUND! DROP YOUR WEAPONS AND DO NOT MOVE! YOU ARE UNDER ARREST!
A1
SWAT
POLICE
CHUT CHUT CHUT
TAN, YOU AND THE SLATERS GET THIS CHICKIE ABOARD THE BARGE.
MY FREAKS-- TEAR THESE DIRTBAGS APART!
DUT DUT DUT
OPEN FIRE!

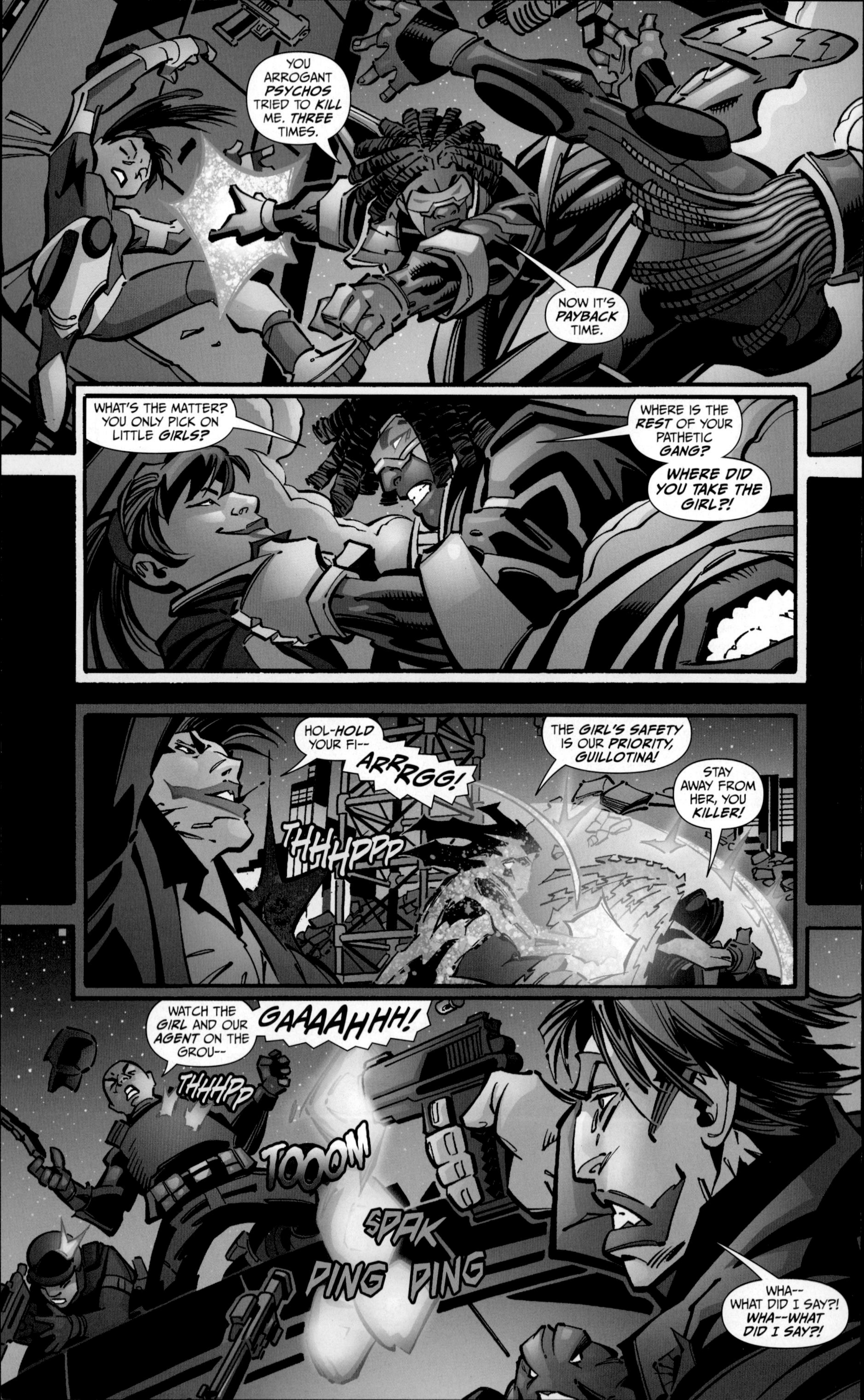
YOU ARROGANT PSYCHOS TRIED TO KILL ME. THREE TIMES.
NOW IT'S PAYBACK TIME.
WHAT'S THE MATTER? YOU ONLY PICK ON LITTLE GIRLS?
WHERE IS THE REST OF YOUR PATHETIC GANG?
WHERE DID YOU TAKE THE GIRL?!
HOL-HOLD YOUR FI-- ARRRGG!
THHHPPP
THE GIRL'S SAFETY IS OUR PRIORITY, GUILLOTINA!
STAY AWAY FROM HER, YOU KILLER!
WATCH THE GIRL AND OUR AGENT ON THE GROU--
GAAAAHHH!
THHHPP
TOOOM
SPAK
PING PING
WHA-- WHAT DID I SAY?! WHA--WHAT DID I SAY?!

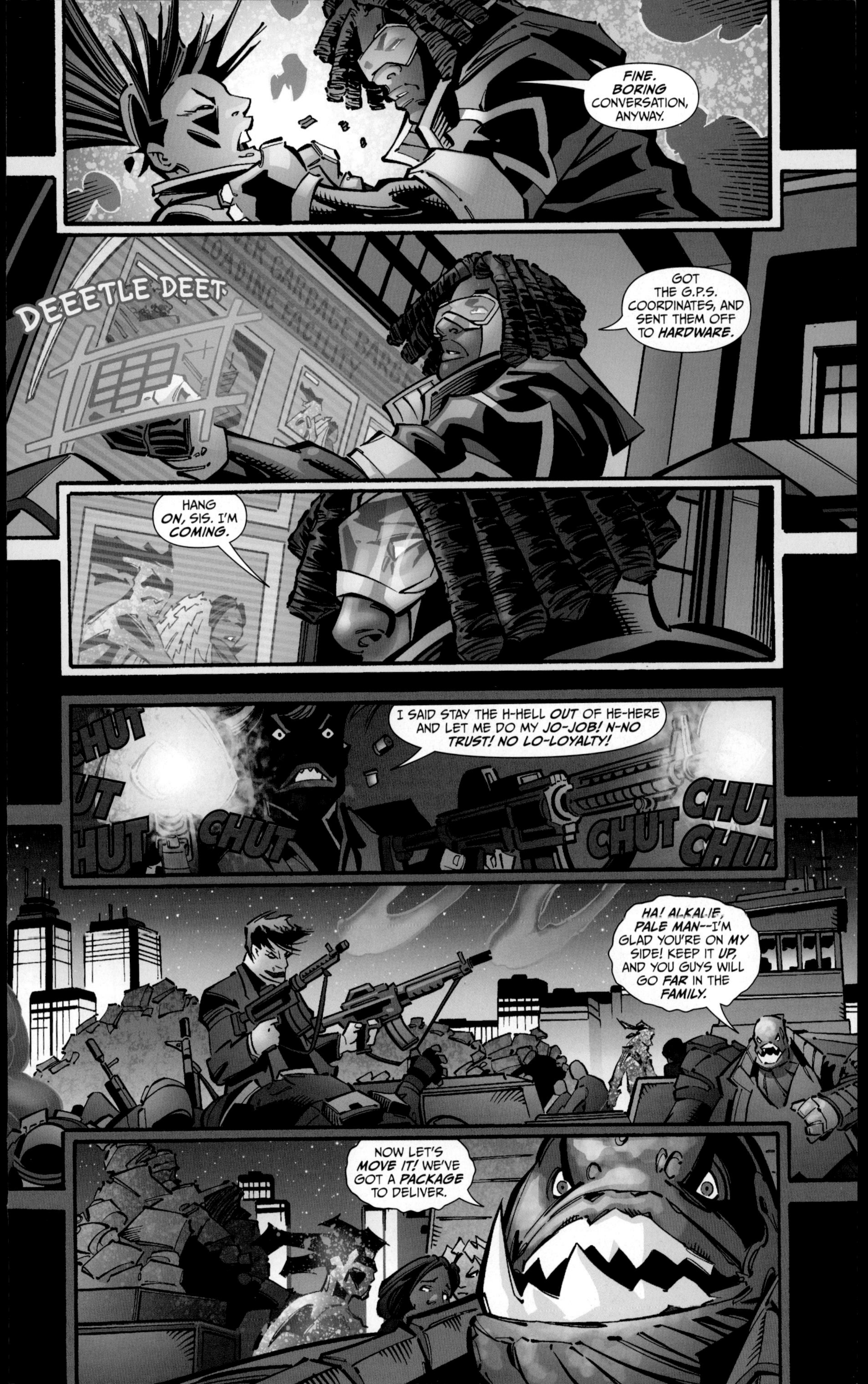
FINE. BORING CONVERSATION, ANYWAY.
DEEETLE DEET
GOT THE G.P.S. COORDINATES, AND SENT THEM OFF TO HARDWARE.
HANG ON, SIS. I'M COMING.
I SAID STAY THE H-HELL OUT OF HE-HERE AND LET ME DO MY JO-JOB! N-NO TRUST! NO LO-LOYALTY!
CHUT CHUT CHUT CHUT CHUT CHUT
HA! ALKALIE, PALE MAN--I'M GLAD YOU'RE ON MY SIDE! KEEP IT UP, AND YOU GUYS WILL GO FAR IN THE FAMILY.
NOW LET'S MOVE IT! WE'VE GOT A PACKAGE TO DELIVER.

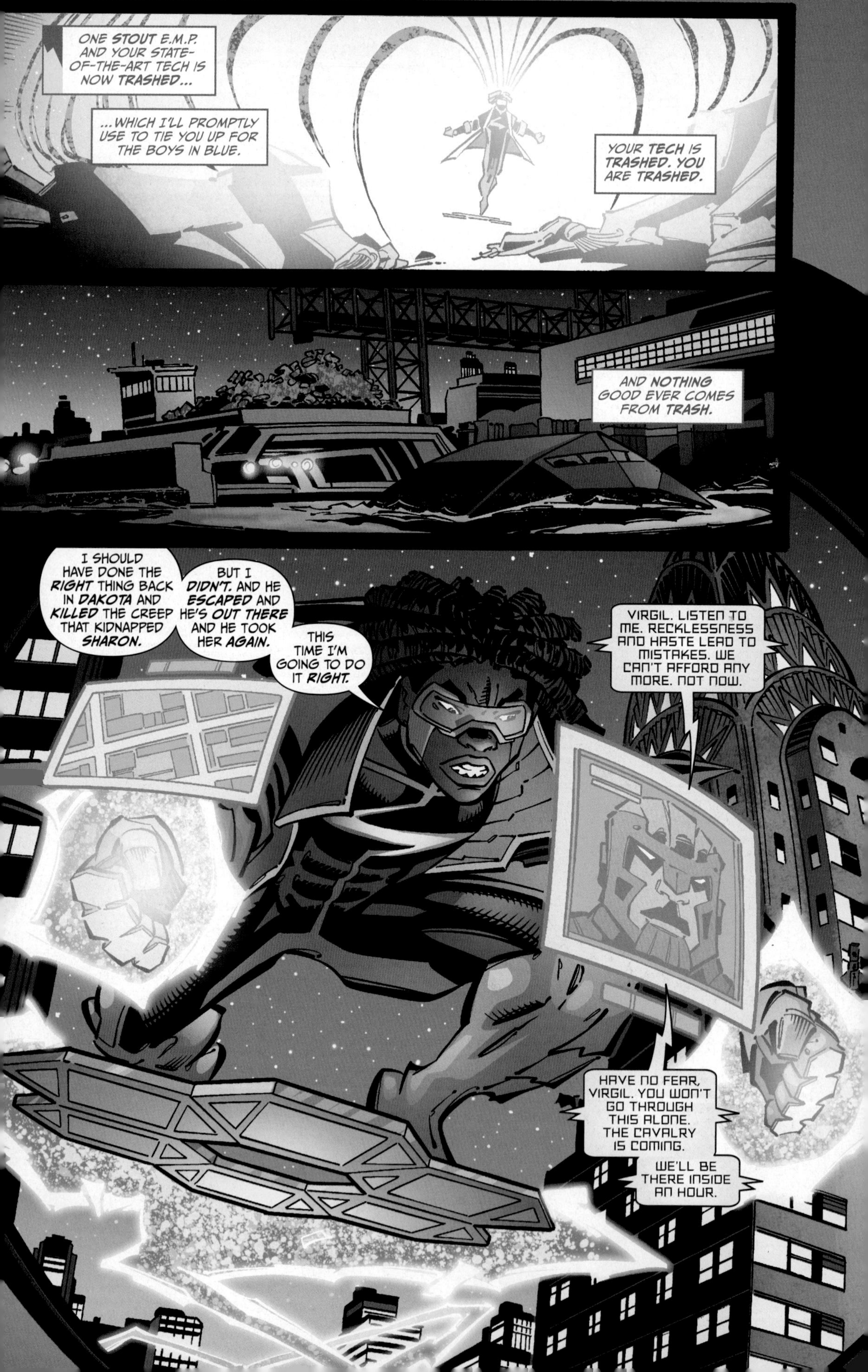
ONE STOUT E.M.P. AND YOUR STATE-OF-THE-ART TECH IS NOW TRASHED...
...WHICH I'LL PROMPTLY USE TO TIE YOU UP FOR THE BOYS IN BLUE.
YOUR TECH IS TRASHED. YOU ARE TRASHED.
AND NOTHING GOOD EVER COMES FROM TRASH.
I SHOULD HAVE DONE THE RIGHT THING BACK IN DAKOTA AND KILLED THE CREEP THAT KIDNAPPED SHARON.
BUT I DIDN'T. AND HE ESCAPED AND HE'S OUT THERE AND HE TOOK HER AGAIN.
THIS TIME I'M GOING TO DO IT RIGHT.
VIRGIL. LISTEN TO ME. RECKLESSNESS AND HASTE LEAD TO MISTAKES. WE CAN'T AFFORD ANY MORE. NOT NOW.
HAVE NO FEAR, VIRGIL. YOU WON'T GO THROUGH THIS ALONE. THE CAVALRY IS COMING.
WE'LL BE THERE INSIDE AN HOUR.

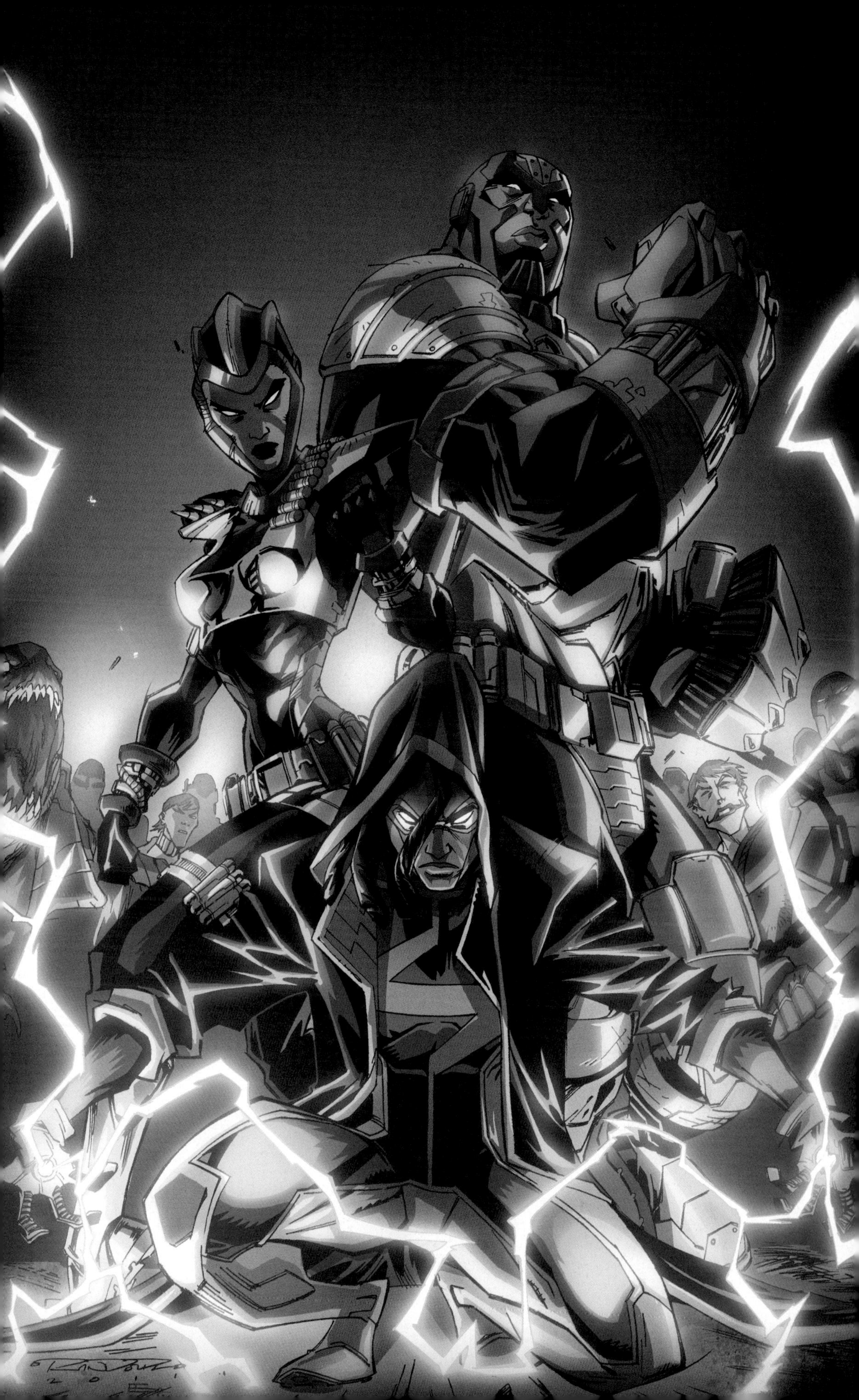

cover art by
KHARY RANDOLPH, LE BEAU UNDERWOOD
& EMILIO LOPEZ

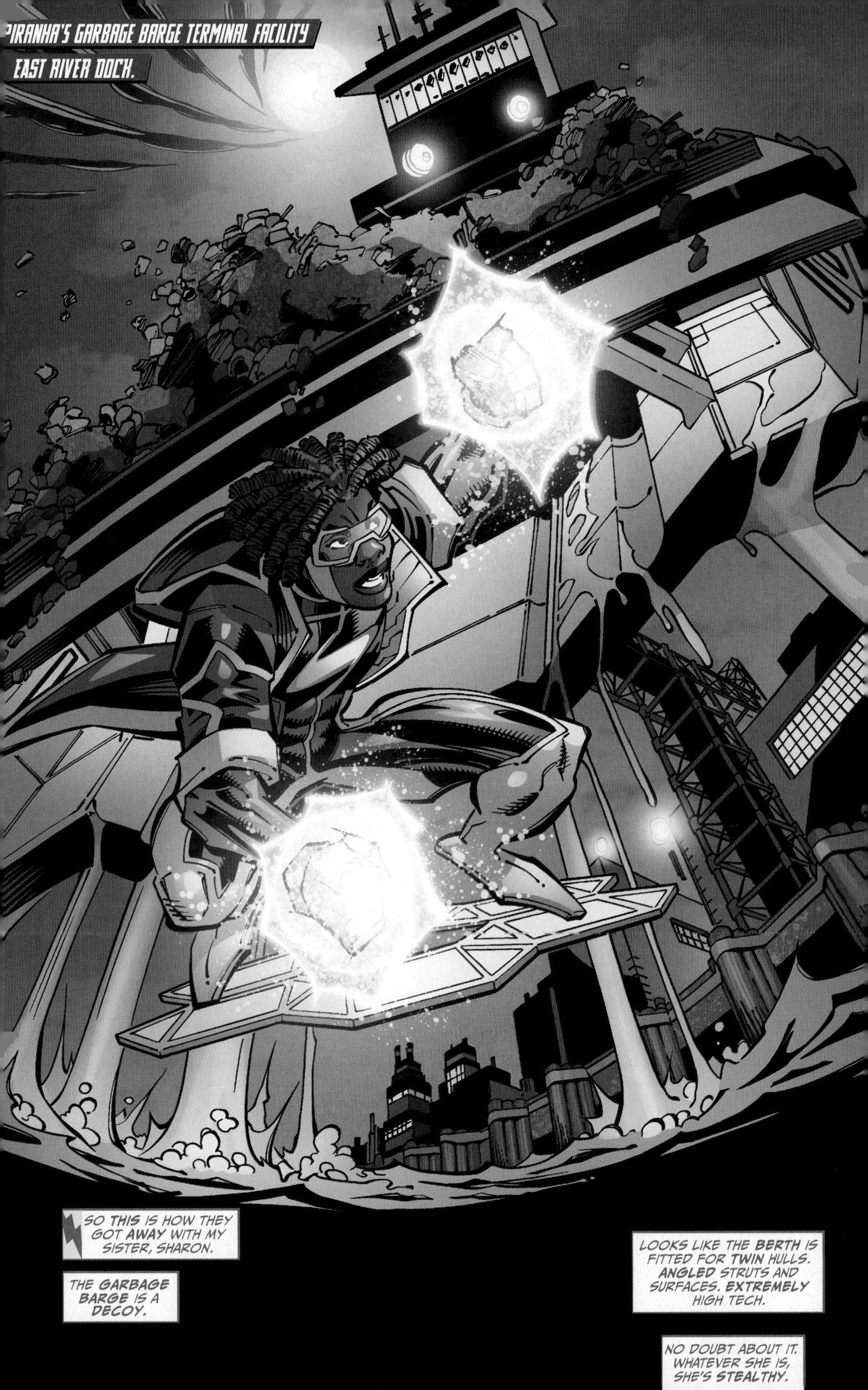
PIRANHA'S GARBAGE BARGE TERMINAL FACILITY
EAST RIVER DOCK.
SO THIS IS HOW THEY GOT AWAY WITH MY SISTER, SHARON.
THE GARBAGE BARGE IS A DECOY.
LOOKS LIKE THE BERTH IS FITTED FOR TWIN HULLS. ANGLED STRUTS AND SURFACES. EXTREMELY HIGH TECH.
NO DOUBT ABOUT IT. WHATEVER SHE IS, SHE'S STEALTHY.

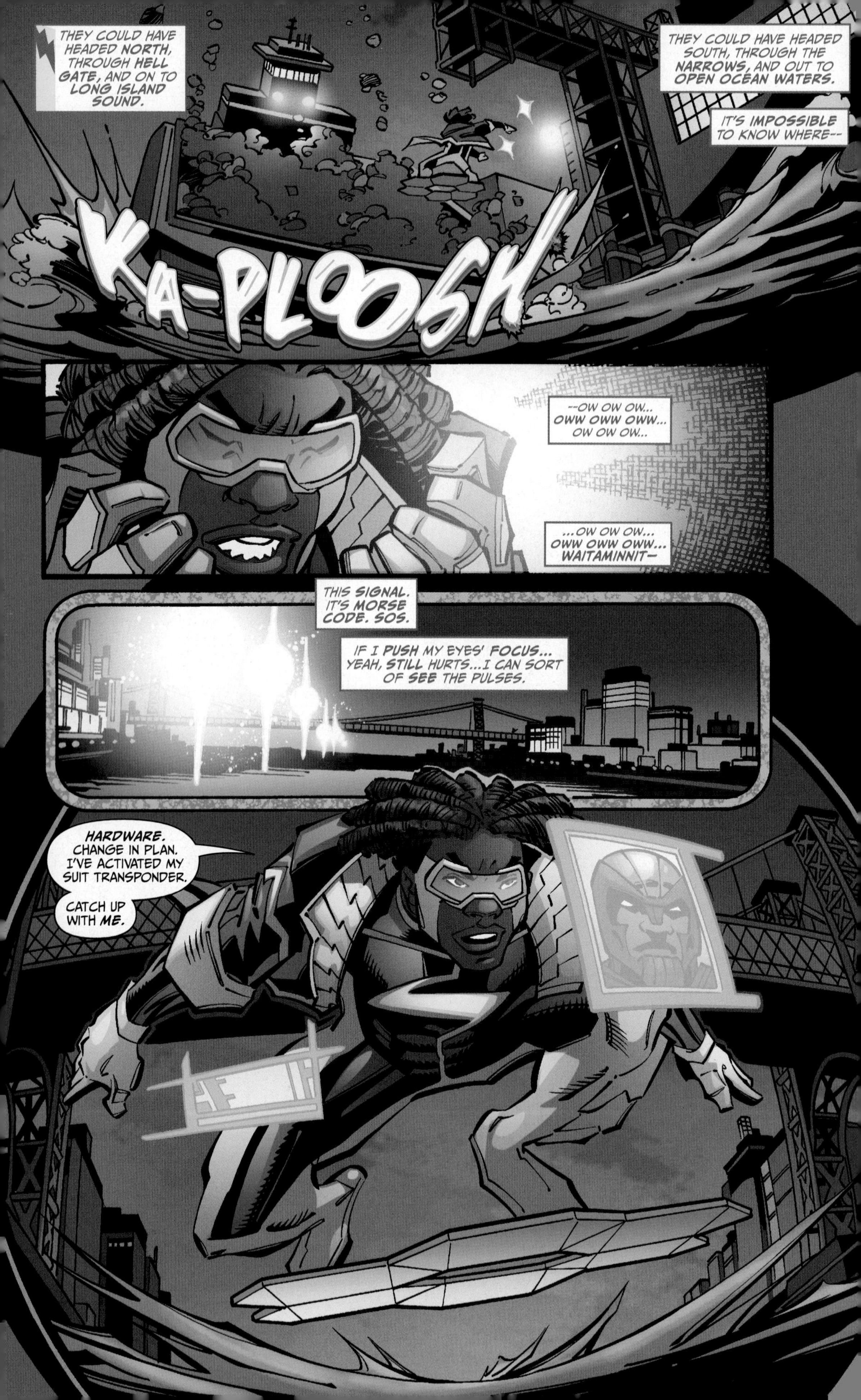

THEY COULD HAVE HEADED NORTH, THROUGH HELL GATE, AND ON TO LONG ISLAND SOUND.
THEY COULD HAVE HEADED SOUTH, THROUGH THE NARROWS, AND OUT TO OPEN OCEAN WATERS.
IT'S IMPOSSIBLE TO KNOW WHERE--
KA-PLOOSH
--OW OW OW... OWW OWW OWW... OW OW OW...
...OW OW OW... OWW OWW OWW... WAITAMINNIT—
THIS SIGNAL. IT'S MORSE CODE. SOS.
IF I PUSH MY EYES' FOCUS... YEAH, STILL HURTS...I CAN SORT OF SEE THE PULSES.
HARDWARE. CHANGE IN PLAN. I'VE ACTIVATED MY SUIT TRANSPONDER.
CATCH UP WITH ME.

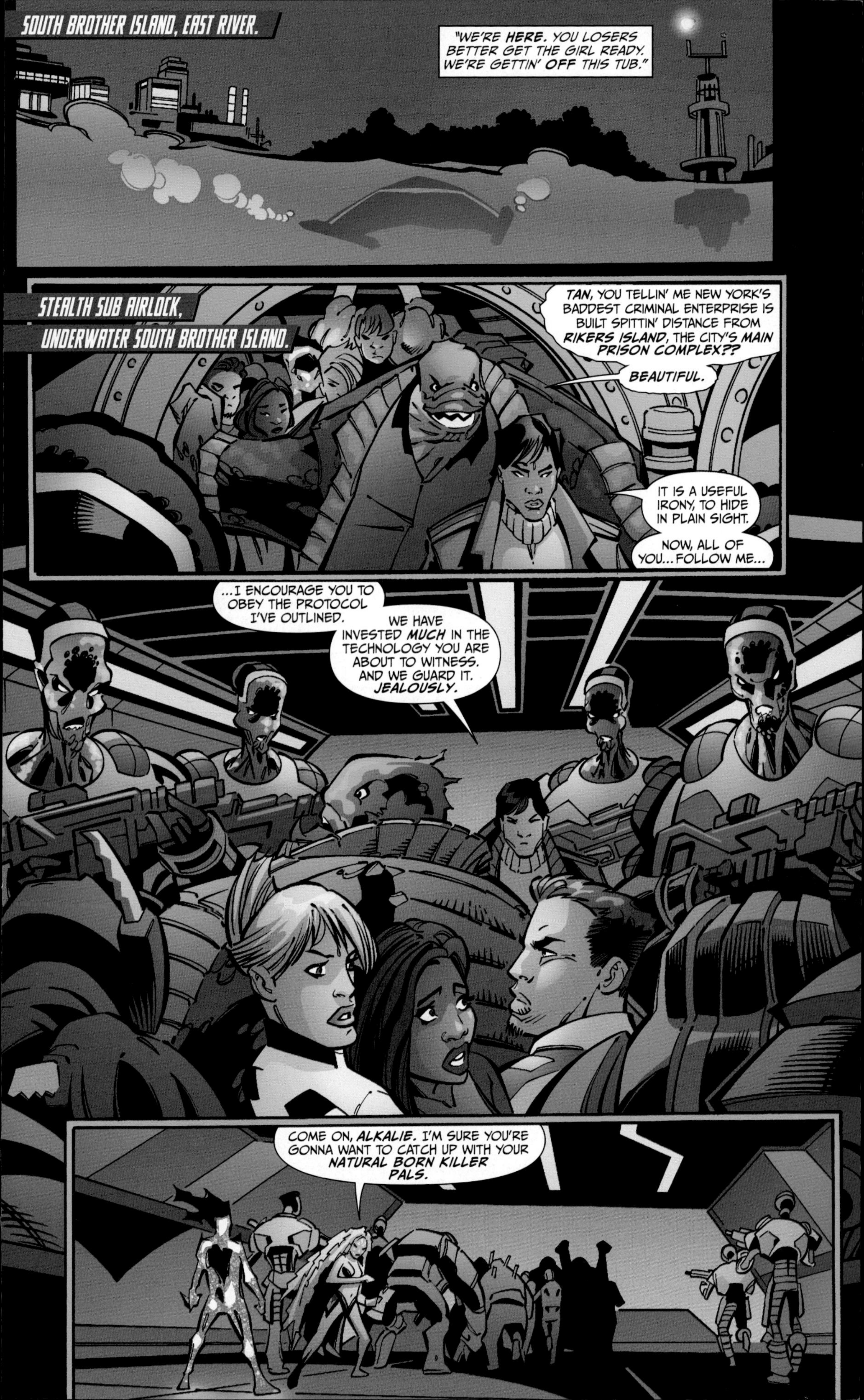
SOUTH BROTHER ISLAND, EAST RIVER.
"WE'RE HERE. YOU LOSERS BETTER GET THE GIRL READY. WE'RE GETTIN' OFF THIS TUB."
STEALTH SUB AIRLOCK, UNDERWATER SOUTH BROTHER ISLAND.
TAN, YOU TELLIN' ME NEW YORK'S BADDEST CRIMINAL ENTERPRISE IS BUILT SPITTIN' DISTANCE FROM RIKERS ISLAND, THE CITY'S MAIN PRISON COMPLEX??
BEAUTIFUL.
IT IS A USEFUL IRONY, TO HIDE IN PLAIN SIGHT.
NOW, ALL OF YOU... FOLLOW ME...
...I ENCOURAGE YOU TO OBEY THE PROTOCOL I'VE OUTLINED.
WE HAVE INVESTED MUCH IN THE TECHNOLOGY YOU ARE ABOUT TO WITNESS. AND WE GUARD IT. JEALOUSLY.
COME ON, ALKALIE. I'M SURE YOU'RE GONNA WANT TO CATCH UP WITH YOUR NATURAL BORN KILLER PALS.

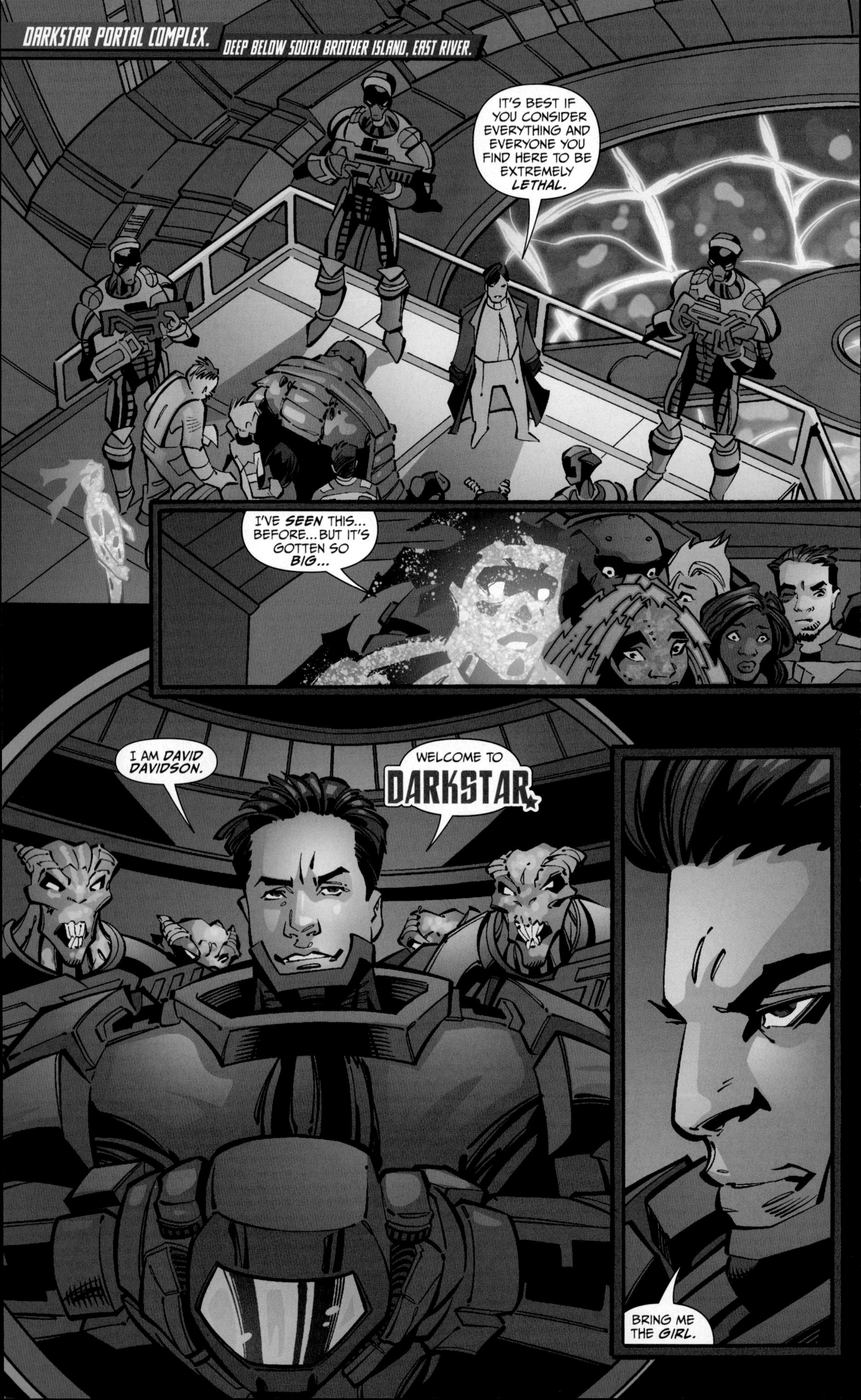
DARKSTAR PORTAL COMPLEX.
DEEP BELOW SOUTH BROTHER ISLAND, EAST RIVER.
IT'S BEST IF YOU CONSIDER EVERYTHING AND EVERYONE YOU FIND HERE TO BE EXTREMELY LETHAL.
I'VE SEEN THIS... BEFORE...BUT IT'S GOTTEN SO BIG...
I AM DAVID DAVIDSON.
WELCOME TO DARKSTAR
BRING ME THE GIRL.

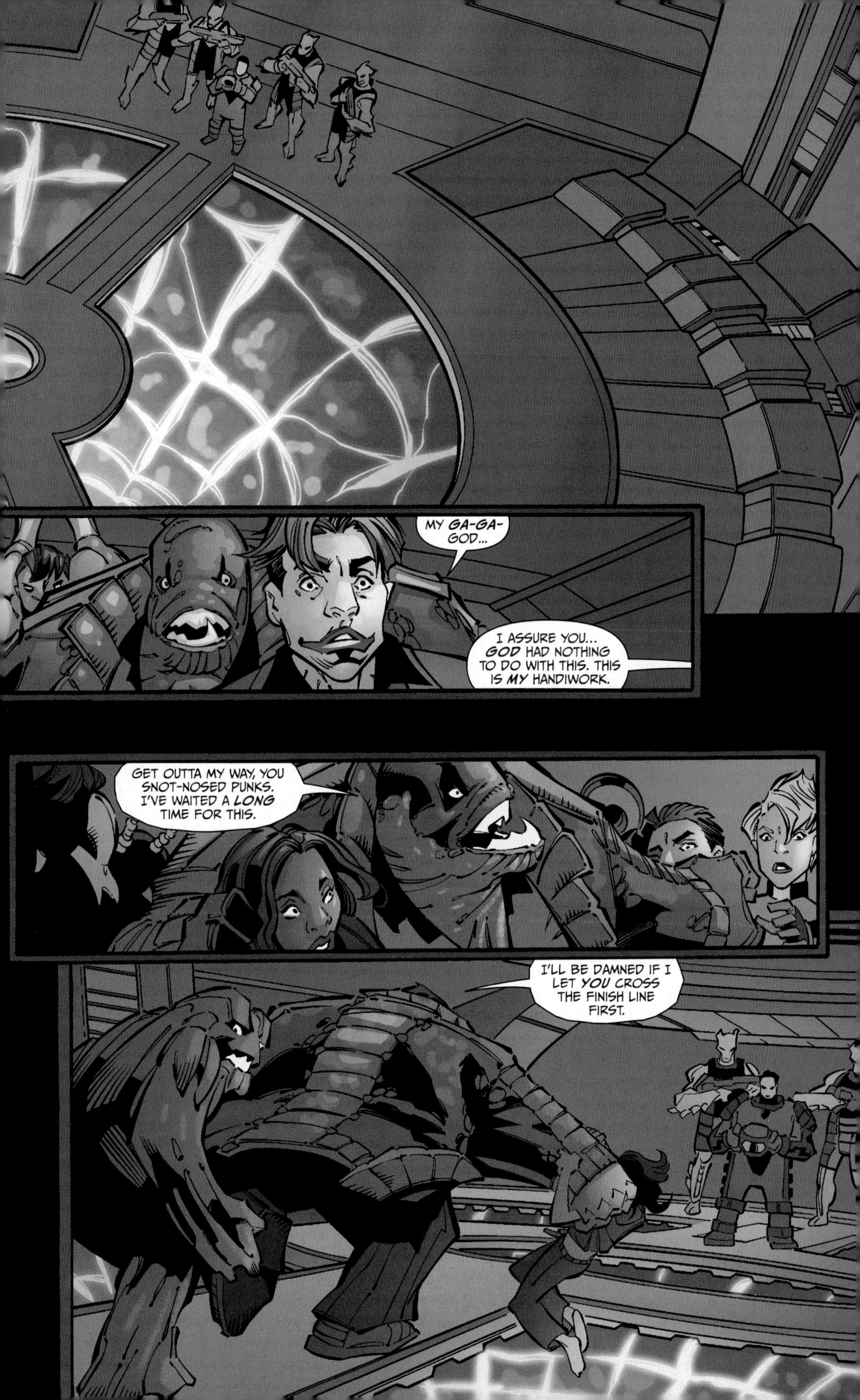
MY GA-GA-GOD...
I ASSURE YOU... GOD HAD NOTHING TO DO WITH THIS. THIS IS MY HANDIWORK.
GET OUTTA MY WAY, YOU SNOT-NOSED PUNKS. I'VE WAITED A LONG TIME FOR THIS.
I'LL BE DAMNED IF I LET YOU CROSS THE FINISH LINE FIRST.

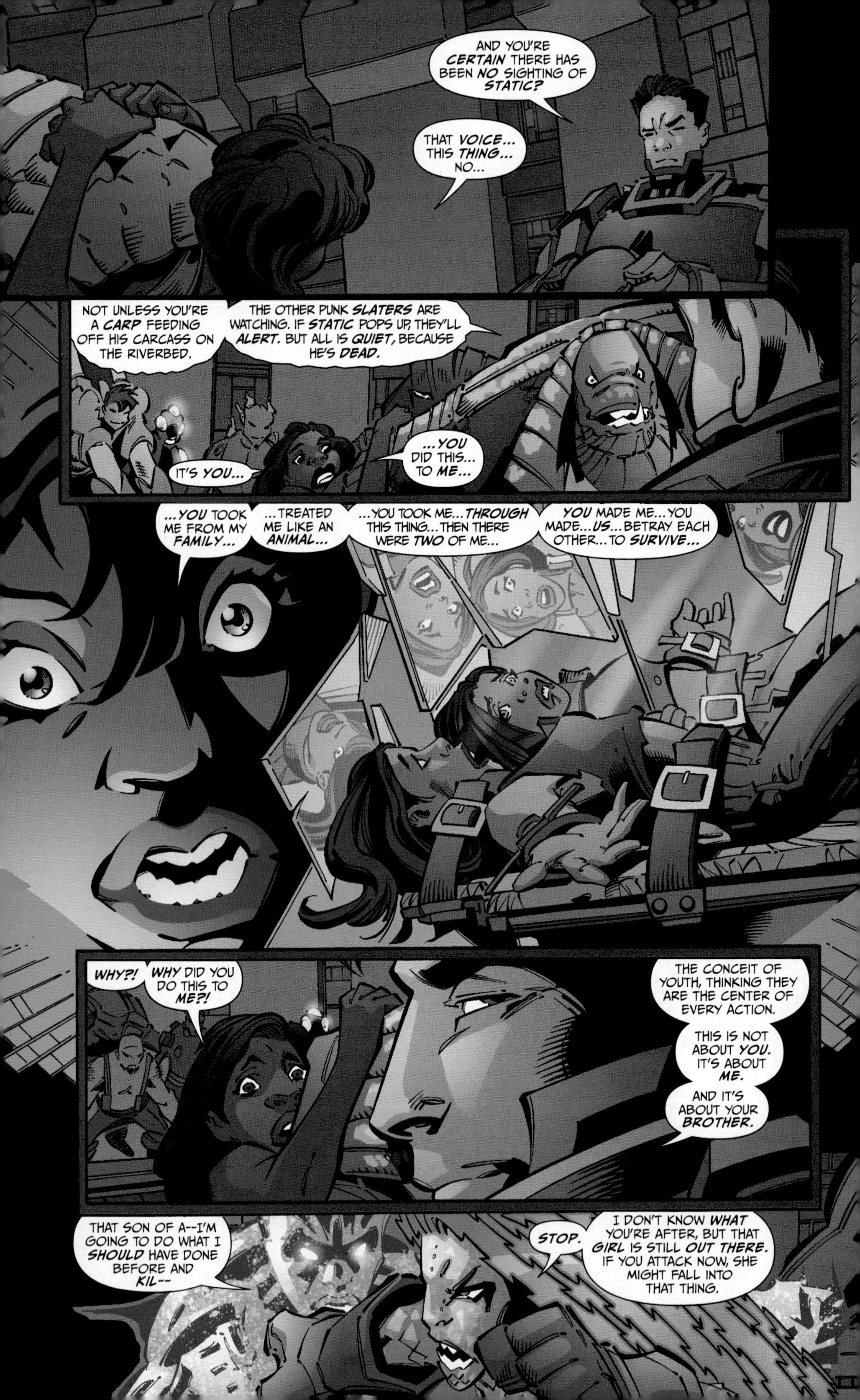
AND YOU'RE CERTAIN THERE HAS BEEN NO SIGHTING OF STATIC?
THAT VOICE... THIS THING... NO...
NOT UNLESS YOU'RE A CARP FEEDING OFF HIS CARCASS ON THE RIVERBED.
THE OTHER PUNK SLATERS ARE WATCHING. IF STATIC POPS UP, THEY'LL ALERT. BUT ALL IS QUIET, BECAUSE HE'S DEAD.
IT'S YOU...
...YOU DID THIS... TO ME...
...YOU TOOK ME FROM MY FAMILY...
...TREATED ME LIKE AN ANIMAL...
...YOU TOOK ME...THROUGH THIS THING...THEN THERE WERE TWO OF ME...
YOU MADE ME...YOU MADE...US...BETRAY EACH OTHER...TO SURVIVE...
WHY?!
WHY DID YOU DO THIS TO ME?!
THE CONCEIT OF YOUTH, THINKING THEY ARE THE CENTER OF EVERY ACTION.
THIS IS NOT ABOUT YOU. IT'S ABOUT ME.
AND IT'S ABOUT YOUR BROTHER.
THAT SON OF A--I'M GOING TO DO WHAT I SHOULD HAVE DONE BEFORE AND KIL--
STOP.
I DON'T KNOW WHAT YOU'RE AFTER, BUT THAT GIRL IS STILL OUT THERE. IF YOU ATTACK NOW, SHE MIGHT FALL INTO THAT THING.

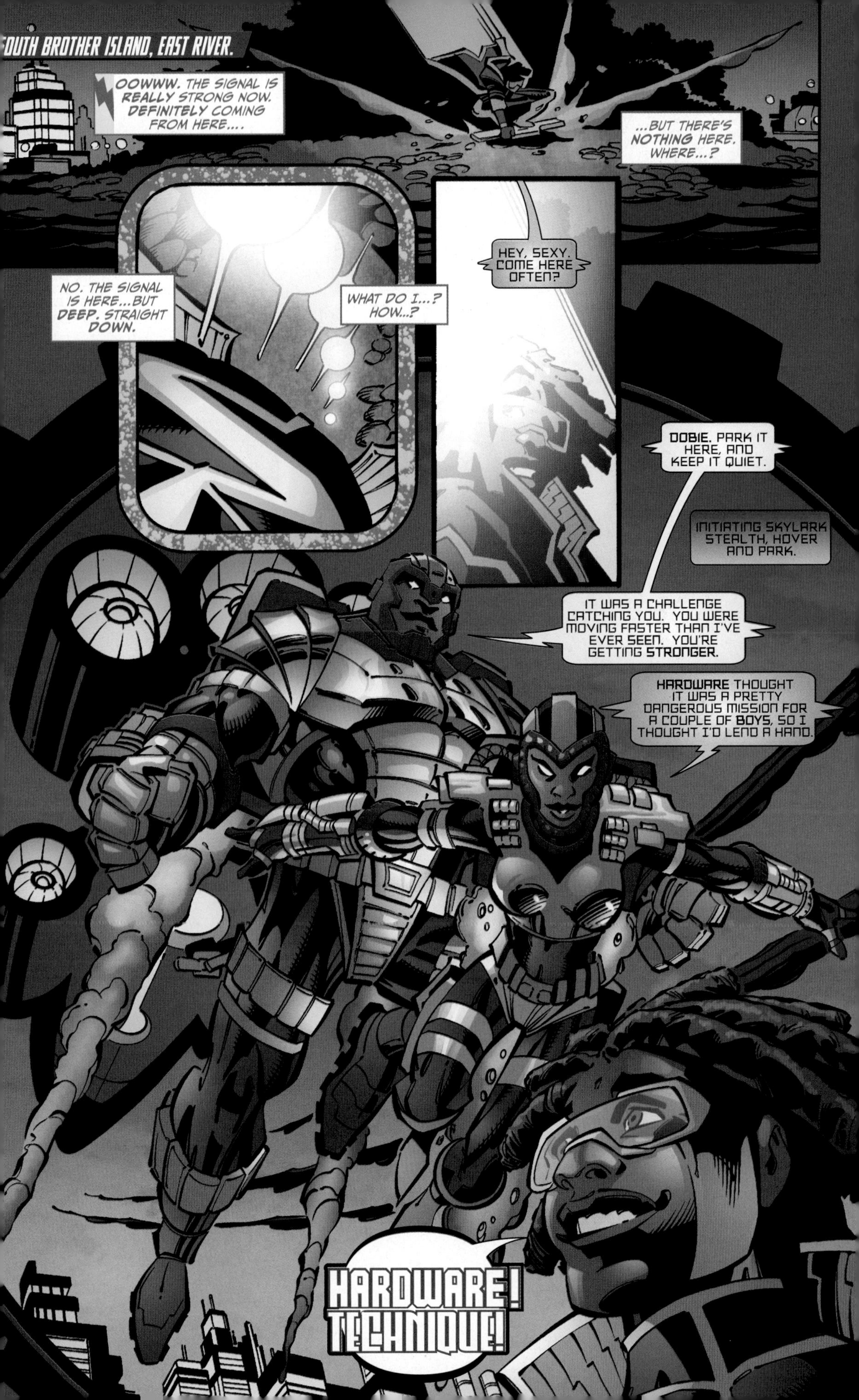

OUTH BROTHER ISLAND, EAST RIVER.
OOWWW. THE SIGNAL IS REALLY STRONG NOW. DEFINITELY COMING FROM HERE....
...BUT THERE'S NOTHING HERE. WHERE...?
NO. THE SIGNAL IS HERE...BUT DEEP. STRAIGHT DOWN.
WHAT DO I...? HOW...?
HEY, SEXY. COME HERE OFTEN?
DOBIE. PARK IT HERE, AND KEEP IT QUIET.
INITIATING SKYLARK STEALTH, HOVER AND PARK.
IT WAS A CHALLENGE CATCHING YOU. YOU WERE MOVING FASTER THAN I'VE EVER SEEN. YOU'RE GETTING STRONGER.
HARDWARE THOUGHT IT WAS A PRETTY DANGEROUS MISSION FOR A COUPLE OF BOYS, SO I THOUGHT I'D LEND A HAND.
HARDWARE! TECHNIQUE!

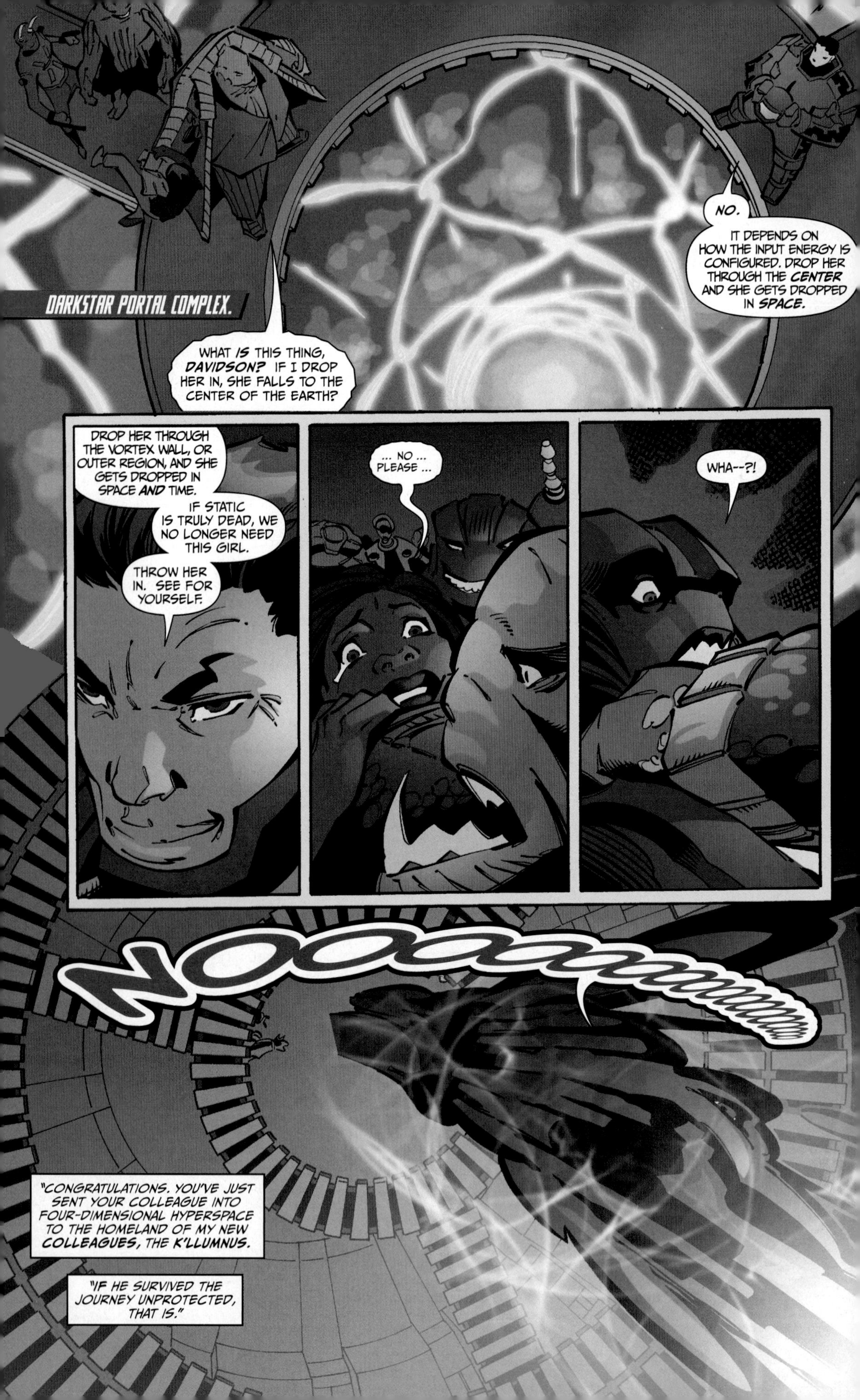
DARKSTAR PORTAL COMPLEX.
WHAT IS THIS THING, DAVIDSON? IF I DROP HER IN, SHE FALLS TO THE CENTER OF THE EARTH?
NO.
IT DEPENDS ON HOW THE INPUT ENERGY IS CONFIGURED. DROP HER THROUGH THE CENTER AND SHE GETS DROPPED IN SPACE.
DROP HER THROUGH THE VORTEX WALL, OR OUTER REGION, AND SHE GETS DROPPED IN SPACE AND TIME.
IF STATIC IS TRULY DEAD, WE NO LONGER NEED THIS GIRL.
THROW HER IN. SEE FOR YOURSELF.
... NO ... PLEASE ...
WHA--?!
NOOOaaaaaaaaaaaa
"CONGRATULATIONS. YOU'VE JUST SENT YOUR COLLEAGUE INTO FOUR-DIMENSIONAL HYPERSPACE TO THE HOMELAND OF MY NEW COLLEAGUES, THE K'LLUMNUS.
"IF HE SURVIVED THE JOURNEY UNPROTECTED, THAT IS."

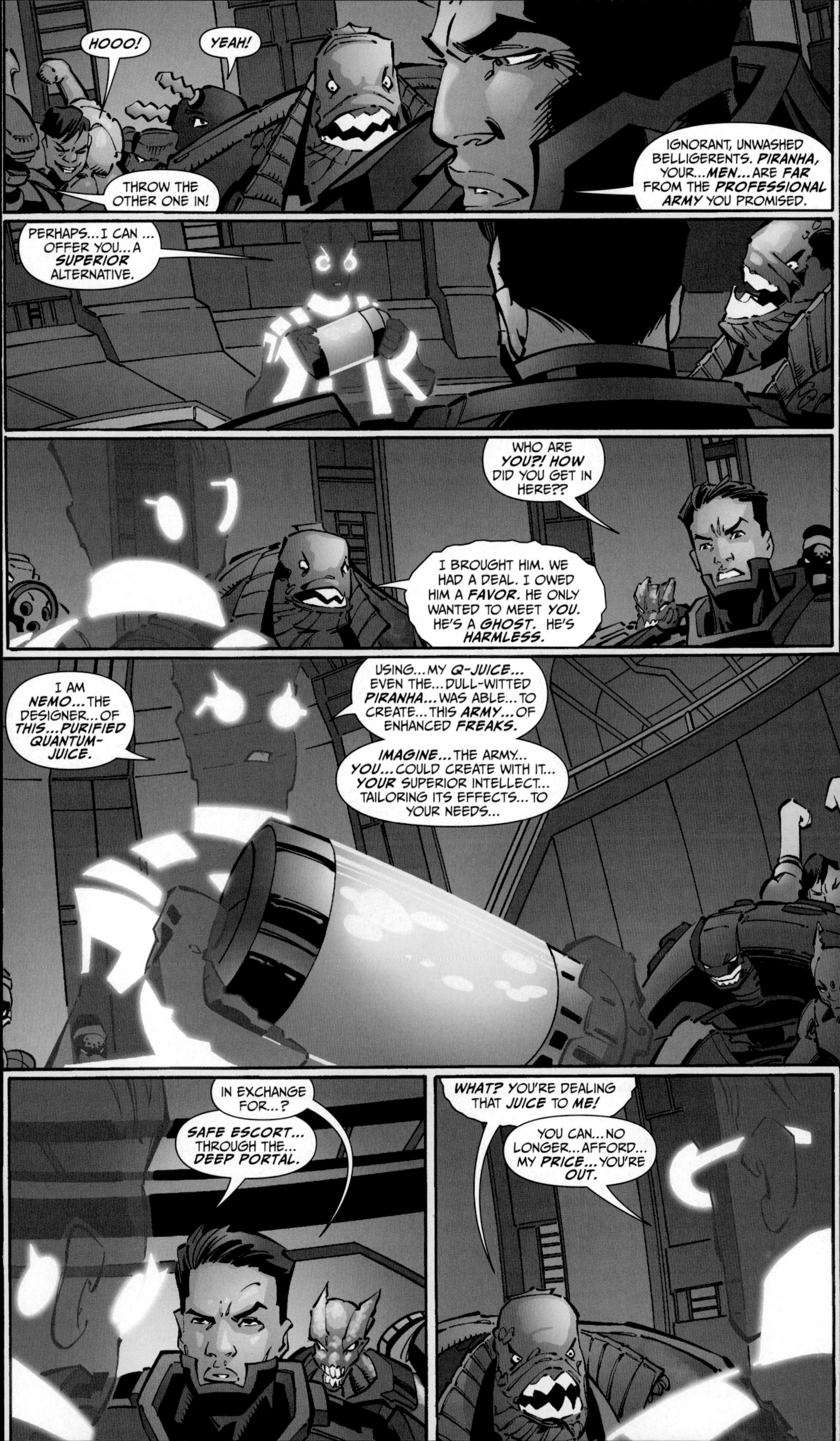
HOOO!
YEAH!
THROW THE OTHER ONE IN!
IGNORANT, UNWASHED BELLIGERENTS. PIRANHA, YOUR...MEN...ARE FAR FROM THE PROFESSIONAL ARMY YOU PROMISED.
PERHAPS...I CAN ... OFFER YOU...A SUPERIOR ALTERNATIVE.
WHO ARE YOU?! HOW DID YOU GET IN HERE??
I BROUGHT HIM. WE HAD A DEAL. I OWED HIM A FAVOR. HE ONLY WANTED TO MEET YOU. HE'S A GHOST. HE'S HARMLESS.
I AM NEMO...THE DESIGNER...OF THIS...PURIFIED QUANTUM-JUICE.
USING...MY Q-JUICE... EVEN THE...DULL-WITTED PIRANHA...WAS ABLE...TO CREATE...THIS ARMY...OF ENHANCED FREAKS.
IMAGINE...THE ARMY... YOU...COULD CREATE WITH IT... YOUR SUPERIOR INTELLECT... TAILORING ITS EFFECTS...TO YOUR NEEDS...
IN EXCHANGE FOR...?
SAFE ESCORT... THROUGH THE... DEEP PORTAL.
WHAT? YOU'RE DEALING THAT JUICE TO ME!
YOU CAN...NO LONGER...AFFORD... MY PRICE...YOU'RE OUT.

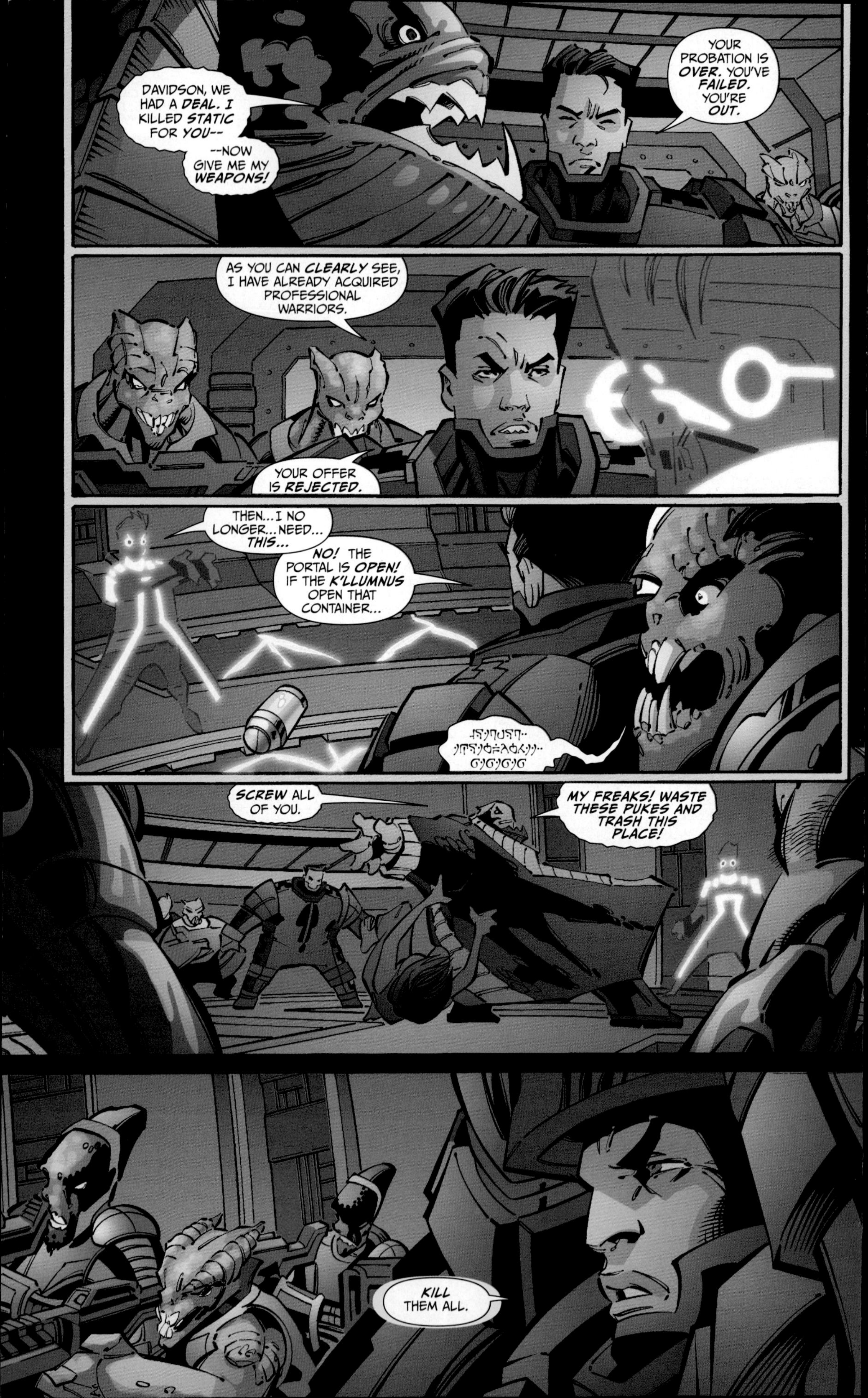

DAVIDSON, WE HAD A DEAL. I KILLED STATIC FOR YOU--
--NOW GIVE ME MY WEAPONS!
YOUR PROBATION IS OVER. YOU'VE FAILED. YOU'RE OUT.
AS YOU CAN CLEARLY SEE, I HAVE ALREADY ACQUIRED PROFESSIONAL WARRIORS.
YOUR OFFER IS REJECTED.
THEN...I NO LONGER...NEED... THIS...
NO! THE PORTAL IS OPEN! IF THE K'LLUMNUS OPEN THAT CONTAINER...
SCREW ALL OF YOU.
MY FREAKS! WASTE THESE PUKES AND TRASH THIS PLACE!
KILL THEM ALL.

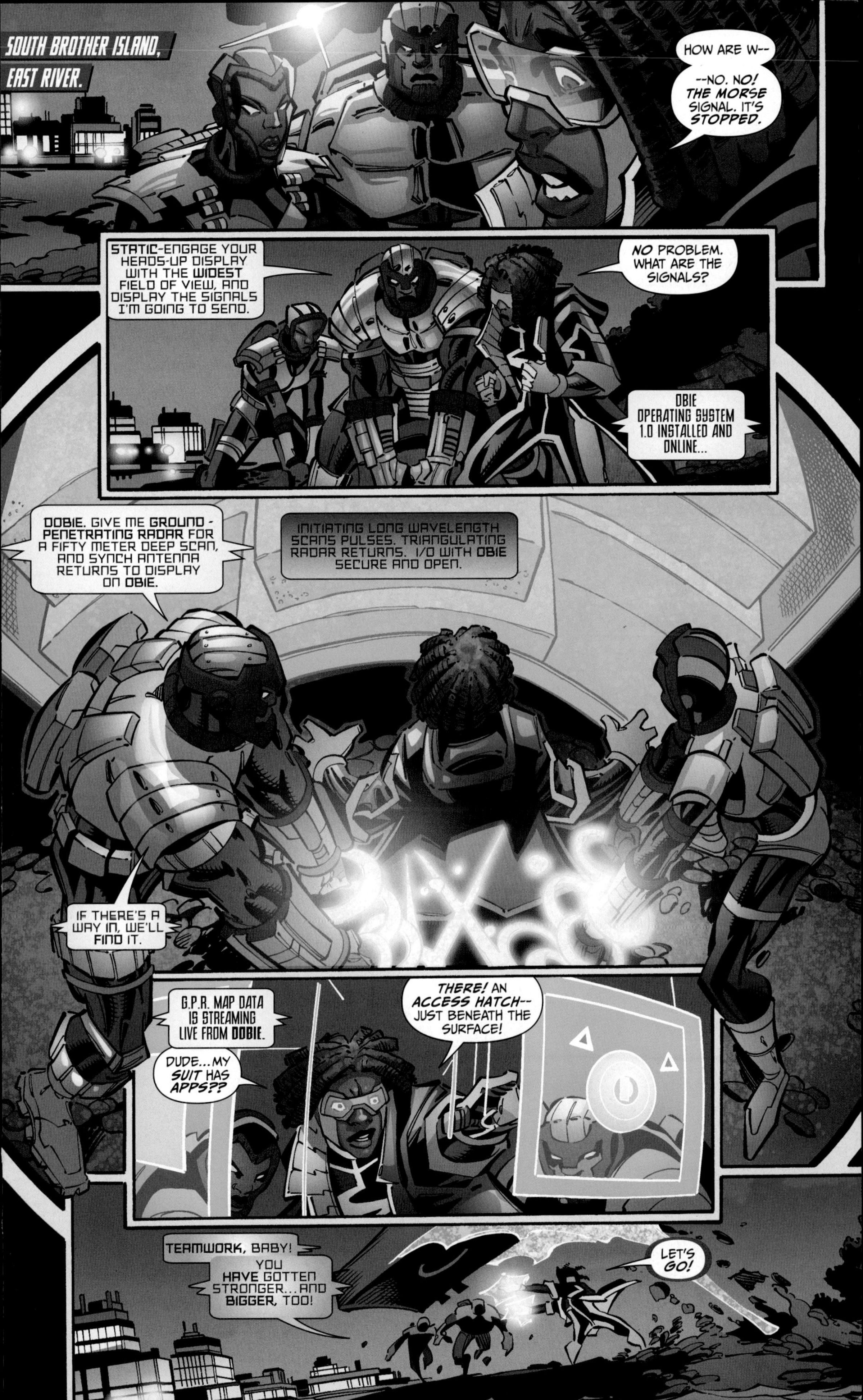

SOUTH BROTHER ISLAND, EAST RIVER.
HOW ARE W--
--NO. NO! THE MORSE SIGNAL. IT'S STOPPED.
STATIC--ENGAGE YOUR HEADS-UP DISPLAY WITH THE WIDEST FIELD OF VIEW, AND DISPLAY THE SIGNALS I'M GOING TO SEND.
NO PROBLEM. WHAT ARE THE SIGNALS?
OBIE OPERATING SYSTEM 1.0 INSTALLED AND ONLINE...
DOBIE. GIVE ME GROUND-PENETRATING RADAR FOR A FIFTY METER DEEP SCAN, AND SYNCH ANTENNA RETURNS TO DISPLAY ON OBIE.
INITIATING LONG WAVELENGTH SCANS PULSES. TRIANGULATING RADAR RETURNS. I/O WITH OBIE SECURE AND OPEN.
IF THERE'S A WAY IN, WE'LL FIND IT.
G.P.R. MAP DATA IS STREAMING LIVE FROM DOBIE.
DUDE...MY SUIT HAS APPS??
THERE! AN ACCESS HATCH--JUST BENEATH THE SURFACE!
TEAMWORK, BABY!
YOU HAVE GOTTEN STRONGER...AND BIGGER, TOO!
LET'S GO!

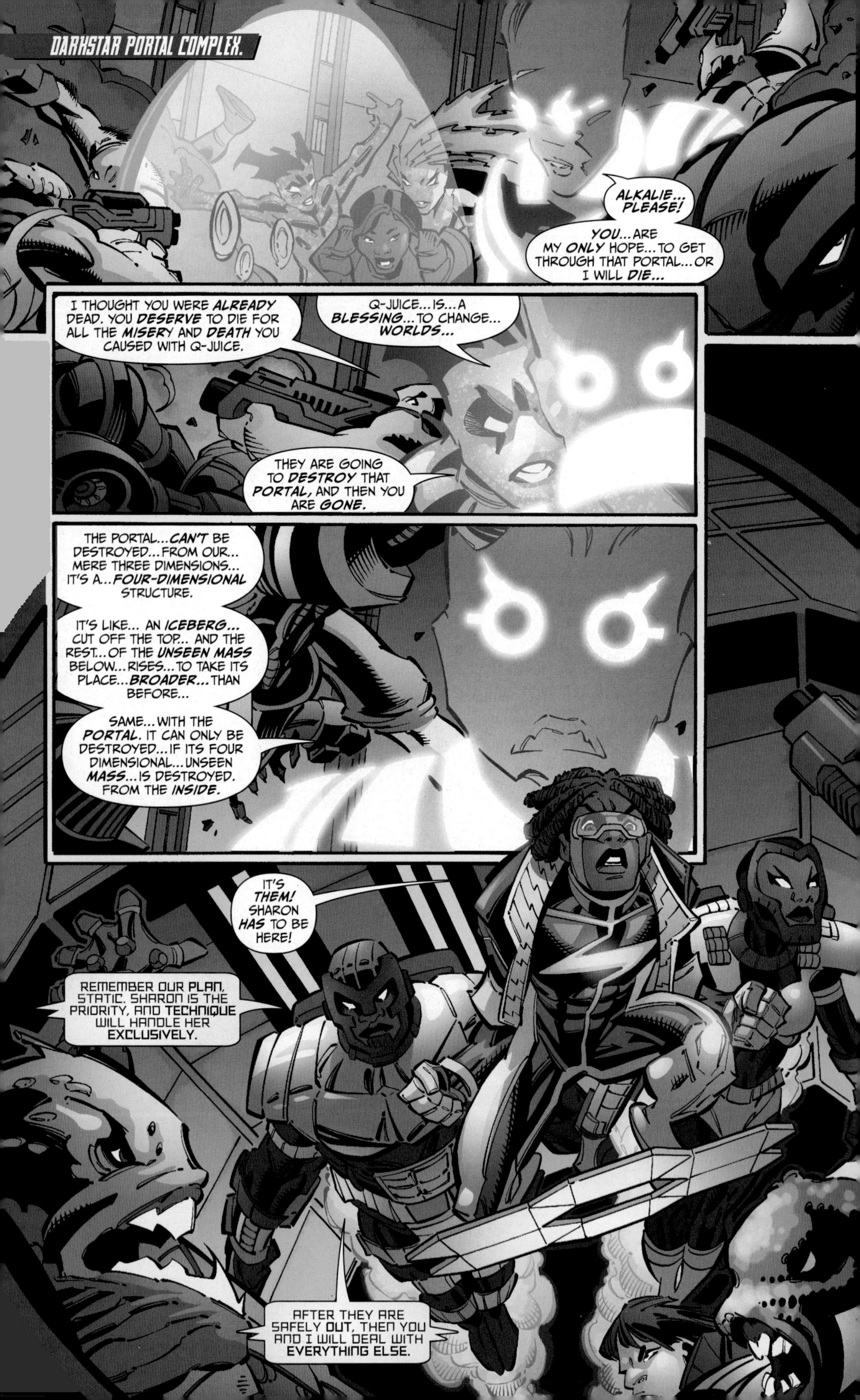
DARKSTAR PORTAL COMPLEX.
ALKALIE... PLEASE!
YOU...ARE MY ONLY HOPE...TO GET THROUGH THAT PORTAL...OR I WILL DIE...
I THOUGHT YOU WERE ALREADY DEAD. YOU DESERVE TO DIE FOR ALL THE MISERY AND DEATH YOU CAUSED WITH Q-JUICE.
Q-JUICE...IS...A BLESSING...TO CHANGE... WORLDS...
THEY ARE GOING TO DESTROY THAT PORTAL, AND THEN YOU ARE GONE.
THE PORTAL...CAN'T BE DESTROYED...FROM OUR... MERE THREE DIMENSIONS... IT'S A...FOUR-DIMENSIONAL STRUCTURE.
IT'S LIKE... AN ICEBERG... CUT OFF THE TOP... AND THE REST...OF THE UNSEEN MASS BELOW...RISES...TO TAKE ITS PLACE...BROADER...THAN BEFORE...
SAME...WITH THE PORTAL. IT CAN ONLY BE DESTROYED...IF ITS FOUR DIMENSIONAL...UNSEEN MASS...IS DESTROYED. FROM THE INSIDE.
IT'S THEM! SHARON HAS TO BE HERE!
REMEMBER OUR PLAN, STATIC. SHARON IS THE PRIORITY, AND TECHNIQUE WILL HANDLE HER EXCLUSIVELY.
AFTER THEY ARE SAFELY OUT, THEN YOU AND I WILL DEAL WITH EVERYTHING ELSE.

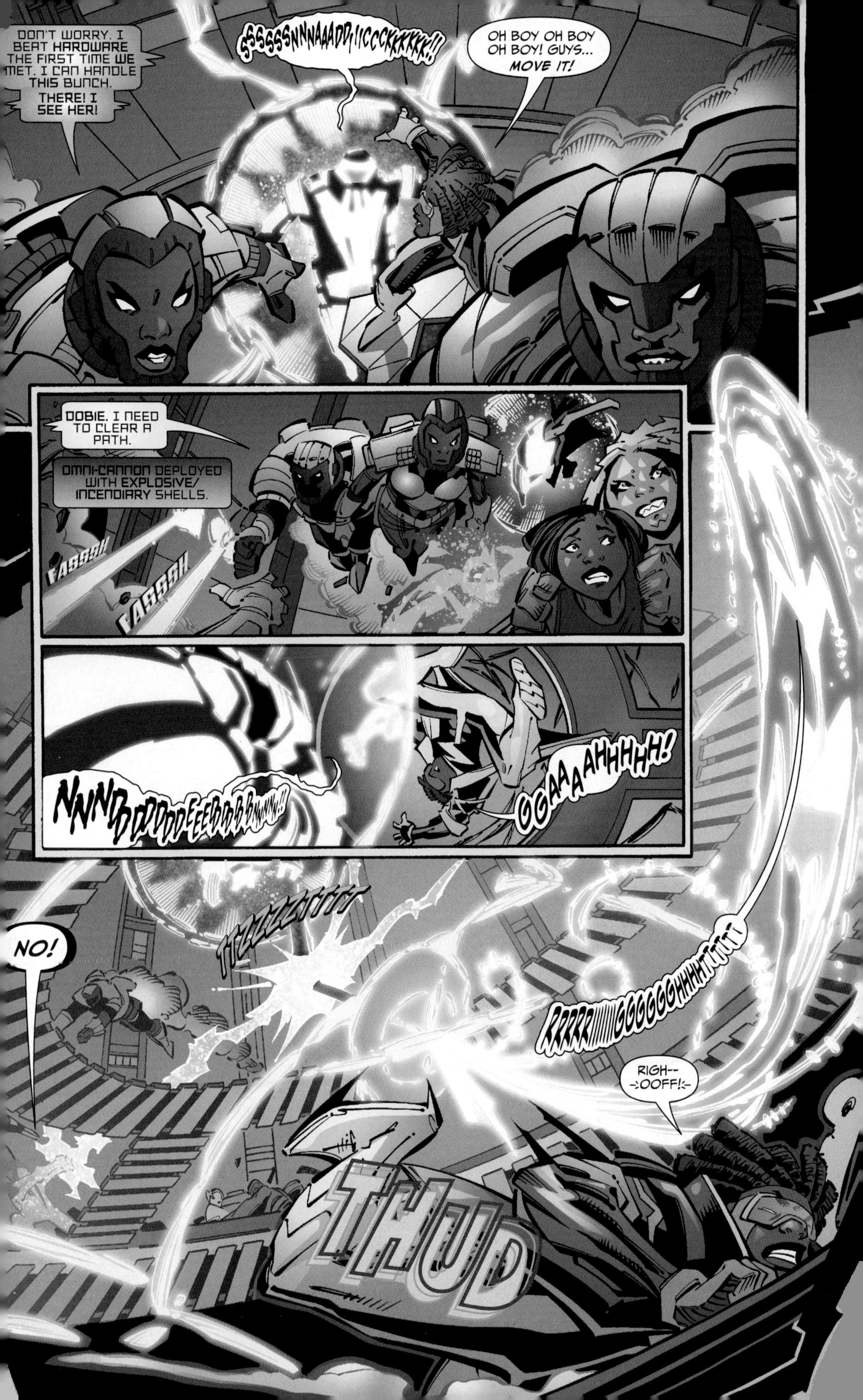

DON'T WORRY. I BEAT HARDWARE THE FIRST TIME WE MET. I CAN HANDLE THIS BUNCH.
THERE! I SEE HER!
SSSSSSNNNAAADD!!CCCKKKKKK!!
OH BOY OH BOY OH BOY! GUYS... MOVE IT!
DOBIE. I NEED TO CLEAR A PATH.
OMNI-CANNON DEPLOYED WITH EXPLOSIVE/ INCENDIARY SHELLS.
FASSSH
FASSSH
NNNDDDDDDEEEDDDBBNNNN!!
OGAAAAHHHHH!
NO!
TTZZZZZTTTTT
RRRRR!!!!!GGGGGGHHHTTTTT
RIGH-- -OOFF!-
THUD

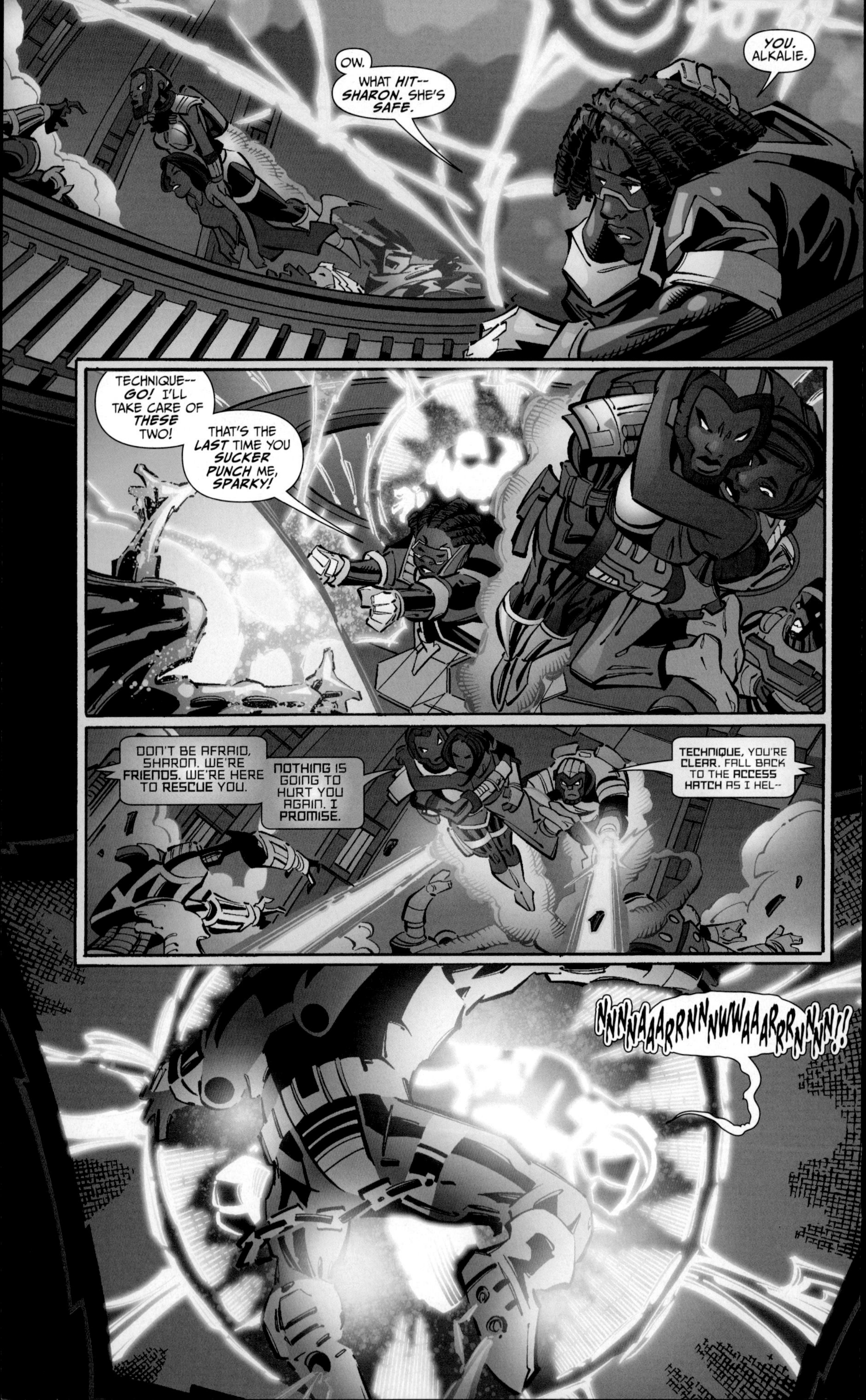
OW.
WHAT HIT--
SHARON. SHE'S SAFE.
YOU. ALKALIE.
TECHNIQUE-- GO! I'LL TAKE CARE OF THESE TWO!
THAT'S THE LAST TIME YOU SUCKER PUNCH ME, SPARKY!
DON'T BE AFRAID, SHARON. WE'RE FRIENDS. WE'RE HERE TO RESCUE YOU.
NOTHING IS GOING TO HURT YOU AGAIN. I PROMISE.
TECHNIQUE, YOU'RE CLEAR. FALL BACK TO THE ACCESS HATCH AS I HEL--
NNNNAAARRNNNWWAAARRRNNNN!!

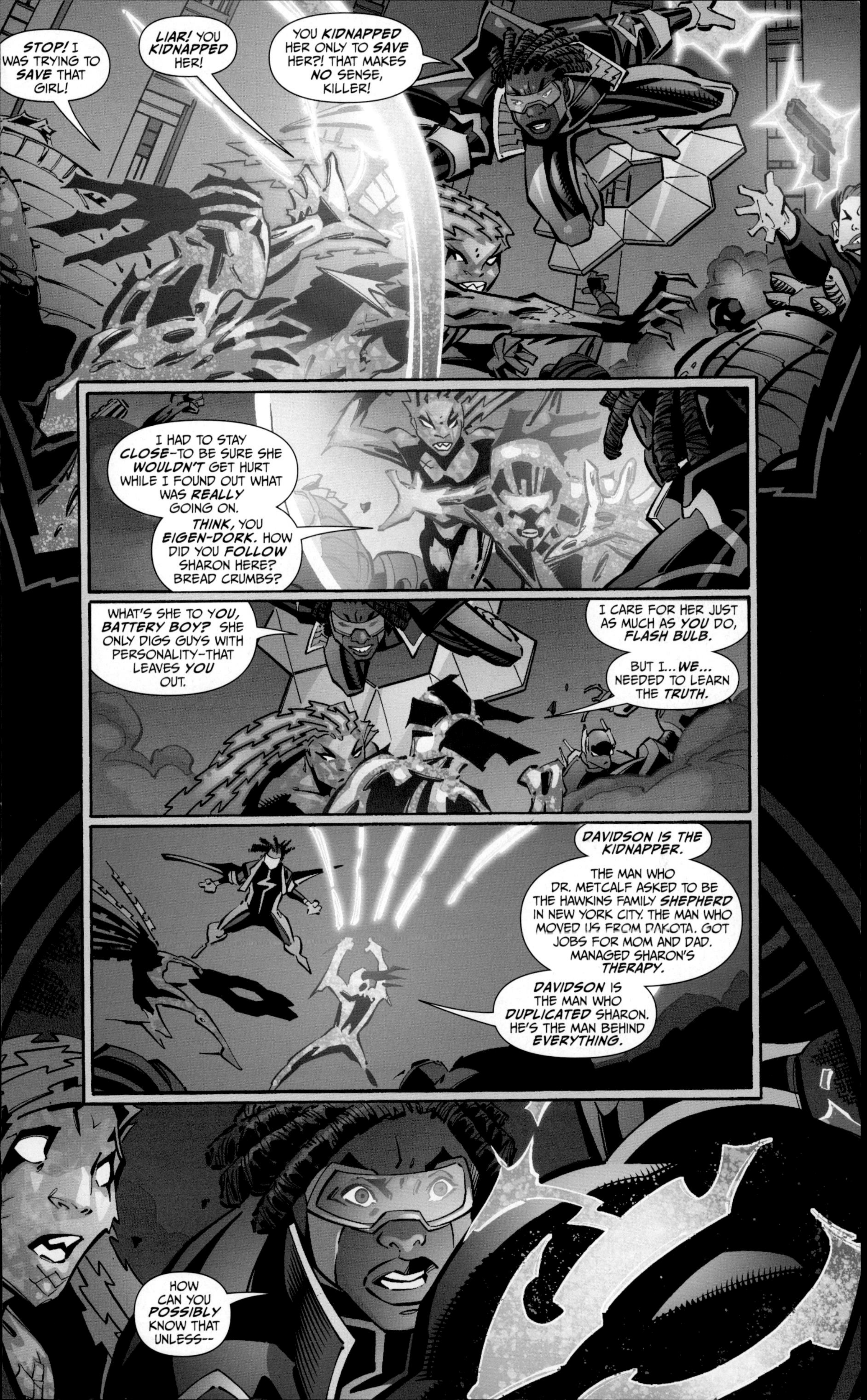
STOP! I WAS TRYING TO SAVE THAT GIRL!
LIAR! YOU KIDNAPPED HER!
YOU KIDNAPPED HER ONLY TO SAVE HER?! THAT MAKES NO SENSE, KILLER!
I HAD TO STAY CLOSE–TO BE SURE SHE WOULDN'T GET HURT WHILE I FOUND OUT WHAT WAS REALLY GOING ON.
THINK, YOU EIGEN-DORK. HOW DID YOU FOLLOW SHARON HERE? BREAD CRUMBS?
WHAT'S SHE TO YOU, BATTERY BOY? SHE ONLY DIGS GUYS WITH PERSONALITY–THAT LEAVES YOU OUT.
I CARE FOR HER JUST AS MUCH AS YOU DO, FLASH BULB.
BUT I...WE... NEEDED TO LEARN THE TRUTH.
DAVIDSON IS THE KIDNAPPER.
THE MAN WHO DR. METCALF ASKED TO BE THE HAWKINS FAMILY SHEPHERD IN NEW YORK CITY. THE MAN WHO MOVED US FROM DAKOTA. GOT JOBS FOR MOM AND DAD. MANAGED SHARON'S THERAPY.
DAVIDSON IS THE MAN WHO DUPLICATED SHARON. HE'S THE MAN BEHIND EVERYTHING.
HOW CAN YOU POSSIBLY KNOW THAT UNLESS--

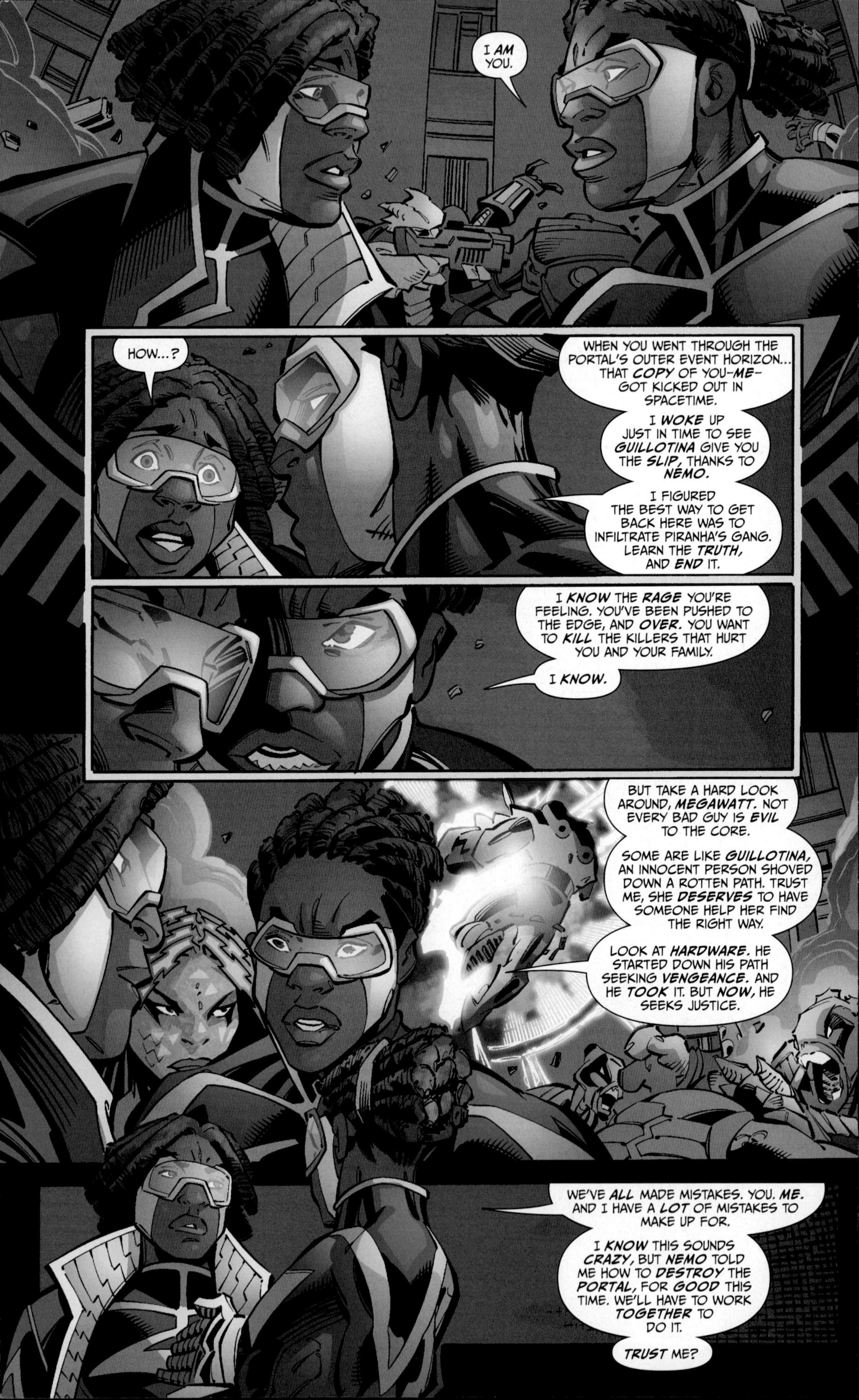
I AM YOU.
HOW...?
WHEN YOU WENT THROUGH THE PORTAL'S OUTER EVENT HORIZON... THAT COPY OF YOU—ME— GOT KICKED OUT IN SPACETIME.
I WOKE UP JUST IN TIME TO SEE GUILLOTINA GIVE YOU THE SLIP, THANKS TO NEMO.
I FIGURED THE BEST WAY TO GET BACK HERE WAS TO INFILTRATE PIRANHA'S GANG. LEARN THE TRUTH, AND END IT.
I KNOW THE RAGE YOU'RE FEELING. YOU'VE BEEN PUSHED TO THE EDGE, AND OVER. YOU WANT TO KILL THE KILLERS THAT HURT YOU AND YOUR FAMILY.
I KNOW.
BUT TAKE A HARD LOOK AROUND, MEGAWATT. NOT EVERY BAD GUY IS EVIL TO THE CORE.
SOME ARE LIKE GUILLOTINA, AN INNOCENT PERSON SHOVED DOWN A ROTTEN PATH. TRUST ME, SHE DESERVES TO HAVE SOMEONE HELP HER FIND THE RIGHT WAY.
LOOK AT HARDWARE. HE STARTED DOWN HIS PATH SEEKING VENGEANCE. AND HE TOOK IT. BUT NOW, HE SEEKS JUSTICE.
WE'VE ALL MADE MISTAKES. YOU. ME. AND I HAVE A LOT OF MISTAKES TO MAKE UP FOR.
I KNOW THIS SOUNDS CRAZY, BUT NEMO TOLD ME HOW TO DESTROY THE PORTAL, FOR GOOD THIS TIME. WE'LL HAVE TO WORK TOGETHER TO DO IT.
TRUST ME?

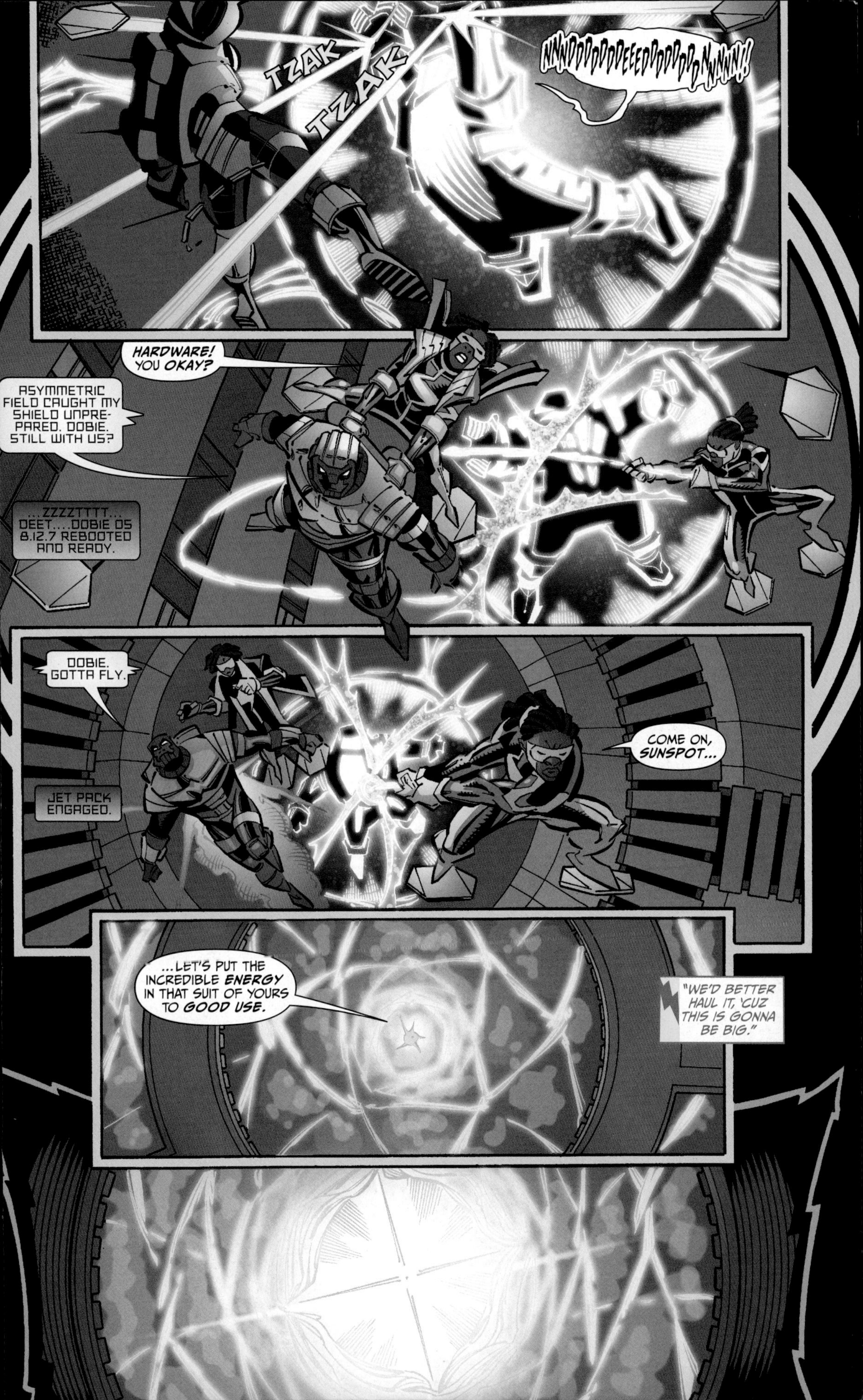
TZAK
TZAK
NNNDDDDDDDEEEDDDDDDNNNN!!
HARDWARE! YOU OKAY?
ASYMMETRIC FIELD CAUGHT MY SHIELD UNPRE-PARED. DOBIE. STILL WITH US?
...ZZZZTTTT... DEET....DOBIE OS 8.12.7 REBOOTED AND READY.
DOBIE. GOTTA FLY.
COME ON, SUNSPOT...
JET PACK ENGAGED.
...LET'S PUT THE INCREDIBLE ENERGY IN THAT SUIT OF YOURS TO GOOD USE.
"WE'D BETTER HAUL IT, 'CUZ THIS IS GONNA BE BIG."

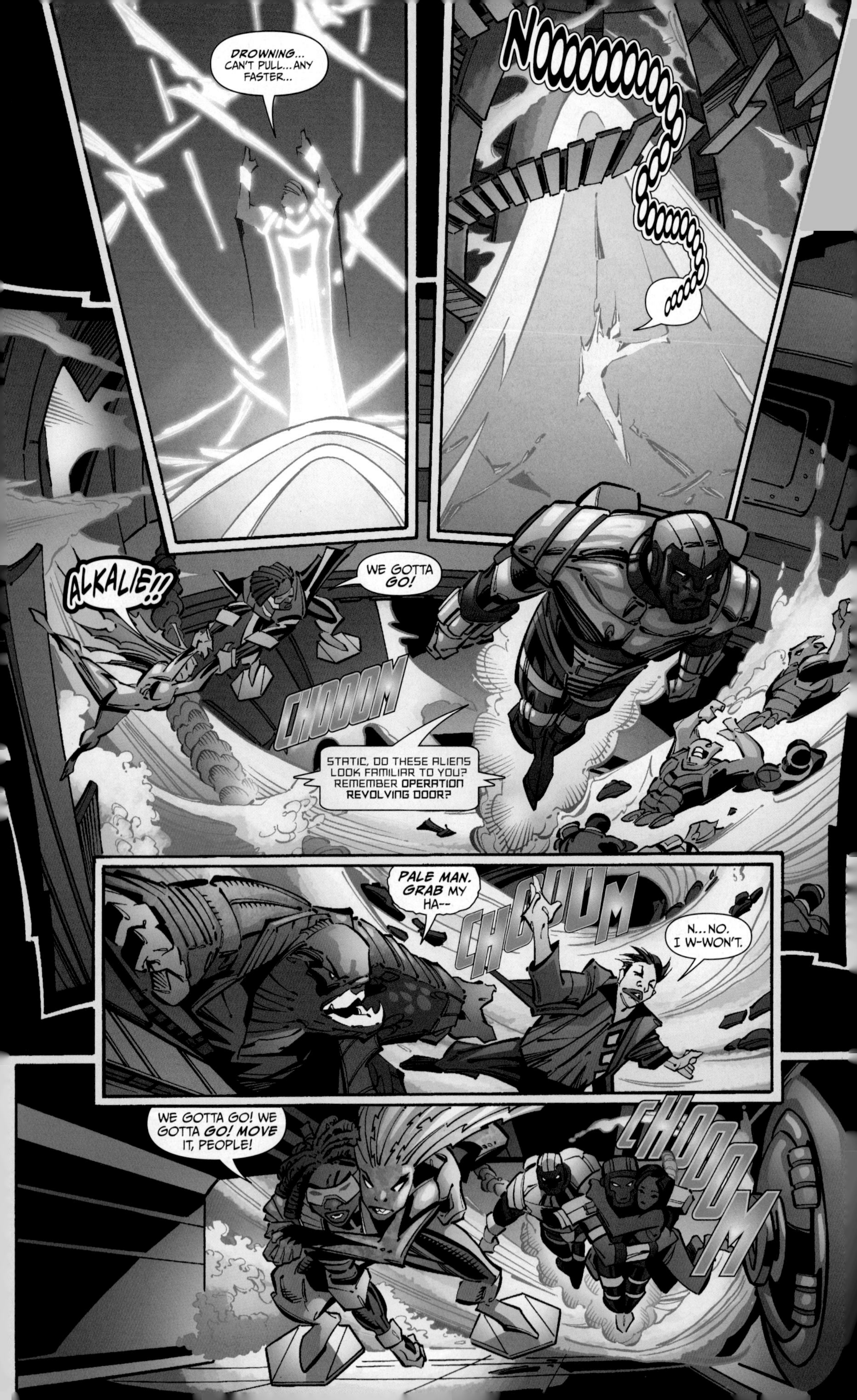
DROWNING... CAN'T PULL... ANY FASTER...
NOOOOOOOOOOOOOOOOOOOOOOOOOOOOOOOOOOOOO
ALKALIE!!
WE GOTTA GO!
CHOOOM
STATIC, DO THESE ALIENS LOOK FAMILIAR TO YOU? REMEMBER OPERATION REVOLVING DOOR?
PALE MAN. GRAB MY HA--
CHOOOM
N...NO. I W-WON'T.
WE GOTTA GO! WE GOTTA GO! MOVE IT, PEOPLE!
CHOOOOM

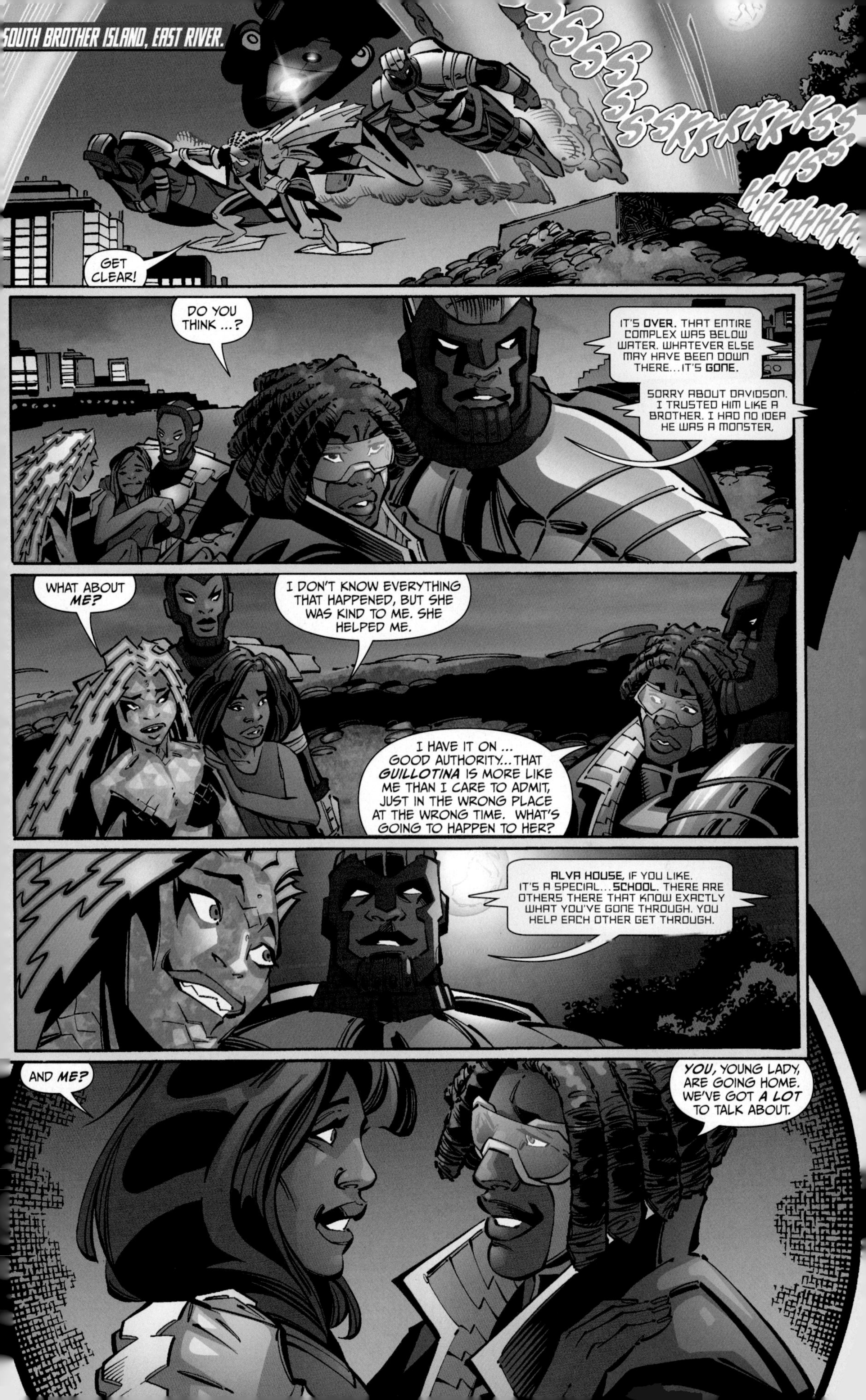
SOUTH BROTHER ISLAND, EAST RIVER.
SSSSSSSSSKKKKKKKSSS HSS HHHHHHHH
GET CLEAR!
DO YOU THINK ...?
IT'S OVER. THAT ENTIRE COMPLEX WAS BELOW WATER. WHATEVER ELSE MAY HAVE BEEN DOWN THERE... IT'S GONE.
SORRY ABOUT DAVIDSON. I TRUSTED HIM LIKE A BROTHER. I HAD NO IDEA HE WAS A MONSTER.
WHAT ABOUT ME?
I DON'T KNOW EVERYTHING THAT HAPPENED, BUT SHE WAS KIND TO ME. SHE HELPED ME.
I HAVE IT ON ... GOOD AUTHORITY... THAT GUILLOTINA IS MORE LIKE ME THAN I CARE TO ADMIT, JUST IN THE WRONG PLACE AT THE WRONG TIME. WHAT'S GOING TO HAPPEN TO HER?
ALVA HOUSE, IF YOU LIKE. IT'S A SPECIAL... SCHOOL. THERE ARE OTHERS THERE THAT KNOW EXACTLY WHAT YOU'VE GONE THROUGH. YOU HELP EACH OTHER GET THROUGH.
AND ME?
YOU, YOUNG LADY, ARE GOING HOME. WE'VE GOT A LOT TO TALK ABOUT.

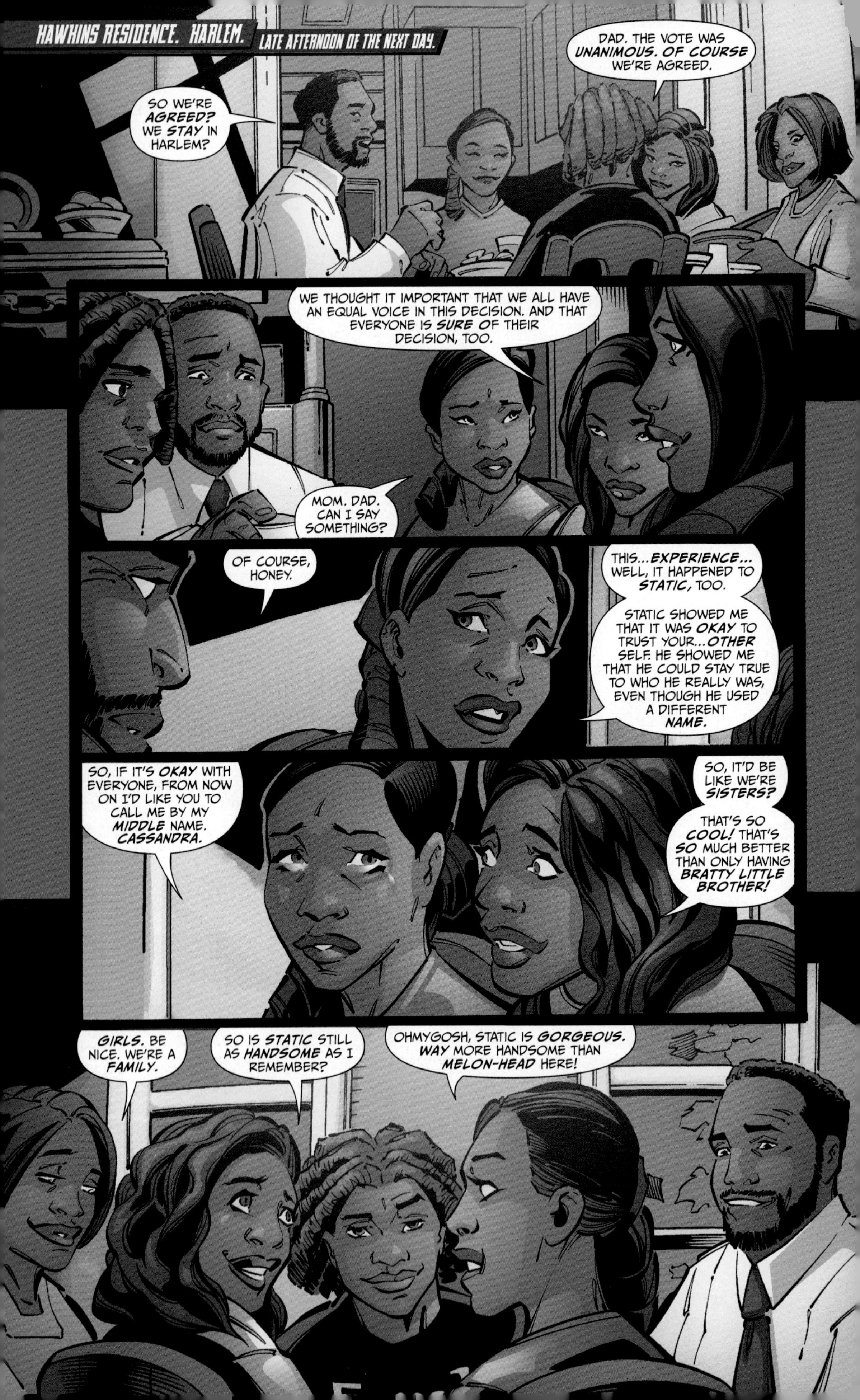
HAWKINS RESIDENCE. HARLEM.
LATE AFTERNOON OF THE NEXT DAY.
SO WE'RE AGREED? WE STAY IN HARLEM?
DAD. THE VOTE WAS UNANIMOUS. OF COURSE WE'RE AGREED.
WE THOUGHT IT IMPORTANT THAT WE ALL HAVE AN EQUAL VOICE IN THIS DECISION. AND THAT EVERYONE IS SURE OF THEIR DECISION, TOO.
MOM. DAD. CAN I SAY SOMETHING?
OF COURSE, HONEY.
THIS...EXPERIENCE... WELL, IT HAPPENED TO STATIC, TOO.
STATIC SHOWED ME THAT IT WAS OKAY TO TRUST YOUR...OTHER SELF. HE SHOWED ME THAT HE COULD STAY TRUE TO WHO HE REALLY WAS, EVEN THOUGH HE USED A DIFFERENT NAME.
SO, IF IT'S OKAY WITH EVERYONE, FROM NOW ON I'D LIKE YOU TO CALL ME BY MY MIDDLE NAME. CASSANDRA.
SO, IT'D BE LIKE WE'RE SISTERS?
THAT'S SO COOL! THAT'S SO MUCH BETTER THAN ONLY HAVING BRATTY LITTLE BROTHER!
GIRLS. BE NICE. WE'RE A FAMILY.
SO IS STATIC STILL AS HANDSOME AS I REMEMBER?
OHMYGOSH, STATIC IS GORGEOUS. WAY MORE HANDSOME THAN MELON-HEAD HERE!

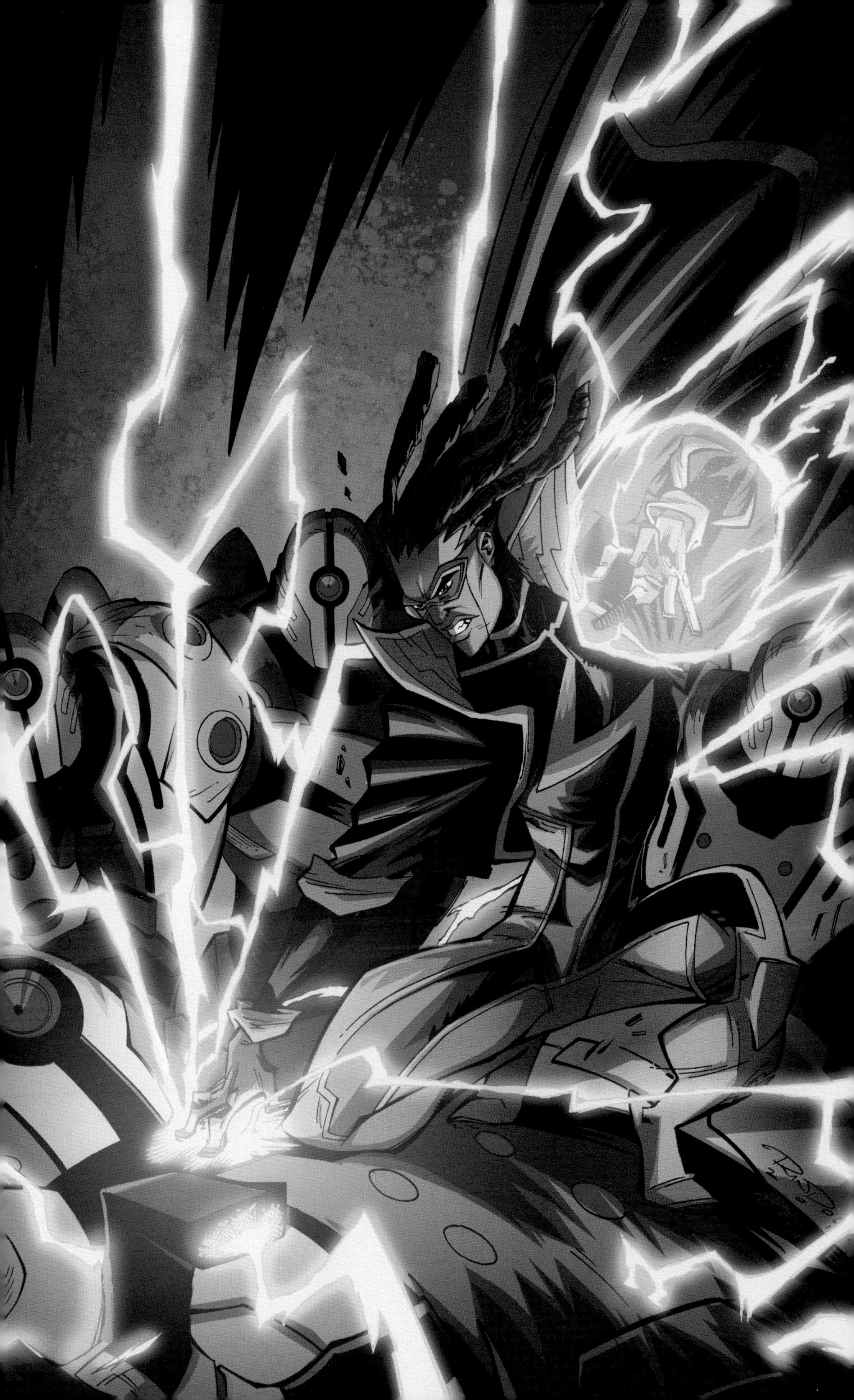

cover art by
KHARY RANDOLPH, LE BEAU UNDERWOOD
& EMILIO LOPEZ

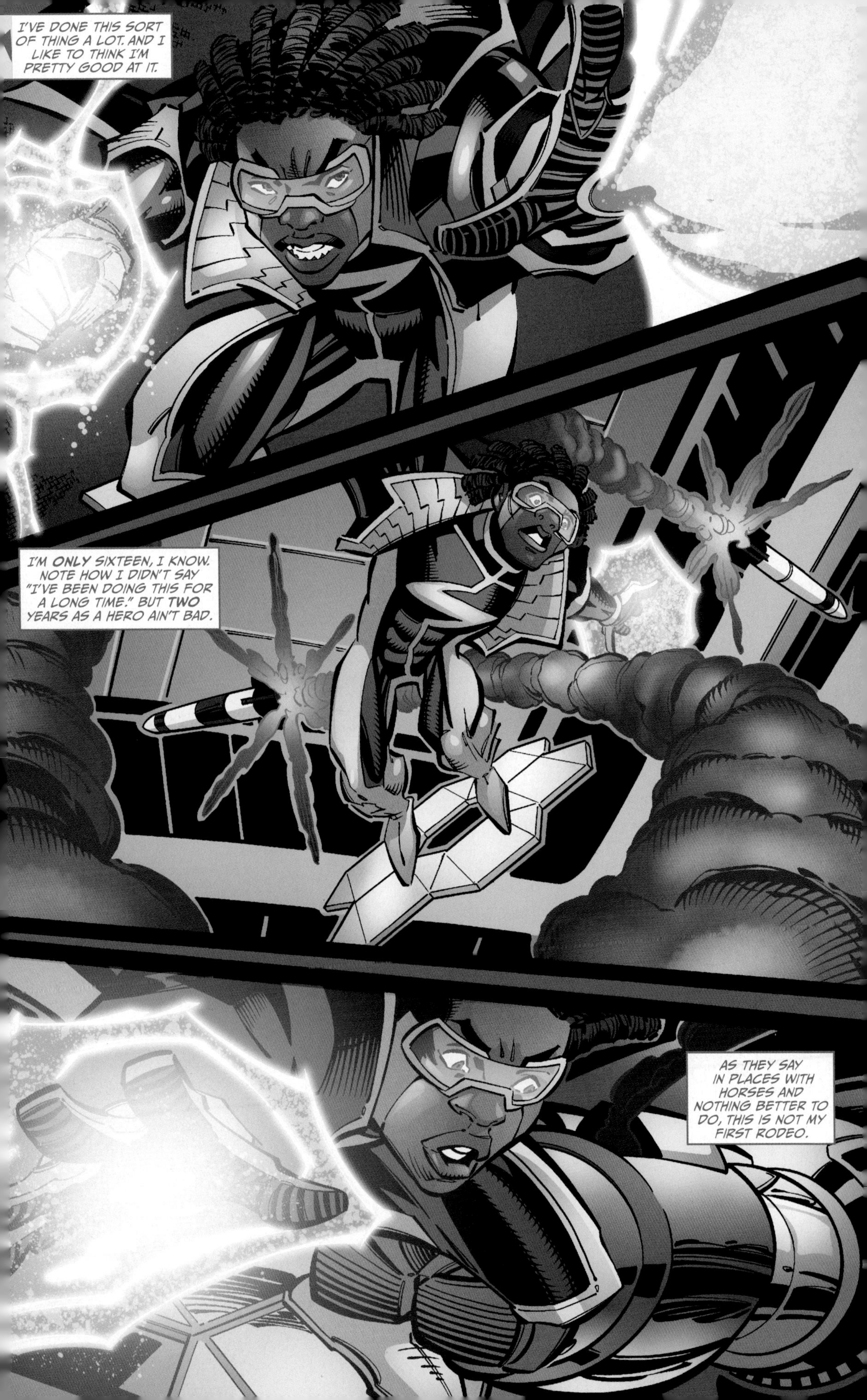
I'VE DONE THIS SORT OF THING A LOT. AND I LIKE TO THINK I'M PRETTY GOOD AT IT.
I'M **ONLY** SIXTEEN, I KNOW. NOTE HOW I DIDN'T SAY "I'VE BEEN DOING THIS FOR A LONG TIME." BUT **TWO** YEARS AS A HERO AIN'T BAD.
AS THEY SAY IN PLACES WITH HORSES AND NOTHING BETTER TO DO, THIS IS NOT MY FIRST RODEO.

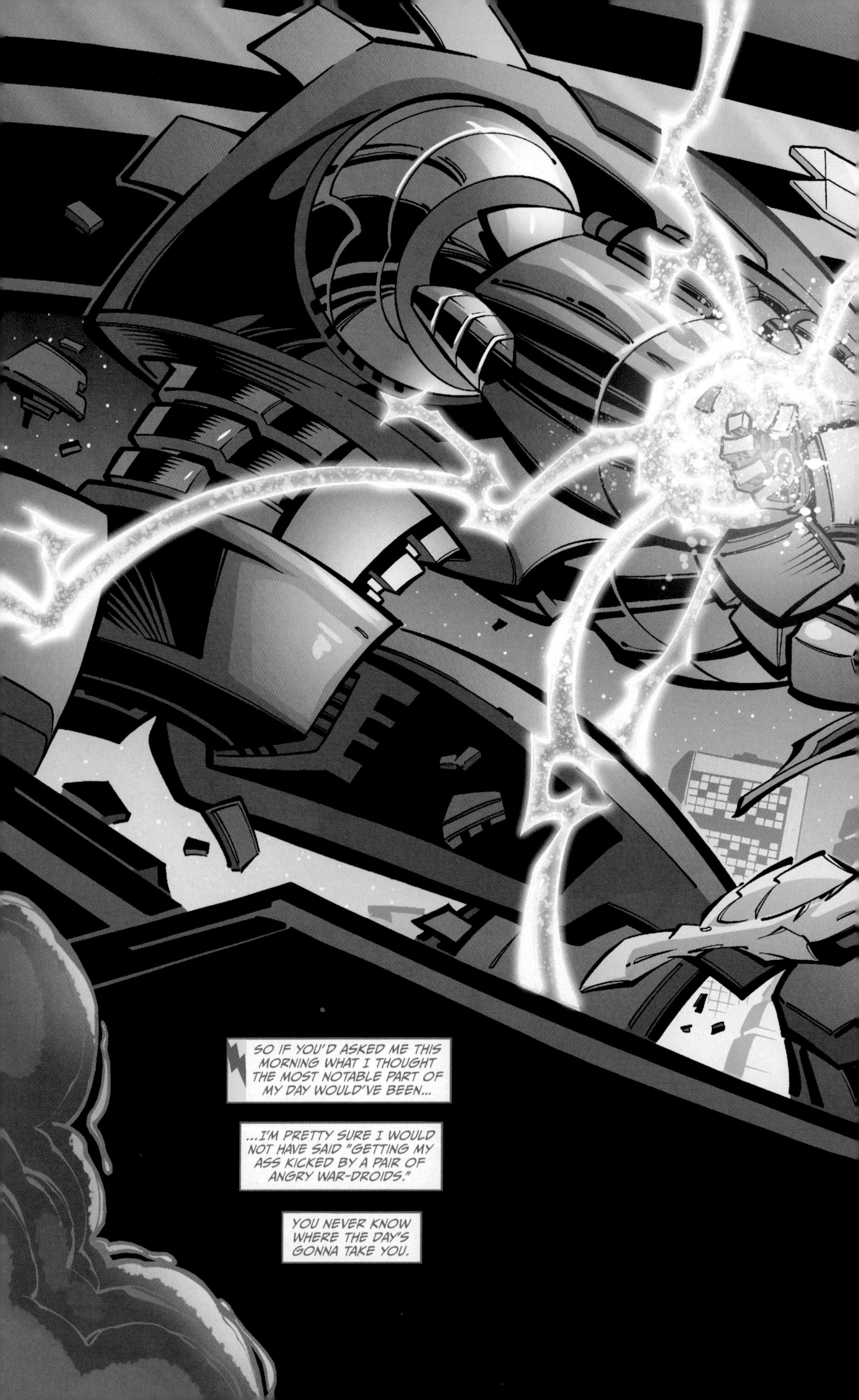
SO IF YOU'D ASKED ME THIS MORNING WHAT I THOUGHT THE MOST NOTABLE PART OF MY DAY WOULD'VE BEEN...
...I'M PRETTY SURE I WOULD NOT HAVE SAID "GETTING MY ASS KICKED BY A PAIR OF ANGRY WAR-DROIDS."
YOU NEVER KNOW WHERE THE DAY'S GONNA TAKE YOU.

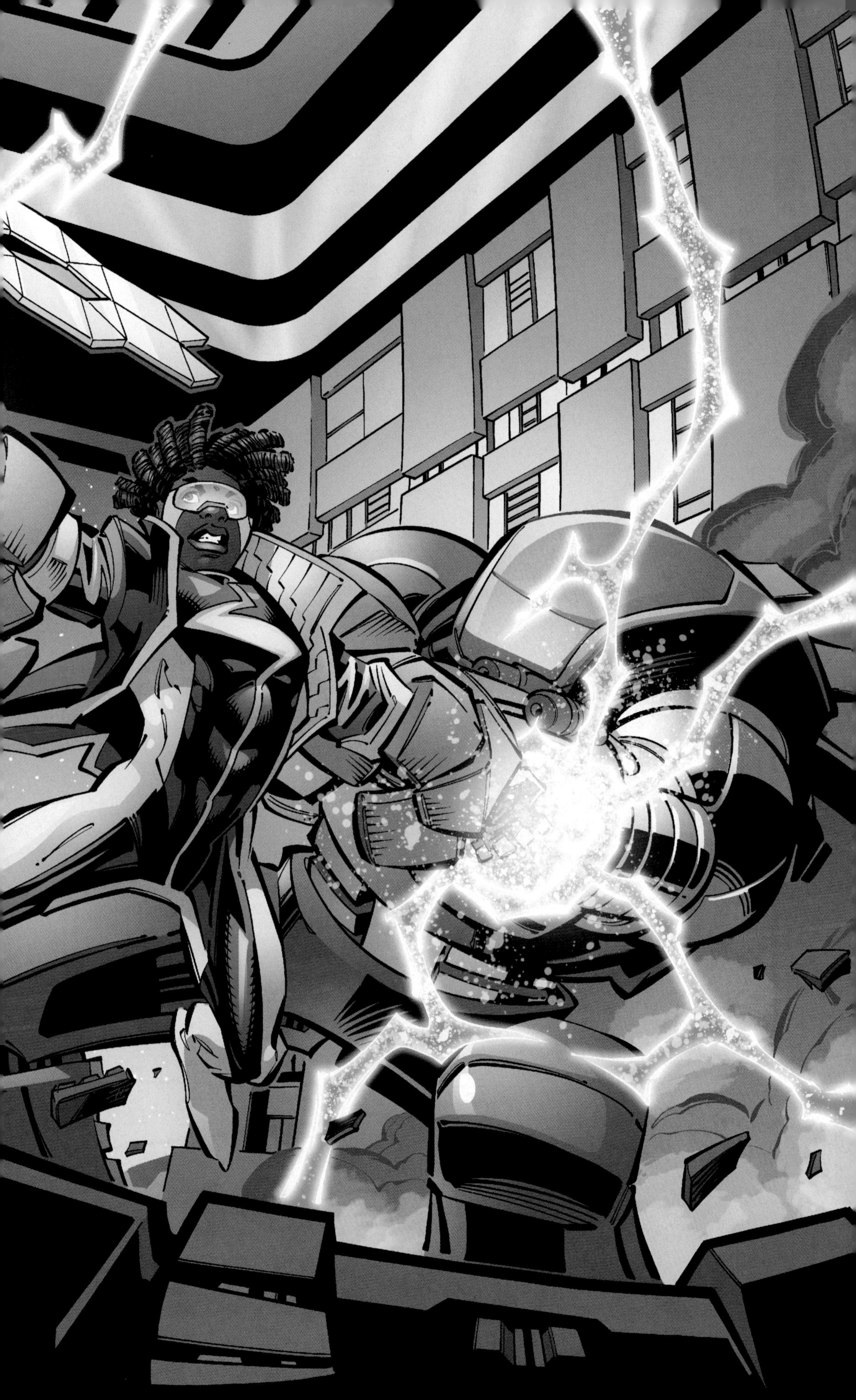

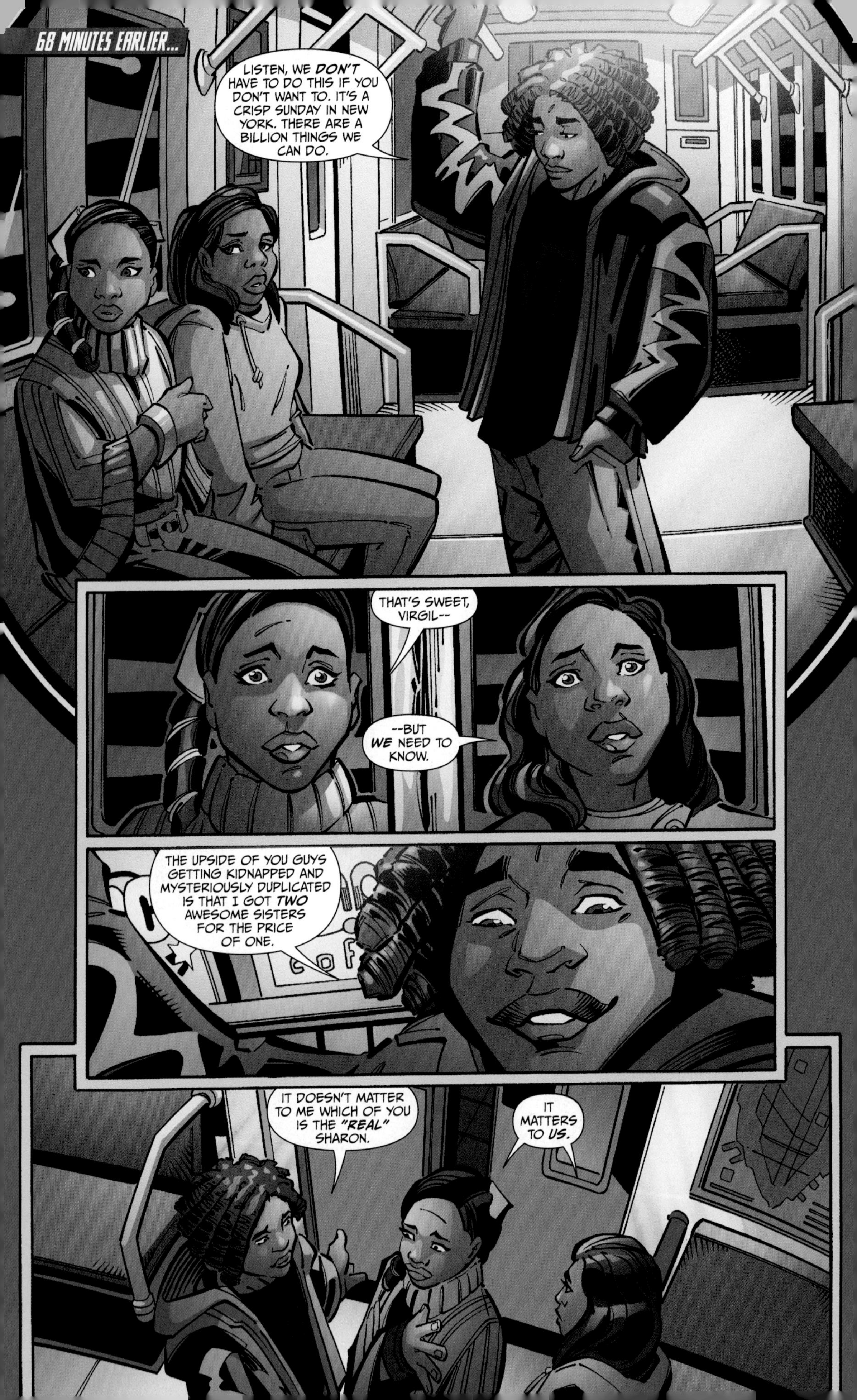
68 MINUTES EARLIER...
LISTEN, WE DON'T HAVE TO DO THIS IF YOU DON'T WANT TO. IT'S A CRISP SUNDAY IN NEW YORK. THERE ARE A BILLION THINGS WE CAN DO.
THAT'S SWEET, VIRGIL--
--BUT WE NEED TO KNOW.
THE UPSIDE OF YOU GUYS GETTING KIDNAPPED AND MYSTERIOUSLY DUPLICATED IS THAT I GOT TWO AWESOME SISTERS FOR THE PRICE OF ONE.
IT DOESN'T MATTER TO ME WHICH OF YOU IS THE "REAL" SHARON.
IT MATTERS TO US.

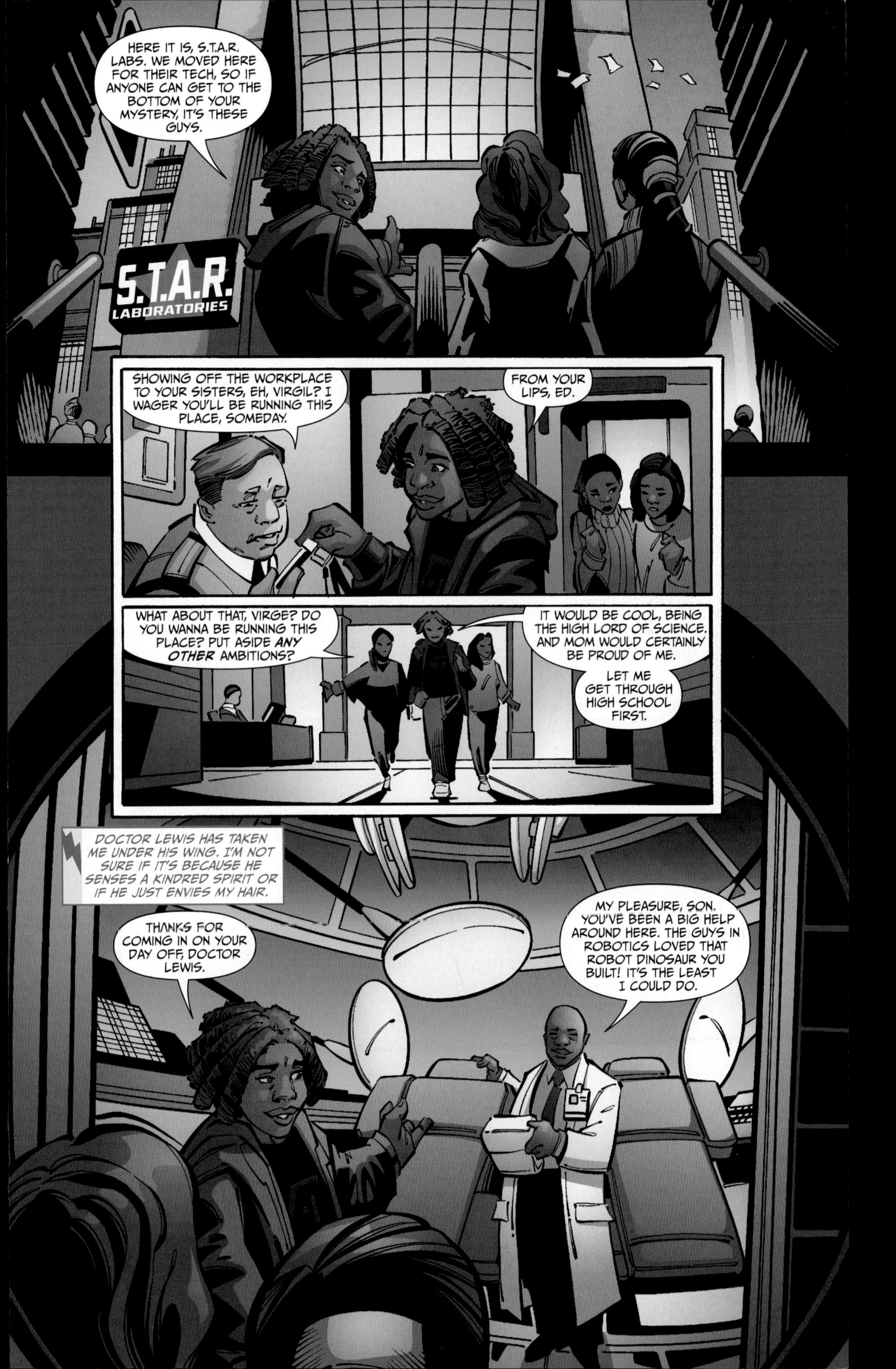

HERE IT IS, S.T.A.R. LABS. WE MOVED HERE FOR THEIR TECH, SO IF ANYONE CAN GET TO THE BOTTOM OF YOUR MYSTERY, IT'S THESE GUYS.
S.T.A.R. LABORATORIES
SHOWING OFF THE WORKPLACE TO YOUR SISTERS, EH, VIRGIL? I WAGER YOU'LL BE RUNNING THIS PLACE, SOMEDAY.
FROM YOUR LIPS, ED.
WHAT ABOUT THAT, VIRGE? DO YOU WANNA BE RUNNING THIS PLACE? PUT ASIDE ANY OTHER AMBITIONS?
IT WOULD BE COOL, BEING THE HIGH LORD OF SCIENCE. AND MOM WOULD CERTAINLY BE PROUD OF ME.
LET ME GET THROUGH HIGH SCHOOL FIRST.
DOCTOR LEWIS HAS TAKEN ME UNDER HIS WING. I'M NOT SURE IF IT'S BECAUSE HE SENSES A KINDRED SPIRIT OR IF HE JUST ENVIES MY HAIR.
THANKS FOR COMING IN ON YOUR DAY OFF, DOCTOR LEWIS.
MY PLEASURE, SON. YOU'VE BEEN A BIG HELP AROUND HERE. THE GUYS IN ROBOTICS LOVED THAT ROBOT DINOSAUR YOU BUILT! IT'S THE LEAST I COULD DO.

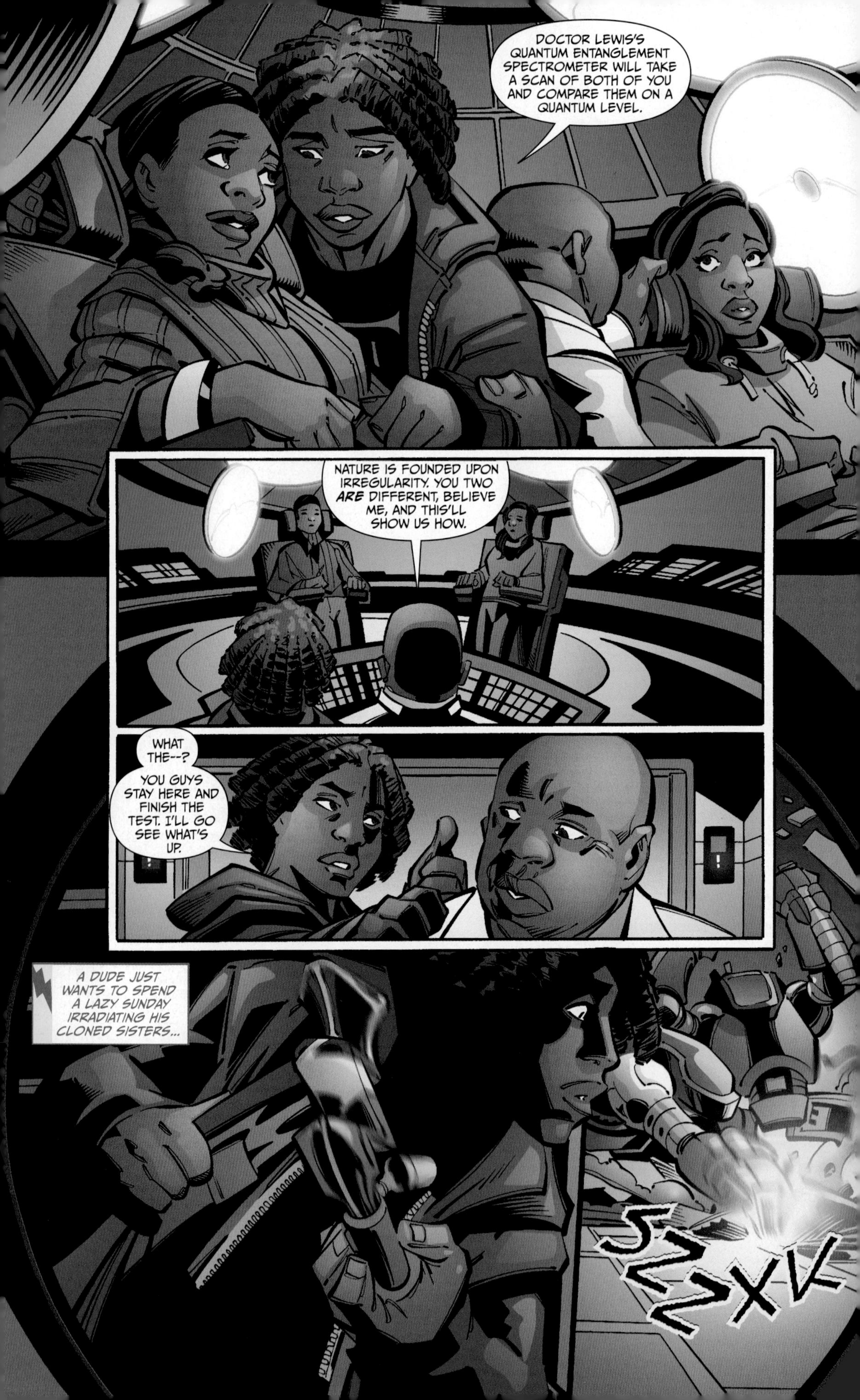
DOCTOR LEWIS'S QUANTUM ENTANGLEMENT SPECTROMETER WILL TAKE A SCAN OF BOTH OF YOU AND COMPARE THEM ON A QUANTUM LEVEL.
NATURE IS FOUNDED UPON IRREGULARITY. YOU TWO *ARE* DIFFERENT, BELIEVE ME, AND THIS'LL SHOW US HOW.
WHAT THE--?
YOU GUYS STAY HERE AND FINISH THE TEST. I'LL GO SEE WHAT'S UP.
A DUDE JUST WANTS TO SPEND A LAZY SUNDAY IRRADIATING HIS CLONED SISTERS...
SZZXK

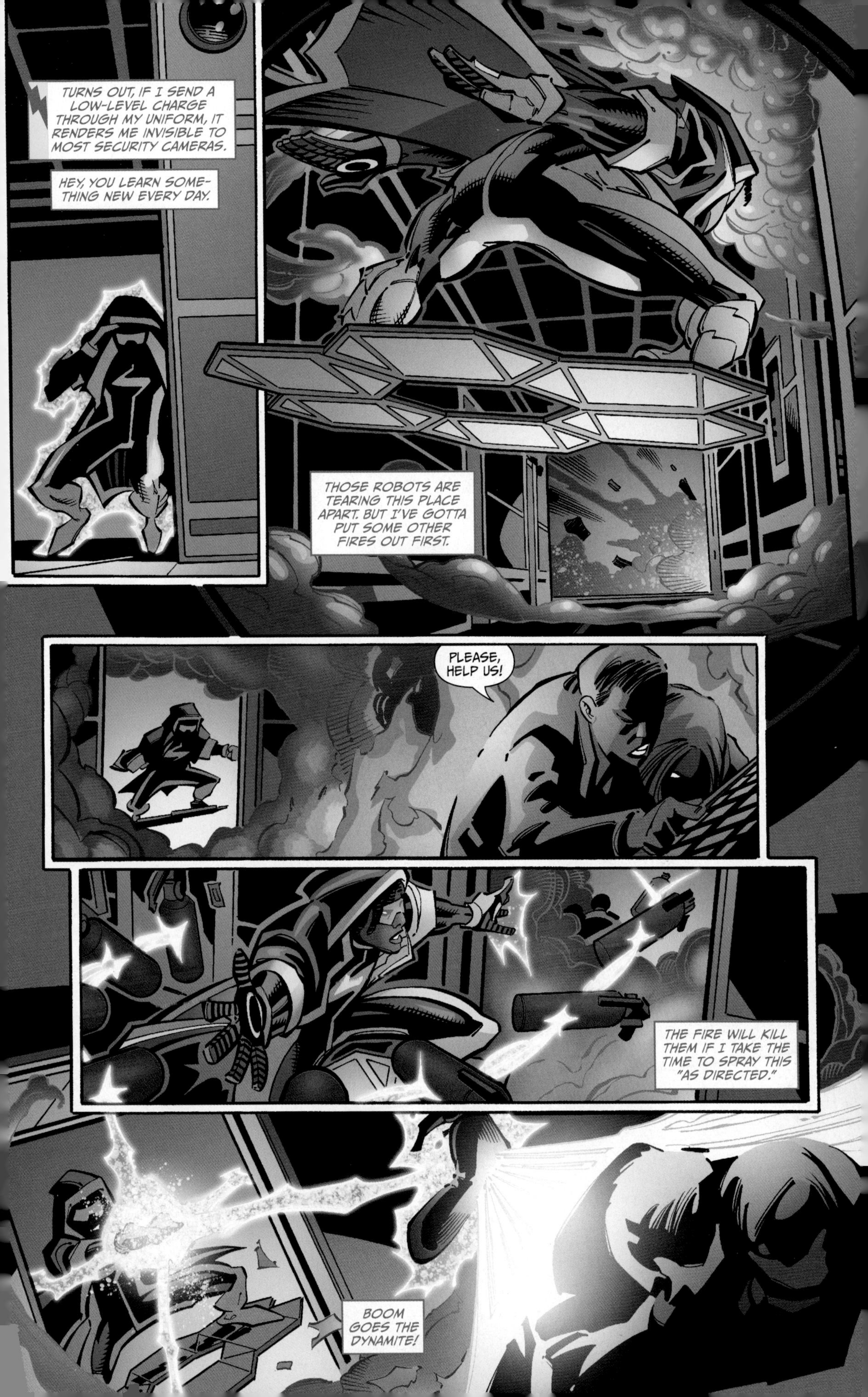
TURNS OUT, IF I SEND A LOW-LEVEL CHARGE THROUGH MY UNIFORM, IT RENDERS ME INVISIBLE TO MOST SECURITY CAMERAS.
HEY, YOU LEARN SOMETHING NEW EVERY DAY.
THOSE ROBOTS ARE TEARING THIS PLACE APART. BUT I'VE GOTTA PUT SOME OTHER FIRES OUT FIRST.
PLEASE, HELP US!
THE FIRE WILL KILL THEM IF I TAKE THE TIME TO SPRAY THIS "AS DIRECTED."
BOOM GOES THE DYNAMITE!

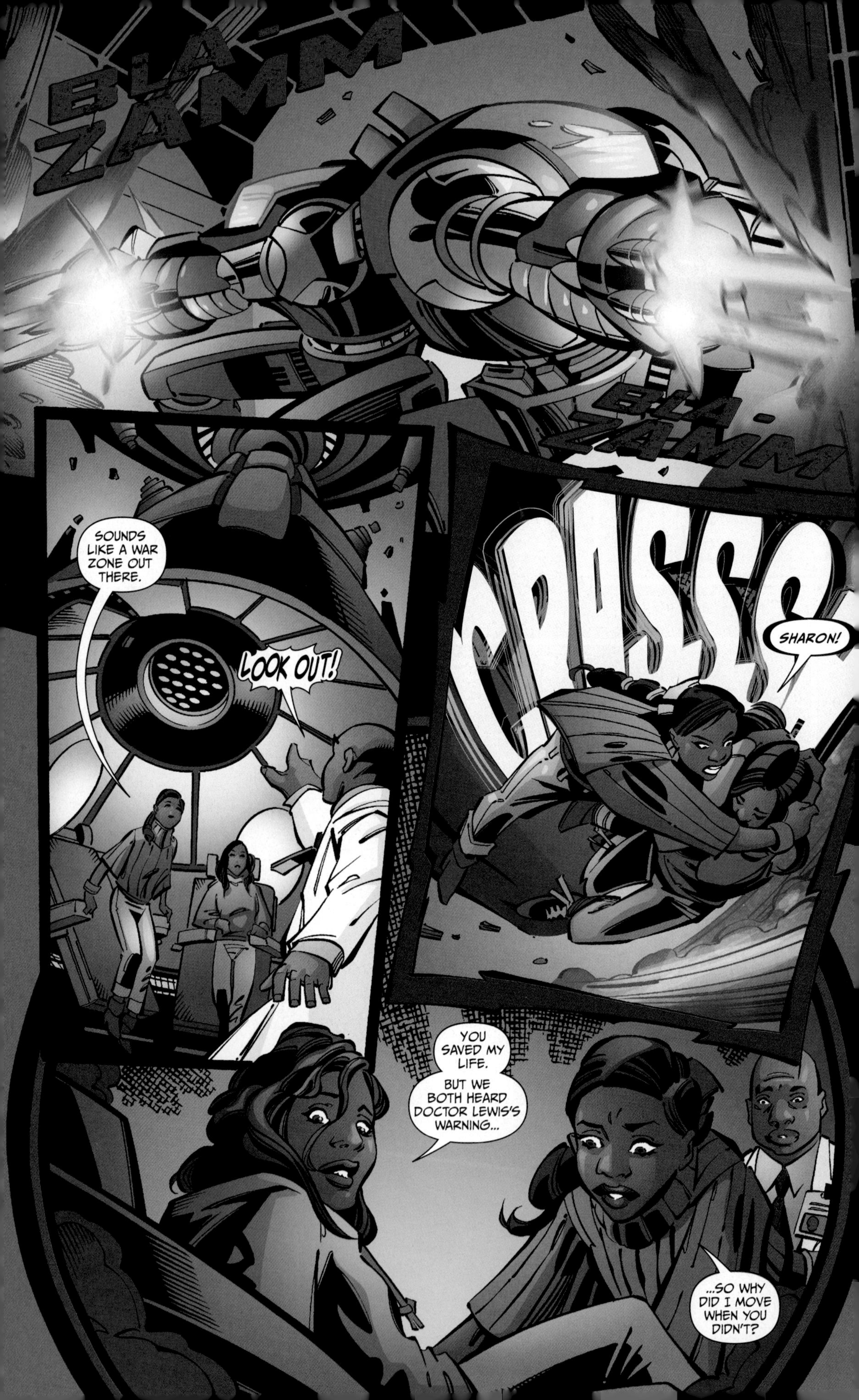
BLA-ZAMM
BLA-ZAMM
SOUNDS LIKE A WAR ZONE OUT THERE.
LOOK OUT!
CRASSSH
SHARON!
YOU SAVED MY LIFE.
BUT WE BOTH HEARD DOCTOR LEWIS'S WARNING...
...SO WHY DID I MOVE WHEN YOU DIDN'T?

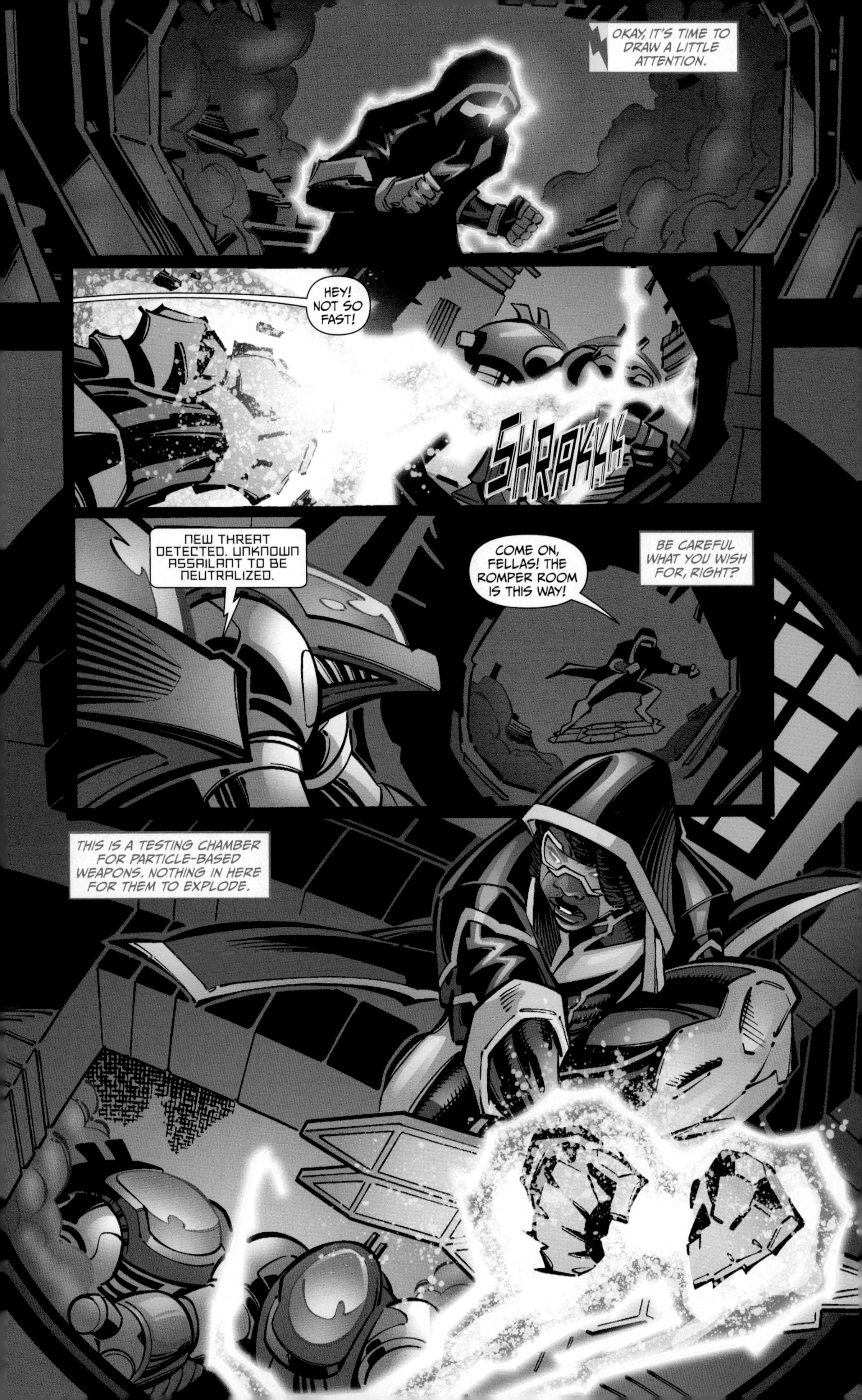
OKAY, IT'S TIME TO DRAW A LITTLE ATTENTION.
HEY! NOT SO FAST!
SHRAKKK
NEW THREAT DETECTED. UNKNOWN ASSAILANT TO BE NEUTRALIZED.
COME ON, FELLAS! THE ROMPER ROOM IS THIS WAY!
BE CAREFUL WHAT YOU WISH FOR, RIGHT?
THIS IS A TESTING CHAMBER FOR PARTICLE-BASED WEAPONS. NOTHING IN HERE FOR THEM TO EXPLODE.

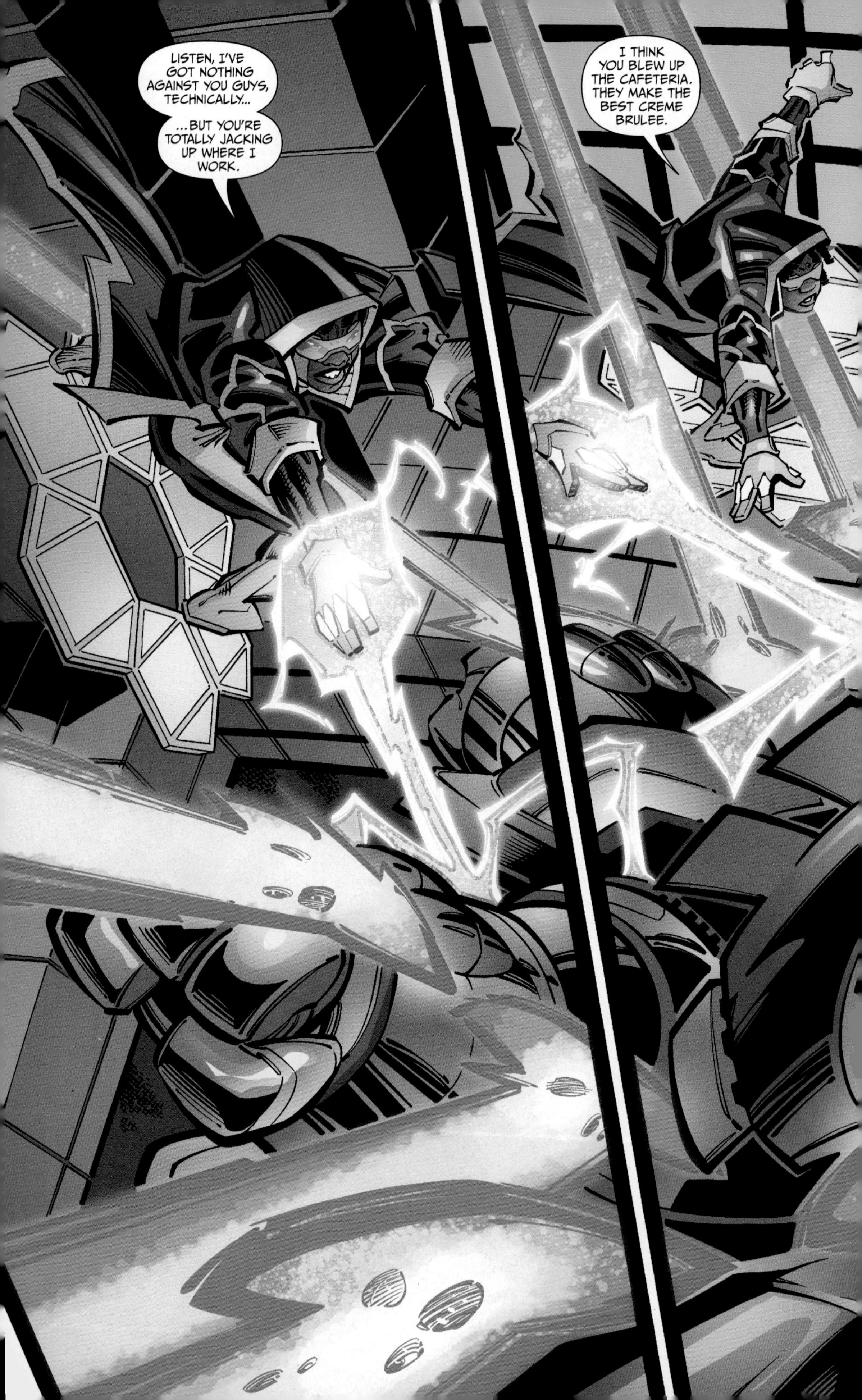
LISTEN, I'VE GOT NOTHING AGAINST YOU GUYS, TECHNICALLY...
...BUT YOU'RE TOTALLY JACKING UP WHERE I WORK.
I THINK YOU BLEW UP THE CAFETERIA. THEY MAKE THE BEST CREME BRULEE.

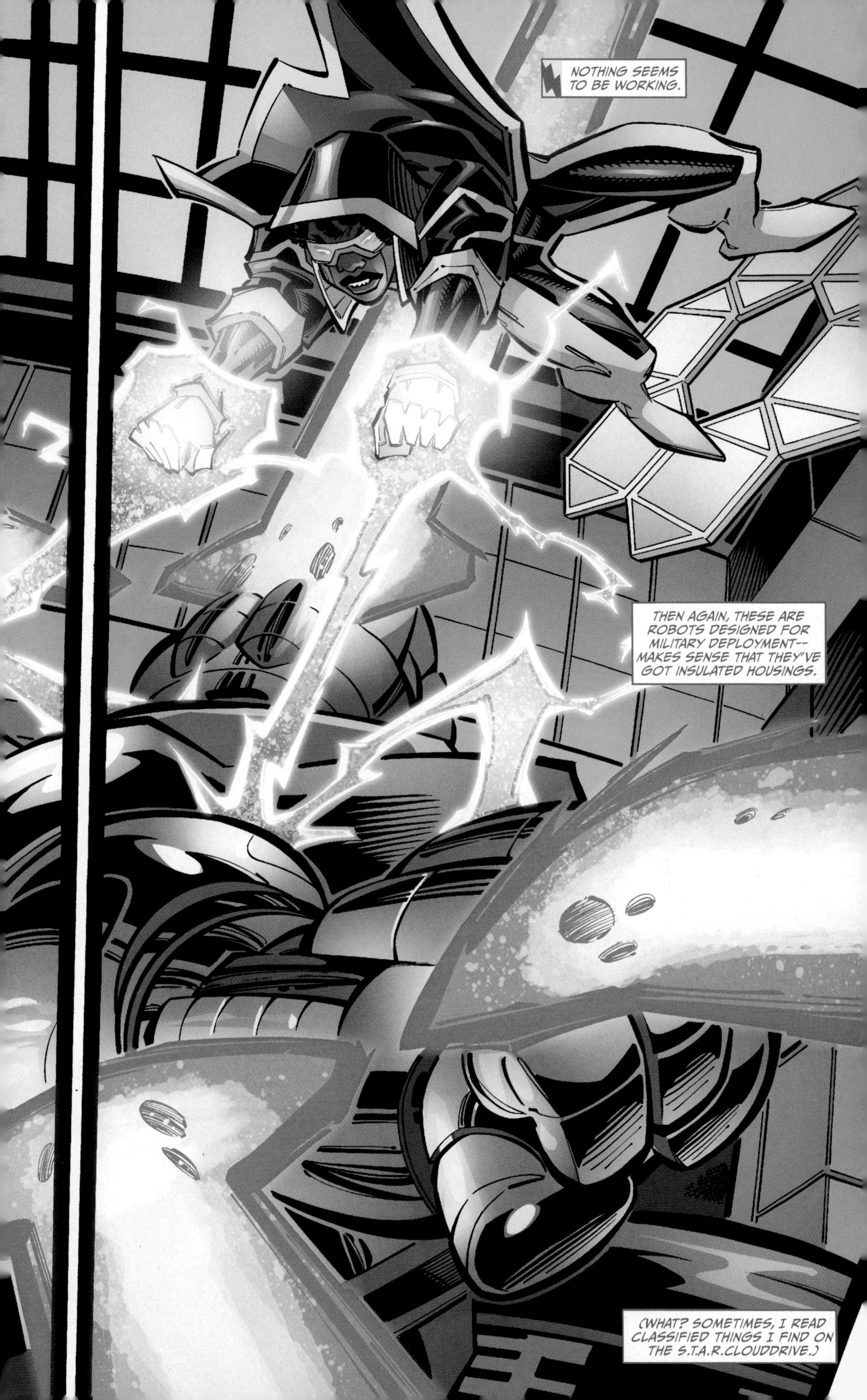
NOTHING SEEMS TO BE WORKING.
THEN AGAIN, THESE ARE ROBOTS DESIGNED FOR MILITARY DEPLOYMENT--MAKES SENSE THAT THEY'VE GOT INSULATED HOUSINGS.
(WHAT? SOMETIMES, I READ CLASSIFIED THINGS I FIND ON THE S.T.A.R.CLOUDDRIVE.)

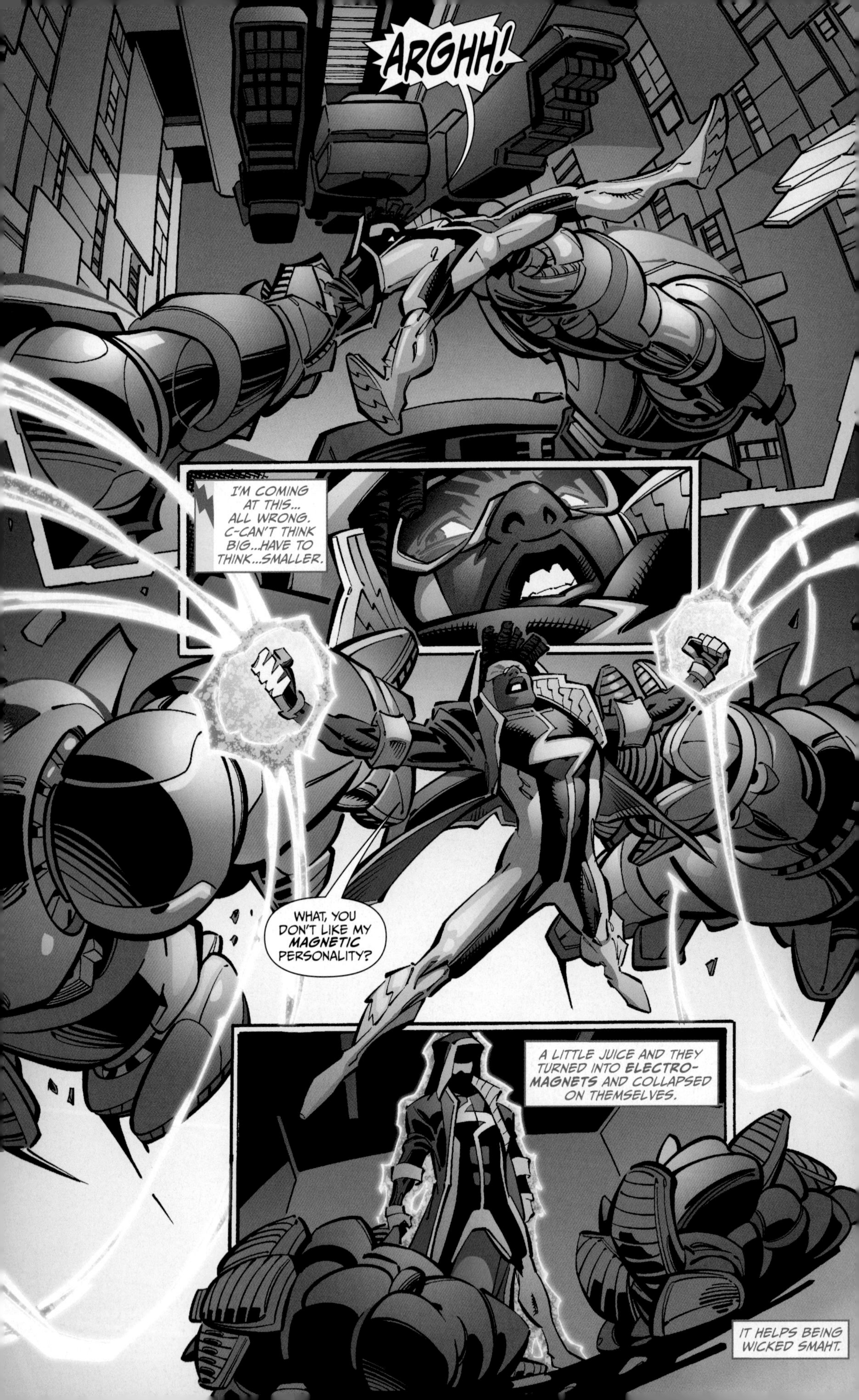
ARGHH!
I'M COMING AT THIS... ALL WRONG. C-CAN'T THINK BIG...HAVE TO THINK...SMALLER.
WHAT, YOU DON'T LIKE MY MAGNETIC PERSONALITY?
A LITTLE JUICE AND THEY TURNED INTO ELECTRO-MAGNETS AND COLLAPSED ON THEMSELVES.
IT HELPS BEING WICKED SMAHT.

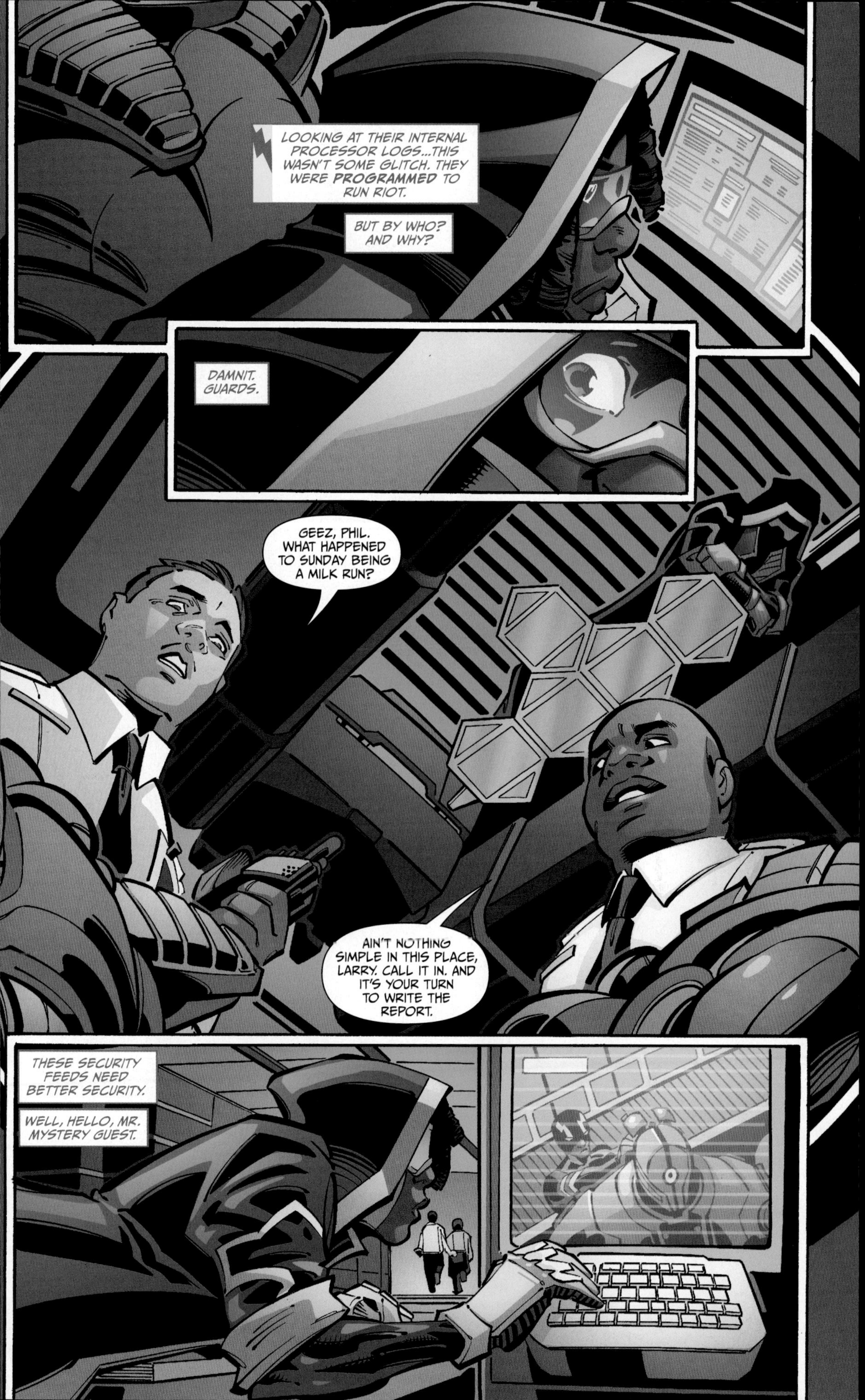

LOOKING AT THEIR INTERNAL PROCESSOR LOGS...THIS WASN'T SOME GLITCH. THEY WERE **PROGRAMMED** TO RUN RIOT.
BUT BY WHO? AND WHY?
DAMNIT. GUARDS.
GEEZ, PHIL. WHAT HAPPENED TO SUNDAY BEING A MILK RUN?
AIN'T NOTHING SIMPLE IN THIS PLACE, LARRY. CALL IT IN. AND IT'S YOUR TURN TO WRITE THE REPORT.
THESE SECURITY FEEDS NEED BETTER SECURITY.
WELL, HELLO, MR. MYSTERY GUEST.

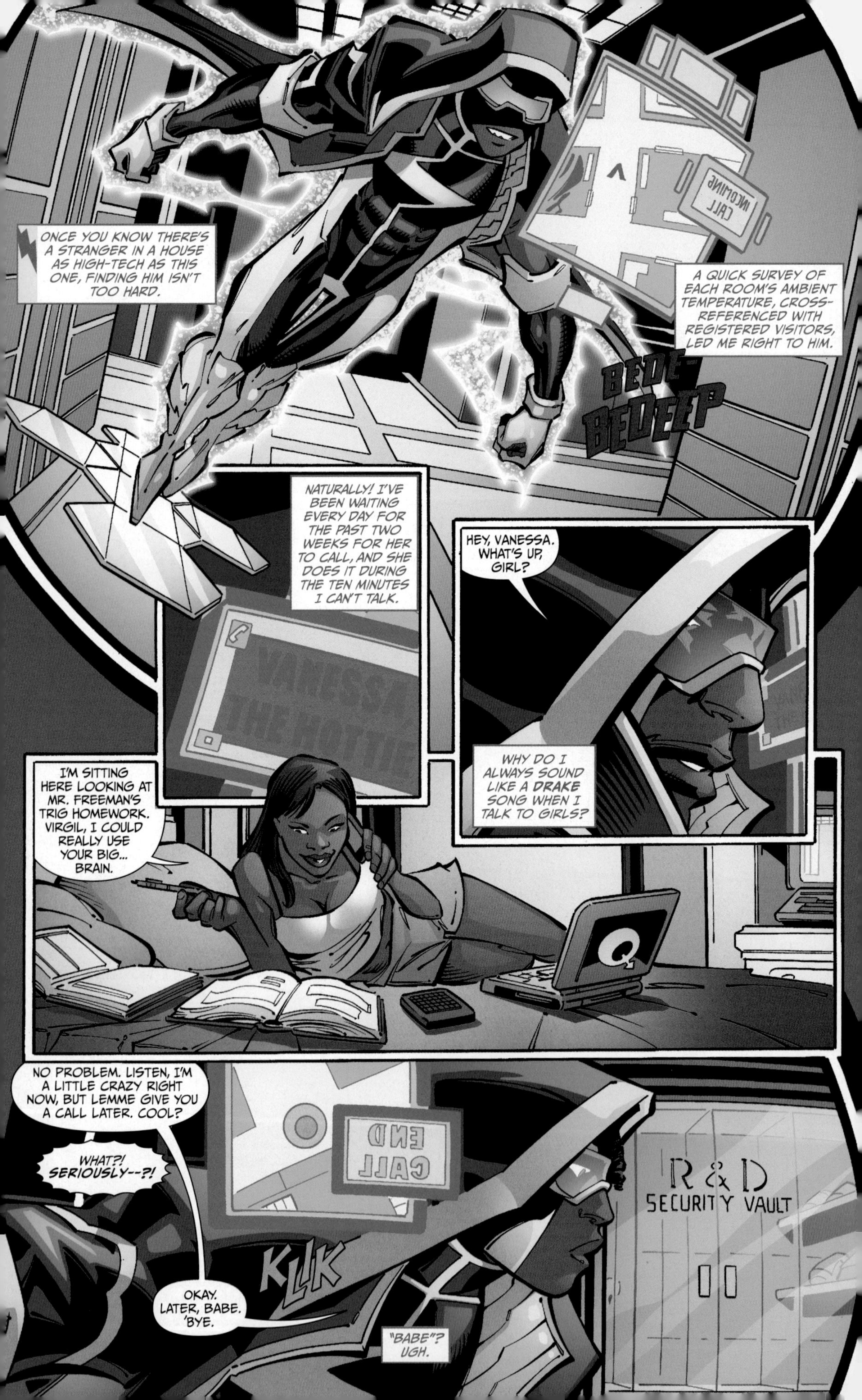

ONCE YOU KNOW THERE'S A STRANGER IN A HOUSE AS HIGH-TECH AS THIS ONE, FINDING HIM ISN'T TOO HARD.
INCOMING CALL
A QUICK SURVEY OF EACH ROOM'S AMBIENT TEMPERATURE, CROSS-REFERENCED WITH REGISTERED VISITORS, LED ME RIGHT TO HIM.
BEDE-BEDEEP
NATURALLY! I'VE BEEN WAITING EVERY DAY FOR THE PAST TWO WEEKS FOR HER TO CALL, AND SHE DOES IT DURING THE TEN MINUTES I CAN'T TALK.
VANESSA THE HOTTIE
HEY, VANESSA. WHAT'S UP, GIRL?
WHY DO I ALWAYS SOUND LIKE A **DRAKE** SONG WHEN I TALK TO GIRLS?
I'M SITTING HERE LOOKING AT MR. FREEMAN'S TRIG HOMEWORK. VIRGIL, I COULD REALLY USE YOUR BIG... BRAIN.
NO PROBLEM. LISTEN, I'M A LITTLE CRAZY RIGHT NOW, BUT LEMME GIVE YOU A CALL LATER. COOL?
END CALL
WHAT?! SERIOUSLY--?!
R & D SECURITY VAULT
KLIK
OKAY. LATER, BABE. 'BYE.
"BABE"? UGH.

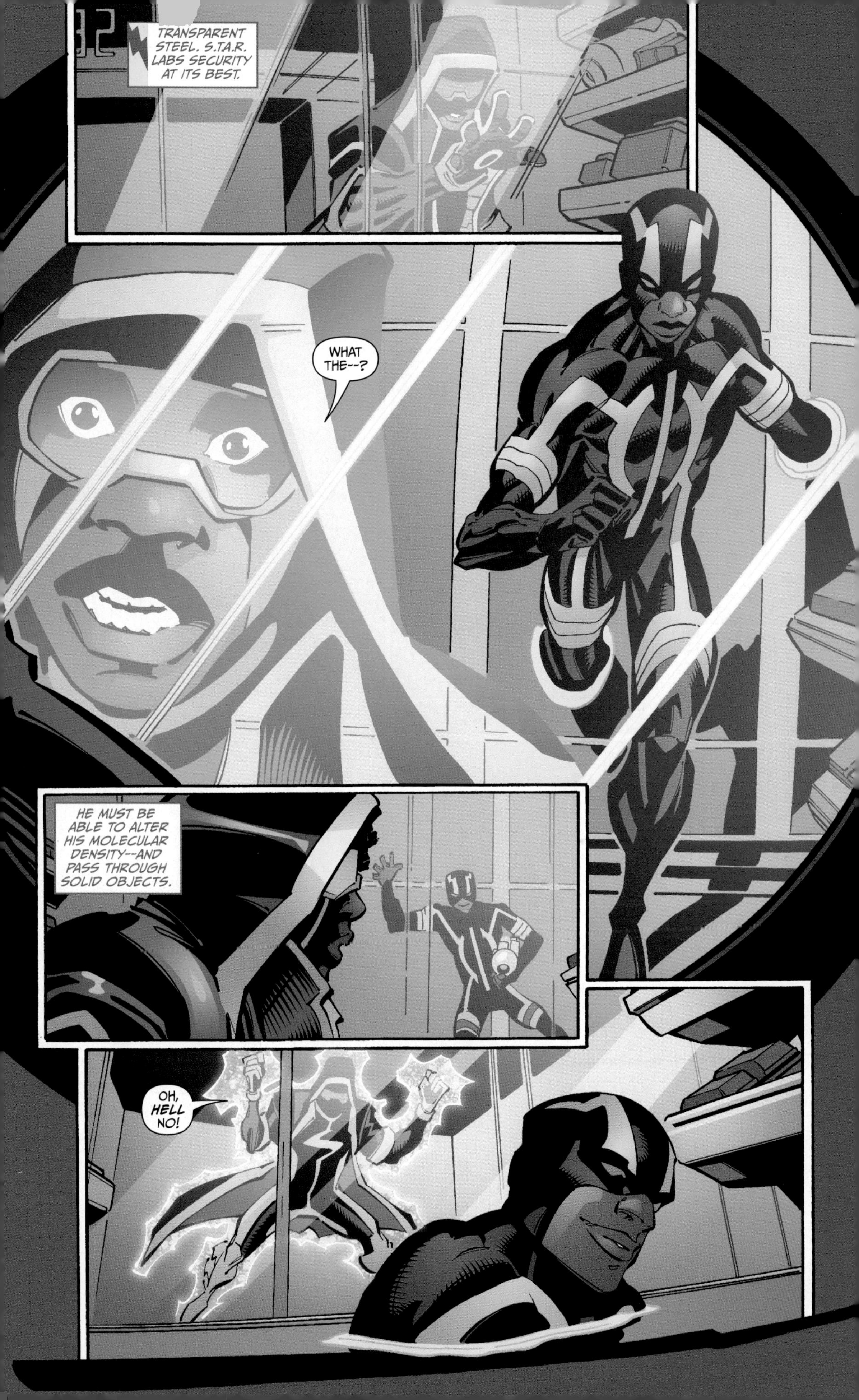
32
TRANSPARENT STEEL. S.T.A.R. LABS SECURITY AT ITS BEST.
WHAT THE--?
HE MUST BE ABLE TO ALTER HIS MOLECULAR DENSITY--AND PASS THROUGH SOLID OBJECTS.
OH, **HELL** NO!

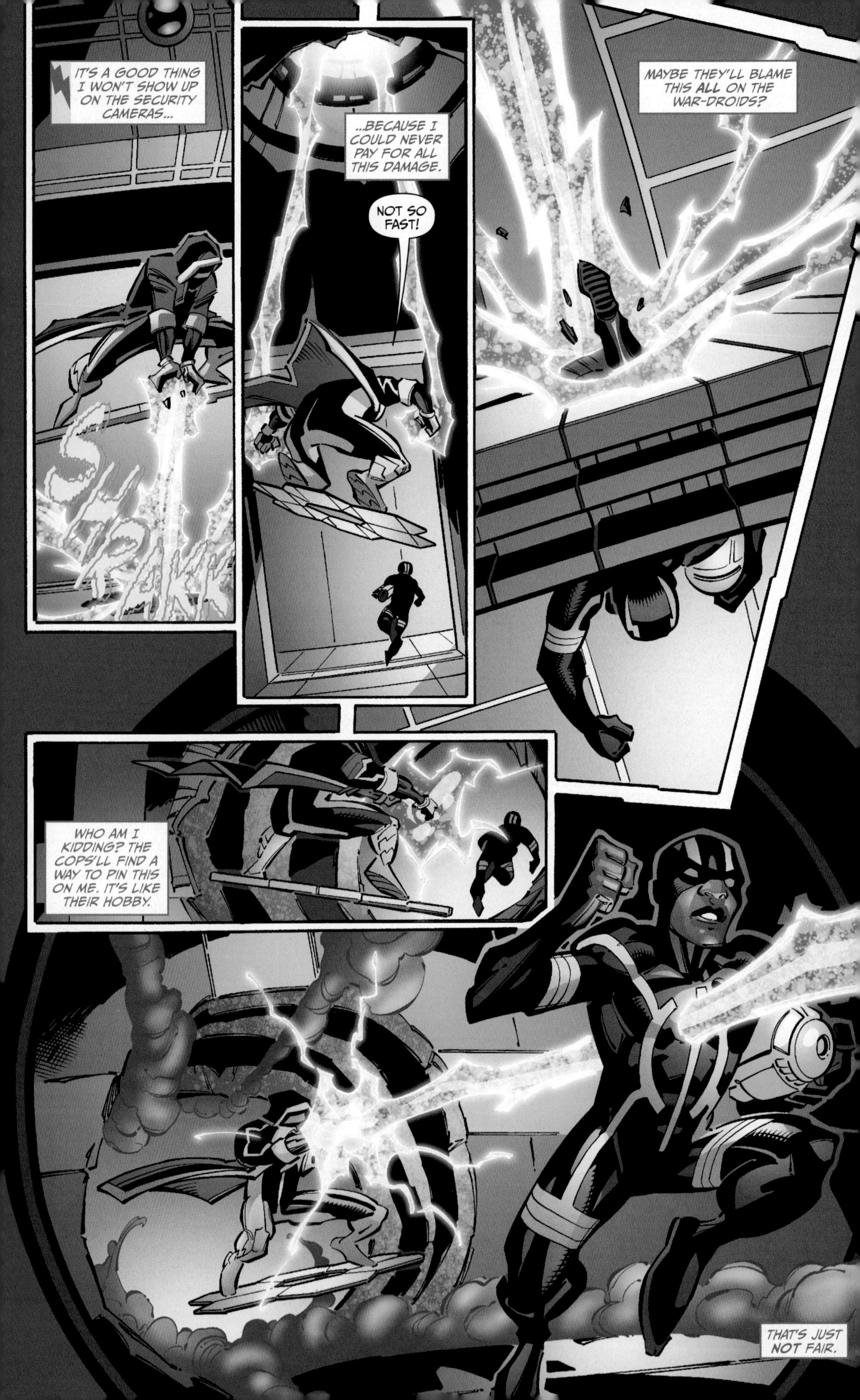

IT'S A GOOD THING I WON'T SHOW UP ON THE SECURITY CAMERAS...
...BECAUSE I COULD NEVER PAY FOR ALL THIS DAMAGE.
NOT SO FAST!
MAYBE THEY'LL BLAME THIS ALL ON THE WAR-DROIDS?
WHO AM I KIDDING? THE COPS'LL FIND A WAY TO PIN THIS ON ME. IT'S LIKE THEIR HOBBY.
THAT'S JUST NOT FAIR.

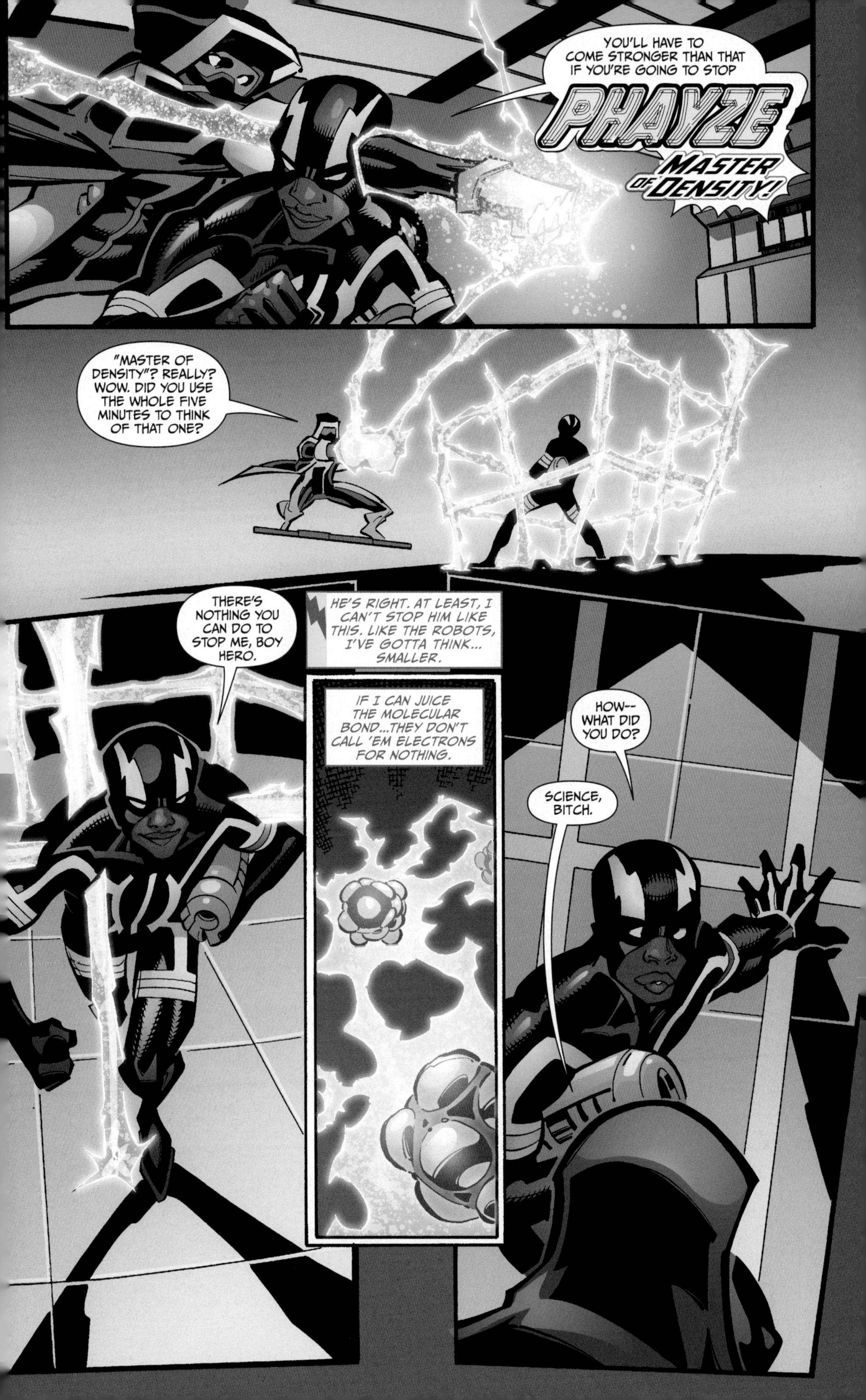
YOU'LL HAVE TO COME STRONGER THAN THAT IF YOU'RE GOING TO STOP
PHAYZE
MASTER OF DENSITY!
"MASTER OF DENSITY"? REALLY? WOW. DID YOU USE THE WHOLE FIVE MINUTES TO THINK OF THAT ONE?
THERE'S NOTHING YOU CAN DO TO STOP ME, BOY HERO.
HE'S RIGHT. AT LEAST, I CAN'T STOP HIM LIKE THIS. LIKE THE ROBOTS, I'VE GOTTA THINK... SMALLER.
IF I CAN JUICE THE MOLECULAR BOND...THEY DON'T CALL 'EM ELECTRONS FOR NOTHING.
HOW-- WHAT DID YOU DO?
SCIENCE, BITCH.

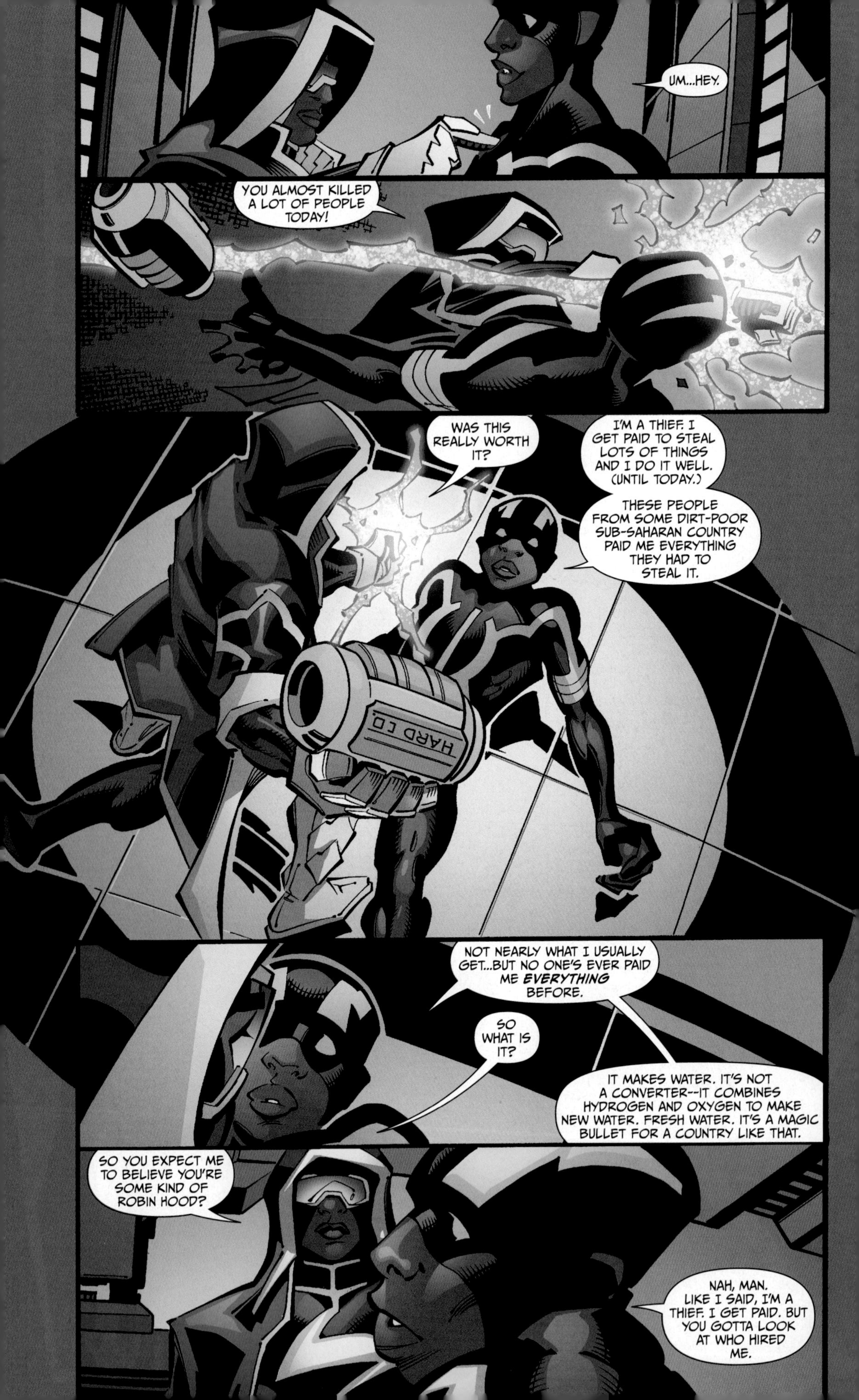
UM...HEY.
YOU ALMOST KILLED A LOT OF PEOPLE TODAY!
WAS THIS REALLY WORTH IT?
I'M A THIEF. I GET PAID TO STEAL LOTS OF THINGS AND I DO IT WELL. (UNTIL TODAY.)
THESE PEOPLE FROM SOME DIRT-POOR SUB-SAHARAN COUNTRY PAID ME EVERYTHING THEY HAD TO STEAL IT.
HARD CD
NOT NEARLY WHAT I USUALLY GET...BUT NO ONE'S EVER PAID ME *EVERYTHING* BEFORE.
SO WHAT IS IT?
IT MAKES WATER. IT'S NOT A CONVERTER--IT COMBINES HYDROGEN AND OXYGEN TO MAKE NEW WATER. FRESH WATER. IT'S A MAGIC BULLET FOR A COUNTRY LIKE THAT.
SO YOU EXPECT ME TO BELIEVE YOU'RE SOME KIND OF ROBIN HOOD?
NAH, MAN. LIKE I SAID, I'M A THIEF. I GET PAID. BUT YOU GOTTA LOOK AT WHO HIRED ME.

HARDWARE? IT'S ME, STATIC. I'VE GOT A GUY HERE WHO TRIED TO JACK ONE OF YOUR INVENTIONS FROM THE S.T.A.R. VAULT. IT'S LIKE A HYDRO-SYNTHESIZER.

YEAH, FOR SOME BROKE AFRICAN COUNTRY. YOU DO? I SHOULD? OKAY.

YOU'RE LUCKY I KNOW THE GUY WHO BUILT THIS AND HE'S GOT ANOTHER. BUT IF THAT DOESN'T GET TO WHERE IT'S SUPPOSED TO GO, OR IF YOU COME BACK HERE FOR ANYTHING ELSE...

...I BEAT YOU ONCE AND I CAN DO IT AGAIN. ALL FRAKKIN' DAY.

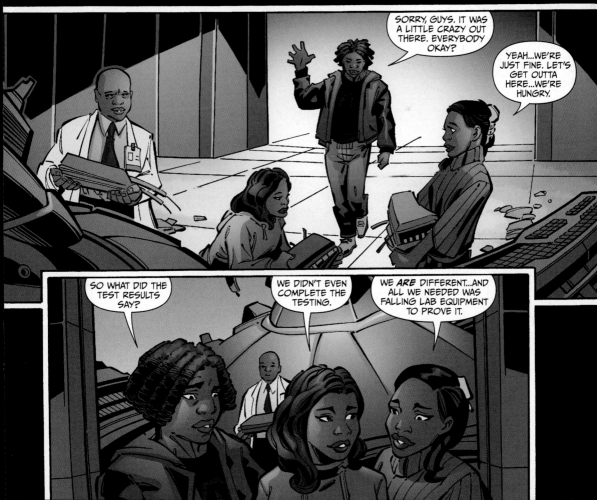

SORRY, GUYS. IT WAS A LITTLE CRAZY OUT THERE. EVERYBODY OKAY?

YEAH...WE'RE JUST FINE. LET'S GET OUTTA HERE...WE'RE HUNGRY.

SO WHAT DID THE TEST RESULTS SAY?

WE DIDN'T EVEN COMPLETE THE TESTING.

WE ARE DIFFERENT...AND ALL WE NEEDED WAS FALLING LAB EQUIPMENT TO PROVE IT.

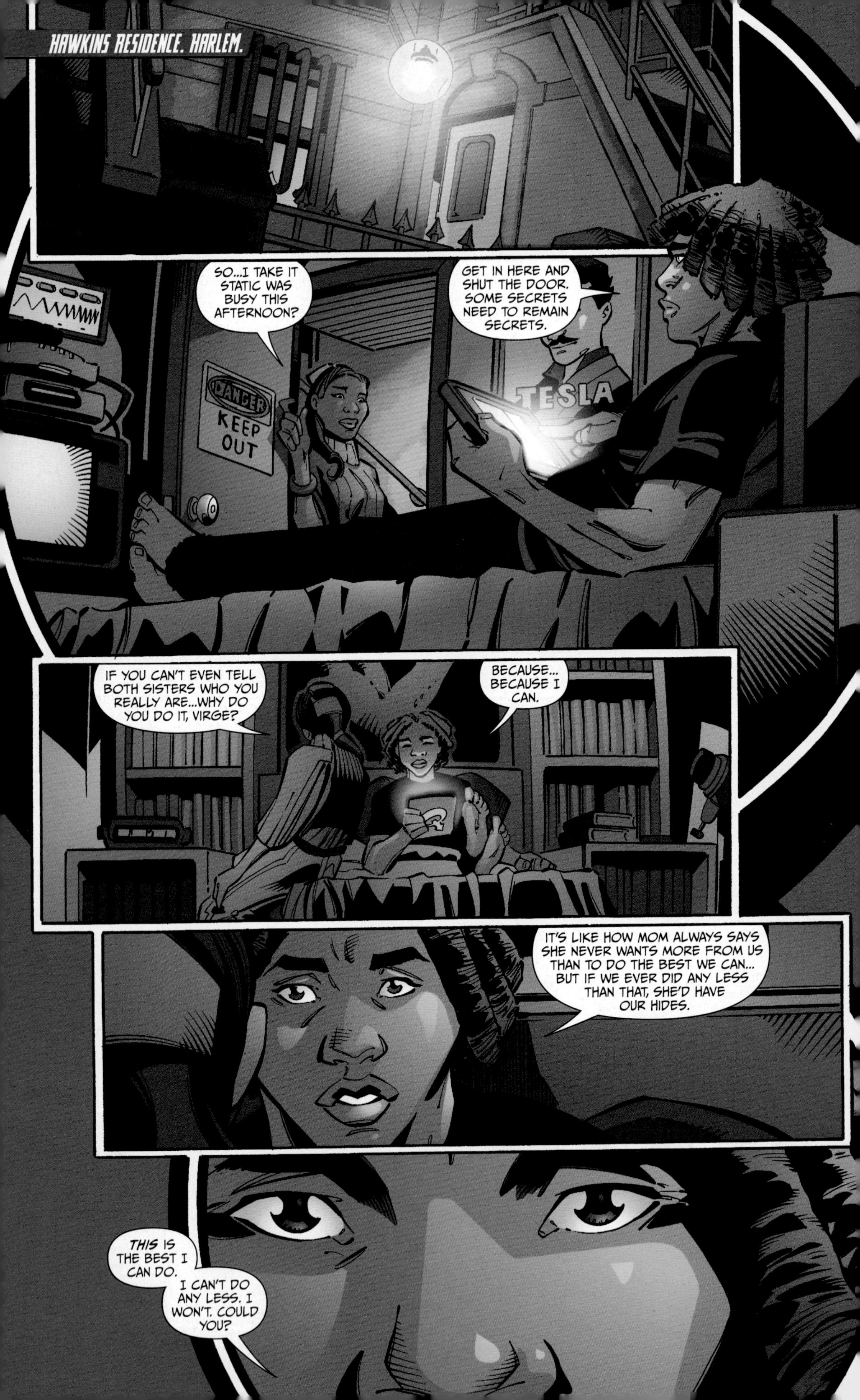
HAWKINS RESIDENCE. HARLEM.
SO...I TAKE IT STATIC WAS BUSY THIS AFTERNOON?
GET IN HERE AND SHUT THE DOOR. SOME SECRETS NEED TO REMAIN SECRETS.
DANGER KEEP OUT
TESLA
IF YOU CAN'T EVEN TELL BOTH SISTERS WHO YOU REALLY ARE...WHY DO YOU DO IT, VIRGE?
BECAUSE... BECAUSE I CAN.
IT'S LIKE HOW MOM ALWAYS SAYS SHE NEVER WANTS MORE FROM US THAN TO DO THE BEST WE CAN... BUT IF WE EVER DID ANY LESS THAN THAT, SHE'D HAVE OUR HIDES.
THIS IS THE BEST I CAN DO.
I CAN'T DO ANY LESS. I WON'T. COULD YOU?

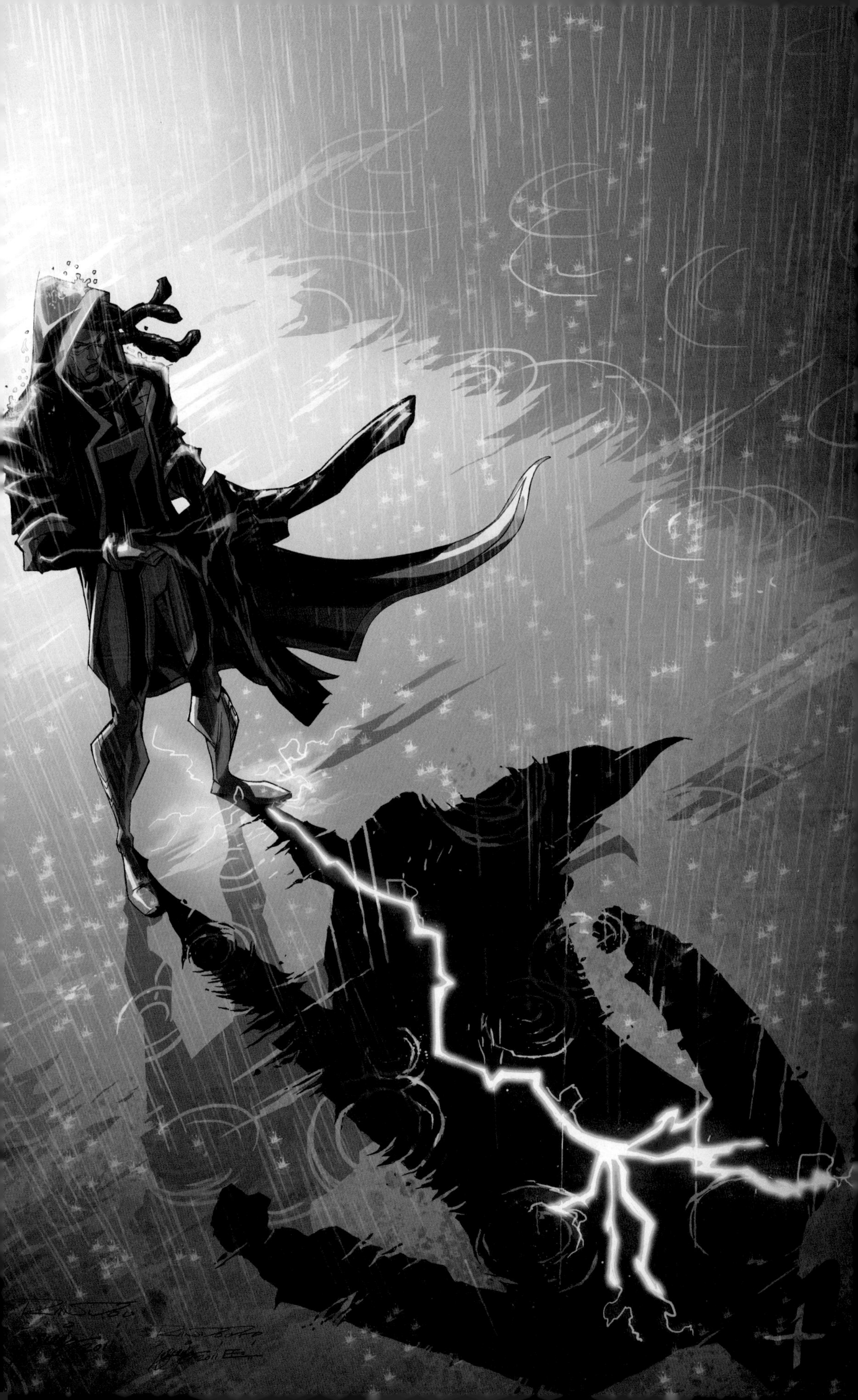

cover art by
KHARY RANDOLPH, LE BEAU UNDERWOOD
& EMILIO LOPEZ

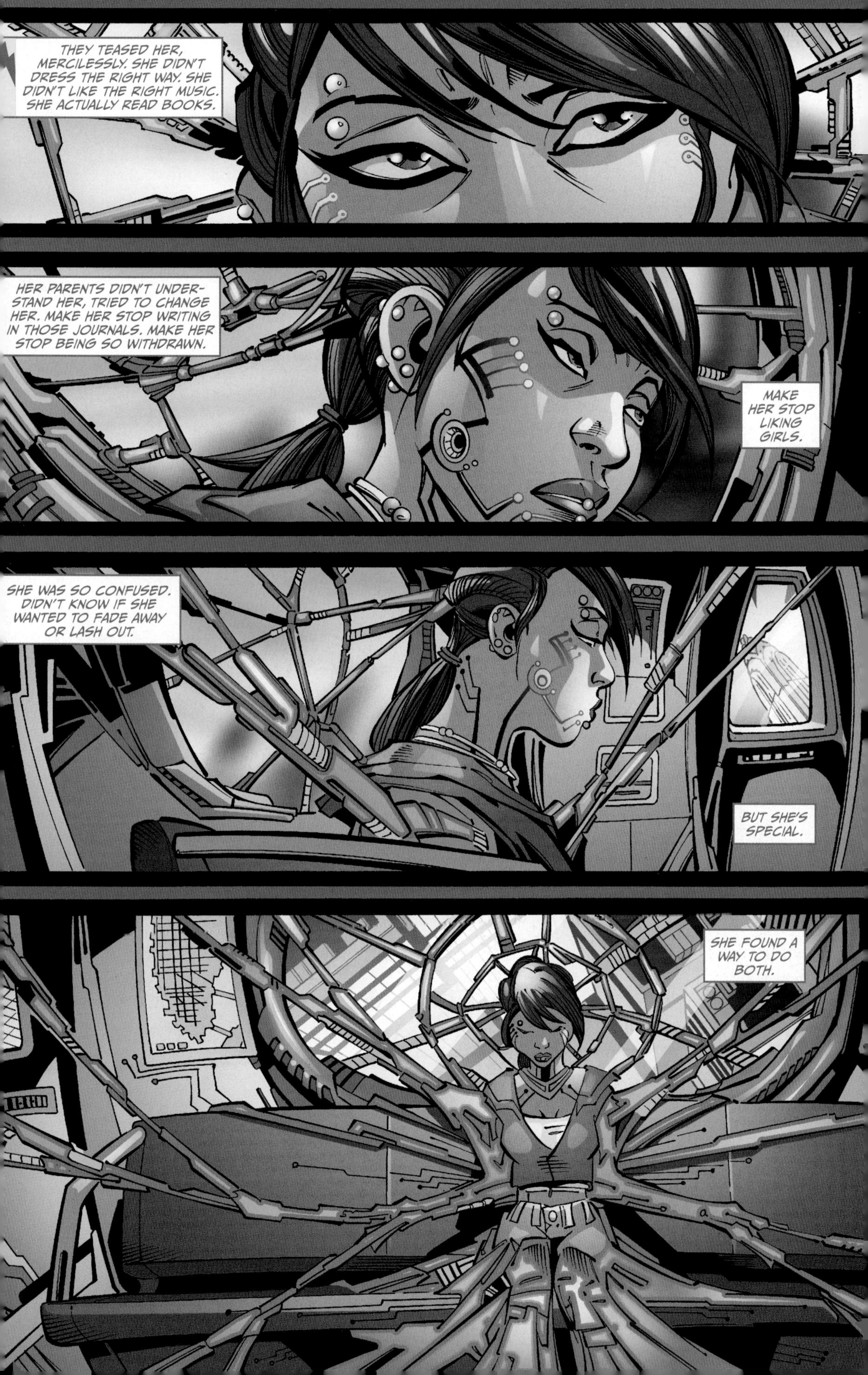
THEY TEASED HER, MERCILESSLY. SHE DIDN'T DRESS THE RIGHT WAY. SHE DIDN'T LIKE THE RIGHT MUSIC. SHE ACTUALLY READ BOOKS.
HER PARENTS DIDN'T UNDERSTAND HER, TRIED TO CHANGE HER. MAKE HER STOP WRITING IN THOSE JOURNALS. MAKE HER STOP BEING SO WITHDRAWN.
MAKE HER STOP LIKING GIRLS.
SHE WAS SO CONFUSED. DIDN'T KNOW IF SHE WANTED TO FADE AWAY OR LASH OUT.
BUT SHE'S SPECIAL.
SHE FOUND A WAY TO DO BOTH.

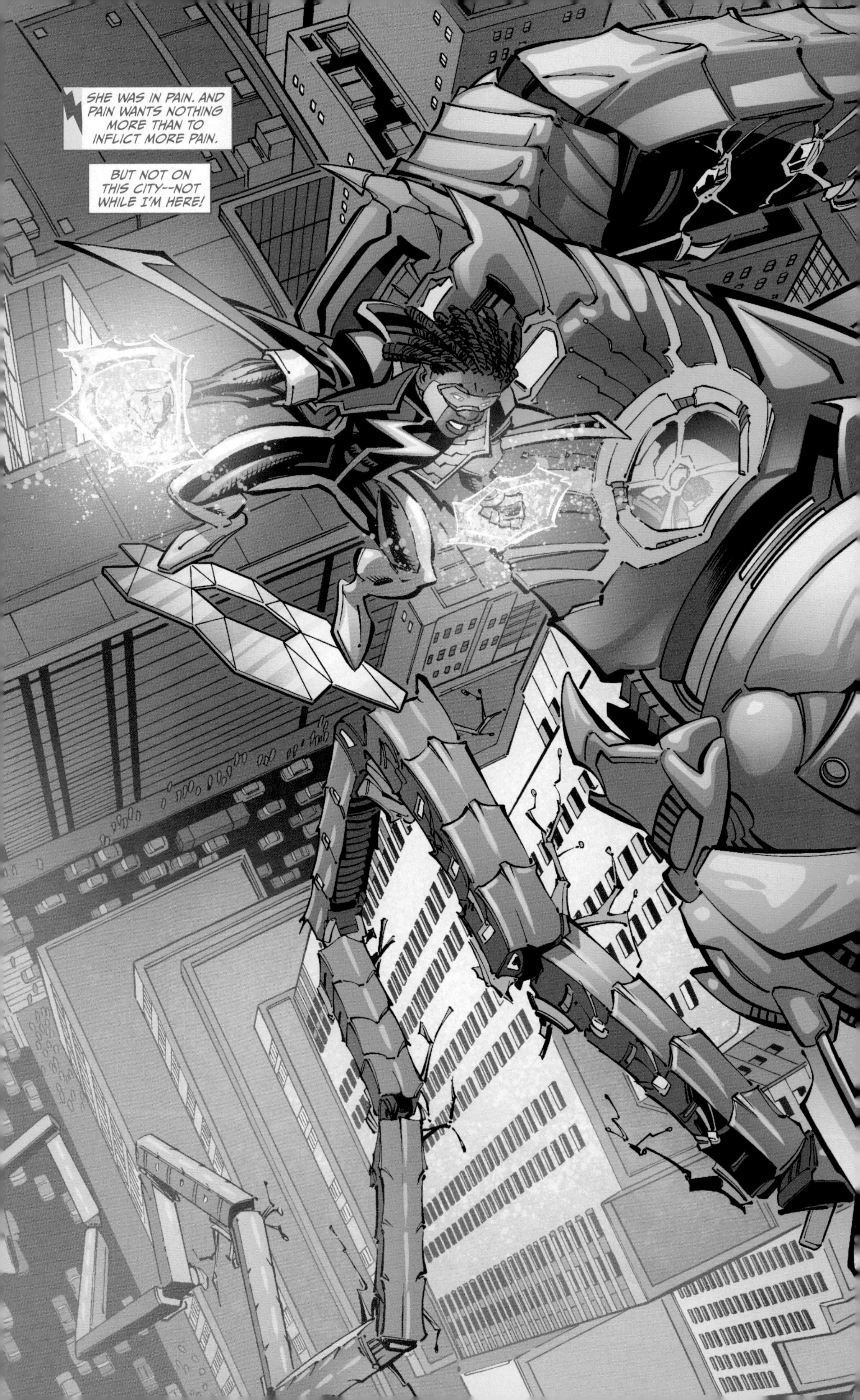
SHE WAS IN PAIN. AND PAIN WANTS NOTHING MORE THAN TO INFLICT MORE PAIN.
BUT NOT ON THIS CITY--NOT WHILE I'M HERE!

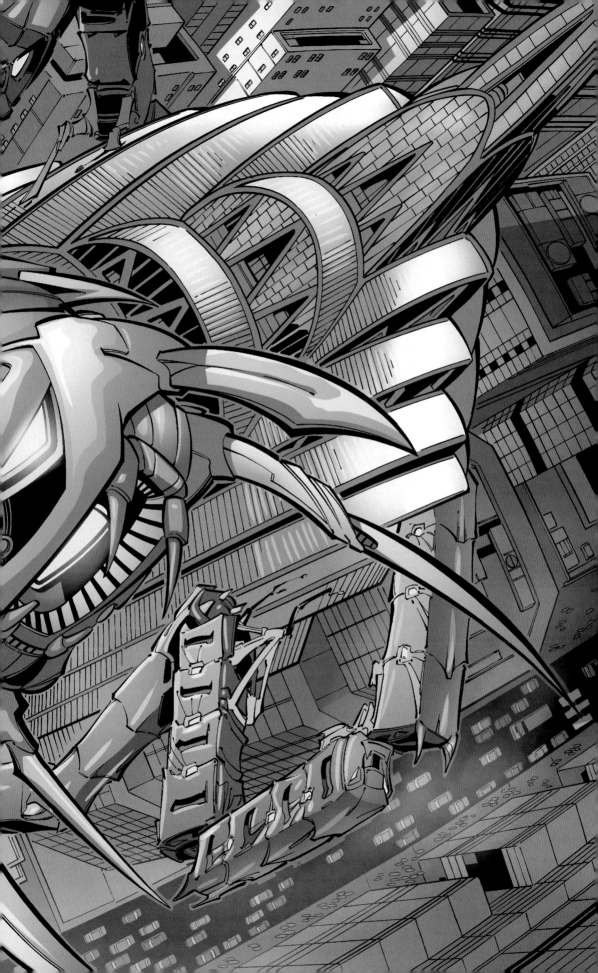

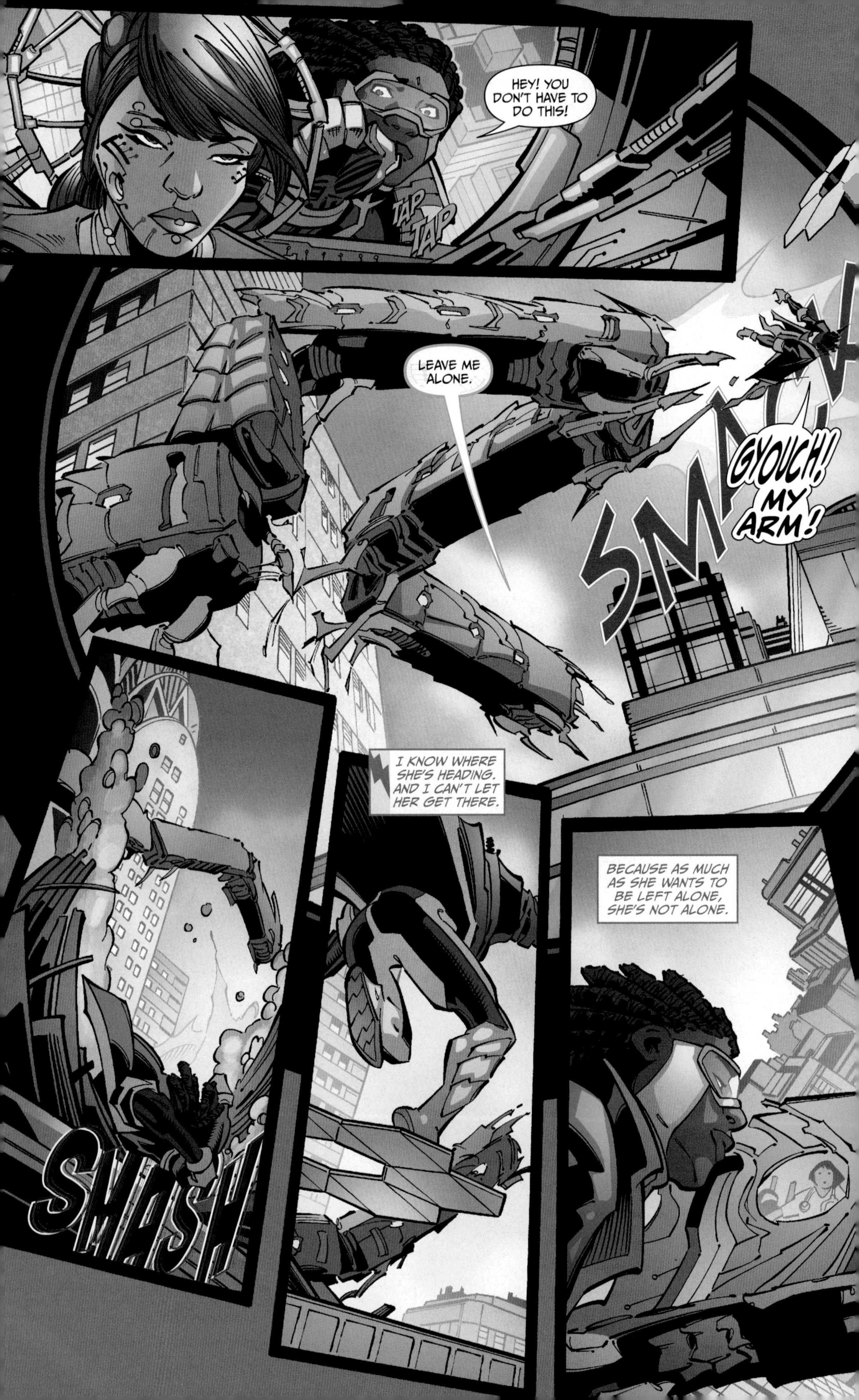
HEY! YOU DON'T HAVE TO DO THIS!
TAP TAP
LEAVE ME ALONE.
SMACK
GYOUCH! MY ARM!
SMASH
I KNOW WHERE SHE'S HEADING. AND I CAN'T LET HER GET THERE.
BECAUSE AS MUCH AS SHE WANTS TO BE LEFT ALONE, SHE'S NOT ALONE.

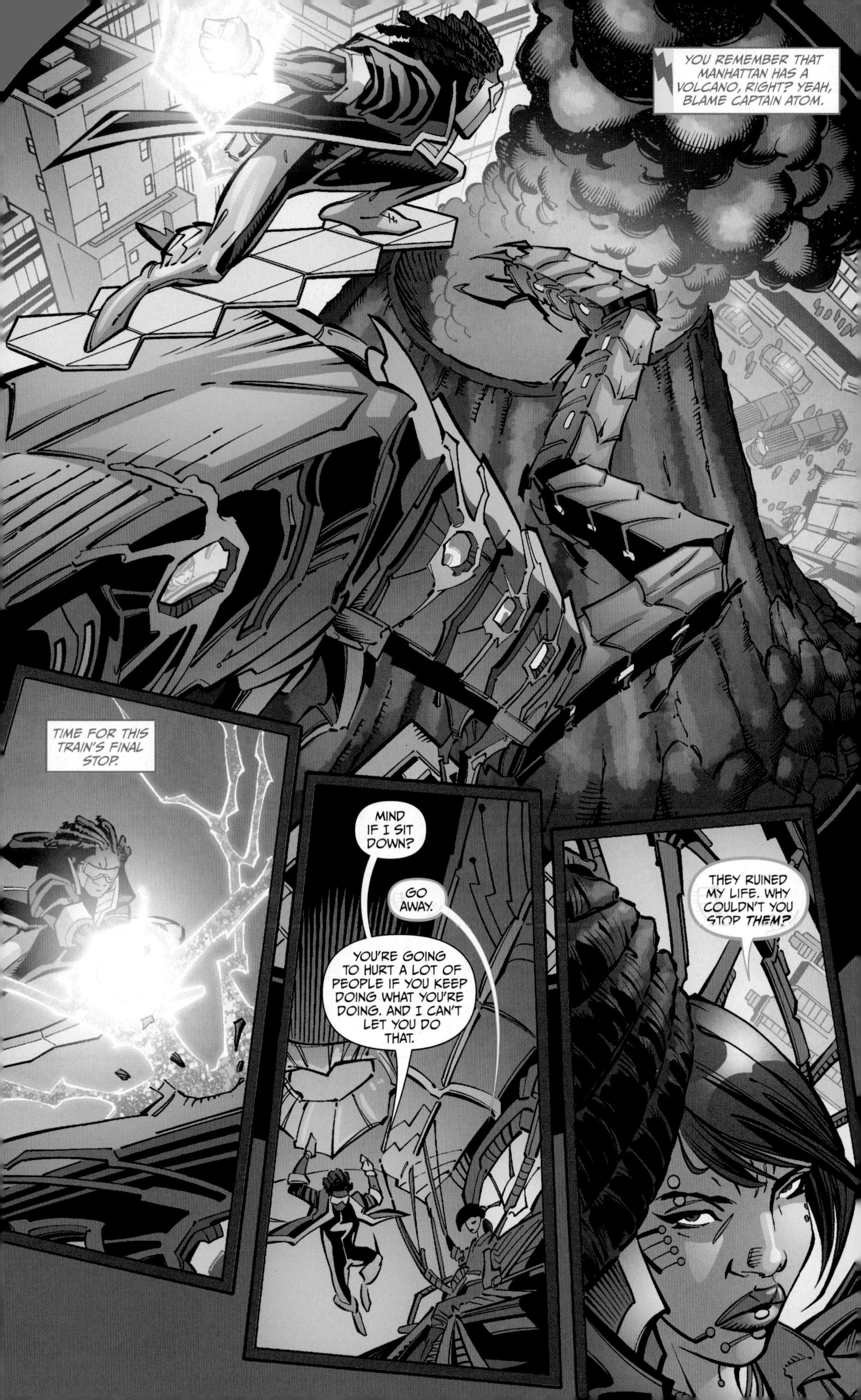
YOU REMEMBER THAT MANHATTAN HAS A VOLCANO, RIGHT? YEAH, BLAME CAPTAIN ATOM.
TIME FOR THIS TRAIN'S FINAL STOP.
MIND IF I SIT DOWN?
GO AWAY.
YOU'RE GOING TO HURT A LOT OF PEOPLE IF YOU KEEP DOING WHAT YOU'RE DOING. AND I CAN'T LET YOU DO THAT.
THEY RUINED MY LIFE. WHY COULDN'T YOU STOP THEM?

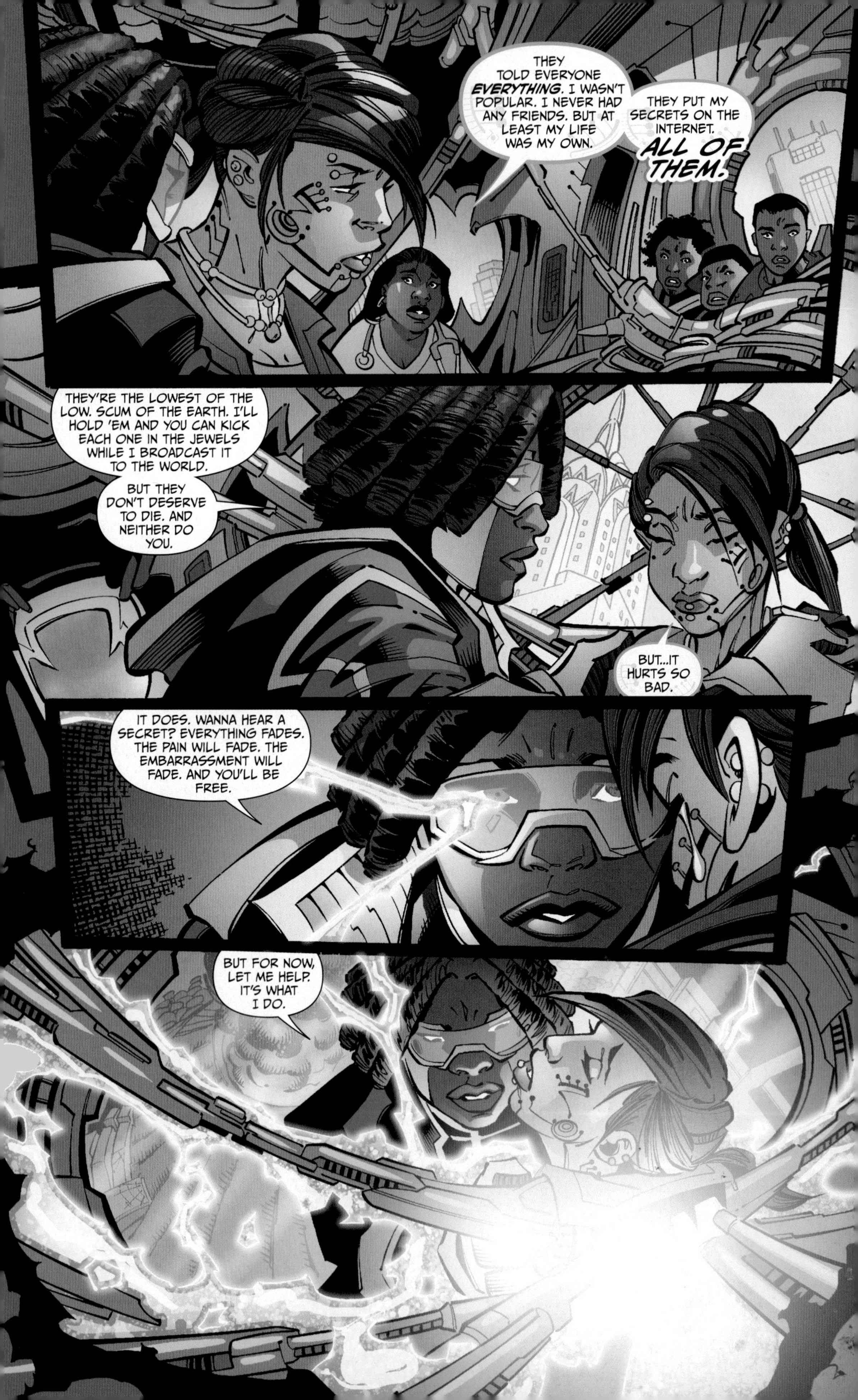
THEY TOLD EVERYONE EVERYTHING. I WASN'T POPULAR. I NEVER HAD ANY FRIENDS. BUT AT LEAST MY LIFE WAS MY OWN.
THEY PUT MY SECRETS ON THE INTERNET. ALL OF THEM.
THEY'RE THE LOWEST OF THE LOW. SCUM OF THE EARTH. I'LL HOLD 'EM AND YOU CAN KICK EACH ONE IN THE JEWELS WHILE I BROADCAST IT TO THE WORLD.
BUT THEY DON'T DESERVE TO DIE. AND NEITHER DO YOU.
BUT...IT HURTS SO BAD.
IT DOES. WANNA HEAR A SECRET? EVERYTHING FADES. THE PAIN WILL FADE. THE EMBARRASSMENT WILL FADE. AND YOU'LL BE FREE.
BUT FOR NOW, LET ME HELP. IT'S WHAT I DO.

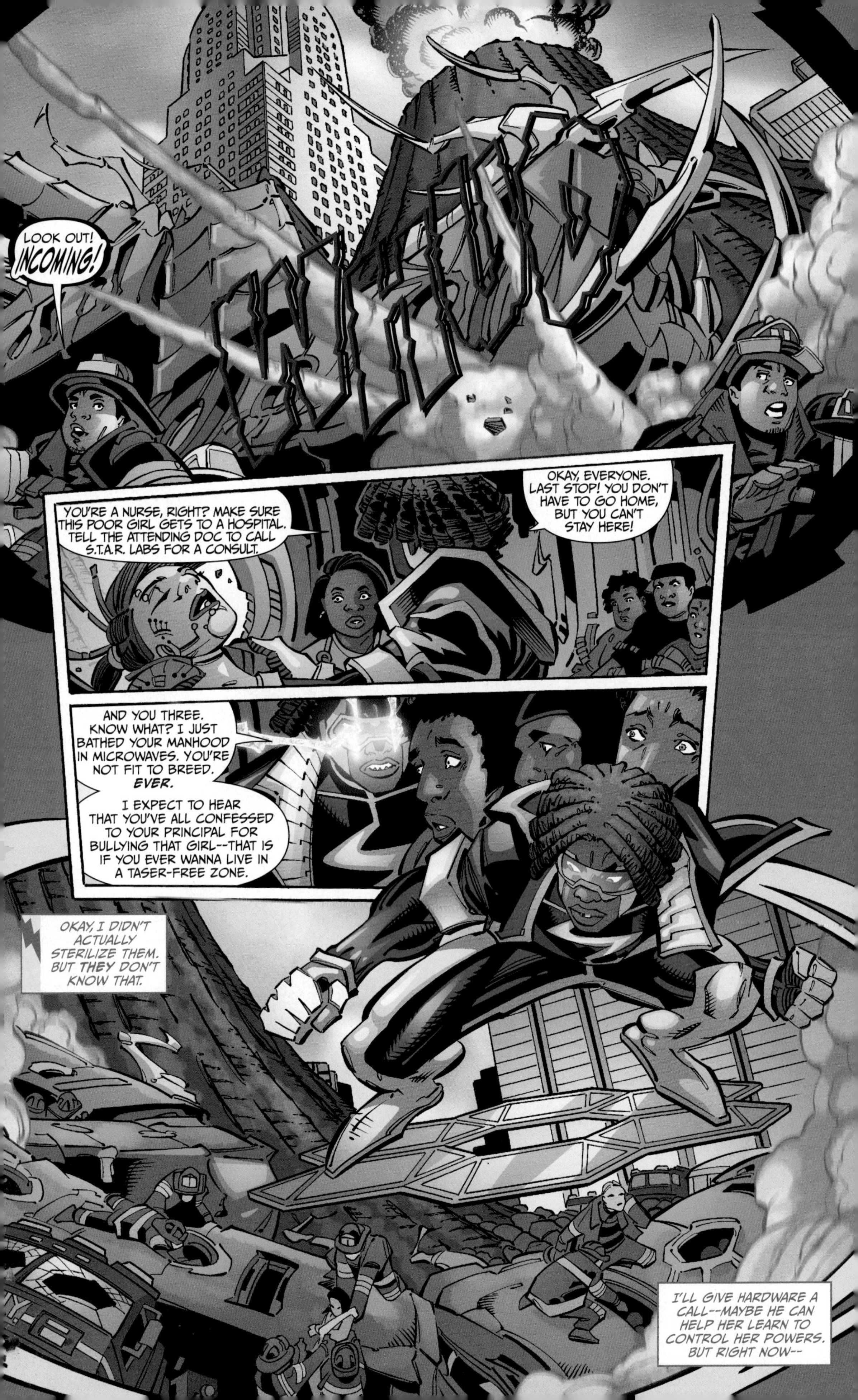
LOOK OUT! INCOMING!
YOU'RE A NURSE, RIGHT? MAKE SURE THIS POOR GIRL GETS TO A HOSPITAL. TELL THE ATTENDING DOC TO CALL S.T.A.R. LABS FOR A CONSULT.
OKAY, EVERYONE. LAST STOP! YOU DON'T HAVE TO GO HOME, BUT YOU CAN'T STAY HERE!
AND YOU THREE. KNOW WHAT? I JUST BATHED YOUR MANHOOD IN MICROWAVES. YOU'RE NOT FIT TO BREED. EVER.
I EXPECT TO HEAR THAT YOU'VE ALL CONFESSED TO YOUR PRINCIPAL FOR BULLYING THAT GIRL--THAT IS IF YOU EVER WANNA LIVE IN A TASER-FREE ZONE.
OKAY, I DIDN'T ACTUALLY STERILIZE THEM. BUT THEY DON'T KNOW THAT.
I'LL GIVE HARDWARE A CALL--MAYBE HE CAN HELP HER LEARN TO CONTROL HER POWERS. BUT RIGHT NOW--

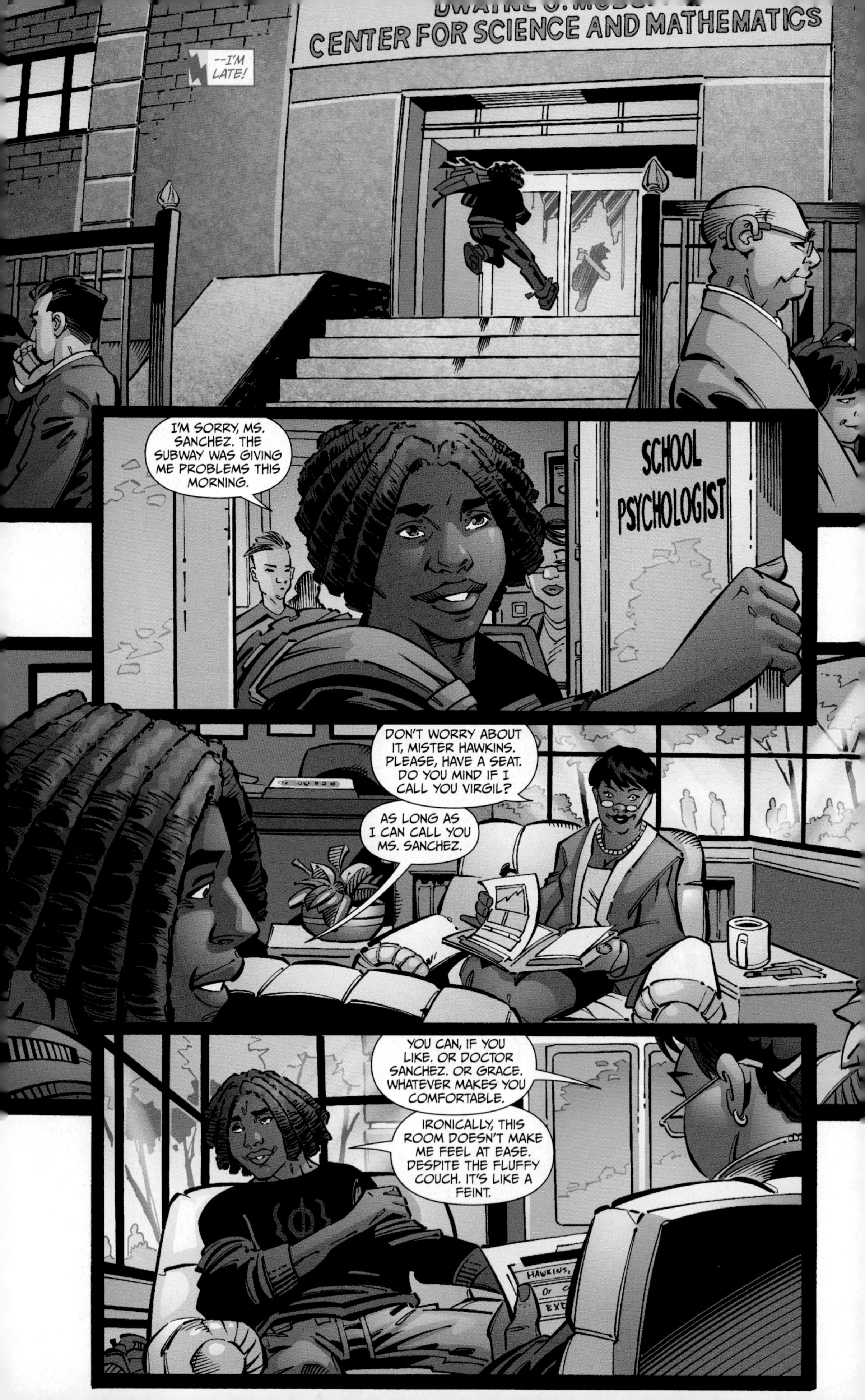
CENTER FOR SCIENCE AND MATHEMATICS
--I'M LATE!
I'M SORRY, MS. SANCHEZ. THE SUBWAY WAS GIVING ME PROBLEMS THIS MORNING.
SCHOOL PSYCHOLOGIST
DON'T WORRY ABOUT IT, MISTER HAWKINS. PLEASE, HAVE A SEAT. DO YOU MIND IF I CALL YOU VIRGIL?
AS LONG AS I CAN CALL YOU MS. SANCHEZ.
YOU CAN, IF YOU LIKE. OR DOCTOR SANCHEZ. OR GRACE. WHATEVER MAKES YOU COMFORTABLE.
IRONICALLY, THIS ROOM DOESN'T MAKE ME FEEL AT EASE. DESPITE THE FLUFFY COUCH. IT'S LIKE A FEINT.
HAWKINS,

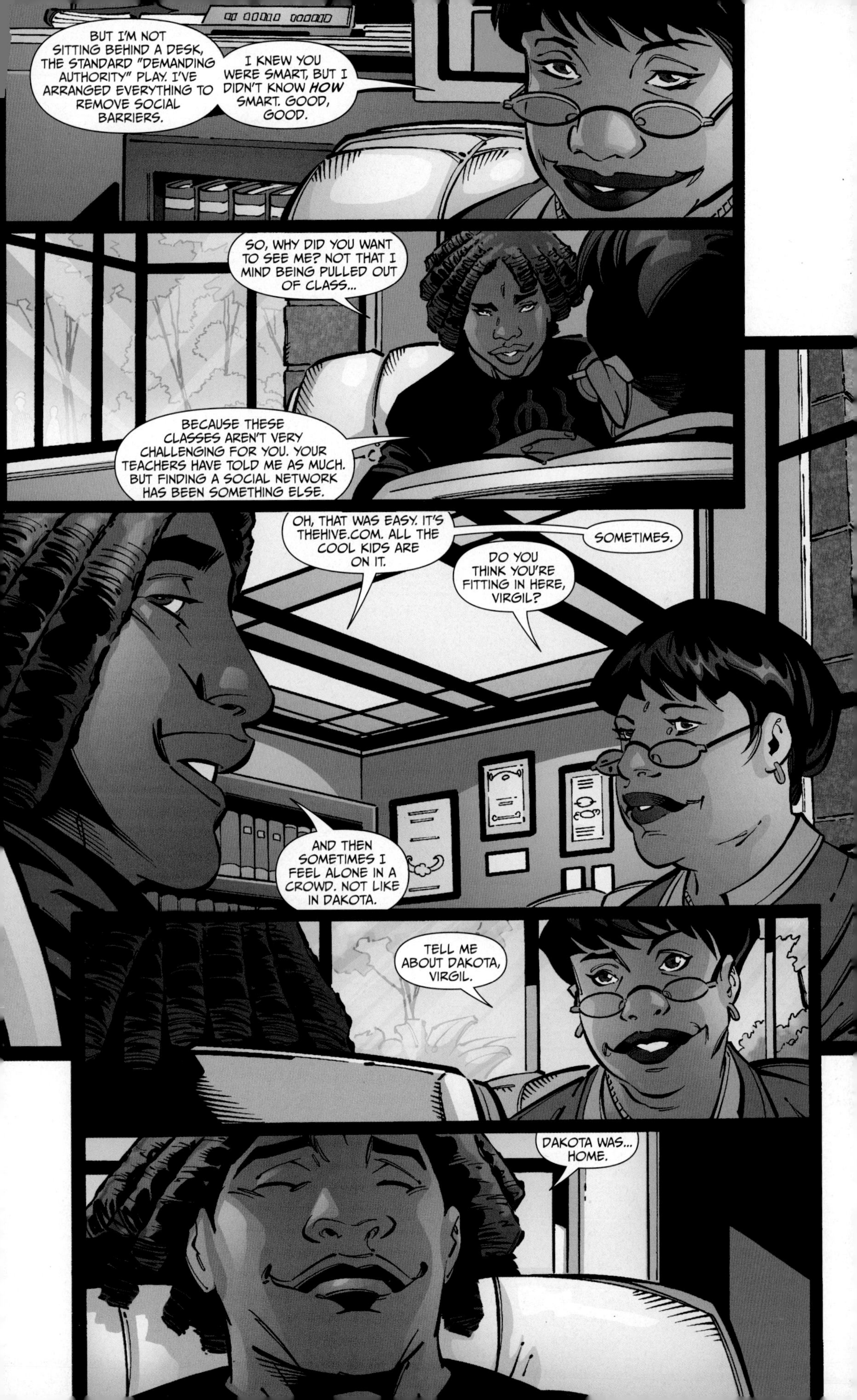
BUT I'M NOT SITTING BEHIND A DESK, THE STANDARD "DEMANDING AUTHORITY" PLAY. I'VE ARRANGED EVERYTHING TO REMOVE SOCIAL BARRIERS.
I KNEW YOU WERE SMART, BUT I DIDN'T KNOW HOW SMART. GOOD, GOOD.
SO, WHY DID YOU WANT TO SEE ME? NOT THAT I MIND BEING PULLED OUT OF CLASS...
BECAUSE THESE CLASSES AREN'T VERY CHALLENGING FOR YOU. YOUR TEACHERS HAVE TOLD ME AS MUCH. BUT FINDING A SOCIAL NETWORK HAS BEEN SOMETHING ELSE.
OH, THAT WAS EASY. IT'S THEHIVE.COM. ALL THE COOL KIDS ARE ON IT.
SOMETIMES.
DO YOU THINK YOU'RE FITTING IN HERE, VIRGIL?
AND THEN SOMETIMES I FEEL ALONE IN A CROWD. NOT LIKE IN DAKOTA.
TELL ME ABOUT DAKOTA, VIRGIL.
DAKOTA WAS... HOME.

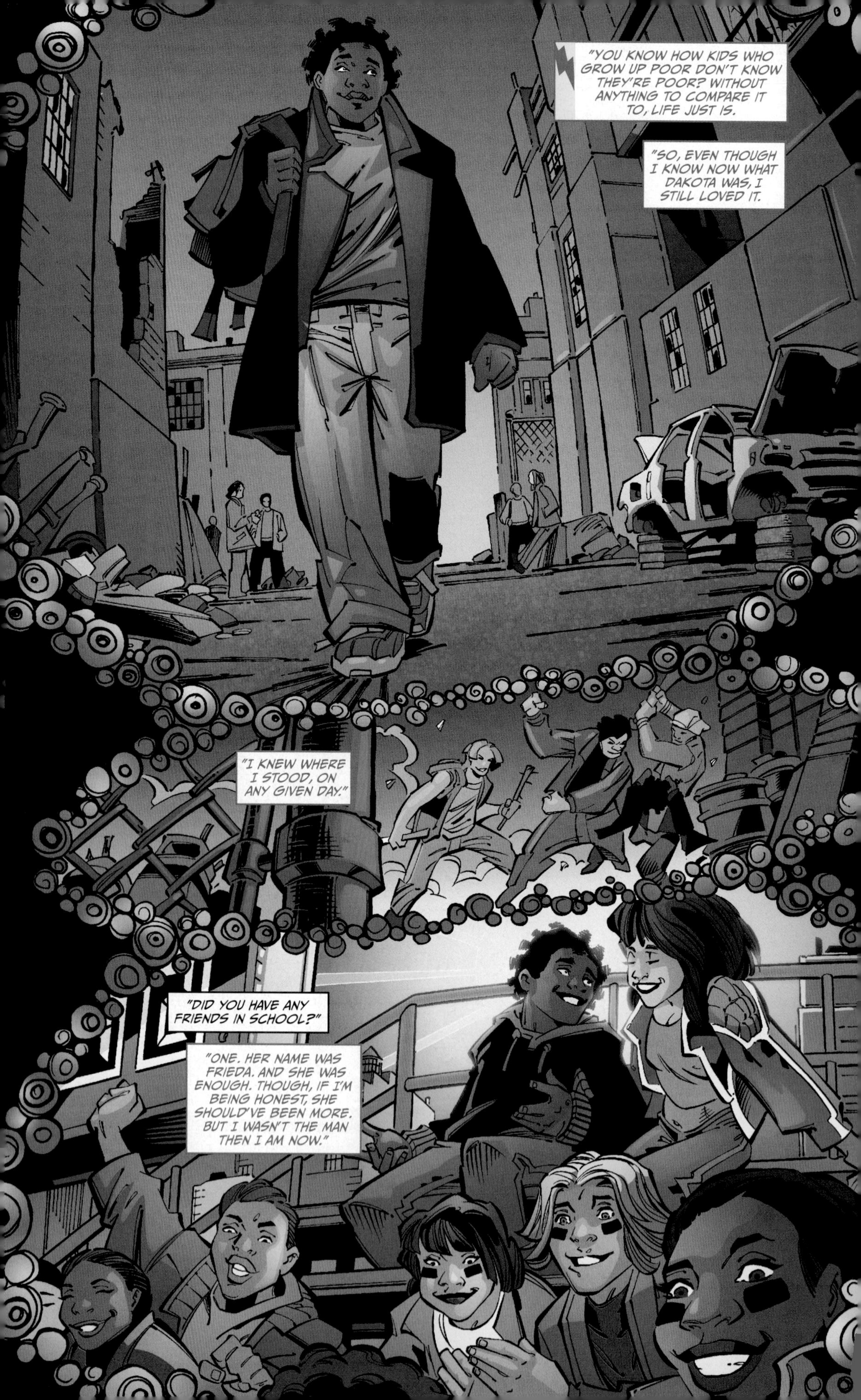
"YOU KNOW HOW KIDS WHO GROW UP POOR DON'T KNOW THEY'RE POOR? WITHOUT ANYTHING TO COMPARE IT TO, LIFE JUST IS.
"SO, EVEN THOUGH I KNOW NOW WHAT DAKOTA WAS, I STILL LOVED IT.
"I KNEW WHERE I STOOD, ON ANY GIVEN DAY."
"DID YOU HAVE ANY FRIENDS IN SCHOOL?"
"ONE. HER NAME WAS FRIEDA. AND SHE WAS ENOUGH. THOUGH, IF I'M BEING HONEST, SHE SHOULD'VE BEEN MORE. BUT I WASN'T THE MAN THEN I AM NOW."

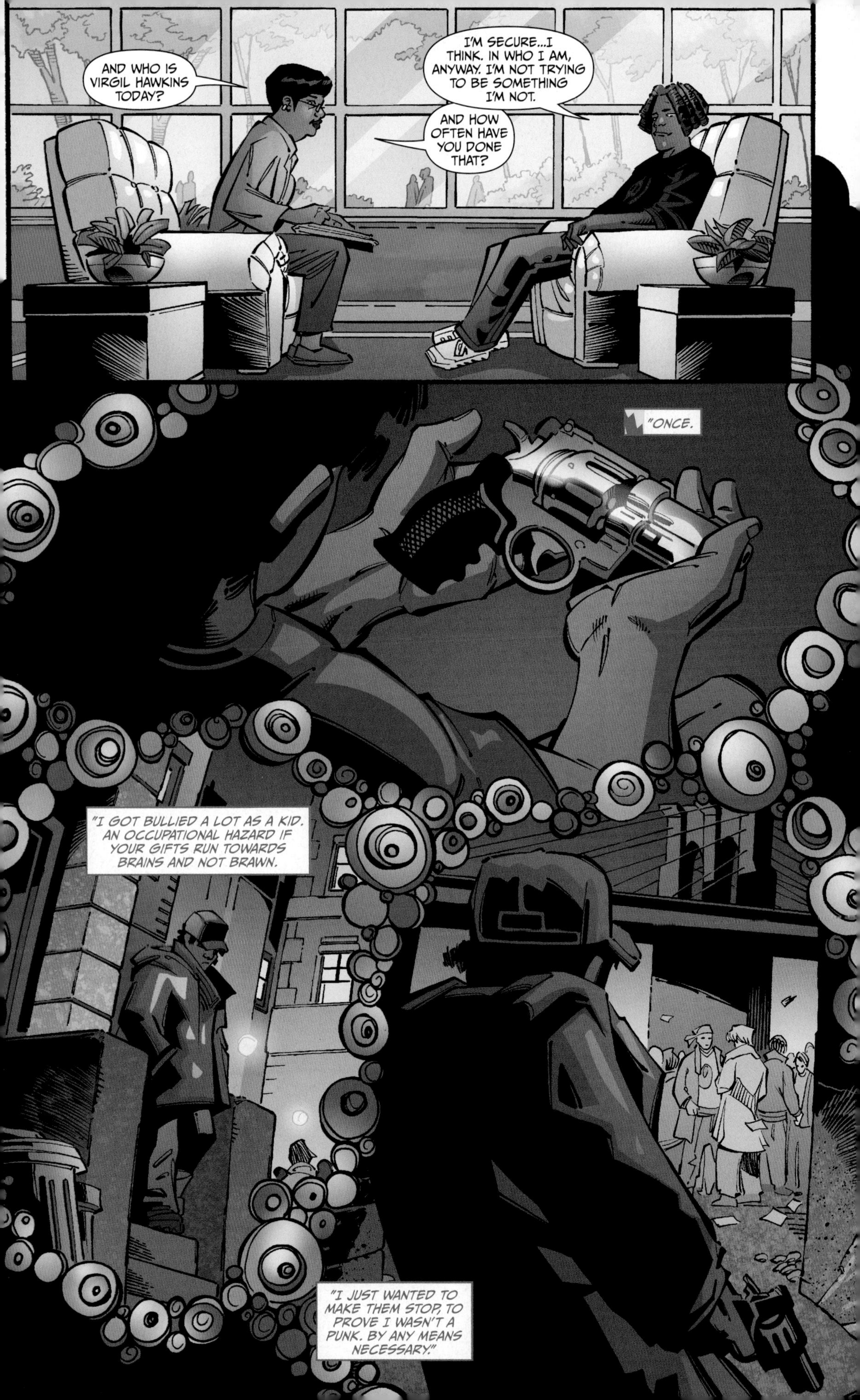
AND WHO IS VIRGIL HAWKINS TODAY?
I'M SECURE...I THINK. IN WHO I AM, ANYWAY. I'M NOT TRYING TO BE SOMETHING I'M NOT.
AND HOW OFTEN HAVE YOU DONE THAT?
"ONCE.
"I GOT BULLIED A LOT AS A KID. AN OCCUPATIONAL HAZARD IF YOUR GIFTS RUN TOWARDS BRAINS AND NOT BRAWN.
"I JUST WANTED TO MAKE THEM STOP, TO PROVE I WASN'T A PUNK. BY ANY MEANS NECESSARY."

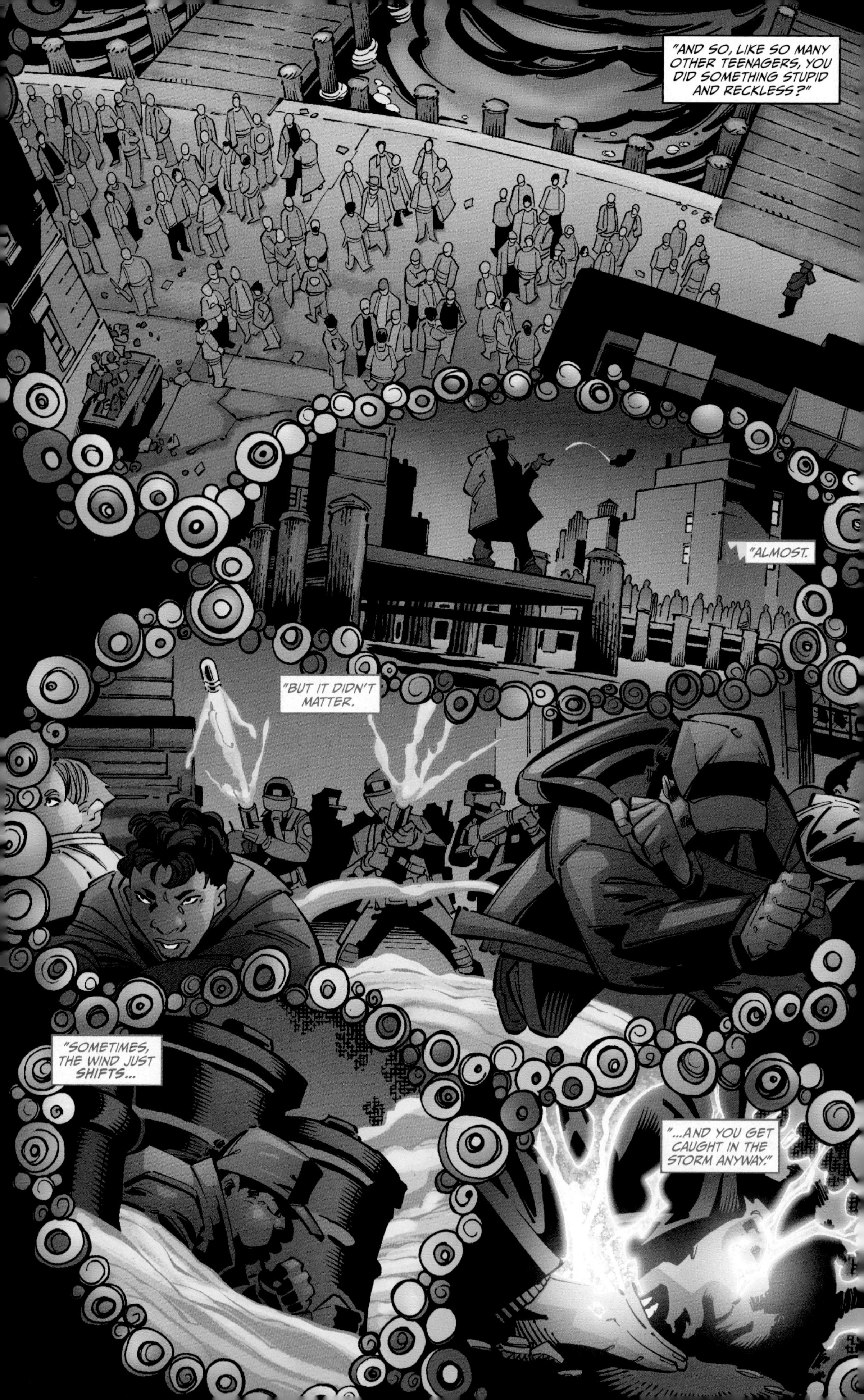
"AND SO, LIKE SO MANY OTHER TEENAGERS, YOU DID SOMETHING STUPID AND RECKLESS?"
"ALMOST.
"BUT IT DIDN'T MATTER.
"SOMETIMES, THE WIND JUST SHIFTS...
"...AND YOU GET CAUGHT IN THE STORM ANYWAY."

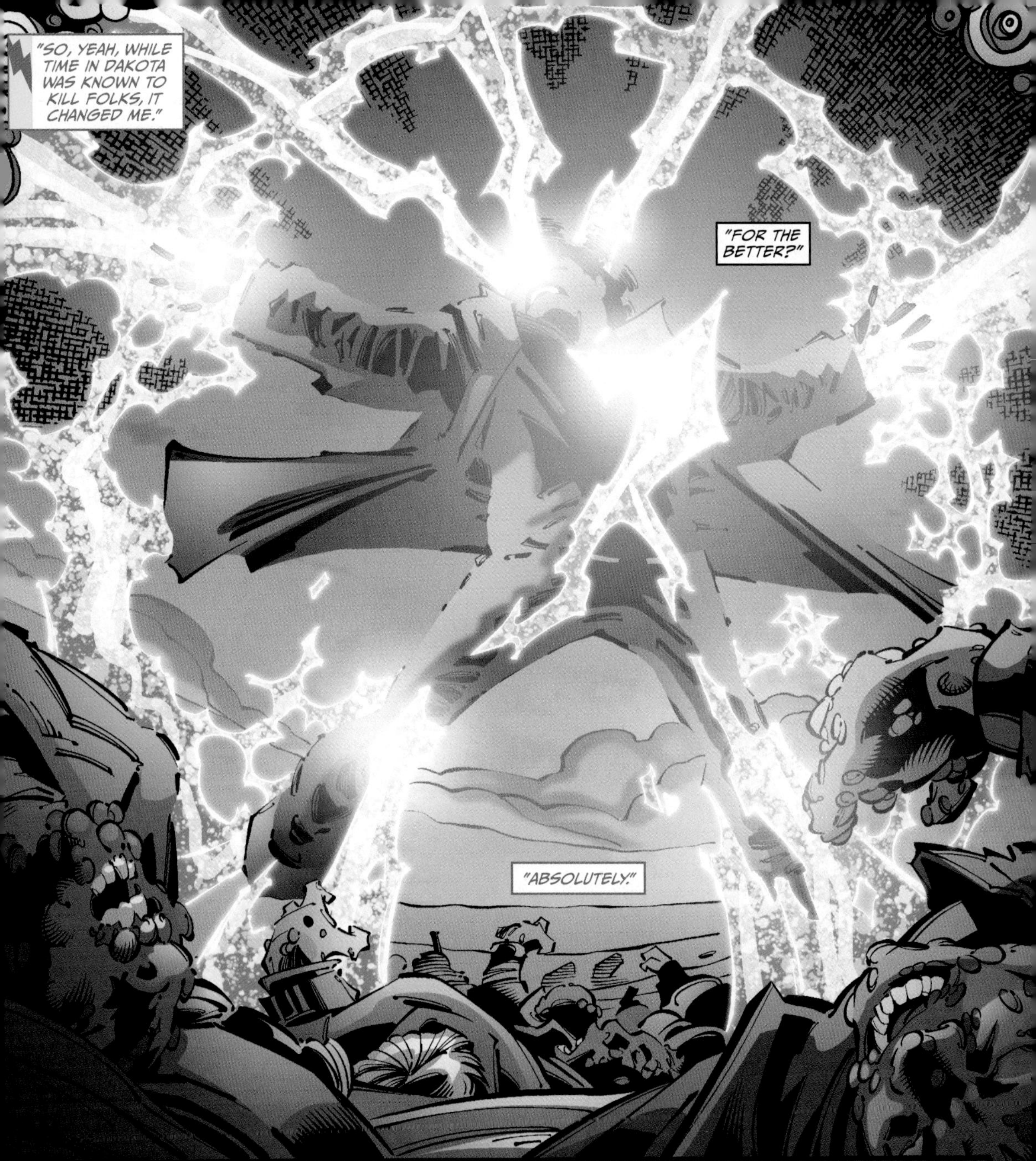
"SO, YEAH, WHILE TIME IN DAKOTA WAS KNOWN TO KILL FOLKS, IT CHANGED ME."
"FOR THE BETTER?"
"ABSOLUTELY."

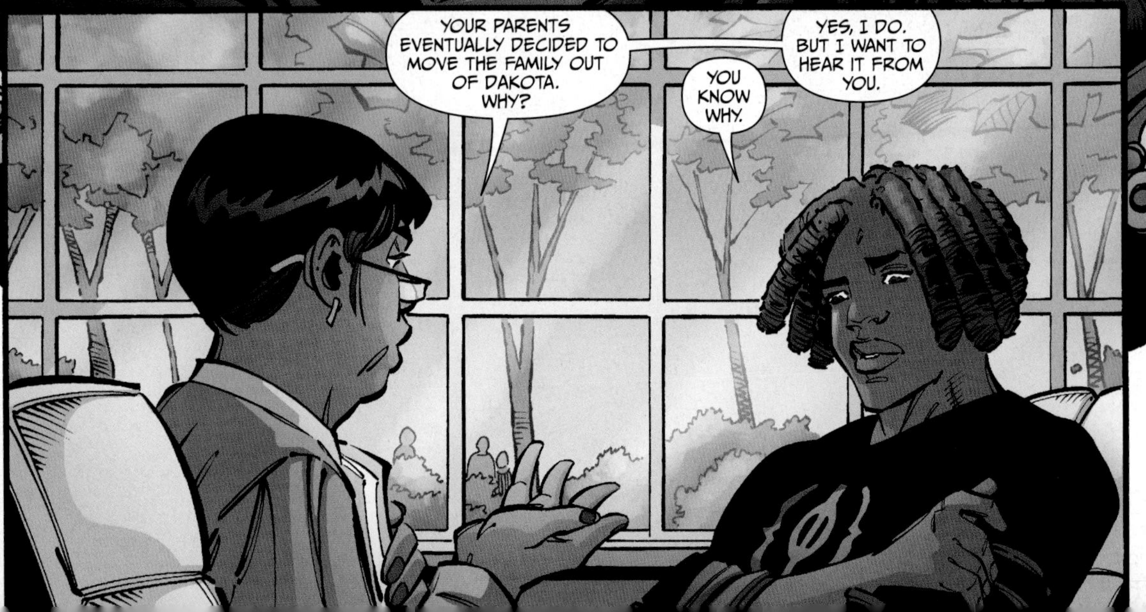
YOUR PARENTS EVENTUALLY DECIDED TO MOVE THE FAMILY OUT OF DAKOTA. WHY?
YOU KNOW WHY.
YES, I DO. BUT I WANT TO HEAR IT FROM YOU.

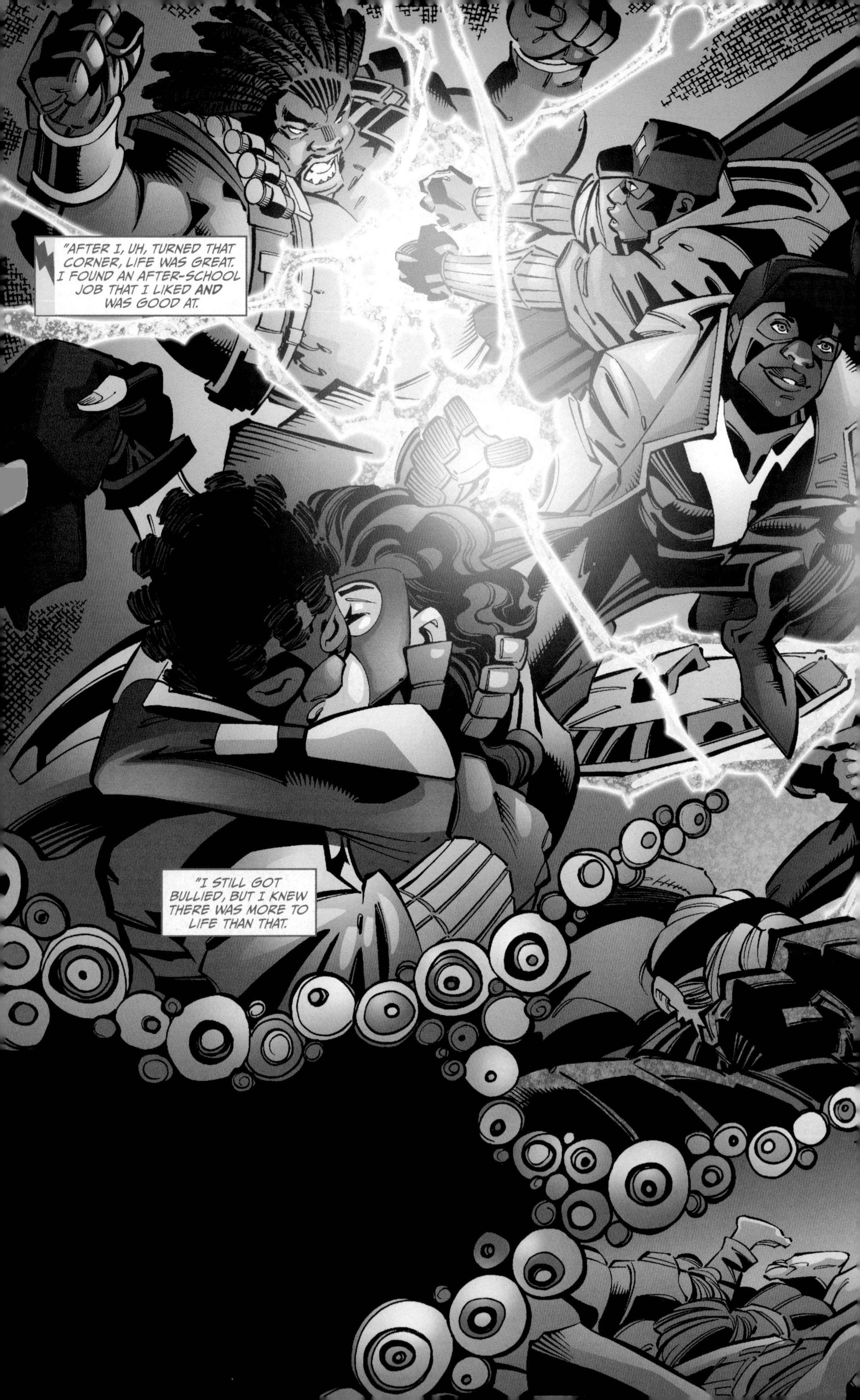
"AFTER I, UH, TURNED THAT CORNER, LIFE WAS GREAT. I FOUND AN AFTER-SCHOOL JOB THAT I LIKED AND WAS GOOD AT.
"I STILL GOT BULLIED, BUT I KNEW THERE WAS MORE TO LIFE THAN THAT.

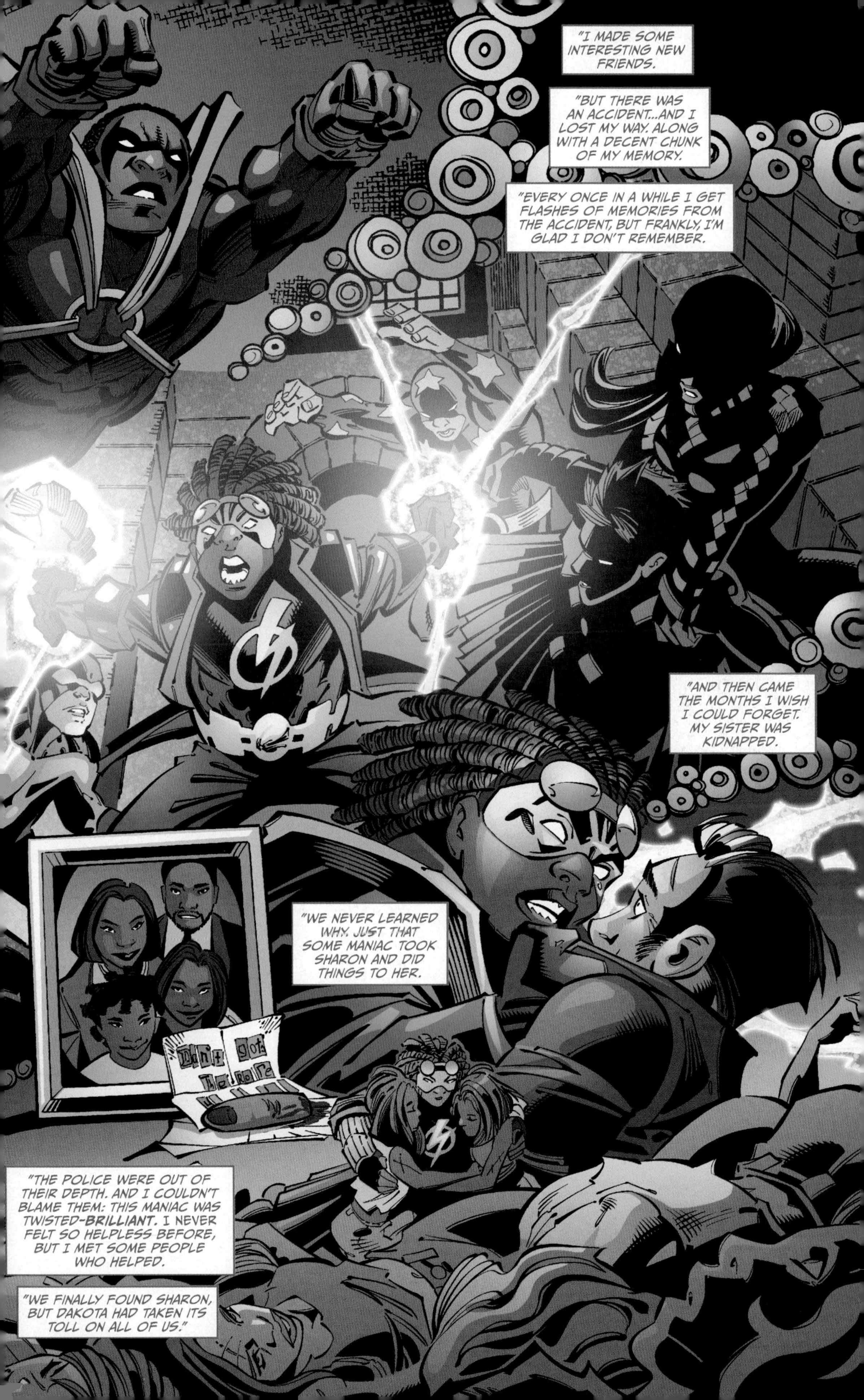
"I MADE SOME INTERESTING NEW FRIENDS.
"BUT THERE WAS AN ACCIDENT...AND I LOST MY WAY. ALONG WITH A DECENT CHUNK OF MY MEMORY.
"EVERY ONCE IN A WHILE I GET FLASHES OF MEMORIES FROM THE ACCIDENT, BUT FRANKLY, I'M GLAD I DON'T REMEMBER.
"AND THEN CAME THE MONTHS I WISH I COULD FORGET. MY SISTER WAS KIDNAPPED.
"WE NEVER LEARNED WHY. JUST THAT SOME MANIAC TOOK SHARON AND DID THINGS TO HER.
"THE POLICE WERE OUT OF THEIR DEPTH. AND I COULDN'T BLAME THEM: THIS MANIAC WAS TWISTED-BRILLIANT. I NEVER FELT SO HELPLESS BEFORE, BUT I MET SOME PEOPLE WHO HELPED.
"WE FINALLY FOUND SHARON, BUT DAKOTA HAD TAKEN ITS TOLL ON ALL OF US."

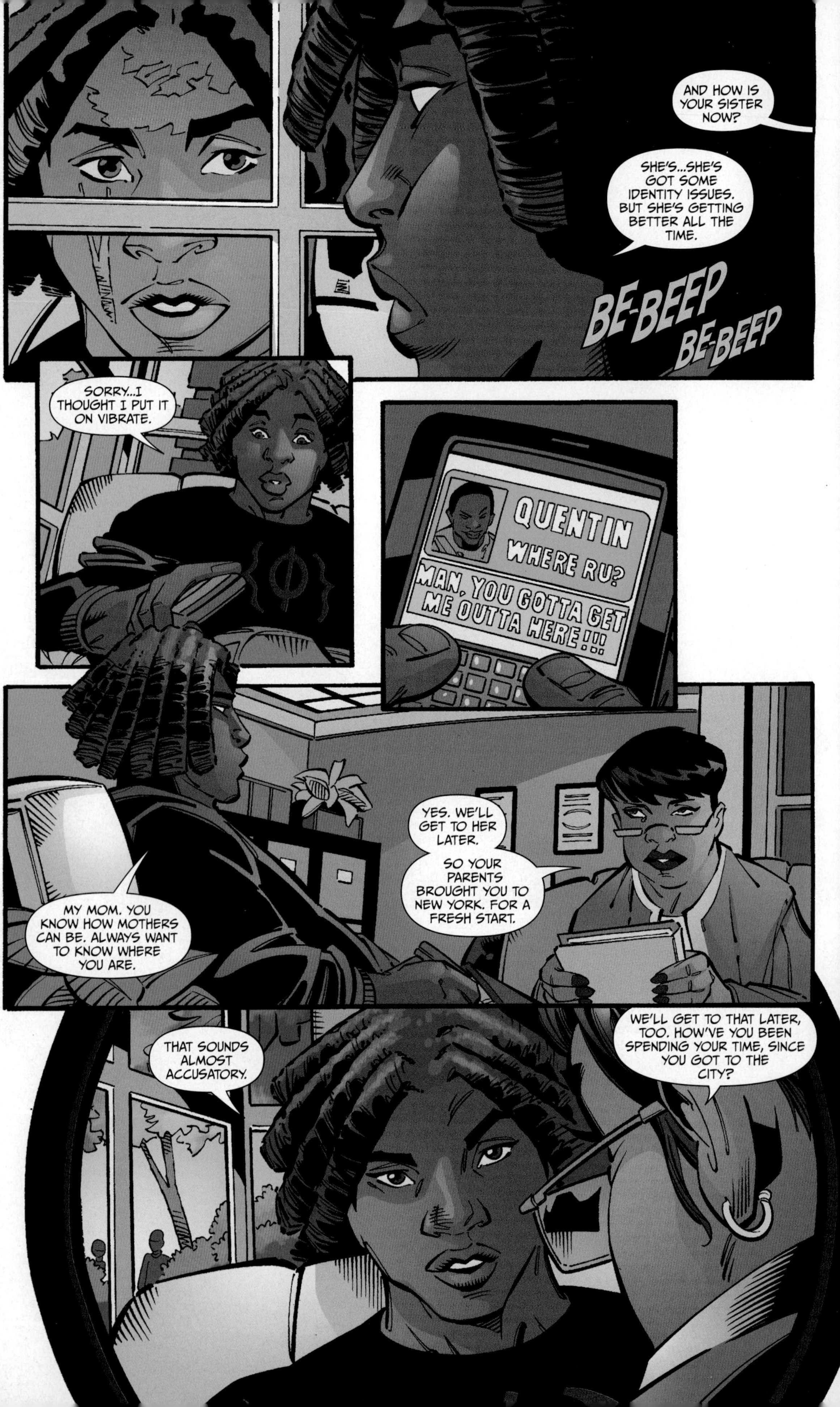
AND HOW IS YOUR SISTER NOW?
SHE'S...SHE'S GOT SOME IDENTITY ISSUES. BUT SHE'S GETTING BETTER ALL THE TIME.
BE-BEEP
BE-BEEP
SORRY...I THOUGHT I PUT IT ON VIBRATE.
QUENTIN
WHERE RU?
MAN, YOU GOTTA GET ME OUTTA HERE!!!
YES. WE'LL GET TO HER LATER.
SO YOUR PARENTS BROUGHT YOU TO NEW YORK. FOR A FRESH START.
MY MOM. YOU KNOW HOW MOTHERS CAN BE. ALWAYS WANT TO KNOW WHERE YOU ARE.
THAT SOUNDS ALMOST ACCUSATORY.
WE'LL GET TO THAT LATER, TOO. HOW'VE YOU BEEN SPENDING YOUR TIME, SINCE YOU GOT TO THE CITY?

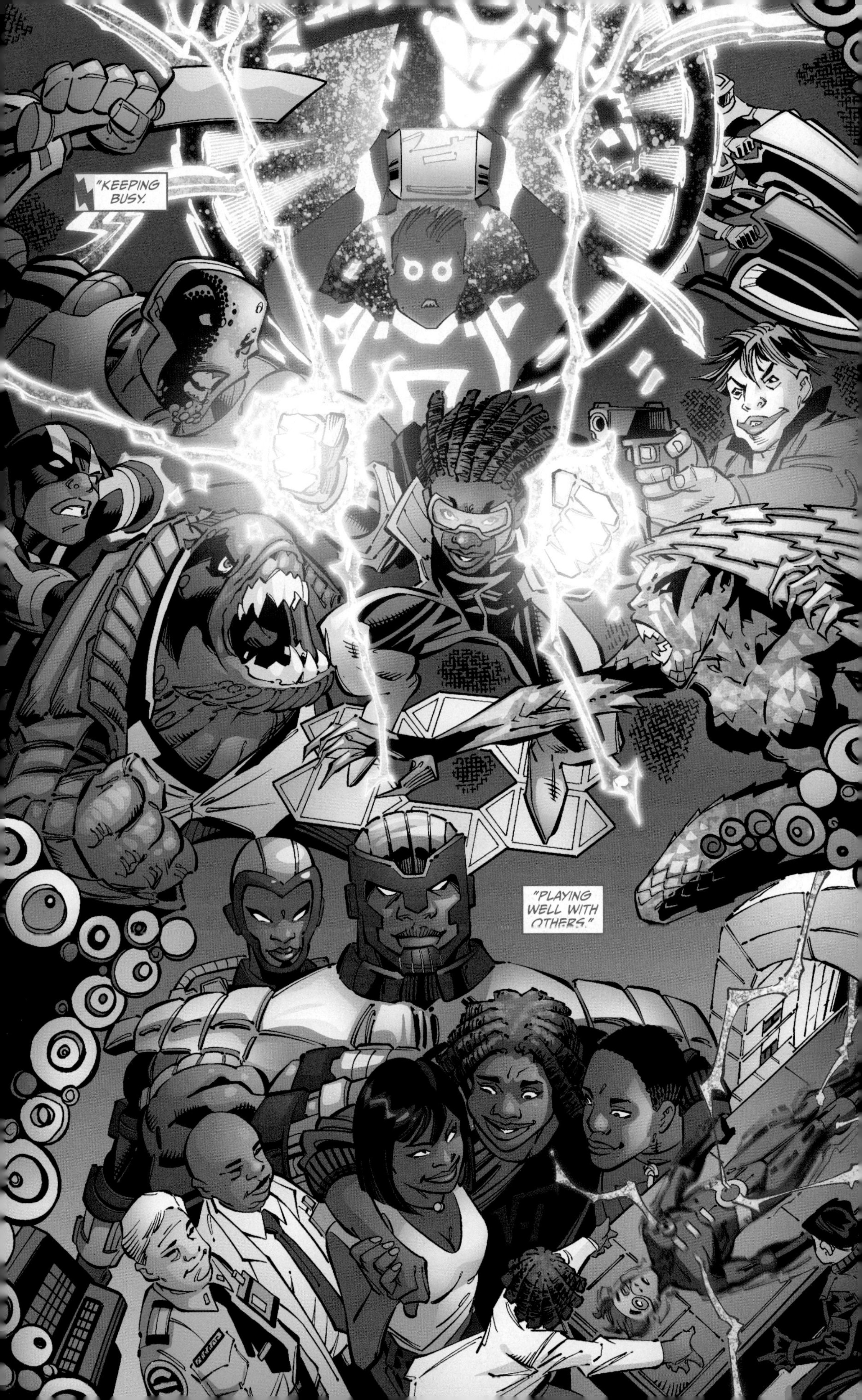
"KEEPING BUSY.
"PLAYING WELL WITH OTHERS."

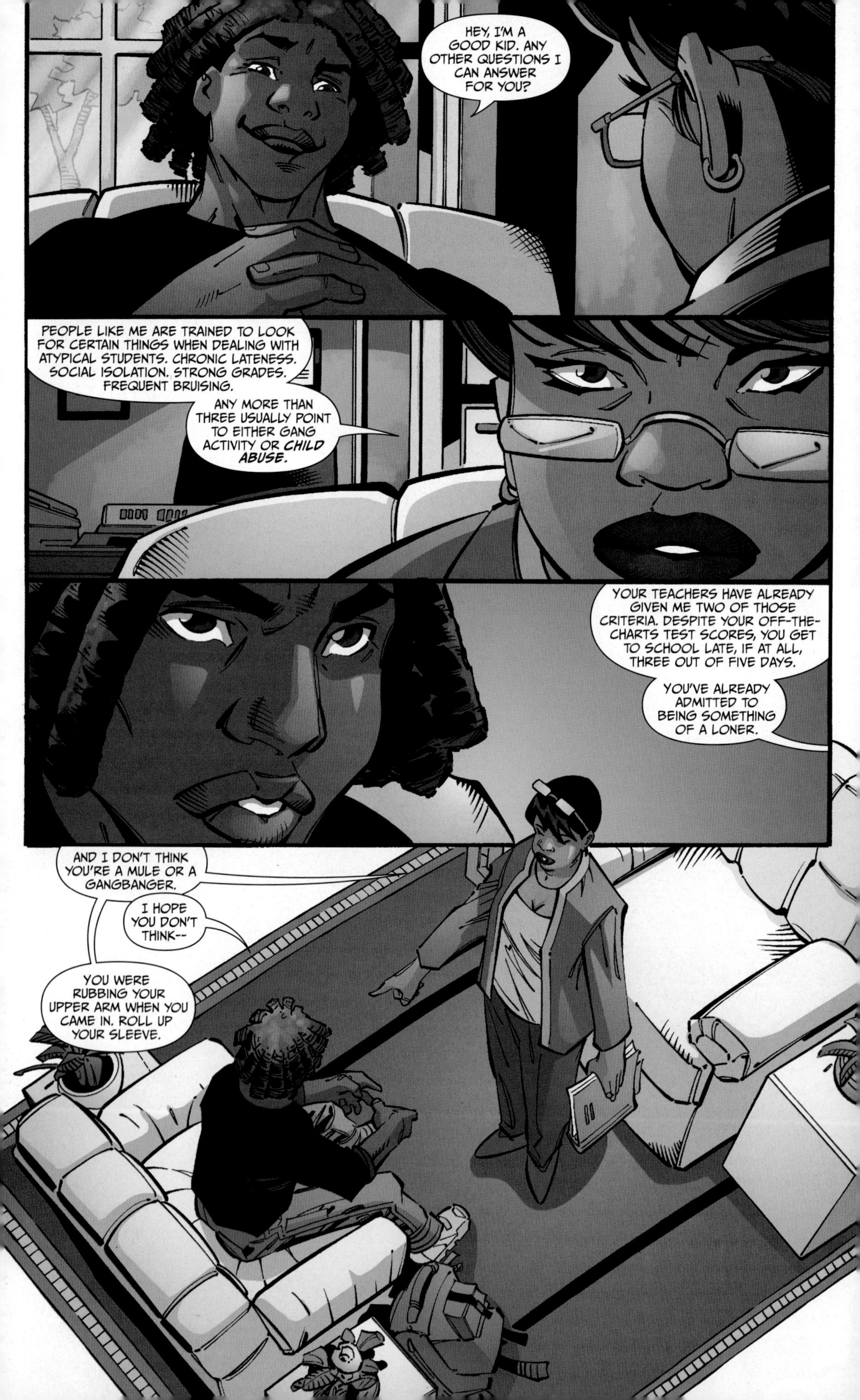
HEY, I'M A GOOD KID. ANY OTHER QUESTIONS I CAN ANSWER FOR YOU?
PEOPLE LIKE ME ARE TRAINED TO LOOK FOR CERTAIN THINGS WHEN DEALING WITH ATYPICAL STUDENTS. CHRONIC LATENESS. SOCIAL ISOLATION. STRONG GRADES. FREQUENT BRUISING.
ANY MORE THAN THREE USUALLY POINT TO EITHER GANG ACTIVITY OR CHILD ABUSE.
YOUR TEACHERS HAVE ALREADY GIVEN ME TWO OF THOSE CRITERIA. DESPITE YOUR OFF-THE-CHARTS TEST SCORES, YOU GET TO SCHOOL LATE, IF AT ALL, THREE OUT OF FIVE DAYS.
YOU'VE ALREADY ADMITTED TO BEING SOMETHING OF A LONER.
AND I DON'T THINK YOU'RE A MULE OR A GANGBANGER.
I HOPE YOU DON'T THINK--
YOU WERE RUBBING YOUR UPPER ARM WHEN YOU CAME IN. ROLL UP YOUR SLEEVE.

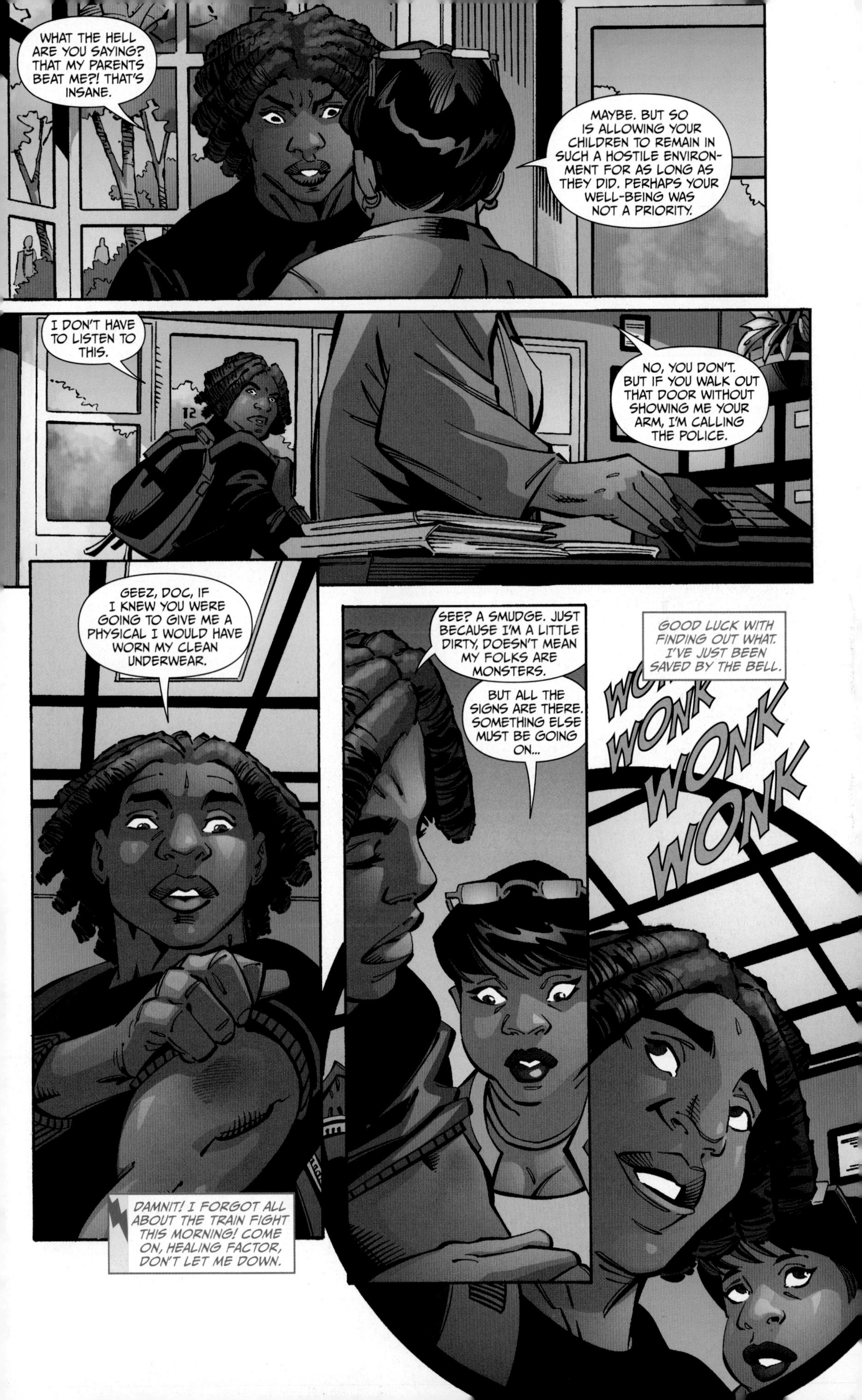
WHAT THE HELL ARE YOU SAYING? THAT MY PARENTS BEAT ME?! THAT'S INSANE.
MAYBE. BUT SO IS ALLOWING YOUR CHILDREN TO REMAIN IN SUCH A HOSTILE ENVIRONMENT FOR AS LONG AS THEY DID. PERHAPS YOUR WELL-BEING WAS NOT A PRIORITY.
I DON'T HAVE TO LISTEN TO THIS.
NO, YOU DON'T. BUT IF YOU WALK OUT THAT DOOR WITHOUT SHOWING ME YOUR ARM, I'M CALLING THE POLICE.
GEEZ, DOC, IF I KNEW YOU WERE GOING TO GIVE ME A PHYSICAL I WOULD HAVE WORN MY CLEAN UNDERWEAR.
DAMNIT! I FORGOT ALL ABOUT THE TRAIN FIGHT THIS MORNING! COME ON, HEALING FACTOR, DON'T LET ME DOWN.
SEE? A SMUDGE. JUST BECAUSE I'M A LITTLE DIRTY, DOESN'T MEAN MY FOLKS ARE MONSTERS.
BUT ALL THE SIGNS ARE THERE. SOMETHING ELSE MUST BE GOING ON...
GOOD LUCK WITH FINDING OUT WHAT. I'VE JUST BEEN SAVED BY THE BELL.
WONK WONK WONK WONK

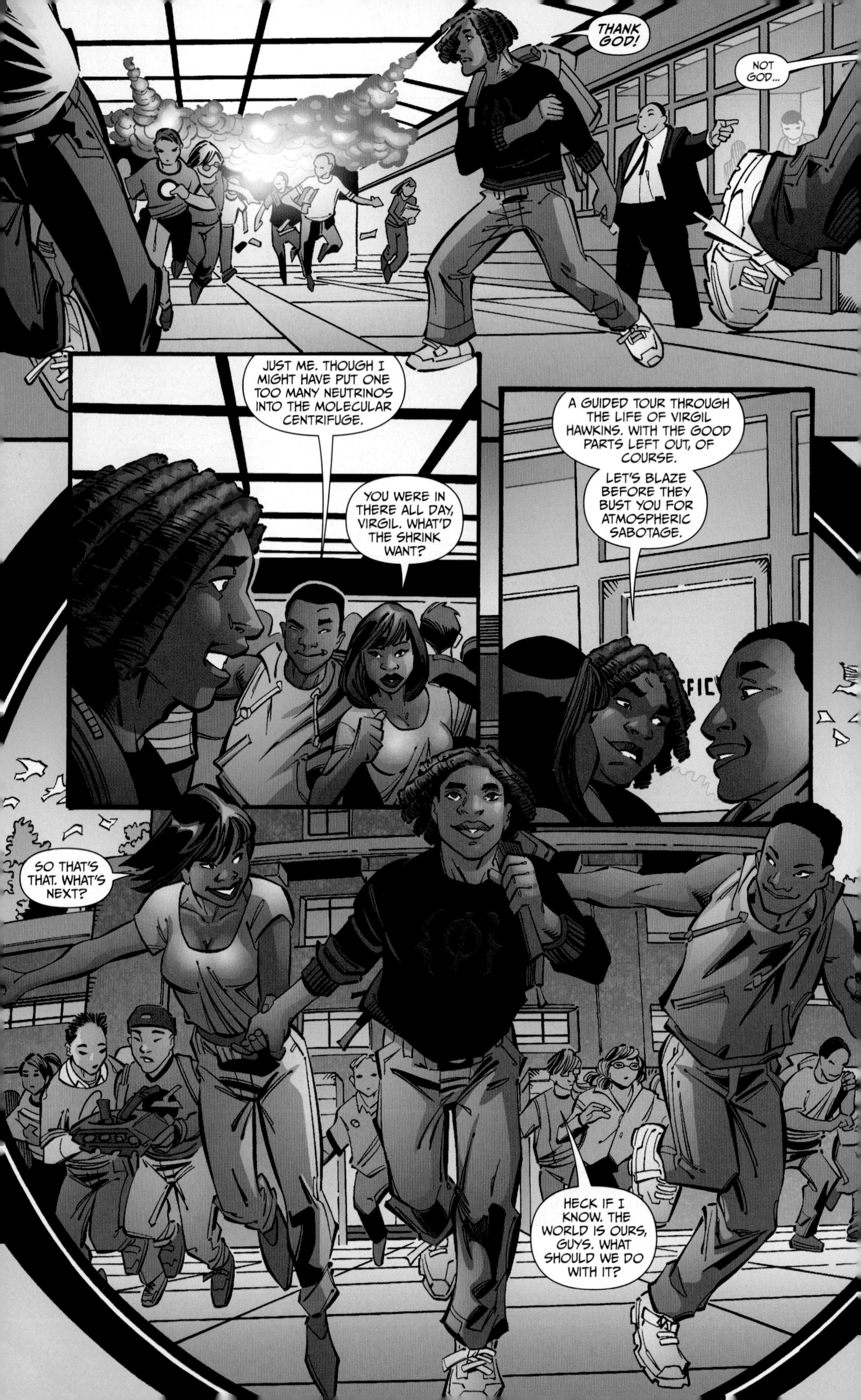
THANK GOD!
NOT GOD...
JUST ME. THOUGH I MIGHT HAVE PUT ONE TOO MANY NEUTRINOS INTO THE MOLECULAR CENTRIFUGE.
YOU WERE IN THERE ALL DAY, VIRGIL. WHAT'D THE SHRINK WANT?
A GUIDED TOUR THROUGH THE LIFE OF VIRGIL HAWKINS. WITH THE GOOD PARTS LEFT OUT, OF COURSE.
LET'S BLAZE BEFORE THEY BUST YOU FOR ATMOSPHERIC SABOTAGE.
SO THAT'S THAT. WHAT'S NEXT?
HECK IF I KNOW. THE WORLD IS OURS, GUYS. WHAT SHOULD WE DO WITH IT?

## STATIC
### EYEWEAR

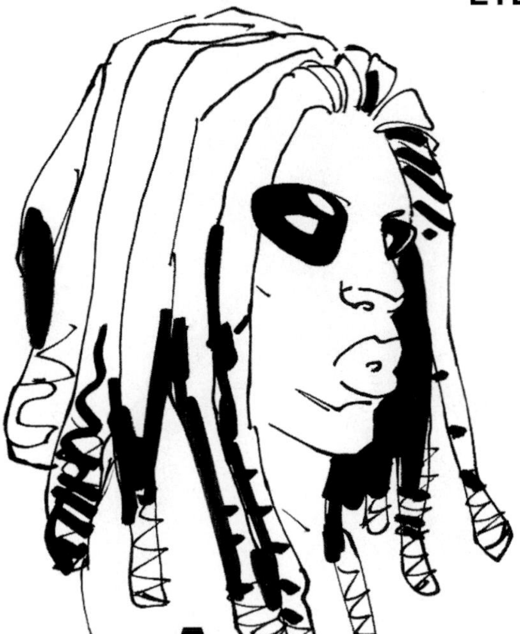

A

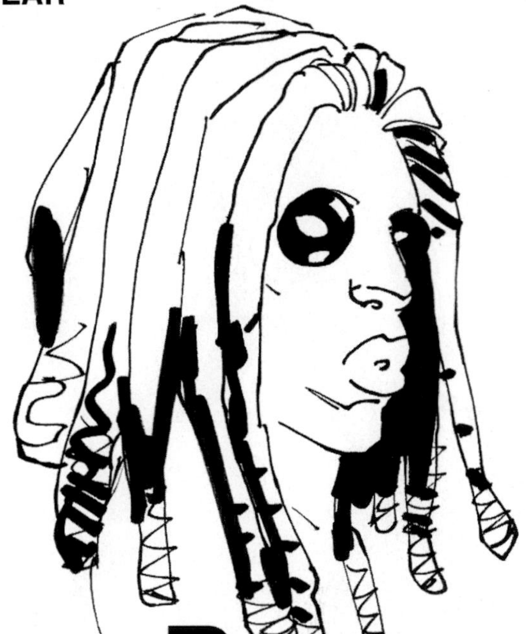

B

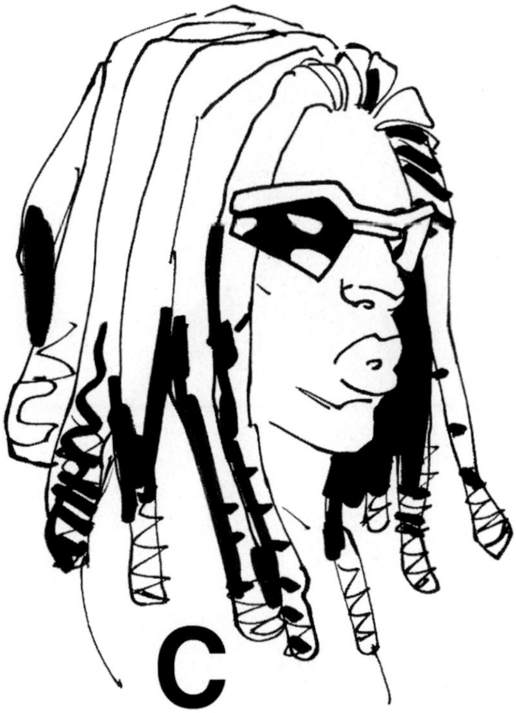

C

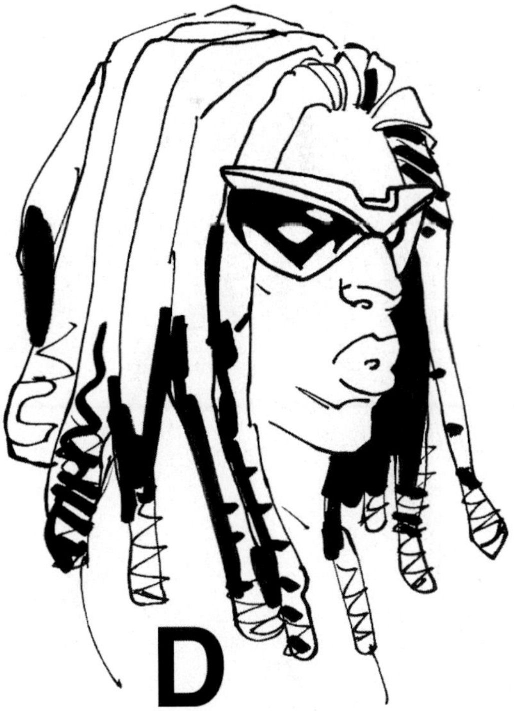

D

## STATIC

### COSTUME DESIGN

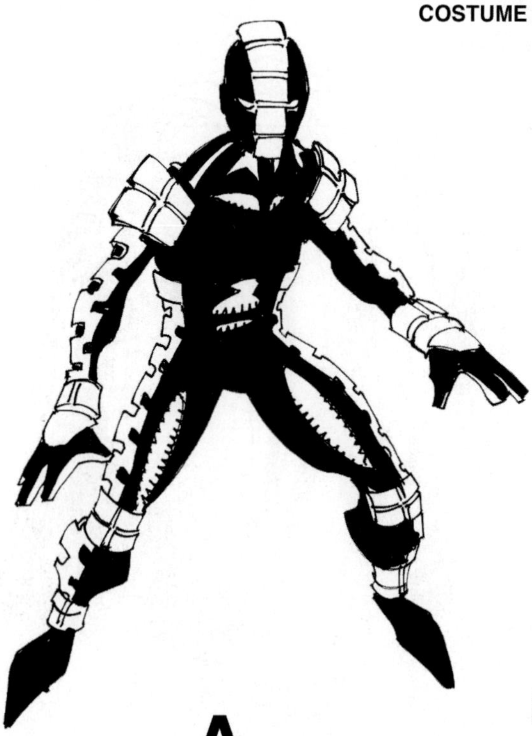

A

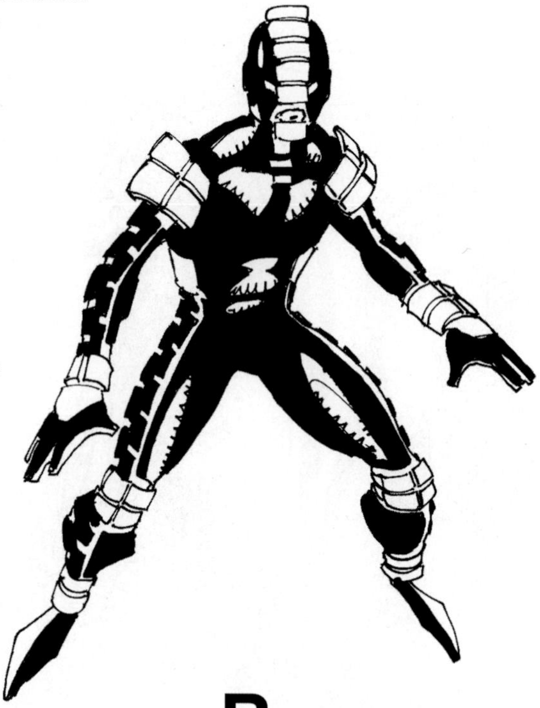

B

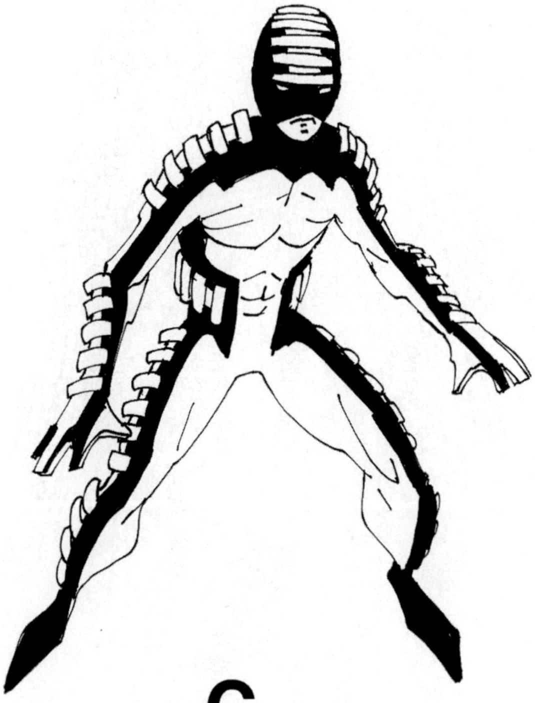

C

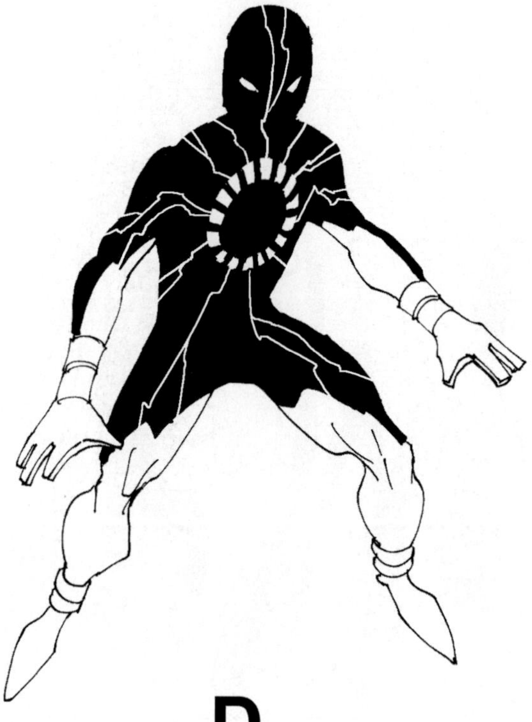

D

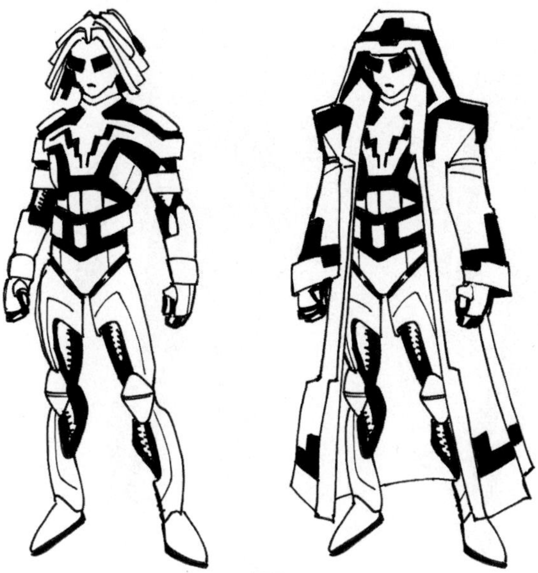

E

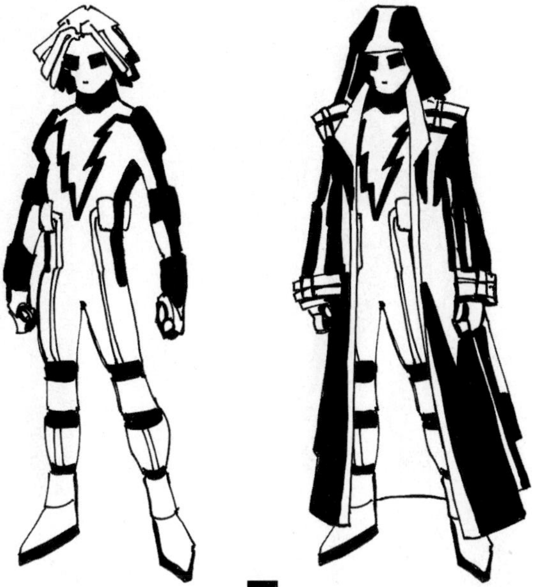

F

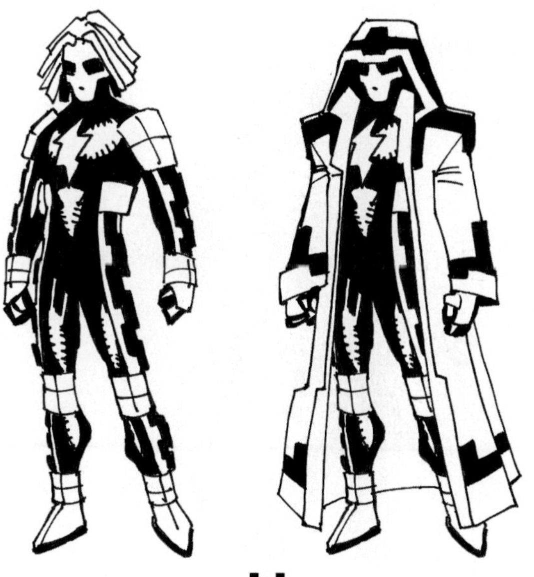

H

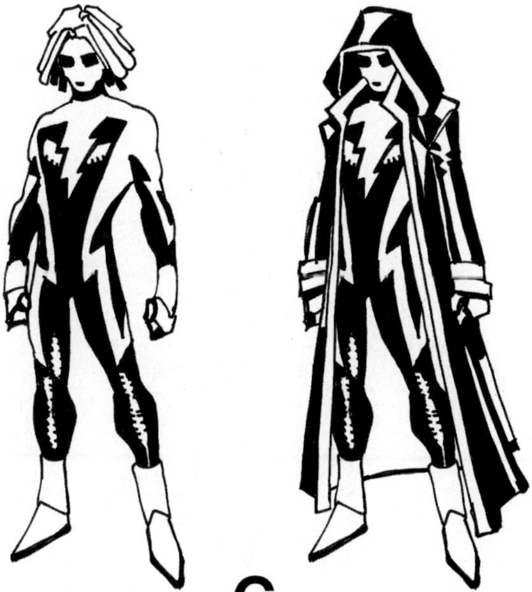

G

## STATIC
COSTUME DESIGN

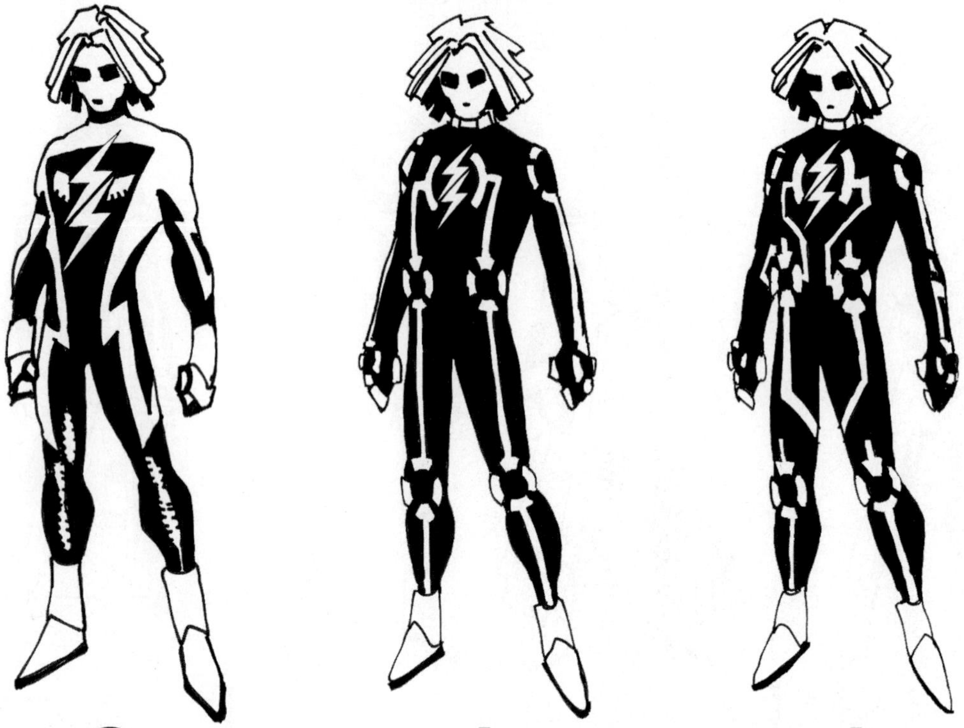

G I J

## STATIC
COSTUME DESIGN

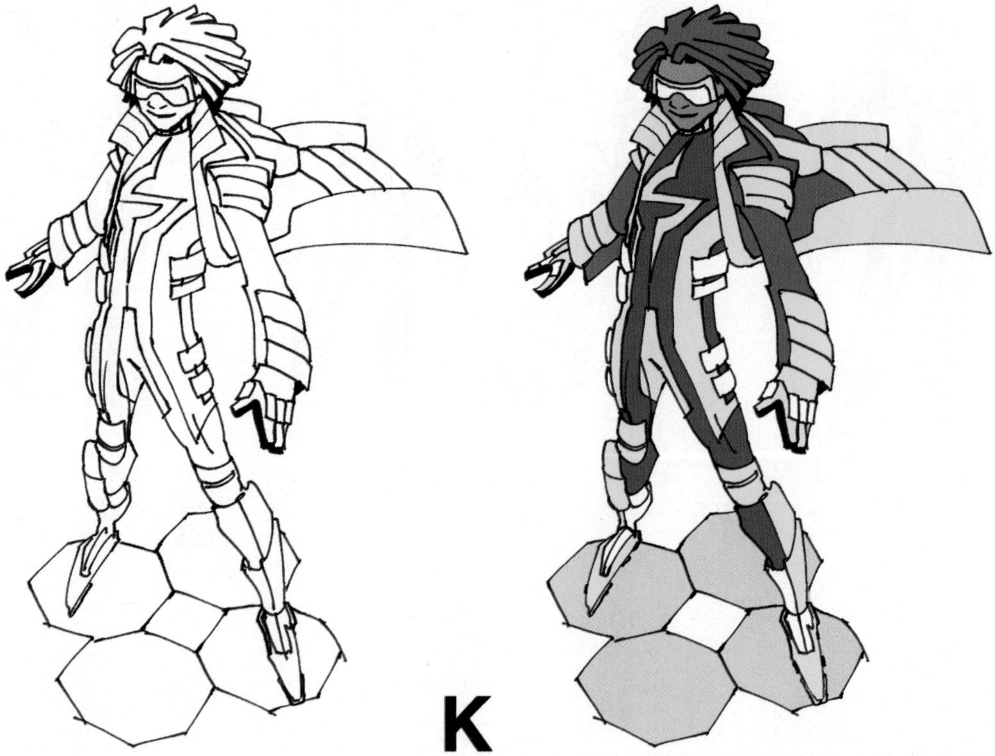

K

# STATIC
## COSTUME DESIGN

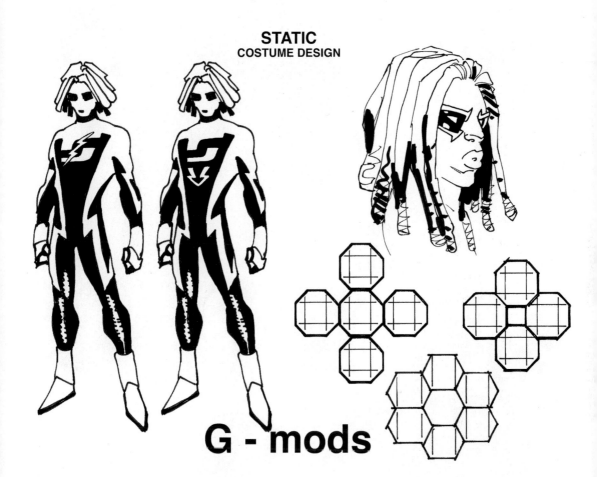

G - mods

# STATIC SHOCK
## CHARACTER SKETCHES BY SCOTT MCDANIEL

**THE PALE MAN**

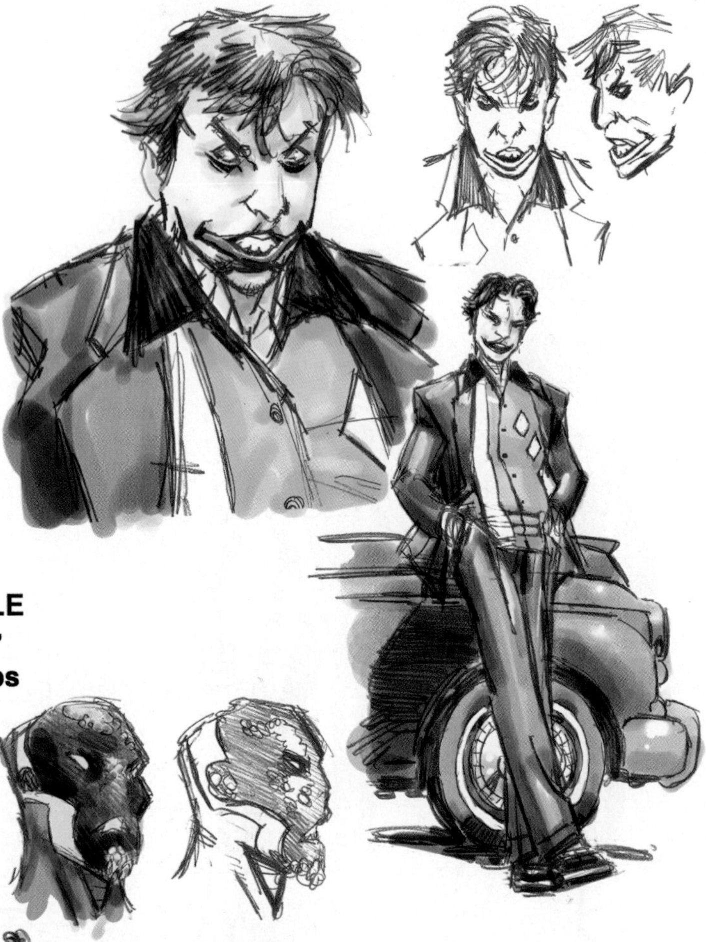

**VIRULE**
**7' 0"**
**275 lbs**

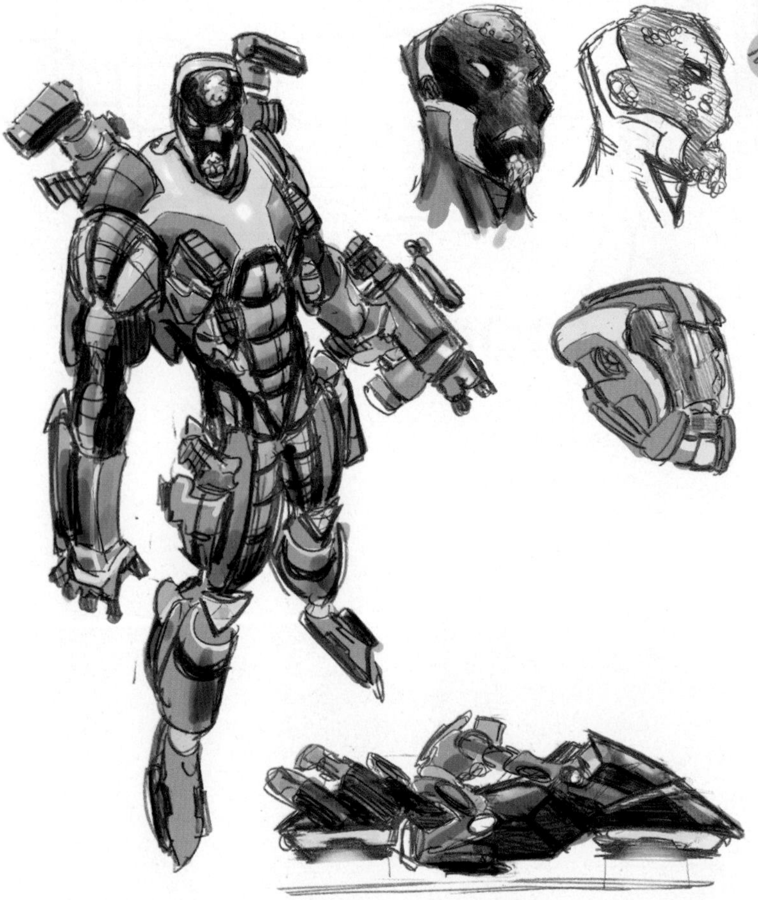

## JOEY "PIRANHA" SCROCCONE

**6' 6"**
**350 lbs**

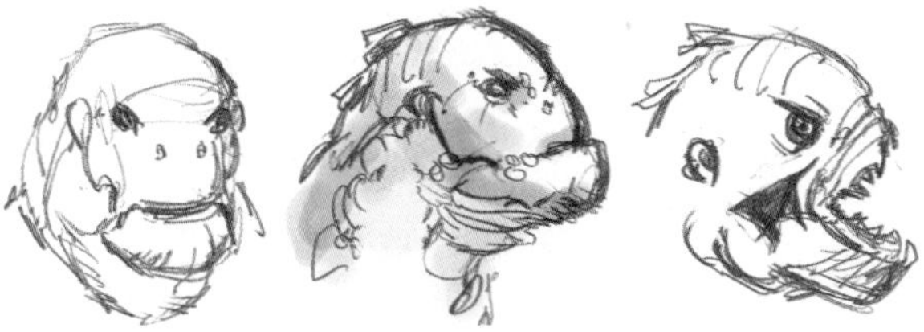

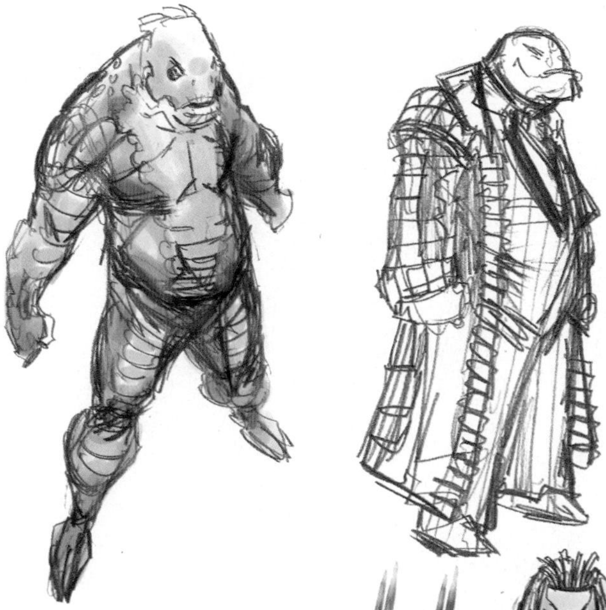

## GUILLOTINA
## INITIAL CONCEPT

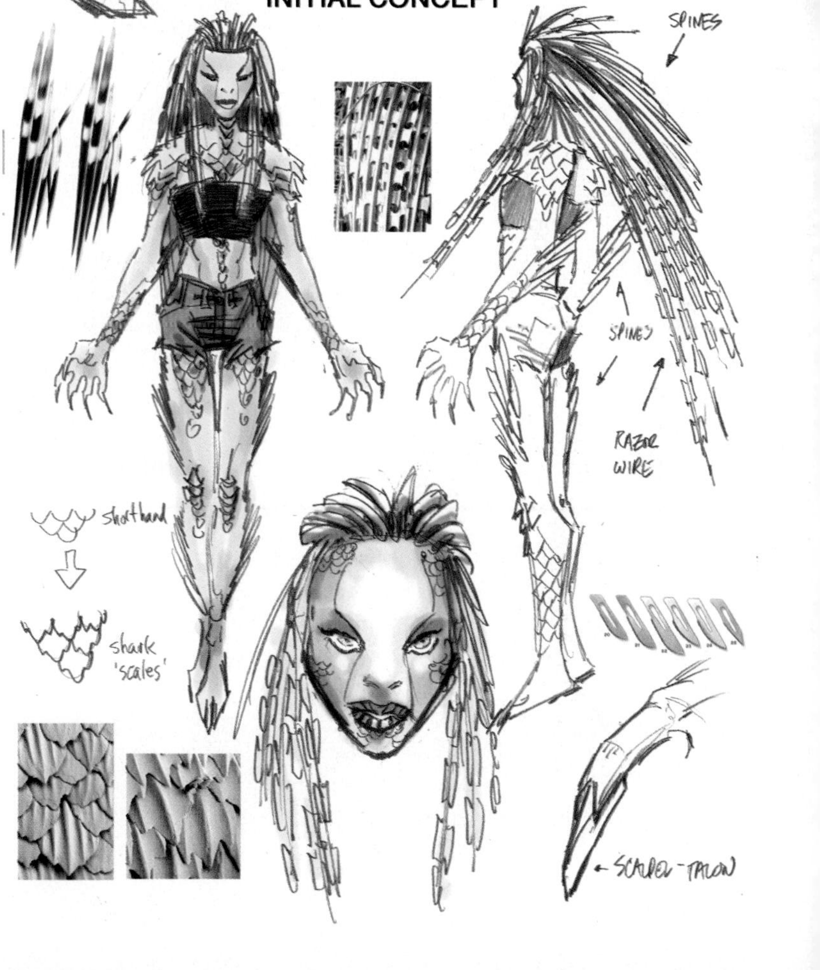
SPINES
SPINES
RAZOR WIRE
shorthand
shark 'scales'
SCALPEL-TALON

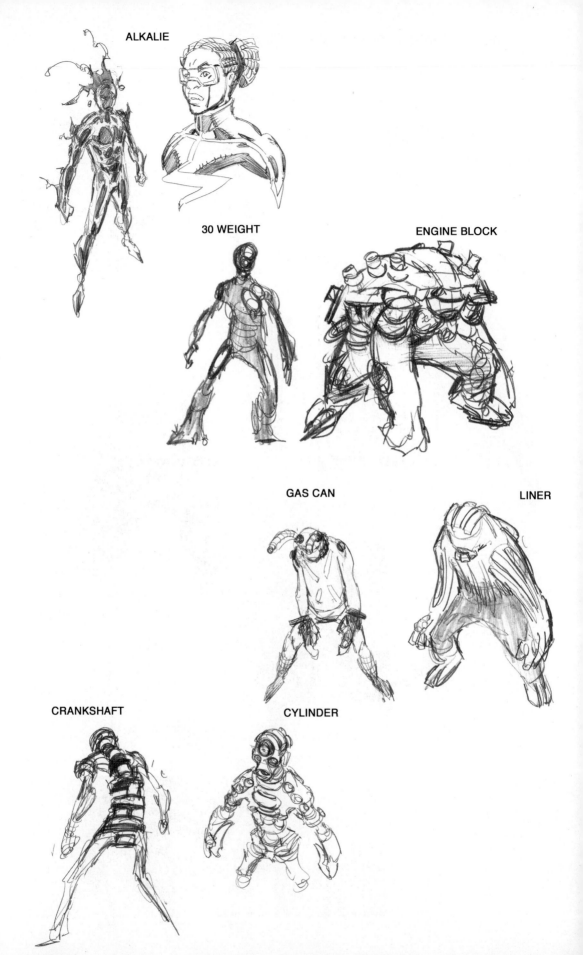

ALKALIE

30 WEIGHT

ENGINE BLOCK

GAS CAN

LINER

CRANKSHAFT

CYLINDER

WINDSHIELD

RETREAD

LIFTER

HEADLIGHT

REBAR

RECIP

JAWS

TERMINAL

DIESEL

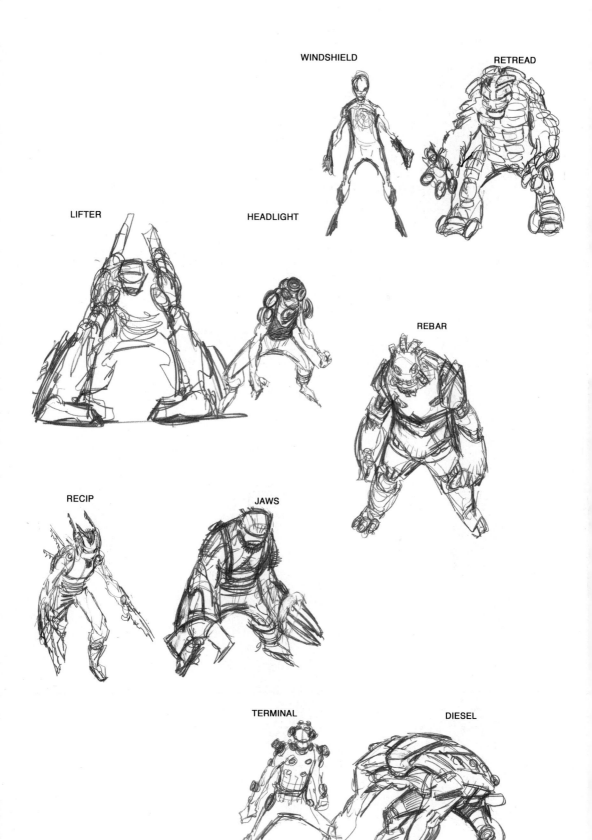

NEMO'S AGENT

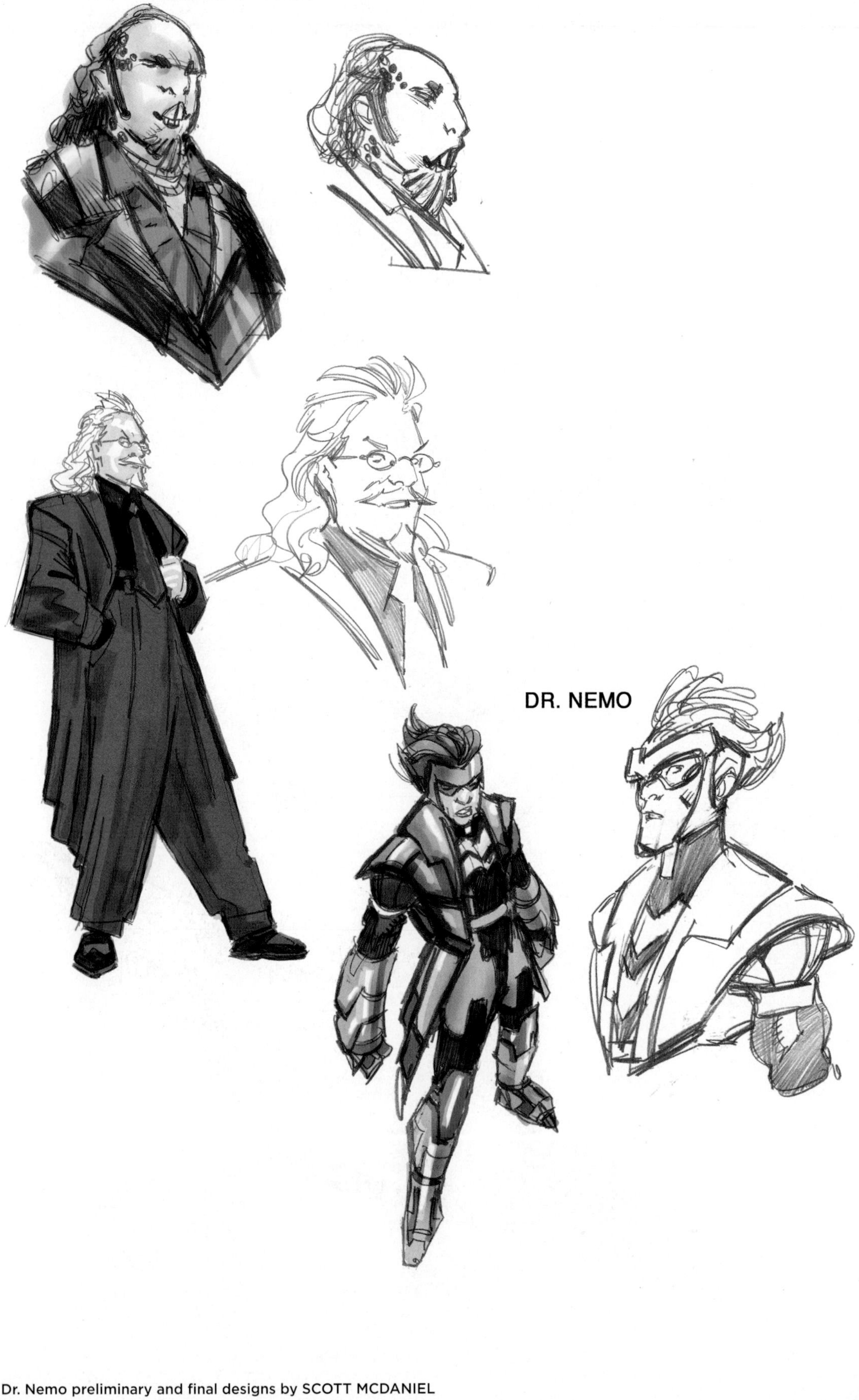
DR. NEMO

Dr. Nemo preliminary and final designs by SCOTT MCDANIEL

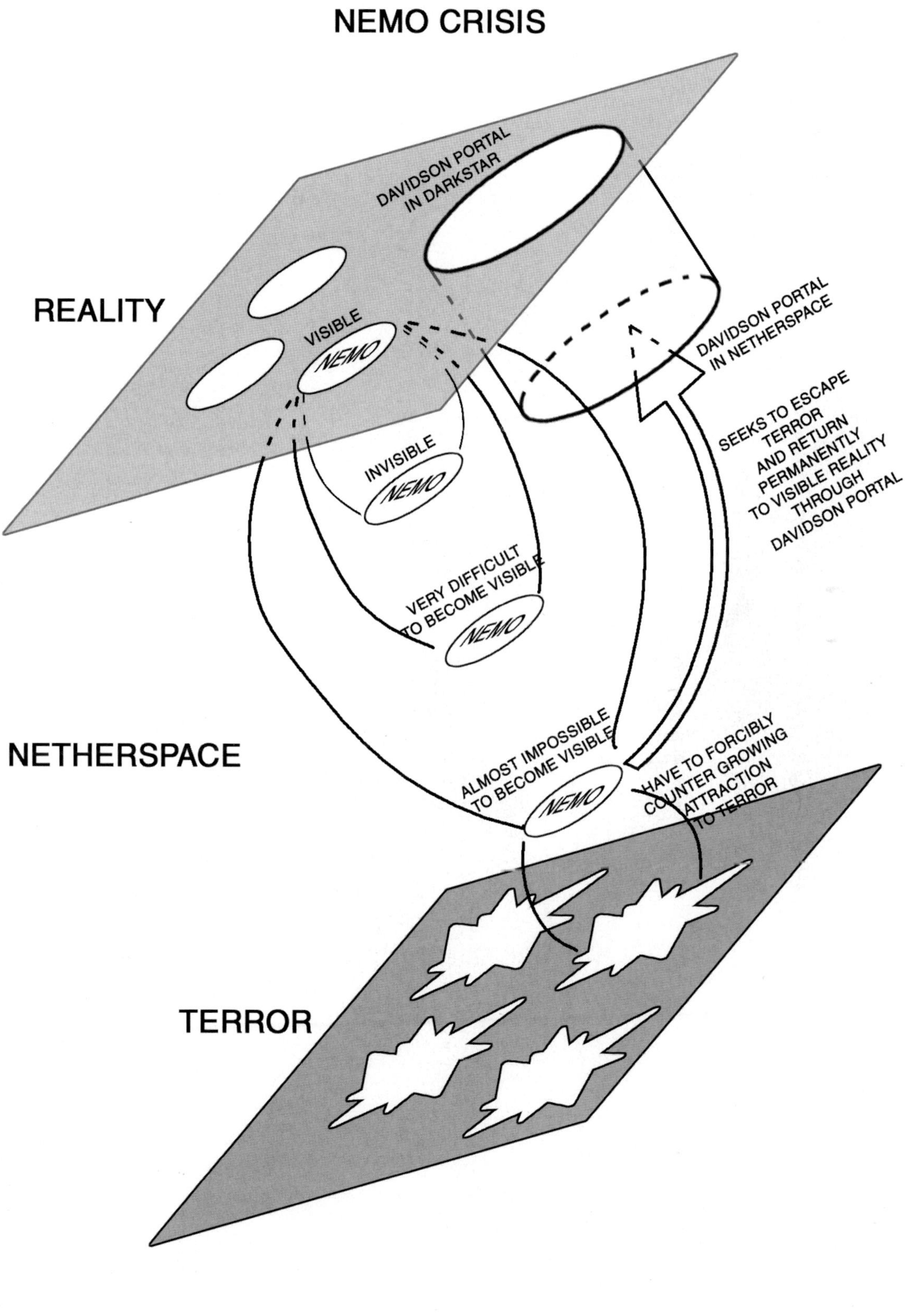
NEMO CRISIS
REALITY
DAVIDSON PORTAL
IN DARKSTAR
VISIBLE
NEMO
DAVIDSON PORTAL
IN NETHERSPACE
INVISIBLE
NEMO
SEEKS TO ESCAPE
TERROR
AND RETURN
PERMANENTLY
TO VISIBLE REALITY
THROUGH
DAVIDSON PORTAL
VERY DIFFICULT
TO BECOME VISIBLE
NEMO
NETHERSPACE
ALMOST IMPOSSIBLE
TO BECOME VISIBLE
NEMO
HAVE TO FORCIBLY
COUNTER GROWING
ATTRACTION
TO TERROR
TERROR

# STATIC SHOCK
SKETCH BY JIM LEE

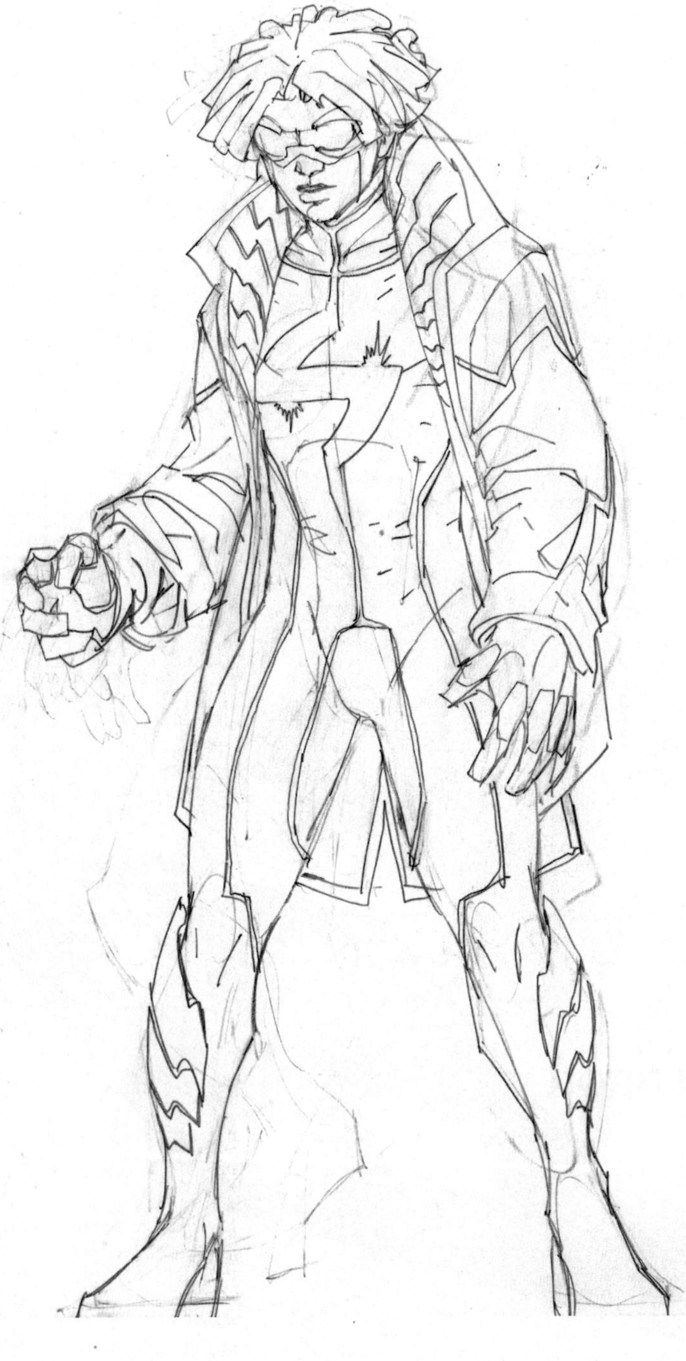